The 2001–2002 Traveler's Companions
ARGENTINA • AUSTRALIA • BALI • CALIFORNIA • CANADA • CHILE • CHINA •
COSTA RICA • CUBA • EASTERN CANADA • ECUADOR • FLORIDA • HAWAII •
HONG KONG • INDIA • INDONESIA • IRELAND • JAPAN • KENYA •
MALAYSIA & SINGAPORE • MEDITERRANEAN FRANCE • MEXICO • NEPAL •
NEW ENGLAND • NEW ZEALAND • NORTHERN ITALY • PERU • PHILIPPINES •
PORTUGAL • RUSSIA • SOUTH AFRICA • SOUTHERN ENGLAND • SPAIN • THAILAND •
TURKEY • VENEZUELA • VIETNAM, LAOS AND CAMBODIA • WESTERN CANADA

Traveler's CHINA Companion

First published 2001
The Globe Pequot Press
246 Goose Lane, PO Box 480
Guilford, CT 06437 USA
www.globe-pequot.com

© 2001 by The Globe Pequot Press, Guilford CT, USA

ISBN: 0-7627-0895-6

Distributed in the European Union by
World Leisure Marketing Ltd, Unit 11
Newmarket Court, Newmarket Drive,
Derby, DE24 8NW, United Kingdom
www.map-guides.com

Created, edited and produced by
Allan Amsel Publishing, 53, rue Beaudouin
27700 Les Andelys, France.
E-mail: Allan.Amsel@wanadoo.fr
Editor in Chief: Allan Amsel
Editor: Anne Trager
Original design concept: Hon Bing-wah
Picture editor and designer: David Henry

Printed by Samhwa Printing Co. Ltd., Seoul, South Korea

T R A V E L E R ' S
C H I N A
C O M P A N I O N

by Derek Maitland and Chris Taylor

photographs by Adrian Bradshaw and Nik Wheeler

The
Globe
Pequot
Press

GUILFORD
CONNECTICUT

Contents

Transportation • The Millionaire
Syndrome • The Main Attraction •
Can I Help You? • The Changing Scene

The Cultural Safe-Deposit • The Distant
Dawning • The Iron Emperor • The Age
of the Han • Chaos and the Canal •
The Golden Tang • The Age of Art •
The Wrath of Khan • The Glory of
the Ming • The Last Dynasty •
The Republican Failure •

TRAVELER'S
CHINA
COMPANION

RUSSIA

Shihezi
Ürümqi
Kuga
Aksu
Turpan
Korla
Hami (Kumui)
Kashgar
XINJIANG
Shache
Argan
Lop
Nur
GANSU
Dunhuang
Jiayuguan
Jiuquan
Khotan
Gus Hu
Da Qaidam
Tianjun
Huangzhong
Golmud
Dulan
QINGHAI
Gyaring Hu
TIBET (XIZANG)
Nagqu
Shigatse
Lhasa
Tingri
Gyantse
Sakya
NEPAL
BHUTAN
Derong
INDIA
Lijiang
Dali
Baoshan
Tengchong
YUNN
MYANMAR
(BURMA)
Jinghong
Menghai
Xishuang

M

NE

LAOS

TOP SPOTS

The Great Wall

IT'S FITTING PERHAPS THAT, AS THE SYMBOL OF CHINA, THE GREAT WALL SHOULD YIELD UP ITS SECRETS SO RELUCTANTLY. Academics wonder when it came into being. Then there's the question of its length. Nearly every reference gives a conflicting figure. The Chinese themselves call it formally the *wanli changcheng*, or the "10,000 *li*-long wall," a *li* being a Chinese measurement of length that equals around half a kilometer. This would make the wall 5,000 km (3,100 miles) long. But other sources quote anything from 3,500 km to 6,000 km. And for that matter, how "great" was it, anyway? As far as Genghis Khan (who is said to have bribed his way across it) was concerned, only as great as "the courage of those who defend it." Marco Polo didn't even bother mentioning it. And, most ironically of all, it didn't even work: Invaders swept across it, and the Europeans and Japanese approached from the wrong side.

The truth is, the Great Wall is many walls. The Qin dynasty original of 2,000 years ago was a much more modest undertaking than the monster that is often mistakenly said to be visible from the moon today. Commencing somewhere around the fifth century BC, kingdoms began walling off their territories during the Warring States Period. When Qinshi Huangdi unified China two centuries later, he began linking the walls as a buffer against outside barbarians. And the building continued off and on for nineteen following centuries, all the way through to the late Ming.

All the more reason to make that pilgrimage from Beijing to Badaling, where the Coca-Cola brigade clamors for small change and the approach swarms with hawkers of "I Climbed the Great Wall" T-shirts. There's even a 360-degree Great Wall Circle Vision Theater that screens 15-minute promotional videos.

Fortunately, it's easy enough to shrug off the crowds. Ignore the lines for the cable-car. Turn left on top and head north. Before long, the crowds thin, leaving the wall deserted. Within one and a half kilometers (one mile) the new, reconstructed section of the wall ends, crumbling into ruins.

It's here that the greatness of this wall becomes apparent. Look at it climbing and descending through a lonely landscape. Imagine the soldiers patrolling it, one eye nervously on the barbaric wastes to the west, the other longingly on hearth and home to the east. The soldiers were conscripts more likely than not, as were the wall's builders. Nobody knows how many tens of thousands perished building, defending and attacking this edifice. It's a disturbing thought, but one that slips away on the walk back to the shops and

OPPOSITE and ABOVE: The Great Wall — contrasting views of serenity and activity.

restaurants and souvenir stands. Today the armies that populate the wall are a different breed from those of old. But as of old, they are easily given the slip.

Tread in the Footsteps of the Celestial Emperor

WHAT CAN POSSIBLY BE MORE INVITING THAN THE FORBIDDEN? Off limits to the masses for 500 years, the gilded nest of 24 Ming and Qing dynasty emperors, their concubines, princesses and scheming eunuchs, is now open to anyone who can afford the price of an admission ticket.

Founded in 1420, the Forbidden City awes and astounds. For a start it's big — 720,000 sq m (over two million square feet) to be precise. More than 900 rooms (an auspicious 999 according to legend) are hidden away in the buildings that overlook sweeping courtyards, gardens and squares. The palace walls are 10 m (33 ft) high and stretch for 3.4 km (2.2 miles). Surrounding all this is a 52-m-wide (170-ft) moat. Then there's the uniquely Chinese poetry of the names: the Hall of Terrestrial Tranquillity, the Hall of Celestial Purity, the Hall of Supreme Harmony, the Hall of Literary Glory, the Hall of Military Prowess. The "Purple Forbidden City" is what it's called in Chinese, a reference to the purple palace of the Emperor of Heaven, whose home is in the faraway reaches of space, near the North Star. The Forbidden City is truly an attempt to duplicate all the glory of the heavens.

It's easy to be swept away by the vast grandeur of it all and miss the details: the carved marble carriageways underfoot, the haughty expressions of stylized fury on the

faces of the sculpted lions (the male with the pomegranate symbol of power in his right paw, the female with a cub beneath her left), the gold filigree depicting dragons and other mythological creatures.

Entry is via the Meridian Gate in the southern walls of the city. This is the grand main gate, the largest of all the many gates in the city, and in times past, ceremonial drums would sound from the gates to announce important occasions. The gate opens out into an expanse of courtyard, where once the emperor paraded with an imperial guard that included Burmese elephants in its ranks. Today it bustles with tourists, many of them lingering on the five marble bridges that symbolize the five Confucian virtues.

This is the Outer Palace. The "Great Within," as it was referred to, is approached by the Gate of Supreme Harmony, which lies

ahead. This gate in turn leads into another vast courtyard, so big that at special ceremonies it could accommodate the entirety of the imperial court, which at its height numbered upwards of 100,000.

At the end of the courtyard is the first and the most magnificent of the palace halls, the Hall of Supreme Harmony, where only the most important affairs of state were performed. Ahead lies the Hall of Middle Harmony, where the visiting heads of faraway vassal states might be ushered to kowtow before the emperor, and ahead again lies the Hall of Preserving Harmony, where the empire's best and brightest scholars took examinations for positions as mandarins in the exalted imperial service.

Thus the inner sanctum of the Celestial Empire is approached in stages. The emperor faced the outside world from the Meridian

Gate; he addressed his court from the Gate of Supreme Harmony; he disposed of state affairs in the Hall of Middle Harmony; he appointed the inner core of his administration in the Hall of Preserving Harmony; and beyond lay the imperial living quarters, the preserve of the emperor, his concubines and an army of court eunuchs.

Today even the Son of Heaven's living quarters are open. This was once the heart of an empire, in the old Chinese scheme of things the center of the world. To think that its last inhabitant, Pu Yi, was banished from here to see out his days as a municipal gardener in Beijing. It seems a long way to fall.

OPPOSITE: Flower beds surround the Forbidden City, Beijing. ABOVE: A light blanket of snow softens the imperial architecture of the Ming dynasty's most dramatic legacy, the Forbidden City, in Beijing.

A Day on the Bund

WHEN TRAVELERS ARRIVED IN SHANGHAI BY BOAT, BACK IN THE OLD DAYS, THE BUND WAS THEIR FIRST GLIMPSE OF THE CITY. As the cliché goes, a fusion of Manhattan and the Liverpool docks, the Bund may be an unlikely confluence of architectural styles but it remains one of China's most memorable sights and one of its most fascinating trips down memory lane. At every step the ghosts of a bygone era clamor for attention.

At its southern extent, on the river side, sits a peculiar, elongated white tower ringed with three red bands. A meteorological observatory built by the Jesuits in 1865, today it houses a modest but interesting museum that documents the Bund in its glory days. It's a minor attraction, but the black-and-white photographs from the colonial era make a good introduction to a walking tour of the Bund.

Diagonally opposite, at No. 3, is one of the Bund's most historically interesting edifices. Formerly the Shanghai Club, and until recently the Tung Feng Hotel (undergoing renovations and vacant at the time of publication), in its day it was Shanghai's most exclusive gathering place. Built in 1909, it was home to the Long Bar, a 34-m (111-ft) sweep of marble bar top. Famously, the club excluded women and Chinese, and even for those of the right sex and skin color was only accessible by the right kind of invitation.

The architecturally less interesting gray building at No. 5 was formerly the headquarters of a Japanese shipping magnate. Now it's worthy of mention for its M on the Bund ((21) 6350-9988, a fashionable Continental restaurant that makes a perfect place to lunch and gaze out at the bristling Pudong skyline across the river.

Further north at No. 12 lies the Bund's most famous building. Built by the Hongkong and Shanghai Bank in 1925, it now houses the Pudong Development Bank, which has financed a tasteful refurbishment of the building. Even the building's two flanking lions — long thought to have been melted by the Japanese for scrap iron during World War II — are back in place, though they are replicas. The originals, recently uncovered, sit in the Shanghai Museum on Renmin Square.

Note the entrance lobby's eight-sided mosaic, which at the time of building represented the Hongkong and Shanghai Bank's eight worldwide branches.

Next door, at No. 13, is the 1927 Customs House. Its tower clock — known in its day as the "big Ching" — is allegedly inherited from an original 1847 structure that stood on the same spot.

With its clean lines, the art-deco structure next door was once the German Asiatic Bank. Now it is home to the Federation of Labor Unions.

The American insurance company AIA is one of the few original tenants of a building to reclaim their space on the Bund at No. 17. In actual fact, though, their tenancy was brief and limited to only two floors — the building mostly housed the *North China Daily News*, in its day China's number-one English-language newspaper, the northern rival to Hong Kong's *South China Morning Post*.

No. 19 is now the southern wing of the Peace Hotel, but was once the Palace Hotel. The northern wing of the Peace, meanwhile, was the Cathay Hotel, a wonderful piece of *fin de siècle* elegance — Noel Coward wrote *Private Lives* ensconced in a suite here. Both the Palace and the Cathay were built by Sir Ellice Victor Sassoon, a Jewish playboy whose

LEFT: The Bund, Shanghai's unforgettable waterfront skyline. RIGHT: The crowds on Shanghai's Nanjing Road are not for the faint-hearted.

extravagant ballroom parties were the celebration of 1920s Shanghai and in no small part responsible for the city's infamy as a place of debauch.

Farther north, past the crumbling edifice that once captained the Jardine & Matheson's empire (No. 27), is the former Banque de l'Indochine Building at No. 29, with its impressive marble façade and columns.

Across the way, and the best place to finish up a Bund tour, is Huangpu Park, once home to that notorious sign that allegedly read "No Chinese or dogs allowed." Today it's a lively place with a trendy café, the perfect place to relax with a latte and watch the crowds of strolling Chinese families or gaze back on China's most illustrious skyline.

Into the Sea of Clouds

CHINA'S SACRED PEAKS ARE SCATTERED THE LENGTH AND BREADTH OF THE COUNTRY; pilgrims have toiled up their slopes and artists sought inspiration in their views for centuries. Most peaks are either Buddhist or Daoist: Emeishan in Sichuan, for example, is Buddhist, while Taishan in Shandong province is Daoist; but a few peaks — such as Huangshan in Anhui province — have been sanctified by their beauty alone.

Whether Buddhist, Daoist or simply beautiful, climbing one of China's sacred mountains is like slipping through a magical backdoor into the world of the Chinese watercolor. Those fluted rocks surmounted by a lone pine, roiling clouds lapping at gnarled roots, really do exist. The catch? Getting up there invariably demands serious exertions.

At Anhui province's Huangshan, perhaps the most gorgeous of all China's sacred mountains, the path up into the clouds is long and arduous, and — as the song goes — "with many a winding turn." The scenic western approach, which includes precipitous steps hewn out of rock faces, and a vertiginous approach up to the Heavenly Capital Peak, is a full 15 km (10 miles) of climbing. Even the very fit can expect some aches and pains the next day.

Of course — and there are those who will resent such modern encroachments — the inevitable has happened, and at the most popular sacred mountains a cable-car will be waiting to whisk you to the summit. In the case of Huangshan, the cable-car does the trip in just eight minutes. Contrast this with the quickest walking route — the eastern approach — which takes a minimum of three

grueling hours, and the temptation to do the ascent sitting down becomes difficult to resist. A good compromise is to take the cable-car one way and walk the other. Up or down, it's hard either way, but at least momentum and gravity are willing helpers on the descent. And when weariness strikes, spare a thought for the famed Chinese artist Liu Haisu, who climbed Huangshan for the tenth time in 1988... at the age of 93! He stayed on the mountain for two months and knocked off 46 paintings.

At Huangshan, like other peaks, the chief attraction at the summit is what the Chinese poetically call *yunhai* — the "sea of clouds." With the advent of mass tourism in China, heaving crowds of oohing and aahing local tourists can be guaranteed at the most popular mountains. Strike off on the side trails, however, and the crowds soon thin. It's usually still possible to find some quiet corner where the clouds roll lazily against the rocky shore far below, offering a solitary moment to commune with nature as have so many poets and brush-masters of times past.

For the true pilgrim experience, Buddhist Emeishan, in Sichuan province, is the most accessible. Even here there's a shortcut, by way of a minibus service that whisks travelers to the Jieyin Hall, where a cable-car awaits latter-day pilgrims in need of a quick summit ascent. But the real attraction of Emeishan is the opportunity to slowly scale the heights, stopping overnight at Buddhist monasteries and temples with the Chinese pilgrims (armed with staves that double as walking sticks and monkey-deterrents). One night is enough to get up the mountain and down again, but two nights is better. Some of the temple and monastery hotels, such as the one at Wannian Temple, are eight centuries old or more. A night spent in circumstances of such antiquity is a rare privilege indeed in the new China.

Ironically, given that Daoism is the more otherworldly of the two faiths, Taishan is a far more touristy climb than Emeishan. The mountain that has brought countless emperors to its slopes and summit to make sacrifices to heaven and earth is today a toiling sea of people. Still, here and there, among the crowds, it's still possible to occasionally catch a glimpse of a bearded Daoist monk trudging skyward alongside the tourists. It's a reminder that even in today's rush-to-riches China a faint pulse of old traditions continues to beat.

Huangshan's watercolor landscapes have inspired artists for centuries.

Cormorants, Caves and Limestone Peaks

A CHINESE SAYING GOES, GUILIN IS THE MOST BEAUTIFUL PLACE ON EARTH, BUT YANGSHUO IS EVEN MORE BEAUTIFUL. The cruise boats from Guilin glide down-river past the hulking limestone monoliths that the region is famous for and stop in Yangshuo, from where tourists are taken back to Guilin in tour buses. But many travelers skip the bus and stay on in Yangshuo instead.

Backpackers discovered this charming village nearly two decades ago, and despite the fact that the restaurants and hotels continue to grow in number, Yangshuo is far from being overrun. Feisty traders presiding over piles of cabbages and fruit inhabit the back streets; clumps of talkative retirees squat outside their homes on wicker stools, whiling away the hours with noisy games of mahjong. Ten minutes out of town by bicycle are paddy fields stretching away between the limestone peaks.

It's possible to while away a week in Yangshuo doing very little but taking in the scenery. The bicycle ride to nearby Moon Hill is a veritable rite of passage. From its huge natural arch a patchwork of paddy fields can be seen, the karst monsters marching away into the horizon. Many travelers bring lunch and make a picnic of it, before spending an afternoon exploring the recently discovered Black Buddha and Black Dragon caves. These cave systems are still being explored, but in the meantime enterprising locals are only too willing to take small tours on the tried-and-tested routes into the caves. It's a muddy, damp experience, but one not to be missed.

Another popular Yangshuo activity is splashing around in the river. Renting inner tubes and lazily drifting with the current, apart from being wonderfully relaxing, is a good way to get a close-up look at local village life. Another way is to jump aboard one of the many boats that putter past every now and again crowded with locals going home from market or from work. A boat journey to the rural village of Xingping takes a couple of hours and about the same to return by bicycle, a popular round trip.

Evenings see travelers flocking to the cormorant fishing displays. For a small fee, locals will row anyone who cares to join them

The eerie karst landscape surrounding Yangshuo, as seen from Moon Hill.

onto the river at dusk, where fishermen ply an age-old trade with the help of trained cormorants. A halter around the cormorant's neck prevents the bird from swallowing the fish, but the fisherman allows the bird to guzzle one down every now and again as a reward for all the hard work. It's an atmospheric scene: The birds lined up on the prow of a small punt in the flickering light of an oil lantern, the last light of the day etched in searing red into the western sky.

Don't worry about missing dinner, though, the village main street is packed with restaurants, many of them open until late. Order an inexpensive bottle of the local brew, Guilin beer, in anticipation of dinner — fish perhaps.

Silk Dreams

IMAGINE IF THE CANS AND JARS WE SO CASUALLY TOSS INTO OUR BASKETS AT SUPERMARKETS HAD TRAVERSED CANALS IN JUNKS, crossed deserts on camel back, survived marauding bandits and Mediterranean pirates. (There probably wouldn't be a great deal in the supermarkets.)

The most intriguing of the ancient trade routes is the Silk Road, that artery of trade, ideas and culture between the East and the West that survived from around 100 BC until the thirteenth century AD. It's difficult now to comprehend how valuable silk was, or why it so captivated the Romans when they first encountered it in the banners of their enemies in Central Asia. Nobody in Europe knew how the material was produced, and the Chinese guarded the secrets of its production under the pain of death. Such was the popularity of silk in Rome that massive imports built up an imbalance of trade and threatened the Roman economy.

The route started in Chang'an, the ancient Tang dynasty capital now known as Xi'an, and it's perfectly possible nowadays to follow part of the old Silk Road and witness scenes that have changed very little in the centuries that have passed since the route fell into disuse (shipping and the discovery of sericulture in Europe brought about the road's demise). For today's China travelers the ultimate Silk Road destination is Kashgar, but in times past this five-month journey was just the first stage of the long road west. The journey can be done in a couple of weeks now, though it is an arduous trip. From Xi'an travel by train to Lanzhou, and from there take an Ürümqi-bound train to

A baker and his wares in Turpan, Xinjiang Province, an oasis town on China's legendary Silk Road.

A Night at the Opera

*IT'S NOISY — EAR-PIERCINGLY SO AT TIMES —
THE PLOT OBSCURE,* the stage more often a
bewildering blur of leaping figures clothed in
impractical suits and fitted with hats that on
close inspection border on plain silly, but what
a spectacle it all is. Like Japanese *kabuki* and
Thai *lakhon*, Beijing opera and the various
regional operas found across China are
stylized dance dramas accompanied by boom-
crash orchestras of startling sounds and a
chorus of octave-leaping vocal effects.

Beijing is the famous place for opera, and
catching a show is a highlight of any visit to
the capital. For a truly authentic performance
in a traditional opera venue, the only place to
go in Beijing is the Zhengyici Theater ((10)
6318-9454, 220 Xiheyuan Dajie. The nightly
performances last for around two hours, and
as in times past, the audience munches on
food and swills back drinks as the performers
do their thing. The Liyuan Theater ((10) 6301-
6688, extension 8860, at the Qianmen Hotel,
has nightly opera shows of a more touristic
nature — the shows are shorter and come with
minimal English translations.

For a more intimate insight into Chinese
opera, watch a performance of Sichuan opera
in Chengdu. Any of the travel agents at the
Traffic Hotel ((28) 555-1017, 77 Jinjiang Lu,
can arrange that rarest of treats, a visit
backstage at the Shudu Theater to watch the
actors applying their makeup. There was a
time when all roles, including female parts,
were played by male actors; nowadays, both
men and women perform, though the
occasional bit of cross-dressing may still turn
up in a performance for comic effect. The
makeup can take a long time to apply;
essentially, the performer is creating a mask of
his or her face with greasepaint and a startling
array of different-sized brushes.

Backstage is a hive of activity, the
performers hunched over mirrors, busily
dusting and brushing away at their faces,
while the stars of the show are hustled
through their makeup routines by teams of
fussing helpers, the people who take care of
the elaborate costumes and hairstyles.
The result of all this work is that performers
emerge godlike, reminiscent of the
mythological figures who adorn Chinese
temples, which is indeed the intention.

Although it helps to know the plot
beforehand, it's not essential. Betrayal and
revenge, mistaken identities and unrequited
love, and the great dramatic themes all make

Liuyuan. Liuyuan is a 130-km (80-mile) bus
journey from the first of the great Silk Road
oasis towns, Dunhuang. In Dunhuang the Silk
Road lives on, not just in its Buddhist cave art
— all that remains of a Buddhist Silk Road
culture — but in the massive rolling sand
dunes that surround the town, a reminder of
the landscape that would have surrounded
ancient caravans for weeks on end.

From Dunhuang the road forks: Buses rattle
along desert roads to Hami, an oasis town
famed for its melons; while back in Liuyuan it's
possible to travel to Turpan by train. Turpan
lies at the edge of the feared Takla Makan
Desert (Taklimakan Shamo), and for Silk Road
traders marked the start of one of the most
arduous sections of the entire route. A series of
Buddhist cities once lay between Turpan and
faraway Kashgar, but today they are ruins.
Some of the ruins can be visited from Turpan.
In the summer months they simmer under a
ferocious sun, so hot that locals proudly claim
that it's possible to cook an egg on the broken
doorstops and tumbledown walls. But, despite
the fact that it's a furnace in the summer,
Turpan, its streets a leafy forest of grape
trellises, is a charming town with Old World
Silk Road markets and friendly people.

The old towns of Kuqa and Khotan, once
important stops on the Silk Road, are now
mere shadows of their former glory and can
easily be skipped. In this case, fly from
Ürümqi to Kashgar. Said to be the farthest
town from the sea in the world, this city of
mosques and kebabs and Middle Eastern
fabrics is the quintessential Silk Road
destination.

ABOVE: Beijing opera performer dons vibrant
traditional makeup. OPPOSITE: The splendid
pomp of Beijing opera.

an appearance. Because there are no props at all on an opera stage, every gesture and action must speak loudly, much in the way that mime does. An actor with a whip in his hand galloping around the stage is obviously riding a horse, the young beauty bashfully simpering behind a sleeve is obviously embarrassed.

As in Beijing, performances at Chengdu's Shudu Theater are a medley of high points from the best of the opera tradition (a traditional opera performance can last four hours or more). Moments of high drama collide with swashbuckling action, where the stage comes alive with whirling, leaping fighters armed with spears and swords. There's something joyous about these noisy, acrobatic, dazzling events, so that even those who came prepared for the worst end up thundering their applause as the performance draws to a close.

An Army in Stone

ONE OF THE MOST REMARKABLE ARCHEOLOGICAL DISCOVERIES OF THE TWENTIETH CENTURY CAME ABOUT IN 1974, when Shaanxi peasants digging a hole for a well uncovered a huge underground vault. Inside the vault were over 1,000 life-size terracotta figures. In the years that followed an estimated further 7,000 figures were found.

Unwittingly, the well-digging peasants had stumbled upon a vast stone army grouped in defense of the mausoleum of Qinshi Huangdi who, in 221 BC, had become the first leader of a unified China. Qinshi Huangdi achieved much, standardizing the written language and weights and measures, but the stone army on display today near Xi'an says everything about his methods. China's first emperor, the man who started work on the Great Wall, has passed into history as a tyrant, and is remembered more for his decrees that all books not written to the glory of the Qin dynasty be destroyed than for his success in bringing the squabbling states of the time under a unified leadership.

The terracotta warriors, as Qinshi Huangdi's army has come to be known, are at their most impressive in Vault 1. The warriors are *in situ* and in battle formation, protected from the elements by a huge hangar. The only pity is that their hands — which once held real weapons — are now empty, most of the wooden sections of spears and bows having long ago rotted away. Strolling along the

The serried ranks of Xi'an's famous terracotta warriors.

elevated walkways that overlook the ranked troops, it's the expressions and features of the faces that amaze. Some scholars have theorized that the faces may be modeled on actual members of the imperial guard, an astounding thought considering there is believed to be a total of 10,000 soldiers (including the groups in two other vaults). Each soldier's rank is displayed and the uniforms of knee-length protective tunics and armored tunics were once brightly colored. Note the soldiers' hair, which is tied up in buns.

It's worth making several swoops around the Vault 1 hangar. The other two vaults are smaller. Vault 2 comprises archers and charioteers, some of which are superbly executed. Vault 3 is speculated to have been the guard of honor, perhaps the leadership core of Qinshi Huangdi's army, leading the 10,000 into battle. Nowadays they are witness to daily skirmishes between army staff and visiting tourists determined to surreptitiously break the no-photographs rule. Snapping from the waist, nonchalantly reeling off a couple of shots from within a crowd, the tourists sneak their photographs in, while the museum staff stand by in thwarted vigilance. The army in stone seem oblivious; their job is to defend an empire, after all.

All Roads Lead to Lhasa

THE TIBETAN PLATEAU, AN AREA THE SIZE OF WESTERN EUROPE, with altitudes that average around 3,600 m (11,800 ft), is a place of nomads, villages and just one city worth the name, Lhasa. Tibetans in faraway Qinghai and Gansu provinces whisper the city's name with reverence. Villagers from hundreds of miles distant make that once-in-a-lifetime pilgrimage to Lhasa on their bellies — measuring themselves on the ground every second step — and arrive months later, dusty, mantra-muttering, to prostrate their way around the city's holiest of holies, the Jokhang Temple. The pilgrim circuit (*kora*) around the Jokhang is known as the Barkhor, and starts at Barkhor Square. With its magnificent views of the entrance to the Jokhang and its bustling market for pilgrim accessories (prayer wheels, prayer flags, leather padding for the knees and elbows, amulets and the like), it's easy to while an hour or so away here before joining the clockwise flow of faith around the temple. Alleys disappear into markets selling yak

Prayer flags flutter at the base of Lhasa's Potala Palace, former residence of the Dalai Lama.

cheeses and yak yogurt, alfresco pool tables sit in dusty corners surrounded by proud Tibetan nomads dressed to the nines in felt capes and sturdy boots, Tibetan carpets hang against whitewashed walls. The tableau is medieval (apart from the pool tables), and in that sedately moving crowd of the faithful, a pilgrim several steps ahead climbing wearily to his feet from the cobblestones, it is difficult to imagine how such a place could continue to survive into the dawn of the twenty-first century.

After the Barkhor *kora*, it's time to enter the Jokhang. Everything about this ancient temple (it dates back to the seventh century) is otherworldly. In the forecourt a steady stream of pilgrims prostrate themselves in front of the heavy curtains draped over the entrance. Directly inside are four Guardian Gods, two on each side, and the air is thick with that odor that is unique to Tibetan temples. It is the smell of yak-butter candles, an oily, sweet and sour odor so strong that in the darkness it creates the feeling of having entered another realm where the sense of smell reigns over that of sight.

In the ghostly candlelight, murmuring crowds (they're all muttering that holiest of mantras: *Om mani padme hum*) file in a clockwise circuit of the Jokhang's many chapels, each enshrining a sacred image. Directly to the rear of the temple is Tibet's holiest sanctuary: a small chapel that houses Jowo Sakyamuni, the Lord Buddha, aged 12. As pilgrims approach this holiest of images, they are absorbed with devotion, their lips flickering repetitively, their fingers kneading at strings of prayer beads. They touch their foreheads to the leg of the boy Buddha and depart.

Not that this need be the end of a visit to the Jokhang. Stairs lead to the roof, where

engineer a funicular railway on such steep gradients. Three years later the scoffers were cheering. The 554-m-tall (1,817-ft) peak on Hong Kong Island, formerly only approachable by jolting sedan chair (or, heaven forbid, on foot) was suddenly accessible in a mere eight minutes.

The Peak Tram, as it is called, has never looked back. It starts at Garden Road, Central, and creaks its way up 373 m (1,224 ft) to just below the summit of the Peak. Not that today's Peak Tram is exactly the same as the 1888 original. The carriages date from 1989, and the upper terminal was torn down and replaced with a completely new structure in 1996. But little else has changed.

The tram is mostly a tourist attraction nowadays. It was long ago supplanted as the primary means of transport for the area's wealthy elite (who tend to prefer chauffeur-driven limousines to trams) the first road to the peak was completed in 1924. But that is no reason to avoid the tram. The journey is easily one of Hong Kong's most fun outings, and the views (take a right-hand seat) of the soaring Central skyscrapers and office blocks, as banyan creepers slide past an arm's length away, are spectacular. There are even a few thrilling moments when the gradient steepens to the point that passengers are almost laid flat, as if in a G-force experiment.

The Peak itself is no longer restricted to elite housing as it once was. Indeed the tram terminal is now incorporated into the Peak Galleria, a modern shopping mall and entertainment complex that for some may be a disappointment after the antique rattle of the tram. Such distractions are easily escaped. From the Peak Galleria, four roads lead north and west. The middle one, Mount Austin Road, leads to the very top of the peak, home to Victoria Peak Garden and once the site of the Governor's Residence. To the west is Harlech Road, which joins up with Lugard Road, between them forming an approximately one-hour walk around the Peak and offering unsurpassed views en route.

The traditional way to end an afternoon stroll on the Peak is to drop into the Peak Café for a drink or a bite to eat. Renovation work has robbed the place of some of its atmosphere, but the terrace rattan chairs are still an unbeatable place to take in the Hong Kong skyline. So much for the scoffers.

there are monks' quarters, soaring gilded eaves, and walls painted in the muted reds and browns of Tibetan design. And then there is the view: The prostrating pilgrims directly beneath, and beyond them Barkhor Square, and beyond the square, dominating the middle ground between the city and the distant snowcapped mountains, the Potala, the palace of the Dalai Lamas.

In Tibet, all roads lead to Lhasa. And, before such a scene, the reason is clear.

Anyone for the Peak?

THE ELITE OF HONG KONG SCOFFED WHEN PHINEAS KYRIE AND WILLIAM KERFOOT HUGHES ANNOUNCED THEY WERE GOING TO BUILD A TRAMWAY TO THE TOP OF VICTORIA PEAK IN 1885. It seemed an impossible task. Nobody anywhere in the world had attempted to

The Star Ferry, perhaps the world's cheapest cross-harbor cruise (the new wing of The Peninsula hotel rises in the background).

YOUR CHOICE

outdoors is never far away, whether it be scenes of farmers toiling with oxen in fields, or the seemingly endless deserts of the far west.

FAMED BEAUTY SPOTS

Chinese attitudes to China's sweeping geography don't quite align with those of Westerners who visit the country. Scenes, for example, that Westerners might find nostalgically bucolic are likely to be seen as simply poor and undeveloped by Chinese.

When nature is celebrated in China, it is usually in aesthetic terms that have historical precedent or are authenticated by religious impulses. Nowhere is this more so than China's sacred mountains. The Buddhist peak of **Emeishan** in Sichuan province is a place of pilgrimage, as is the less impressive Taoist peak **Taishan** in Shandong province (see INTO THE SEA OF CLOUDS, page 17 in TOP SPOTS).

Non-religious scenic destinations include **Guilin**, whose craggy limestone rock formations and winding rivers are the subject of misty watercolors hung in hotel lobbies the length and breadth of the land. Guilin is probably China's most famous landscape. Poets and painters have celebrated its beauty for centuries, and from the moment you arrive you understand why. There are few sights in China that compare with these marching rows of limestone pinnacles, a patchwork of fields and the wandering threads of the Li River at their feet. The picturesque nearby village of **Yangshuo** has been turned by backpackers into a budget vacation resort (see CORMORANTS, CAVES AND LIMESTONE PEAKS, page 18 in TOP SPOTS).

The Great Outdoors

In the popular imagination, China is a place that teems with people. But China is vast, almost a continent, with geographical extremes that range from the world's lowest-altitude town (Turpan — 80 m or 265 ft below sea level) to the world's highest peak (Everest, on the border with Nepal), and from the dusty deserts of Xinjiang to the palm-lined beaches of Hainan island. The people? Most of them are crowded into the lush coastal provinces in the east. Go west is the answer if the unending rollcall of push-and-shove cities gets too much. No matter whether it's the north or the south, the farther west the traveler goes the more accessible China's natural vistas become.

Perhaps China, unlike neighboring Nepal, is not the first place that comes to mind when you want to commune with nature, but all the same it is a country where the great

Scenes of rural Yunnan Province — OPPOSITE: The terraced hills of China's deep south. ABOVE: Fields of rape provide a brilliant contrast in rolling farmland.

Equally famous is **Huangshan** in Jiangxi province, not far from Shanghai. An overnight stay on the mountain, with a day of hiking on either side, surrounded by hordes of toiling latter-day pilgrims is one of the highlights of any China journey.

SAND AND SURF

With the exception of Russians and Koreans, few people visit China for the same reasons they might visit, say, Thailand. Still, China is not without its beach resorts, and the best of them by far is on the southern, subtropical island of **Hainan**.

Easily accessible from Guangzhou by air, Hainan's top beaches are at Sanya, which local tourist officials have taken to calling the "Hawaii of the East." The best of the beaches is Dadonghai, and while few people go to China to sprawl out in the sun, a visit at least provides a fascinating insight into Chinese beach culture.

MOUNTAINS, FORESTS AND MINORITIES

Some of China's most exciting landscapes can be found in the southwest of the country — notably in Yunnan and Sichuan provinces.

In Yunnan, the **Stone Forest (Shilin)**, a popular day trip from Kunming, the provincial capital, is akin to a high-density version of Guilin, where limestone pillars jostle together in a scene that is immediately suggestive of the area's poetic name. Elsewhere in Yunnan, the Dai minority town of Dali offers the prospect of boat trips on **Erhai Lake** and extended hikes into the surrounding countryside. It is also possible to rent a bicycle and strike off for a day of relaxed pedaling with the turquoise lake on one side and the vertiginous face of the snowcapped Cangshan Mountains on the other. **Lijiang**, home of the matriarchal Naxi tribe and a day's bus ride to the north of Dali, is another popular hiking region, though mainly with backpacking travelers.

North of here, Sichuan province is another region with scope for exploration in the outdoors. With the exception of the Buddhist sacred mountain, Emeishan, however, most of Sichuan is remote and seldom visited. **Jiuzhaigou**, in the mountainous deep north of the province, is held to be one of the most stunning destinations in all China; accommodation — mostly Tibetan — is primitive and access by road is dangerous. Sichuan is also one of the last places where pandas still roam wild. The **Wolong Nature Reserve**, around 150 km (93 miles) northwest of Chengdu, is difficult to reach unless you join a tour (widely available in Chengdu); in addition, pandas are notoriously shy creatures, and sightings are rare.

GRASSLANDS AND DESERT

It's out beyond the Great Wall that China becomes a land of open spaces. In Inner Mongolia tours are operated from **Hohhot** to the grasslands, from whence the Mongol tribes once swept down on China and claimed the Celestial Throne as their own. Summer is the time to visit, if you want the grasslands to be the color of grass — in winter the plains turn a frostbitten brown. Today you can venture out into these regions and stay in the Mongolian's traditional yurt dwellings.

In Xinjiang autonomous region, the Chinese Turkestan of yore, through which the Silk Road once passed, you can travel to the edge of the feared Takla Makan Desert and stay at **Turpan**. From Turpan it is possible to rent jeeps and journey out to ruined Silk Road cities of **Jiaohe** and **Gaochang**, the remnants of a Buddhist civilization that disappeared centuries ago. For those with more time, the road continues farther to **Kashgar**, the fabled oasis town at the far western extreme of the Chinese Silk Road. Continue on from here and you are on the Karakorum Highway destined for Islamabad in Pakistan, a route only for the most intrepid and hardy of travelers.

A similarly demanding trail is the high road to **Lhasa** in Tibet. There are flights from Chengdu in Sichuan province, but for the adventurous traveler the road leads from Xi'an to Lanzhou and from there by train to Xining and Golmud. At Golmud a 30-hour bus trip to the roof of the world awaits. The train journey between Xining and Golmud itself is worth all

OPPOSITE: The remarkable Stone Forest (Shilin) was formed by massive upheaval and erosion of limestone. A giant panda ABOVE at Xi'an Zoo. Rare and protected, they are indigenous to Western China.

the hardship of the journey, Qinghai Lake a ribbon of blue in the foreground, mountain ranges behind it, and occasionally the pinprick suggestion of a camel train wending its way through the intervening dunes.

Sporting Spree

China is many things, but a compelling sporting destination it is not. Recreational sports with snob appeal such as golf are gaining headway in China, but for most other sports travelers will find themselves at the mercy of their hotel facilities.

MARTIAL ARTS

A good resource for martial arts information in China and elsewhere is the **Martial Arts Pages** WEB SITE www.martial-arts-network.com/ link_pg.htm. And, as anyone who takes a look at this site will discover, Chinese martial arts is a vast, complex subject with a huge range of competing forms to choose from.

The Chinese martial arts have evolved probably over millennia and are today known collectively as *wushu*. Although the Chinese government did much to standardize and limit their study (particularly the more martial forms) after the Communist takeover, the last decade has seen an enormous revival of all forms of Chinese martial arts, particularly the modern styles.

Although there is a bewildering plethora of forms, essentially Chinese martial arts can be divided into soft forms — such as the famous tai chi, or *taiji* — and hard forms, such as kung fu, or *gongfu*. The harder, or "external," forms are usually associated with Buddhism, as with the famous Shaolin Temple near Zhengzhou, where monks have evolved kung fu fighting styles over centuries, based on the movements of animals. The softer, or "internal" forms like tai chi are collectively known as *neigong* in China, and despite their denomination provide formidable efficiency in combat. They are usually associated with Daoism, with its emphasis on harmony with nature, and with the sacred Daoist mountains of Wudang Shan in Hubei province. There the mythical Zhang Sanfeng is said to have created tai chi after having observed a crane and a snake fighting.

A popular Chinese saying goes, "If in the north Shaolin rules, in the south Wudang stands." Nevertheless, the commonly accepted distinction between the internal forms from Wudang and the external forms from Shaolin is not entirely accurate, as the different forms developed from a complex intermingling of diverse influences.

A company that offers study courses and tours for *wushu* in China is **EducAsian** ((1 917) 432-1609 FAX (1 212) 535-2501 E-MAIL info@educasian.com, 1441 Third Avenue, Suite 12C, New York, New York 10028. They also have an office in Beijing ((10) 6234-7904 FAX (10) 6234-7905, Third Floor, Building One, Xijiao Hotel, Haidian, Beijing, and in Australia ((61 414) 764056 FAX (61 891) 683164 E-MAIL australia@educasion, Suite 6, Mallee Court, Kununurra, WA 6743, Australia. Courses in qiqong, taiji and wushu are offered at the Beijing University of Physical Education and can be combined with Chinese language courses.

Another similar organization is **World Link Education** ((10) 6239-5067 FAX (10) 6239-5067, Xijiao Hotel, 18 Wangzuang Road, Haidian, Beijing 100083. Their WEB SITE www.study-in-china.com contains full details of a wide range of courses.

It's also possible to organize study of Chinese martial arts yourself. One school with regular classes for foreigners is the **Northern China Shaolin Martial Arts Academy** ((434) 549-6648 FAX (434) 3290265, Yehe Ancient Castle, Si Ping city, Jilin province 136523, which runs regular courses through the year aimed at foreigners. Courses are conducted in English and are intensive, running from 5 AM until 8 PM. Don't bother inquiring unless you are seriously interested in studying martial arts. In the province of Guangdong, near Zhangjiang, try the **International Institute for Traditional Martial Arts** (/FAX (795) 227-7197 E-MAIL wan.laisheng@wanadoo.fr, which offers courses for all levels in traditional styles, both internal and external. For information on schools and monasteries at Wudang Shan, contact the **Wudang Federation** ((719) 522-3531 FAX (719) 522-7401 E-MAIL wudang@public.sy.hb.co.

GOLF

Following the lead of Japan, Taiwan and the other booming Asian economies, golf is popular among China's growing executive class. The sport is in its early days, however, and as you would expect the best greens are in Hong Kong.

The **Royal Hong Kong Golf Club Fanling** ((852) 2670-1211 FAX (852) 2679-5183, New Territories, is one of Asia's first, established in 1908. It has three courses: the Old Course, the New Course, and the Eden Course, each with 18 holes. The Old Course is the easiest of the three.

The **Royal Hong Kong Golf Club Deepwater Bay** ((852) 2812-7979 FAX (852) 2812-7111, Hong Kong, is a par-28 course, measuring 1,650 yards, parts of which overlap.

The Hong Kong Golf Club Fanling, New Territories.

The **Kau Sai Chau Public Golf Course**
((852) 2791-3388 FAX (852) 2792-0982 is as the
name suggests a public course, but in order to
play you will have to produce a handicap
certificate or take part in a beginner's clinic.

Some of the best courses outside Hong
Kong are in neighboring Guangdong
province. **Sand River Golf Club** ((755) 660-
9270, in Shenzhen Bay, Shenzhen, is a 27-hole
Gary Player-designed course. The **Shenzhen
Golf Club** ((755) 330-8888 FAX (755) 330-4992
is one of China's oldest.

WATER SPORTS

Despite its long eastern coastline, China has
little in the way of water sports, or indeed
anywhere for swimming.

Sanya and **Yalong Bay** are beach resorts
on Hainan Island, where swimming and
sunbathing (still not popular with the Chinese,
for whom fair skin is considered an asset)
is the main attraction. Scuba diving and
snorkeling are also available at Sanya. Other
popular beach resorts can be found at
Qingdao, in Shandong province, and at
Beidaihe, 300 km (187 miles) east of Beijing —
the latter having been for many years the
off-limits preserve of exalted cadres.

In Hong Kong swimming is popular
through the summer months, but pollution
and sharks are both concerns. Shark nets
have been installed at popular beaches and
pollution levels are closely monitored —
check with the **Hong Kong Tourist
Association** ((852) 2508-1234 for details.
On weekends and public holidays during
the official swimming season (April 1 to
October 31) the most popular beaches (e.g.,
at Stanley on Hong Kong Island) are packed
with swimmers and sunbathers. There are
good facilities at these major beaches —
lifeguards, warning flags for rough seas,
changing rooms and toilets and sometimes
even beachside cafés or snack stalls. The
biggest and most glorious stretch of beach in
Hong Kong is Cheung Sha on Lantau; there
are facilities at both ends of the beach, with
a couple of Chinese restaurants at its
easternmost end (Lower Cheung Sha).

CYCLING

With more motorized traffic taking to the
roads with each passing day, China is not the
cyclist's dream that it was when the entire
country got around on two wheels. But
touring China (or at least parts of it) by
bicycle is still an attractive proposition.

Some keen cyclists bike over the border
from Hong Kong or even from Kathmandu
(a long uphill slog) and tour across China solo.

While this is certainly not impossible, it is not
easy. A less arduous way to see China by
bicycle is to join a specialized tour.
Alternatively, take your bike with you and
bundle it onto the roof of buses or into the
goods vans of trains for the long sectors, and
leave your cycling for the parts of China where
touring is rewarded by breathtaking views.

Backroads ((800) 462-2848 FAX (510) 527-
1444 WEB SITE www.backroads.com, 801 Cedar
Street, Berkeley, California 94710, is a tour
organizer that specializes in adventure and
cycling tours. **Himalayan Travel** ((800) 225-
2380 FAX (203) 359-3669 E-MAIL
himalayantravel@cshore.com WEB SITE
www.gorp.com/himtravel/default.htm, 112
Prospect Street, Stamford, Connecticut 06901,
is another operator with cycling tours to
China. In London, **Imaginative Traveller**
((020) 8742-8612 FAX (020) 8742-3113 E-MAIL
info@imaginative-traveller.com WEB SITE
www.imtrav.com, 14 Barley Mow Passage,
London W4 4PH, has trekking and cycling
tours in China.

The Open Road

Only since the beginning of the 1990s has
China begun to grapple with the huge task of
bringing its roads up to scratch. Add to this
the fact that increasing numbers of
inexperienced drivers are taking to the roads
armed only with a horn and a dim
understanding of traffic rules, and most
visitors will agree that the sensible thing is to
leave your international license at home.

Car rental is available in China, and the car
will usually come with a driver. There are very
few roads that foreigners are permitted to
drive themselves — the Shenzhen–Guangzhou
superhighway is one; the highway between
Beijing and Tianjin is another, and it's also
possible to drive yourself in Hong Kong,
Macau and Sanya on Hainan island.

Cycling on a rented bicycle is as close as
most travelers will come to experiencing the
joys of the open road in China. In rural areas
such as Yangshuo in Guangxi autonomous
region and Dali in Yunnan province, cycling
can still be a joy. In many of the larger cities,
where once bicycles were the only mode of
transportation besides buses, there are now
armies of honking cars and trucks. Always
take a good look at traffic conditions before
launching off on a pedal-power journey of
discovery in a new town.

A typical rural street scene in the environs of
historic Xi'an.

Backpacking

THE BACKPACKING TRAILS

When China first opened up to individual travelers in the early 1980s, adventurous backpackers flooded in. Travel was demanding in those days, but meals, accommodation and transportation were bargains, providing that magical combination of low costs and hardship that the backpacking spirit thrives on. Two and a half decades later, China is both less challenging and more expensive. But this doesn't mean that it's no longer an attractive destination for the budget voyager.

Travelers bent on keeping costs down should minimize their time in booming eastern China — from Beijing all the way south to Hainan Island. Of course, skipping the east altogether means that you miss out on some of China's premiere attractions — Shanghai (now bouncing back with a vengeance), Suzhou (famed for its gardens and canals), Hangzhou (famed for its West Lake), Xiamen and Qingdao (both of which have retained some of their Old World charm), not to mention bustling Guangzhou, and Beijing, the capital. But in most of these destinations accommodation costs have skyrocketed in the last decade, and old backpacker standbys have been renovated to attract a "better class" of guest.

The key is to plan your itinerary on the east coast carefully, and be prepared to go through your money much more quickly there. In Beijing, for example, finding a double room (or even a single room for that matter) for under US$30 is possible but rarely easy, particularly at peak holiday periods. Entry fees to attractions around Beijing are high, and if you drop into a bar in the evening for a drink you will find yourself paying Hong Kong prices.

The solution for many young travelers is to do whirlwind tours of the historical sights of Beijing and then head west or southwest. Few budget travelers bother with the east coast at all, though some stop in Shanghai, which has direct rail connections with Kunming and Guilin, backpacker Meccas.

From Hong Kong, the route of choice is a boat or a train to Guangzhou, and from there a combination of boat (to Wuzhou) and bus (to Yangshuo, with its stunning limestone karst scenery). Yangshuo's cafés are renowned and rooms are available for as little as US$5. From Yangshuo most travelers continue westwards

to Kunming, the capital of subtropical, minority-rich Yunnan.

Although Kunming has witnessed something of a tourist boom in recent years, by the time you are this deep into the southwest of China, day-to-day expenses begin to plummet. In the border regions of Xishuangbanna and Dehong, it is possible to get by on less than US$20, staying in budget hostels, renting bicycles and cycling out to minority villages by day, and in the evenings enjoying the superb local cuisine cooked family-style. The route from here runs up to Dali, an old walled town by the exquisite Erhai Lake, and on to Lijiang, home of the matriarchal Naxi tribe. North of here — and accessible by a combination of bus and train — lies the Buddhist sacred mountain of Emeishan, Leshan with its Grand Buddha (bigger than the one on Hong Kong's Lantau

Island, and around 1,250 years older), and the large cities of Chengdu and Chongqing. The remote — and largely Tibetan — northwest of Sichuan is a magnet for intrepid backpackers, and routes have sprung up from Chengdu to Xining in Qinghai province and to Lanzhou in Gansu province, from either of which it is possible to travel by bus to destinations such as Turpan, Ürümqi and Kashgar in Xinjiang, to Lhasa in Tibet (via Golmud) or to Xi'an, home of the Terracotta Warriors and a city where expenses can still be kept to a reasonable level.

GETTING AROUND

The cheapest way to get around China is by bus. Travel this way tends to be slow, crowded and often dangerous — some drivers appear to be relative newcomers to their vocation. Nevertheless, in many of the more remote destinations in China, bus or minibus will be the only way to get around. In Yunnan, for example, trains link the capital Kunming with Chengdu in Sichuan and Guilin in Guangxi, but elsewhere around the province — to Dali and Xishuangbanna, say — you either take a bus or settle for a relatively expensive flight.

Trains are rarely a bargain in China, but if you're prepared to rough it, there is always the "hard seat" option. Hard seat is the equivalent of third-class, though there are few places in the world where third-class is such a rough-and-tumble proposition. With hard-seat prices weighing in at roughly a quarter the cost of a soft sleeper (first class) ticket, and half the price of a hard sleeper

Dali's fabulous Three Pagodas, mirrored in the placid waters of Erhai Lake.

Living It Up

The toiling masses dream of just one thing nowadays, and it's not Mao's collectivized society, but Deng's dream of being gloriously rich. It's possible to live like a king in the new China, if that's what you wish, though high-flyers will find that China's best is no less expensive than the best anywhere else in the world.

EXCEPTIONAL HOTELS

China's top hotels are where you would expect them to be: in Hong Kong and Beijing. Nevertheless, Shanghai gives the capital a run for its money, and Guangzhou is not without some minor-league contenders.

Hong Kong, of course, has some of the world's most luxurious accommodation. Top of the list are the **Mandarin Oriental** in Central and the **Peninsula** in Tsimshatsui, where you can expect the very best in service, luxury down to the finest detail, and sky's-the-limit room rates.

The palatial **Beijing Hotel** was the first international-style hotel to be built in the capital, and it commands pole position in the heart of the old city, overlooking the Forbidden City. Next door to the Beijing Hotel, the **Grand Hotel** is the new kid on the block. With similar views and levels of luxury, it's an alternative to staying at the Beijing, where service standards come in for some criticism.

Shanghai lacks a truly luxurious hotel on the Bund, which is a pity. The best this historically significant part of town can offer is the **Peace Hotel**, which was formerly known as the Cathay, when it shared a prestige rating that equaled the Peninsula in Hong Kong, the Stanley Raffles in Singapore and the Taj in Bombay. Take one of the suites — perhaps it will be the same one in which Noel Coward wrote *Private Lives*.

For Shanghai at its best, the new **Grand Hyatt** in the upper reaches of the soaring Jinmao building is not only one of the world's highest hotels, but also, with its 29-story atrium, one of the world's most architecturally impressive. Meanwhile, the **Portman Ritz-Carlton Hotel** is an opulent taste of the future that Shanghai is building for itself, it also offers the utmost in convenience, being in Shanghai Center, where you will find most of Shanghai's foreign airlines, consulates and business representatives.

In Guangzhou, **White Swan Hotel** was one of the pioneering joint-venture hotels in the early days of China tourism. Unlike some that have fallen by the wayside, the White Swan has managed to keep apace of rising

(second class) ticket, many budget travelers find the savings irresistible. Those who travel long distances this way often come away with nightmarish horror stories; few do it again.

WHERE TO STAY

In the early days of China travel, the only kind of hotel foreigners could stay in (with the exception of the rare joint-venture) was a *binguan*, or guesthouse. These were usually sprawling, institutional setups that were built to house visiting "foreign experts" and cadres on the move. When individual budget travelers started to arrive in China in the early 1980s, a lot of these guesthouses were discovered to have inexpensive dormitory accommodation, though staff were rarely willing to admit it. Before long, hapless Chinese guesthouse staff, who had no training for such an onslaught, were dealing with a daily deluge of belligerent foreigners in search of value for their yuan.

Things have changed enormously since those days. Most of the old guesthouses have been renovated, some beyond recognition, into three-, four- or even five-star hotels, and dormitory accommodation is difficult to find. Indeed, in the coastal provinces virtually no dormitory accommodation is available for foreigners. But where budget accommodation is available, and most of western and southwestern China falls into this category, getting a dormitory bed or a budget room is still very straightforward.

The best place to seek out inexpensive accommodation is around the main bus or train station. If it's a dormitory bed you're looking for, don't forget that essential word: *sushe*, pronounced "sooshir."

standards, and whatever happens it will always have its delightful location on Shamian Island, the most charming corner of the city. In the northern commercial part of town the **Garden Hotel** has long been the first choice of business travelers, and is a vast place with excellent amenities and some of the city's best dining.

The Shangri-La chain is well represented in China, but it's hard to beat the **Shangri-La Hangzhou**, which has a fabulous setting, overlooking the northern section of Hangzhou's famous West Lake. The Hyatt group, who set consistently high standards throughout China, is superbly represented inside the city walls of ancient Xi'an at the **Hyatt Regency Xi'an**.

The Holiday Inn group also has hotels all over China, including excellent choices in Beijing, Ürümqi and Xiamen, but alas have given up their stake in the Holiday Inn Lhasa, which is now the **Lhasa Hotel**. Remarkably, even under new, less renowned management, the Lhasa still manages, against all odds, to bring the high life to a part of the world that until now has always had the "high" but not the "life" to go with it.

EXCEPTIONAL RESTAURANTS

Given the beating that China's restaurant culture got during the Communist era, not to mention the Cultural Revolution, by which time one of the world's great cuisines was in danger of devolving into greasy spoon canteen slop, it's remarkable to see the renaissance in dining out that is taking place all over China. It will still be some time before China is able to offer the diversity that is found in, for example, Hong Kong and Taipei, which between them arguably command center stage in the Chinese haute cuisine stakes. Still, Hong Kong *is* China these days, so if its exceptional restaurants you want in China, look to Hong Kong first.

The Grand Hyatt's **One Harbour Road** Cantonese restaurant and the Island Shangri-La's **Summer Palace** are two of the best hotel restaurants that Hong Kong has to offer. Out on the streets, **Fook Lam Moon Restaurant**

OPPOSITE: Hainan Island's Yalong Bay is China's slice of tropical paradise. ABOVE: The open-air swimming pool at Kowloon Park.

has long been noted as one of the best in town and is famous for its (very) pricey shark fin dishes, which appear on the first page of a menu designed to shock (if you're paying) and impress (if you're the guest). Remember too that it is not just Chinese cuisine that Hong Kong is celebrated for, but everything from Vietnamese to Mexican.

Over the "border" in China everything changes. For a start, you generally pay far less for your meals than in Hong Kong. To be sure, standards are not as high, but you certainly get value for your money. At famous restaurants such as **Beijing's Qianmen Quanjude Roast Duck** you can sample the capital's famous duck dish in sumptuous surroundings for around US$20. Outside the five-star hotels this is generally about as expensive as dining out in China gets.

Guangzhou has been an open city for some time now, and its proximity to Hong Kong has allowed some famous old restaurants to flourish. The best of these include **Taotaoju Restaurant**, a delightful place that started life as an academy of learning in the seventeenth century; the **North Garden Restaurant**, which has an inner garden courtyard; and the **Panxi Restaurant**, which lays on the old China theme as thickly as you're likely to ever experience it.

In general, the best in Chinese cuisine is sponsored by the five-star hotels in Beijing, Shanghai and Guangzhou. Although quality is improving elsewhere, it will still be some time before restaurants that do justice to China's culinary traditions are commonplace even in the major cities.

NIGHTLIFE

The affluent youth of China are marching to a different drummer than that of their parents. Out are the non-differentiating Mao suits and the puritanical mistrust of boys and girls brought together in anything other than revolutionary zeal, and in are Parisian fashions and the London beat.

Mind you, for most of China a night out means a meal in a restaurant and a sing-along at a karaoke parlor — look for the neon signs ending in the English letters "OK." Karaoke, which originated in Japan and involves singing along to popular hits minus the vocals, is fun to try, but for most foreigners it is of limited appeal, particularly given that the average Chinese is enormously ungifted with a microphone. Add to this the fact that most karaoke "menus" only sport one or two English songs, and after a couple of experiences most Westerners retreat to a Western-style bar for a quiet drink.

In the remoter parts of China, you will only find bars in the top hotels, but as you get closer to the major cities, nightlife becomes increasingly diverse, and by the time you arrive in Beijing, Shanghai or Guangzhou it is positively frenetic. In each of the big three you will find branches of international staples such as the **Hard Rock Café**, and more imitators than anyone would care to list.

In Shanghai, **Shanghai Sally's** was a pioneer in the British pub trend that has taken China's big cities by storm in recent years. Shanghai's Maoming Nanlu is the best area to explore the city's burgeoning pub and bar scene. The British pub, **Poachers Inn** was the pioneer in Beijing. It still survives, but now faces competition from countless innovators, many of them in the Sanlitun "Bar Street" area.

Don't pass up an opportunity to visit one of Beijing's or Shanghai's happening dance clubs. In Shanghai **Maya** is the place for the beautiful people, and in Beijing the warehouse-style **JJ's** packs in thousands of sweaty bodies on the weekends.

Family Fun

Nobody spoils their children the way the Chinese do. If China is at times a trying destination for a family with children to tackle, this open-heartedness of the Chinese is a major compensation.

As is the case elsewhere in Asia, there are some practical concerns if you are planning a family vacation in China. Firstly, have your children had all their vaccinations? Although China is more hygienic than, say, India or Nepal, it is still a poor country and in many regions medical facilities are primitive: ensuring your children remain healthy throughout their travels is the first step towards a successful trip.

Some of the major cities, in particular Shanghai and Guangzhou, are extremely crowded. If you have small children, a baby carrier that straps on to your back or chest is a far better way to get them from point A to point B than in a stroller. This is true in many rural areas as well, where you're unlikely to find sidewalks and where the roads are often rutted and potholed.

On a more positive note, the Chinese are remarkably tolerant of children's antics. Parents dining in restaurants will let their children run wild with little regard for other diners, and this means that you can relax somewhat when dining out.

Around the major cities there are amusement parks for children, and in the smaller cities there will always be a central People's Park (*renmin gongyuan*), where you will often find climbing rails and so on. But mostly, outside the big coastal cities, Western children may be bored by Chinese game areas and cultural attractions. Think ahead and bring games and toys that will keep your children amused. This is particularly true if you are going to be taking long train journeys. Buses are best avoided in China if you are traveling with children.

All things considered, China is a better destination for older children who are able to appreciate the grand adventure of visiting this populous and ancient nation. For the tiny tots, other Asian destinations such as Thailand and Bali, where there are beaches and hotels that are used to dealing with children, are probably much more practical propositions.

The exception to these caveats is Hong Kong, where there are a number of children-friendly attractions. Chief among them is **Ocean Park**, one of Asia's largest oceanariums and fun parks, and which is just half an hour away from Hong Kong Island's Central district (take bus No. 70 from Central and get off immediately after Aberdeen Tunnel or take the special Ocean Park Citybus service from Admiralty MTR station which goes directly to the entrance).

Among its attractions are the massive water play park, called Water World; the world's largest reef aquarium, the Atoll Reef (6,000 fish on three levels); and, the biggest thrill of all, one of the world's longest and fastest roller coasters, a heart-stopping loop-the-loop appropriately called The Dragon. Near the Tai Shue Wan (upper level) entrance, the Middle Kingdom recreates 5,000 years of Chinese history through crafts demonstrations, theater, opera and dance. It's a huge place, and it is easy to eat up whole day and not exhaust its attractions.

Also popular with children are the Space Museum and the Science Museum, both in Kowloon. The **Space Museum**, dominating the Tsimshatsui waterfront with its huge planetarium (featuring Omnimax screenings and sky shows several times daily) has fun and informative shows about astronomy and space technology. Meanwhile the **Science Museum** in Tsimshatsui East has "hands-on" displays on robotics, transportation, computers and virtual reality. The 20-m-tall (65-ft) Energy Machine is worth the visit alone. Wednesdays (free admission day) are best avoided, as the museum gets very crowded.

Smiles all round on a school outing in Kunming.

Cultural Kicks

There are any number of ways to appreciate a country as vast as China. In the big cities you might spend your nights in bars and dance clubs and your days sleeping off the effects. In the country there are sacred mountains to be climbed, otherworldly landscapes such as Guilin to be explored. In the far west, deserts sprawl under a cruel sun, and in Tibet the mountains touch the sky. But for most visitors, the overwhelming attraction is China's cultural tradition, whose lineage, as the Chinese themselves will proudly pronounce, stretches back through some 5,000 years of history.

However, there's very little in China of cultural value that dates back 5,000 years. That anything older than two or three hundred years has lingered into the present, given the turbulence of the last few centuries, is miraculous. Some visitors come away from China disappointed at how "modern" the country is, and complaining that there is so little of historical significance to see. This is true to a certain extent. China has no Venice, no Naples, no Rome, no Paris; the best-preserved Chinese cities are largely ugly growths of factories and faceless housing estates.

If you feel a twinge of disappointment, remind yourself that China's transition into the modern world has been a painful, troubled one that has involved a great deal of disgust with all that went before. In the Western hemisphere the 1960s has been mythologized as a ferment of discontent and youth rebellion. In the Chinese 1960s, during the Great Proletarian Cultural Revolution, the young literally tore the country apart.

Yet China's past survives. You'll find it everywhere you look, if you take the time to slow down. The Cantonese opera burbling out from speakers in a Guangzhou park. The serried ranks of oblivious oldsters performing the dawn ritual of catlike tai chi routines. The roar and sizzle of the roadside stir-fry. The rural street performers and local opera troupes. Then of course, there's the Great Wall, the Buddhist grotto art, the temples coming back to life, the Forbidden City, the artists splashing ink onto paper before limestone landscapes draped in mist...

ARCHITECTURAL LEGACY

Unlike Europe, little of China's architectural has survived through the ages. The main reason for this is that, while the European builder works with the stone, the Chinese master builder works with timber — which is subject to decay and the ravages of fire. Most of the more ancient examples of Chinese architecture still in existence are in fact reconstructions.

Chinese classical architecture reached maturity in the Tang dynasty, with styles that continued to be employed all the way through

until the fall of the Qing in the twentieth century. One defining characteristic, the curved roof of classical Chinese buildings is not in fact Chinese at all but derives from early Tang Chinese contact with Southeast Asian civilizations. More local in origin is the basic plan of the Chinese temple, which is thought to be modeled on the mansions of early rich patrons of the arts and religion. Thus, like a traditional Chinese home, which consisted of a main building and ancillary structures, the height of which reflected the level of residents in the family hierarchy, a Chinese Buddhist temple consists of a main building and secondary buildings set in courtyards linked by galleries.

This basic layout can even be seen in China's most awe-inspiring example of classical architecture: Beijing's **Forbidden City**. Heart of the empire through the Ming and Qing dynasties, the remarkable point about the Forbidden City is the way it maintains such elegant detail over such a vast canvas. If the Forbidden City is unforgettable, it is also overwhelmingly large, so that unless you have plenty of time and can make repeat visits it tends to remain a jumble in your memories after you leave. For a more focussed glimpse of Ming dynasty design, Beijing's **Tiantan** (Temple of Heaven) is undoubtedly Beijing's superlative architectural attraction.

Northeast of Beijing is some of China's finest surviving imperial architecture at **Chengde**. By Chinese standards, the temples

and palaces of Chengde are recent arrivals, the earliest of them being constructed in the first years of the eighteenth century. Indeed, Chengde was the site of a frenzy of building that culminated the construction of a replica of Lhasa's Potala.

Beijing's city walls are long gone, but **Xi'an**, in Shaanxi province, has a well-preserved city wall. Xi'an is the former Tang dynasty capital and has a wealth of other historical attractions. On the architectural front, the 52-m (210-ft) **Dayan (Big Wild Goose) Pagoda** was originally founded in AD 652.

For those on an architectural pilgrimage, there can be few more fascinating destinations than **Qufu**, the home of Confucius in Shandong province. The Kong clan lived in a maze of over 450 rooms, but it is the adjacent **Confucius Temple**, over a kilometer (at least a half mile) in length — which grew to its enormous size from humble beginnings in the fifth century BC — that is the main attraction. It is one of China's most important classical architectural relics. Yunnan, in the southwest of China, is not an obvious destination for architecture buffs, but for those who make it this far west, some more remote destinations

The China every traveler dreams of is still much in evidence in Beijing; OPPOSITE is the Yonghegong Lama Temple. ABOVE: The Reclining Buddha of Dazu, Sichuan Province, sprawls like a sleeping giant.

in Yunnan not covered in this book such as Baoshan and Tengchong have picturesque wooden street architecture that is long gone elsewhere in China.

For the intrepid traveler **Tibet** is a destination with architectural sights you will remember for the rest of your life. The **Potala**, former residence of the exiled Dalai Lama, and the **Jokhang**, spiritual heart of the holy city of Lhasa, alone make Tibet worth a visit.

Ironically, some of China's most imposing architecture reposes in the buildings constructed by the Western imperial powers in the late nineteenth century. The **Bund** in Shanghai is undoubtedly the most famous of these, a skyline that famously evokes Manhattan and dockyard Liverpool by turns. **Tianjin** is another city with some fascinating colonial architecture. More low-key but not without interest is **Shamian Island** in Guangzhou and the delightful island of **Gulangyu**, just off Xiamen, in Fujian province. Xiamen is also home to the 1,000-year-old **Nanputuo Temple**.

CAVE ART

The best of China's cave art, Buddhist in inspiration, is at Dunhuang's Mogao Caves, Datong's Yungang Caves and Luoyang's Longmen Caves.

Of the three it is Dunhuang's **Mogao Caves** that rate as China's most awe inspiring. Started as early as AD 366 by a monk called Lie Zun, Dunhuang's Buddhist Silk Road culture continued to inspire cave art for a further millennium. A Buddhist monk called Wang Yuanlu discovered the caves in 1900, and began excavating them — many were full of sand. The earliest caves are small, featuring a Buddha statue surrounded by brilliantly colored Buddha paintings radiating outwards in tiers. By the time of the Tang dynasty, when Mogao art was at its apogee, the caves were bigger and so was the statuary within — most famous is Cave 96, with its massive 34-m (nearly 112-ft) seated Buddha.

Close to Datong in Shanxi province, the **Yungang Caves** were a massive undertaking that employed tens of thousands of workers over a century. It's thought that many of the craftsmen employed to carve the statuary came from India. Grottoes are carved from a sandstone rockface, and many of them contain massive Buddha images that can startle on first glance. The earliest caves are in the western section and, along with the central section, these are where the majority of the most impressive grottoes can be found.

Equally impressive are the **Longmen Caves** near Luoyang, which contain close to 100,000 pieces of Buddhist statuary carved out of limestone cliffs bordering the Yi River. The product of some 500 years of continuous labor, they rate as one of China's most impressive cultural attractions.

MUSEUMS

China is full of museums. Every provincial capital has one, and most historically significant counties have one too. Unfortunately, they're rarely well maintained, English is almost never featured in the labeling, and the displays have a tendency to shoot off on wild tangents, so that you might move through several thousand years of history in the space of several steps.

The current generation of Chinese museums is best exemplified by the new **Shanghai Museum**, where meticulous attention has been given to labeling, presentation and lighting, making a tour of the museum's displays of ancient artifacts, notably the bronzes, a joy.

In Beijing, the palace area of the **Forbidden City** is in fact a museum, and the constant inward flood of tourist ticket money and ongoing restoration work means that the displays — and indeed the palace — are in the best shape they've been in for over a century. The **Museum of Chinese History** on Tiananmen Square doesn't live up to its promise, but is not without interest. The drawback is the absence of English labeling.

Xi'an, the ancient Tang dynasty capital of Chang'an, has two excellent museums. The **Shaanxi Provincial Museum** is a high-quality version of the typical provincial museum, with little in the way of English explanations, but nevertheless a fascinating collection of Buddhist images and over 1,000 steles. The **Shaanxi History Museum** is a more recent arrival (opened in 1992), tracing the evolution of civilization in Shaanxi province through thoughtfully displayed and clearly labeled exhibits. Along with the Shanghai Museum it is probably the best in the country.

The **Guangzhou Municipal Museum** is another representative of China's new generation of museum. Uncluttered, well-labeled and chronologically following 2,000 years of local Guangdong history. The museum even has a top-floor tea shop.

PERFORMANCES

China isn't as rich in performance as you might hope, but for those coming in on a whirlwind tour of the main Chinese tourist attractions, there will probably be something to see every night.

Snow frosts the simple elegance of Beijing's famous Temple of Heaven.

Shop till You Drop

The major tourist destinations of China are superb for shopping. There's no need, as in the old days, to seek out the nearest "Friendship Store." These days you'll find most things you need and souvenirs for home in department stores and in street markets.

BARGAINING

Bargaining in China is not the way of life it is in some parts of Asia. In most shops prices are marked, and marked prices mean what they say. Out on the streets, it's a different matter. When market shopping, for example, prices quoted, particularly for tourist souvenirs, are likely to be inflated, sometimes grossly.

The first trick is to hang back. Never rush into purchases at the beginning of your trip. It's highly unlikely that a souvenir that has caught your eye will not be available in other places (unless it's an original work, of course). As your China trip progresses, you will find yourself becoming more familiar with how things work and bolder at making counter offers. The second trick is to never look too "hungry." Maintain an engaged but disinterested smile, offer what you feel is the value of the object, and if you think the price is not right walk away. Walking away can often by a very effective strategy for getting a last-minute discount. Never lose your temper when bargaining.

China is no exception to the general Asian rule that, while bargaining is simply about commerce, it's also about relationships. A Chinese who is bargaining for something is likely to spend as much time chatting with salesperson as actually hammering out a deal. This softly-softly approach is invariably very effective, but the language barrier can make it hard to do. In cases where the barrier is not a barrier, come across as relaxed and interested in more than just the task at hand — getting the cheapest deal possible for what you want.

An important thing to note is, if you make an offer and the salesperson agrees to it, you are obligated to buy.

ANTIQUES

Unless you really know what you're doing, China is not a good place to buy genuine antiques. The quality of imitation antiques is simply too good for the average collector to discern the difference. On the other hand, this is good news to those shoppers who are happy buying attractive Chinese articles and don't require the cachet of a genuine antique.

Beijing is the place for opera, and nightly performances are held, though mostly for the benefit of tourists. Check the listings magazine, *Beijing Scene*, for performances of the real thing — whether traditional or avant-garde. Be warned, however, a real performance of Beijing opera is a nonstop actionfest of acrobatics, eardrum-piercing wails, gong clanging and choreographed fight scenes. The **Zhengyici Theater** in Beijing has nightly authentic opera performances that are a must-see. Meanwhile the **Chaoyang Theater** in Beijing is the place to see the capital's amazing performances of acrobatics. Shanghai, however, is the best place to see acrobatics, and performances there take place nightly at the **Shanghai Center** on Nanjing Xilu.

Beijing is famous for its opera, but regional operas can also be found throughout the country. In **Guangzhou** you will probably see small opera ensembles performing in the parks around town; such performances are informal, with everyone dressed casually in flip-flops and T-shirts. Sichuan is one of the few provinces that is actually working to keep its operatic traditions alive, and in **Chengdu** you can enjoy fascinating short opera performances and even backstage visits before and afterwards at the **Shudu Theater**.

ABOVE: The New World department store on Nanjing Lu in Shanghai. RIGHT: The modern shopping district on Tianjin's fashionable Heping Road.

Start your antique hunt at the Friendship Stores. The branches in Beijing and Xi'an are particularly good, and in theory, if you buy a genuine antique from one of the Friendship branches you will receive a letter of authentication. The Friendship Stores will at least give you a good overview of the kinds of antiques that are available, and most of them have shipping facilities.

Like the Friendship Stores, Chinese museums will often have imitations of prize exhibit pieces for sale. These can often be large and expensive, but it's always worth taking a look at the souvenirs section of museum. Travelers with a keen interest in antiques who make it to Beijing should be sure to visit **Beijing Curio City** on Dongsanhuan Lu, a sprawling confluence of nearly 300 stalls selling every imaginable item of alleged and genuine antique value. The best day to go is Sunday. Also worth visiting is the **Hongqiao Market and Department Store**, next to Tiantan Park. It's open daily.

The nearby city of Tianjin is worth a detour for its huge **Antique Market**. It has something for everyone, including items that are the genuine article.

Hong Kong is an excellent place to shop for antiques, though prices can be staggering. The place to go is the area in Central starting from the upper end of Wyndham Street, continuing all the way along Hollywood Road until you reach "Cat Street," just by the Man Mo Temple. Don't imagine for a moment that all the items

displayed in the antique boutiques of this area are Chinese: Chinese and Thai carved Buddhas, Indonesian masks and batiks, Persian and Indian carpets, rosewood furniture, Himalayan artwork and a fascinating array of snuff bottles, porcelain, silver jewelry, Korean and Japanese wooden chests and traditional Chinese silk paintings and scrolls are all on offer.

In Hong Kong, always look out for the Hong Kong Tourist Association (HKTA) membership sign on shop doors, and don't forget to pick up a copy of HKTA's *Official Shopping Guide*. This handy little booklet is packed with information on where to go and who to trust on your shopping spree, and it offers the added guarantee of its own membership system — every retail outlet in the book has the HKTA stamp of approval. If you have any complaints or queries about a member, you can contact the HKTA Hotline ((852) 2508-1234. (There is no equivalent system elsewhere in China.)

ART

You needn't be a connoisseur and you needn't be fabulously wealthy to shop for art in China. Admittedly, a Tang dynasty scroll may be out of the question, but there are legions of artists in China producing exciting art in a variety of media.

At the bottom of the range are inexpensive wall hangings, usually traditional-style watercolor landscapes. The cheaper ones can cost as little as US$20 or US$30, and can be found anywhere in China where there are tourists. The better works will start at US$100 and usually much higher.

Most tourist-class hotels sell Chinese art in their souvenir shops, but the best places to buy are always in the small, privately run studios you'll find in art centers such as **Suzhou**, **Hangzhou** and **Guilin**. In **Kunming** it is common to come across the work of painters whose work — some in watercolors, some in oils — depicts scenes from minority villages. Generally the prices marked on paintings are optimistic, and there is some latitude for bargaining in studios.

CLOTHES

The Chinese become more fashion conscious with every passing day, but it's still not a wildly exciting place to shop for clothes — except, perhaps, in some of the large open-air markets in Beijing where there are a number of bargains, especially in winter clothing and basic silk items, to be had. Outside the major cities, choice is limited and quality is poor. If new clothes are part of your plans, be sure to allocate some time for Hong Kong.

For a quick overview of Hong Kong's shopping possibilities you might start in Central District. Take a look at the high-class boutiques in **Swire House** and the **Mandarin Hotel** and, via pedestrian crossovers, the **Prince's Building**, the **Landmark** and the elegant **Galleria**, an area bristling with names such as Gucci, Chanel, Christian Dior, Lanvin, Hermes, Giorgio Armani, Nina Ricci, Issey Miyake and Salvatore Ferragamo. Close by are more affordable options such as **Marks & Spencer's**, on the corner of Wyndham Street. **Lane Crawford** on Queen's Road Central, is the traditional home of Harrod's-style upper-drawer British shopping.

Causeway Bay is a better area for bargains, though the accent changes from Western to Japanese high fashion and luxury accessories in the giant Tokyo-style department stores, **Mitsukoshi**, **Daimaru**, **Matsuzakaya** and **Sogo**. Just around the corner from Mitsukoshi, between Russell and Sharp streets, you'll find the spectacular **Times Square**, which has virtually everything you could possibly need.

On the other side of the harbor, in Tsimtsui and Tsimshatsui East, is a city of interconnected shopping complexes: **Star House**, **Harbour City** (**Ocean Terminal**, **Ocean Centre** and **Ocean Galleries**) and **China Hong Kong City**. An information desk in the Ocean Terminal, staffed by English-speaking guides, will provide you with maps and even a computer printout of suitable shops to help you find your way through the retail maze.

ELECTRONICS

China may not be famous for its electronics bargains, but Hong Kong certainly is. The electronics shopping districts are mostly on Kowloon side, but you can shop in Central too. Stanley Street, in Central, is the place for photographic goods. **Photo Scientific Appliances** ((852) 2522-1903, 6 Stanley Street, Central, is recommended. Prices are unlikely to be higher here than in Tsimshatsui, and service will probably be much better. For other electrical items, try the two Sony Service Centre's **Chung Yuen Electrical Co. Shop** ((852) 2524-8066, 104–105 Prince's Building, Chater Road, in Central; and ((852) 2890-2998, 2/F In Square, Windsor House, 311 Gloucester Road, in Causeway Bay.

The so-called "Golden Mile" of Tsimshatsui's **Nathan Road** is Hong Kong's famous tourist shopping district. Prices are not usually marked (they are in the non-tourist parts of town), and some of the salespeople operating out of these shops are very unscrupulous. Use care. **Crown Photo Supplies** ((852) 2376-1836, 27 Hankow Road, and the **Camera Shop** ((852) 2730-9227, Shop 121, Ocean Terminal, can be recommended for photographic needs.

For computers, **Silvercord**, 30 Canton Road, and **Star Computer City**, 2/F Star House, 3 Salisbury Road, are two complexes where you can shop around for the latest software and hardware. The **Golden Shopping Arcade** in Shamshuipo is famous for providing software at unbeatable prices. Some legitimate shops also operate out of this maze of computer dens.

OPPOSITE: At a market in Xishuangbanna, Yunnan Province, a minority woman in Menghun displays locally produced handicrafts. ABOVE: Chinese silk is a good buy in Hong Kong.

Short Breaks

China is such a formidably huge place that — for anyone with on brief vacation or a stopover in Hong Kong, Shanghai or Beijing — coming up with a manageable and sensibly conceived itinerary for some out-of-town sightseeing can be daunting. The trick is not to attempt too much. The last thing you want to do is spend so much time getting to where you're going that you're too tired to enjoy it.

HONG KONG

Transportation connections between Hong Kong and the rest of China have improved to the extent that "popping over the border" for a day or two is perfectly reasonable. The obvious destination — it's closest — is **Shenzhen**. Shenzhen, it must be said, is not the most exciting place in China, nor is it endowed with cultural riches. It is, however, a fascinating lesson in what a difference a few hundred meters can make: enter Shenzhen and you instantly feel very far from Hong Kong. Shenzhen has several theme parks, such as Window of the World (see SHENZHEN, page 126 in HONG KONG, MACAU AND THE SOUTH).

A far more worthy China excursion is a trip to **Guangzhou**. Long looked down on as Hong Kong's poor nephew, Guangdong's provincial capital is a vibrant, modern city these days. Visitors from Hong Kong find the dining cheaper, the people friendlier, the room rates vastly lower, and if the roads are chaotic, it lends some adventure to the trip. Guangzhou also has enough sightseeing to keep you busy for a couple of days.

The easy option (and, if you are pushed for time, the best) is a tour, such as the two-day package from CITS (see TAKING A TOUR, page 60) costing around HK$2,000, which starts in Hong Kong and includes a quick visit to Guangzhou, Foshan (famous for its pottery and temples), Zhongshan and Macau.

Macau, the former Portuguese enclave that is now part of China, makes a rewarding day trip in itself (it's only an hour by boat from Central), but for those with time, an overnight stay in Macau is time well spent: Not only will you be able to see most of the cultural sights but you'll also be able to catch Macau's Portuguese flavor most enjoyably by lingering over meals in typical Portuguese style — that means several hours spent over a three-course lunch that naturally includes aperitifs (a dry white port, perhaps), wine and a vintage port

Repulse Bay and its high-cost condominiums that overlook Hong Kong's most popular beach.

with your coffee. Sightseeing after such lunches is invariably a strain — so it's best to follow the Portuguese way and have a quick siesta back at your hotel.

BEIJING

The area around Beijing is blessed with some of China's best attractions. The crowd-pleaser is the **Great Wall**. Most people climb the wall at Badaling, which is around 70 km (43 miles) northeast of Beijing, and an easy day trip from the capital, but if you're looking to escape the crowds (and at Badaling, they're not to be underestimated), **Simatai**, which is 110 km (68 miles) from Beijing is a far more relaxing spot to enjoy the wall. The **Ming Tombs** tend to get tagged onto some Great Wall tours, but are only worth a visit if you've absolutely exhausted Beijing and its environs.

Just 80 km (50 miles) east of Beijing, **Tianjin** gets overlooked by many China travelers. This is a pity. A vibrant port city, Tianjin has some superb colonial architecture, a legacy of its concession days, and probably the best antique market in all China. It takes about two and a half hours by bus or train from Beijing to get to Tianjin, making it a long, but worthwhile day trip.

An interesting option is to spend a morning sightseeing in Tianjin, and then catch an afternoon train to **Beidaihe** or **Shanhaiguan**, two beach resorts around three hours north of Tianjin. Beidaihe got its start as a European beach resort, but its visitors today are overwhelmingly Chinese. Shanhaiguan is the more interesting destination, as it is here that the Great Wall descends into the sea. It's a charming town, and some mid-range accommodation is starting to materialize here as tourists arrive in greater numbers. A train back to Beijing takes four to five hours.

Chengde, around four hours northeast of Beijing by train, has some of China's most splendid imperial architecture. However, there's far too much to see to attempt it as a day trip from Beijing. It's far better to spend a night in Chengde, get up early, join a sightseeing tour, and then head back to Beijing in the late afternoon.

SHANGHAI

Shanghai is something of a bottleneck when it comes to transportation, so it pays to plan ahead for excursions out of town. But do make a point of getting out of town if you can. Shanghai is surrounded by prime attractions, including two of China's most highly rated destinations: **Suzhou** and **Hangzhou**.

Suzhou is well worth overnighting in, though it's just an hour from Shanghai by train and an easy day outing. After Shanghai, Suzhou's canals and alleys lined with souvenir shops and restaurants will seem village-like. But it's the traditional gardens that are the city's main drawcard.

Hangzhou's main attraction is West Lake, which is the model for hundreds of other West Lakes in China, such is its fame. The lake tends to get swamped with tourists, but if you can manage an overnight stay, things tend to quiet down in the late afternoon. Trains from Shanghai take around three hours to reach Hangzhou.

Festive Flings

As anyone who's spent any time in Taiwan will know, the Chinese celebrate a myriad of festivals. Unfortunately in China most of them have been swept away and will probably never be celebrated again. Nowadays the minority regions of China, such as southern Yunnan, are the best places to see colorful festivals, but as these vary from group to group, listing them would require years of research. The most famous minority festival is the Dai **Water Splashing Festival**, which is held in mid-April throughout Xishuangbanna, wherever there are Dai people and buckets.

SPRING

The one festival that everyone has heard of is **Chinese New Year**, known in Chinese as *chunjie*, or Spring Festival. It lasts for the first two weeks of the first lunar month, which usually places it in late January or early February. This is a time for Chinese to be with their families, so it's not realistic to expect a great deal of festive activity on the streets. You may see the occasional lion dance and hear the explosions of fire crackers going off. Sensible China travelers avoid being in China for Chinese New Year because the transportation infrastructure comes under enormous pressure at this time of year (getting a flight or a seat on a train is nearly impossible at short notice). In addition, much of the country shuts down.

Despite the cold, Chinese New Year is a good time to be in Lhasa, as the Tibetans celebrate **Lhosar**, or the Tibetan New Year, with dances, performances and ritual observances. On the fifteenth day of the first lunar month, the **Lantern Festival** is held in Lhasa, with huge yak butter candles gracing the holy Barkhor circuit. A similar Lantern Festival is celebrated on the same day throughout China; it marks the end of New Year and is celebrated by hanging paper lanterns in the street.

In late March or early April, **Guanyin**, the Buddhist goddess of mercy, has her birthday.

Although a Buddhist deity, she gets the most colorful parties at Daoist temples. Also in early April is the national festival and holiday, **Qing Ming**, or Tomb Sweeping Day. This is the day one's thoughts turn to one's ancestors, and respect is shown by a visit to their graves, which are tidied up. Like Chinese New Year, Qing Ming is not the time to be traveling in China, as transportation gets booked up.

SUMMER

The big Chinese summer festival is the **Dragonboat Festival**, held in the fifth lunar month, which usually falls some time around mid-June. This is one festival that can be quite thrilling, with teams of rowers taking to the water in "dragonboats." *Zongzi*, the packets of rice and pork steamed in lotus leaves, is the traditional festival snack. Hong Kong is a good place to see dragonboat races, as is Yueyang in Hunan province and Nanning in Guangxi autonomous region. In most of the rest of China, however, it is something of a nonevent.

AUTUMN

The seventh lunar month (usually some time in August) is **Ghost Month**, an inauspicious time for new business ventures, exams, and buying important things such as a house or a car. For the most part, life goes on as usual, but look for special celebrations at Daoist temples, particularly in Hong Kong. In Tibet, **Shotun**, or the Yogurt Festival, is celebrated in

the first week of the seventh lunar month, with picnics, dances and operas held in Lhasa.

On the fifteenth day of the eighth lunar month (usually some time in September) is the **Moon Festival**, also known as Mid-Autumn Festival. Like New Year, this is a time for family reunions (more traffic jams), though some street activity is to be expected, with firecrackers and lantern displays. The traditional festival snack is the *yuebing*, or moon cake, a pastry with a soft filling that is made from lotus seeds and sugar — there are hundreds of rival recipes for moon cake fillings.

September 28 is **Confucius' Birthday**. Celebrations are held in Confucius temples all over China, but particularly in Qufu, the Great Sage's hometown.

WINTER

The cold winter months are a lean time for festivals in China. China's only notable festival event at this wintry time of the year is the Harbin Ice Lantern Festival, a recent innovation to draw tourists to the frosty northeast of China. Christmas has little significance outside China's small Christian flocks, but it is usually treated as an excuse for a night out and a big meal, as it is in other countries in the East.

ABOVE, LEFT: China's Long March has taken it from Mao suits to high fashion: pictured is Elite Model Look China 1999 winner Zhao Jun. RIGHT: Near Kunming, colorful dancers keep minority traditions alive.

Galloping Gourmets

Food is never far from the thoughts of the average Chinese. A common greeting among friends is, "*Chi fanle, meiyou?*" or, "Have you eaten?" Complete strangers on trains can fall into long, rapturous conversations about the regional delicacies of the towns they grew up in. Indeed, it wouldn't be far from the truth to say that the Chinese are obsessed by food. The world can be thankful for this, for from it springs a cuisine that ranges adventurously across the entire spectrum of tastes and flavors.

Like China's many dialects, the country's cuisine changes from region to region. For convenience it's reasonable to divide China's cuisines broadly into Northern (Beijing and Shandong), Eastern (Shanghai and Zhejiang), Southern (Chaozhou and Cantonese) and Sichuan.

NORTHERN

One of the first things you notice in the north of China is that thick noodles and steamed breads are the staples of the local diet. Even in Beijing's most famous imperial culinary legacy, Beijing (Peking) duck, the bird is wrapped in *chapati*-like pancakes, not eaten with a bowl of rice.

On the streets look for typical northern treats like *congyoubing*, a griddle-fried pancake stuffed with leeks — it's a snack that has to be eaten hot. *Lamian*, literally "pulled noodles," made from wheat have a slightly chewy texture to them when served correctly, and come in a steaming bowl of broth mixed with fresh leeks, chilies and perhaps some pork. Other northern specialties include the famous *jiaozi*, or dumplings, which if they're good can constitute an entire meal. The basic form of *jiaozi* is chopped pork and chives wrapped in dough and boiled. Dipping sauces are created by the diners themselves with a combination of vinegar, sesame oil, soy sauce and chili.

It's the imperial dishes that pull in the crowds. Along with the famous duck, dishes like beggar's chicken (*qigai ji*) — in which a chicken is wrapped in lotus leaves and cooked in a mud pack (it was originally cooked underground), imparting a curious but intriguing taste to the chicken — are famous.

Beijing's meaty barbecue dishes stem from the days of the Mongol Khans and later from the Manchus. If you're in Beijing in the winter,

For the Cantonese, a fondue cooked over charcoal braziers is a favorite dish in winter months.

a Mongolian barbecue (*mengu kaorou*) is obligatory. It should be accompanied with a Mongolian hotpot, in which vegetables are simmered in a spicy broth.

SOUTHERN

While northern cuisine is heavy and dark — both in its tastes and constituents — the food of the south, Guangdong (Canton) in particular, is light and clear. Unlike the northerners, who have grown used to making it through the long cold winters with pickled vegetables, the southern Chinese are able to cook with fresh ingredients all year round. Indeed the Cantonese take this obsession with freshness to the extremes of displaying their ingredients live and kicking: fish, eels and lobsters swimming around tanks of water, live mammals incarcerated miserably in cages.

When it comes to vegetables it's difficult to think of a better approach than the Cantonese way, which is to stir-fry them quickly at super-hot temperatures; touches of garlic and salt add flavor.

Not everything is stir-fried. Steaming is the preferred option for seafood dishes and *dim sum*. Roasting is employed to great effect on duck and pork, the latter in the famous *chashao*. Cantonese casseroles (*bao*) are another not-to-be-missed specialty. The casseroles are actually sealed up before being heated, allowing the ingredients inside to simmer, with delicious results.

In the West, Cantonese cuisine is most famous for *dim sum*. The word actually means literally "little heart" and is pronounced "*dian xin*" in Mandarin. All regional Chinese cuisines have their *dian xin*, but none of them sport the variety that Cantonese does. Traditionally a morning or brunch experience, *dim sum* are meant to be a light snack washed down with endless cups of tea. Some of the more famous *dim sum* (in Mandarin) include *xiajiao* (prawn dumplings), *shaomai* (prawn and pork dumplings), *luobogao* (fried — usually with pork — taro cake), *zheng paigu* (steamed spare ribs with black bean), *chashabao* (steamed roast-pork bun), and for the adventurous, *fengzhua* — literally "phoenix talons" but in fact steamed chicken's feet.

Most Cantonese will tell you that the best in Cantonese cuisine comes not from Guangzhou or Hong Kong but from Chaozhou in the north of the province. Indeed Chaozhou chefs are highly sought after, and Chaozhou restaurants are favored places for splash-out banquets. Using expensive condiments like shark fin and bird's nest, Chaozhou cuisine — outside Chaozhou itself — is rarely cheap.

EASTERN

One of the famous qualities of eastern cuisine (often called *jiangzhe* in Chinese) is the way salty and sweet flavors combine. Wuxi spareribs, from the town of the same name, is a dish in which the ribs are simmered in a red soy sauce broth with sugar. As in the south, rice is the staple, and fish is a favored dish — the Jiangsu and Zhejiang region is referred to by the Chinese as the *yumi zhixiang*, literally the "land of fish and rice," but with the meaning of "land of plenty," or as we might put it, the "land of milk and honey."

Eastern cuisine frequently gets overlooked by foreigners. The Shanghainese, for example, have their own range of tasty tea snacks, or *dian xin*, to rival the *dim sum* of the south, though typically they tend to be sweeter. Try Shanghai's *xiaolongbao* (sometimes called *tangbao*, which literally means "soup dumpling"), a steamed dumpling that you will recognize in shape from the dumplings you had in Beijing and in Guangzhou, but in this case filled with a hot, sweet and salty soup. They're quite delicious, if you don't mind the soup dribbling down your chin.

As in the south, seafood is a big part of eastern cuisine, particularly in Shanghai and Hangzhou. Shanghai in particular tends to use more oil in its food than other parts of China, and is also heavy on the use of preserved and salted condiments — a famous example is Shanghai's black preserved eggs (*pidan*), which are often served sliced with cold bean curd as a side dish. Other Shanghai favorites include the seasonal "hairy crabs" and "drunken chicken."

Jiangsu favorites are represented best by beggar's chicken, similar to that of Northern China and — if done according to tradition — cooked in the ground. Nanjing is famous for its duck dishes — in particular, smoked duck.

SICHUAN

Sichuan is the fiery cuisine from the west. Little can prepare you for the extremes of heat the Sichuanese will put up with, and enjoy, in their food. You might even think you like hot food until you try a Chongqing-style *mala huoguo*, literally a "numb-hot" hotpot. The culprit is not just chili, and you'll see plenty of it swimming around in your food, but little peppercorns called *huajiao*, or "flower peppers."

The famous spicy dishes from Sichuan are *gongbao jiding*, stir-fried chicken with peanuts, and *mapo doufu*, bean curd cooked in a sauce made of ground pork, spring onions, chili and garlic.

Despite the reputation for spices, Sichuan cuisine reaches out in a variety of directions. Few foreigners can resist the tasty novelty of *guoba roupian*, pork in a soupy stir-fry that is dumped on a bed of crispy rice crusts. Sichuan's sauces too are famed throughout China. Fish-flavored sauce may not taste much like fish, but it's still very tasty and is featured in dishes of national renown, such as *yuxiang qiezi*, fish-flavored eggplant. Sichuan's smoked duck is a dish you should sample if you make it to Chengdu or Chongqing — at its best, it rates favorably with China's other famous duck dish.

BEVERAGES

China's number-one beverage is tea. There are hundreds of varieties, grown at varying altitudes, in different climates, picked in different seasons, but the basic varieties you'll encounter in restaurants are jasmine, flower and wulong (also known as Oolong). When you sit down in a restaurant in China, you will usually be served a pot of tea, for which there is a small charge. If you like, you can forego the tea and ask for China's number-two drink: beer.

How beer got to be so popular in China would make an interesting tale. It got its start at Qingdao, in Shandong province, under the Germans, who had a concession there in the late nineteenth century. Tsingtao is still China's top beer and is widely available, but there will always be a cheaper local brew. Try the local beers; they are usually very good, and, as the joke in China runs, cheaper than bottled water.

Other Chinese alcoholic drinks are rarely appreciated by non-Chinese. Syrupy liqueurs distilled from flowers and fruits are the norm; these, or near-lethal spirits, such as Maotai, which is strictly for toasting your host into oblivion and not the thing for a quiet tipple. Foreign wines and prestigious alcoholic drinks such as brandy are making significant inroads into the Chinese market nowadays.

Avoid drinking tap water in China. Bottled water is available everywhere nowadays and costs very little. Hotel rooms are always supplied with a thermos of hot water; if yours is empty or your room doesn't have one, notify your floor staff with a shout of *"kaishui."*

If you can't do without Coca-Cola, Pepsi, Sprite and company, rest assured you'll find them in the remotest of destinations in China. Trudge to the top of a sacred mountain, and there will probably be someone waiting for you at the top with a can of Coke.

Steaming dumplings, a common street scene in Nanjing, Jiangsu Province.

Special Interests

China is not an easy place to pursue special interests in. If you are keen, it's feasible, say, to enroll in a course in watercolor painting at a university in Suzhou or Hangzhou, but you will probably have to learn Mandarin first. You might conceivably study martial arts at Shaolin Temple (some foreigners do), but again some Mandarin would help and it would be unrealistic to expect that applications and even the study program itself will go smoothly.

Before committing yourself to a study program in China always look into the alternatives in Hong Kong and Taiwan. Taiwan is an especially good place to learn Mandarin.

COOKERY CLASSES

Hong Kong is the place for cookery classes. Try contacting one of the following: **Chopsticks Cooking Centre (** (852) 2336-8433, G/F 108 Boundary Street, Kowloon; **Oriental Culinary Institute (** (852) 2881-5528 FAX 2822-3333, 12/F, 22 Yee Woo Street, Causeway Bay; **Hong Kong Electric Company (Home Management Centre) (** (852) 2510-2828, 10/F Electric Centre, 28 City Garden Road, North Point; **Towngas Centre (** (852) 2576-1535, Basement, Leighton Centre, 77 Leighton Road, Causeway Bay.

LANGUAGE COURSES

If you want to speak Mandarin with a prestigious northern burr, the place to go is Beijing. Full degree programs as well as short courses for all levels are available at the **Beijing Language and Culture University**, 15 Xueyuan Road, Haidian District Beijing, 100083, and at the **Beijing Second Institute of Foreign Languages**, Dingfuzhuang, Chaoyang District, Beijing, 100024. Other courses are available in many of China's provincial capitals, but if you're going to be studying Mandarin in China, you may as well do it in Beijing.

For those who don't fancy a long stint in Beijing, the **Yale in China Language Program** at the Chinese University of Hong Kong **(** (852) 2609-6727 FAX (852) 2603-5004, Shatin, New Territories, is recommended.

The best place in the world to study Mandarin is probably Taipei, although the local accent differs from a Chinese northern accent to the extent that British accent differs from a northern American one. Contact the **Mandarin Training Center (** (886-2) 2321-8405, National Taiwan Normal University, 129-1 Hoping East Road, Section 1, Taipei.

Nanjing, where Mandarin is spoken as the local mother-tongue, is also a center for Chinese studies. The most prestigious language course offered there is at the **Hopkins-Nanjing Center (** (202) 663-5800 FAX (202) 663-7729 E-MAIL nanjing@jhu.edu, 1619 Massachusetts Avenue NW, Washington DC 20036-2213. A less expensive alternative is to make direct arrangements with the Institute for International Students at **Nanjing University (** (25) 359-3587 FAX (25) 331-6747 E-MAIL issd@nju.edu.cn, Nanjing University, 22 Hankou Road, Nanjing. The university also has a WEB SITE http://iwww.nju.

Taking a Tour

For visitors who choose the mainstream or organized tour trail, there's a wide variety of package tours and luxury expeditions offered by the leading tour operators and specialized "trailblazer" agencies of Britain, Europe, the United States and Australia. They'll put you on a train in London and deliver you to Beijing via the memorable Trans-Siberian Railway. They'll fly you directly from London, San Francisco, New York, Seattle, Vancouver, Paris, Frankfurt, Geneva or Sydney to Beijing, Shanghai or Guangzhou or to the main staging point for many China tours, Hong Kong. You can take an ocean cruise from Sydney Harbour and call in on Shanghai and Guangzhou, or you can arrive triumphantly in Kashgar or Lhasa aboard a luxury bus.

ABOVE: Girls from the Miao tribe on Hainan Island pose for a photograph. RIGHT: A practitioner of China's ancient art of *qigong,* oblivious to his surroundings in Lu Xun Park, Qingdao.

Travel to China can be less expensive as an individual traveler, but organized group tours are the most comfortable, convenient and predictable way to do it — you have the advantage of being able to roll along with your group knowing that you don't have to lift a finger on your own behalf except to eat, drink and buy souvenirs. Most of the big established operators provide escorts with a sound experience of China travel and Chinese culture, and they also take care of everything from visas to a very welcome short stopover in Hong Kong at the end of the trip. Their prices generally include international travel to and from China, all internal travel, full accommodation and meals, cultural excursions, Chinese interpreters and guides and airport taxes.

TOUR OPERATORS

BRITAIN

Voyages Jules Verne is probably Europe's biggest and most experienced China tour operator, with its own office in Beijing to help smooth out accommodation and itinerary problems. The company has a wide range of tours to China and Tibet that can also takes in North Korea, the Republic of Mongolia and Russia. It also conducts several tours on the Trans-Siberian/China rail route (see THE TRANS-SIBERIAN RAILWAY, below).

ABOVE: The delicate lines of Xichan Pagoda, Fuzhou, Fujian province, are almost definitive of the exoticism of Chinese architecture. RIGHT: A riot of neon competes for attention along Nathan Road, Kowloon.

For brochures and detailed information their London office is **Travel Promotions Ltd.** ((44 20) 7616-1000 FAX (44 20) 7723-8629 E-MAIL sales@vjv.co.uk, 21 Dorset Square, London NW1 6QJ.

Regent Holidays ((44 117) 921-1711, 15 John Street, Bristol, is another tour operator that offers Trans-Siberian packages, but the difference is they're aimed at individual travelers. For those who want the comfort of knowing everything is organized but don't want the group-tour experience, Regent is a good choice.

For the standard package experience with a reliable and well established operator, **Hayes and Jarvis (Travel) Ltd.** ((44 20) 8748-5055 FAX (44 20) 8741-0299, Hayes House, 152 King Street, London W6 0QU, is recommended. Not only do they do some very reasonably priced combination tours that include China, but their basic one-destination packages inclusive of accommodation are amongst the most reasonably priced around.

CONTINENTAL EUROPE

Swiss-based **Kuoni Travel** has tours of all kinds. They have many offices around the region, including one in the United Kingdom: **Kuoni** ((44 1306) 740500 FAX (44 1306) 744222, Kuoni House, Dorking, Surrey, RH5 4AZ, England.
Voyages Kuoni ((33 1) 42 85 71 22 FAX (33 1) 40 23 06 26, 95 rue d'Amsterdam, F-75008 Paris, France.
Reiseburo Kuoni ((49 89) 2311-1630 FAX (49 89) 2311-1650, Furstenfelderstrasse 7, D-80331 Munich, Germany.
Kuoni Travel (Head Office) ((41 1) 277-4444 FAX (41 1) 272-0071, Neue Hard No. 7, CH-8037 Zurich, Switzerland.

UNITED STATES

Abercrombie & Kent International ((1 630) 954-2944 TOLL-FREE (1 800) 323-7308 FAX (1 630) 954-3324 E-MAIL info@abercrombiekent.com, 1520 Kensington Road, Oak Brook, Illinois 60523, is one of the big names of package tourism and offers not only tours to China but to all corners of the world. Tours such as its Highlights of China, an eight-day jaunt around some of the best of China, are extremely popular.

Himalayan Travel, Inc. ((1 203) 359-3711 TOLL-FREE (1 800) 225-2380 FAX (1 203) 359-3669 E-MAIL worldadv@netaxis.com, 112 Prospect Street, Stamford, Connecticut 06901, is a leading operator for more adventurous tours. Groups tend to be small (fewer than 15 people), and comfort levels and price vary according

to the destination and needs of the group. Himalayan also offers cycling tours, as well as specialized tours like its short "Rural China" expedition.

For a company that specializes in China, **China Voyages (** (1 510) 559-3388 TOLL-FREE (1 800) 914-9133 FAX (1 510) 559-8863, 1650 Solano Avenue, Suite A, Berkeley, California 94707, is recommended. Apart from tour packages, they also offer customized tours. A wide variety of tours are on offer at any given time from the United States, Hong Kong and Beijing. China Voyages also offers a number of "flexible city packages" that get travelers to a China destination and provide accommodation, leaving you free to explore under your own steam.

CANADA
Pacific Rim Travel Corporation ((1 250) 380-4888 TOLL-FREE (1 800) 663-1559 FAX (1 250) 380-7917 E-MAIL pacrimtc@pinc.com, 419–1207, 8-1501, Glentana Road, Victoria, BC V9A 7B2, is a tour operator with special interests in China. Along with general China tours, they also offer specialist tours and tours led by China experts.

AUSTRALIA
Adventure World ((61 2) 9956-7766, 76 Walker Street, North Sydney, has the most comprehensive package tours to China of any Australian operator, and also offers specialized tours.

Australia's most well established tour operator is **Flight Centres International — Sydney (** (61 2) 9267-2999 Bathurst Street (corner of George Street), North Sydney 2090; **Melbourne (** (61 3) 9600-0799 TOLL-FREE 1800-679943, Level 7, 343 Little Collins Street, Melbourne 3000; **Brisbane (** (61 7) 3229 5917 TOLL-FREE 1800-500204, Level 13, 157 Ann Street, Brisbane 4000.

HONG KONG
An alternative to taking a package tour directly from your home country is to fly to Hong Kong, enjoy a few days of leisurely shopping and sightseeing, and then take advantage of China trips organized and operated from there. From Hong Kong, tours ranging from a one-day hop over the border to two- to three-week grand tours are offered by China International Travel Service (CITS), China Travel Service (CTS) as well as many other travel and tour agencies:

CITS (Head Office) Kowloon **(** (852) 2732-5888 FAX (852) 2721-7154, 13/F, Tower A, New Mandarin Plaza, 14 Science Museum Road,

Tsimshatsui East; Branch Office **(** (852) 2810-4282, Room 1807, Wing On House, 71 Des Vœux Road, Central.

CTS (Head Office) **(** (852) 2522-0450 FAX (852) 2851-0642, CTS House, 78–83 Connaught Road Central; Hong Kong Branch Office **(** (852) 2521-7163 FAX (852) 877-2033, China Travel Building, 77 Queen's Road Central; Kowloon Branch Office **(** (852) 2721-1331, First Floor; Alpha House, 27–33 Nathan Road, Tsimshatsui.

OTHER AGENCIES
On Hong Kong Island, one of the biggest and most reliable agencies for either tickets or tours into China from Hong Kong is **Abercrombie & Kent (** (852) 865-7818 FAX (852) 2866-0556 E-MAIL akhkg@attmail.com, Nineteenth Floor Gitic Centre, 28 Queen's Road East, Wanchai.

Thomas Cook Travel Services (HK) Ltd.
((852) 2853-9933 FAX (852) 2545-7477 E-MAIL
infobox@thomascook.com.hk, Unit 2210-2218,
Level 22, Tower 1, Millennium City, 388
Kwun Tong Road, Kwun Tong, Kowloon, is
another long-established operator with
standard and customized tours to China.
They are able to handle most China bookings,
including flights, internal train travel and
hotels.

THE CHINA CONNECTION
Information on China International Travel
Service (CITS) and China Travel Service
(CTS) tours and other China travel matters
can also be obtained by contacting their
overseas branches or agents — or you can get
in touch with Chinese tourist offices abroad
(see TOURIST INFORMATION, page 273 in
TRAVELERS' TIPS).

THE TRANS-SIBERIAN RAILWAY
This grand rail journey from London to Hong
Kong, crossing Europe, the former Soviet
Union and China, has been turned into a
series of adventure tours since the Trans-
Siberian Railway joined the mainstream
tourism trail a few years ago.

One of the leading operators is United
Kingdom-based Voyages Jules Verne, with a
selection of tours ranging from the 21-day
London to Hong Kong epic to a 13-day Silk
Road adventure from Samarkand in Central
Asia to Shanghai on luxury trains. For more
details contact **Travel Promotions Ltd.**
((44 20) 7616-1000.

A ferry trip provides a moment to catch up on news,
against the skyline of Shanghai's famous
waterfront, The Bund.

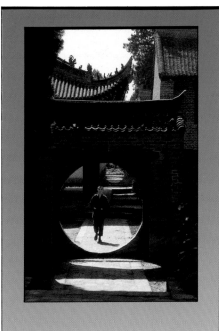

Welcome
to China

REN SHAN, REN HAI — people mountains, people sea — is the saying Chinese use to describe a heaving crowd. They might be talking about China itself. After all, perhaps the most lingering impression that most travelers leave with from China is of the crush of people.

China is also home to a cultural heritage that has endured for thousands of years, making it one of the most fascinating and rewarding travel experiences on earth. But in the end it's the people — more than 1.2 billion of them — that steal the show. They are the players in an ongoing, and increasingly successful, effort to wrest China into the modern world.

That effort has not always had happy results. But one of the many remarkable things about China is that the people, plucky, industrious, enterprising, remain undaunted. The Chinese put their perseverance down to their ability to *chi ku* — swallow bitterness. And there is proof of this wherever you look.

It is the unremitting human struggle that is the most challenging, and yet the most fascinating, aspect of a visit to China. If you're not shielded from it on an official tour you are, in many respects, competing with more than a billion people for services and amenities. But it is this struggle that makes the Chinese who they are, and a China tour so unlike most other travel experiences. And the China traveler is rewarded with countless unbidden acts of charity and kindness — a proffered orange on a long distance train, a helping hand when it's most needed.

And as for that cultural legacy, to be sure it has suffered at the hands of the momentous changes that swept through twentieth-century China, but the last two decades have seen immense restoration efforts. As China modernizes, with it comes new museums, better food, and an increasing awareness of the need to preserve the past.

Still, modern China is a conundrum, a place of extremes of wealth, never-ending change and fascinating juxtapositions of old and new — from the highrise skyline of Shanghai to the towering Potala palace of the exiled Dalai Lama in Tibet. The one constant is the people — at times mystifying, at others like old friends — on the mountains, on the sea, everywhere.

Xuanwu Park is a world apart from the bustle of downtown Nanjing, Jiangsu Province.

The Country and Its People

JUST AS CHINA IS PHYSICALLY VAST, IT IS ALSO A LAND OF VIVIDLY CONTRASTING TERRAIN AND CLIMATE. It is the third largest country on earth after Russia and Canada, its territory covering seven percent of the world's total land surface, an area of nearly 10 million sq km (3.8 million sq miles) including Tibet. It stretches 5,500 km (3,410 miles) from its northern to southern borders and almost the same distance from east to west.

Dotted around its 14,000-km (8,680-mile) eastern and southern coastline are nearly 5,000 islands, some of them, such as Hainan off the southern coast, large enough to support substantial farming and fishing communities. The island of Taiwan, where the Nationalist Guomindang forces fled in the revolution of 1949, is considered by the Beijing leadership to be part of China and pressure mounts on the island to come back into the mainland fold. The tiny, once Portuguese-administered enclave of Macau returned to China in 1999, following the former British colonial possession of Hong Kong — that remarkable capitalist industrial and trading center which has thrived and fattened over the years as the communist giant's principal source of foreign exchange — which returned to full Chinese sovereignty on July 1, 1997.

The terrain within all this territory is so varied and contrasting that, for the relatively casual visitor, it needs to be approached in its simplest terms. In one sense it has the same basic architecture as its traditional man-made temples and pavilions with their sweeping, multitiered eaves. If you take Tibet in the far west as the tip of the roof (and Tibet is, in fact, popularly termed the "Roof of the World"), the rest of the terrain sweeps and falls away to the east in a series of descending plateaus and plains, arriving finally at sea level along the eastern seaboard.

The landscape is dominated by two great river systems, the Yellow River (Huanghe) in the north and the mighty Yangzi (Changjiang) to the central southwest. Both originate in the upper reaches of the Tibet–Qinghai Plateau and surge downhill toward the eastern coast, and both have acted as the landscape's principal sculptors. Over many thousands of years the Yellow River has deposited and then carved its way through a vast plain of soft loess soil, creating a dramatic and sometimes bizarre pattern of winding canyons, rounded bluffs and strangely shaped outcroppings where harder soil and rock have resisted its knife. To the south, the Yangzi has carved the narrow, precipitous Yangzi gorges of Sichuan and Hubei provinces, and beyond that its southern tributaries have rushed and seeped through a wide belt of limestone to form a similarly dramatic landscape of karst — geological formations in which erosion has left spear-shaped pinnacles, underground caverns and abruptly-shaped

mounds and hills that have given the city of Guilin and its Guangxi–Zhuangzu autonomous region its fairyland character.

These river systems have been both life-giving and death-dealing over the many centuries of recorded Chinese history. Both have periodically unleashed terrible floods which have destroyed croplands and wiped out whole communities, killing countless numbers of people. The Yellow River, known in the past as "China's Sorrow," has breached its banks and dikes more than 1,000 times, changed its course on at least 20 occasions, and during the 2,000 years from the Han to Qing dynasties, the Yangzi has gone on the rampage in more than 200 disastrous floods.

Elsewhere, the landscape sprawls and soars through climates that range from frigid-temperate with permafrost in the far north to temperate, subtropical and tropical as it sweeps south. In winter the far northern reaches, lashed by bitter winds from the Siberian steppes, are bleak and forbidding, either dry and frozen or, as one of Mao Zedong's many poems depicted them, "a thousand miles sealed with ice, 10,000 miles of swirling snows." Meanwhile, in the far south, the sun beats down upon lush rainforests, bamboo groves and rice paddies below the Tropic of Cancer. In summer the entire country boils in the south and bakes in the drier north, with the temperature at a national average of 25°C (77°F).

OPPOSITE: Picturesque Sky Lake lies in the Tian Range near Urumqi — revered as heaven by ancient Xiongnü nomads. ABOVE: Turkic-speaking merchant from Urumqi.

The western mountains of Yunnan, Sichuan and Qinghai provinces rise majestically to heights of 7,000 m (23,000 ft) or more to form the foothills of the awesome Himalayas; the deserts and dust bowls, including the dreaded Takla Makan (Taklimakan) and the harsh Turpan Depression — 154 m (505 ft) below sea level, one of the lowest land surfaces on earth — are moonscapes of relentlessly shifting sands under which the houses, temples and bones of the fabled Silk Road and the frontiers of Chinese civilization lie buried. And in between these stark contrasts there lies a wide diversity of prairies, jungles, "green seas" of bamboo, spectacular rivers — some 1,500 of them — 370 large lakes, gentle streams and jagged coastlines.

GAZELLES AND GINGKOS

Despite its huge land space, only about 15% of China is suitable for agriculture and extensive human settlement, and this means that in some areas there is an abundance and similar diversity of vegetation and wildlife. In all, China claims to have some 32,000 species of higher plants and more than 4,500 species of animals and birds, including more than 400 species of mammals, or 10% of the world total.

Some of this natural heritage, including the giant panda and the gingko tree of Sichuan province, is native only to China. And as the near-arctic

ABOVE: Industrialization and intense people-pressure have led to the construction of huge public housing projects in the major cities. RIGHT: China's Muslim minority of Xinjiang Province remain distinct in dress and custom from their Han Chinese counterparts.

forest wildernesses of the north give way to sweeping grasslands and the lush tropical river plains of the south, there are tigers, bears, moose, deer and gazelle, wild horses and camels, wolves and foxes, snow leopards, yaks, antelopes, monkeys, civet cats and even elephants.

However, that's not to say that the country is one vast and flourishing natural habitat. The giant panda hasn't been adopted as the emblem of the World Wildlife Fund for Nature just for its cuddly features and striking colors — hunting, land clearance and centuries of deforestation of many areas have reduced the giant panda population, and many other animal species in China, to crisis point.

Industrialization has also taken its toll, and so have the immense pressure for food and the wholesale slaughter of wildlife for ingredients for traditional Chinese medicine; if you climb Mount Emei in Sichuan, for example, you'll come across a far less illustrious symbol of Chinese conservation — skeletal dried monkey carcasses set up on stalls to advertise herbal and animal medicines.

THE PEOPLE PRESSURE

The most stunning feature of China, however, is its population of 1.2 billion people, a quarter of the human race, packed into 15% of the country's land surface. It has created a stark contrast of its own — teeming eastern and southern cities, with Shanghai and its municipal zone crammed with no fewer than 13 million people, and comparatively deserted wildernesses in parts of the north and in the northwest. It has also created a society whose entire character is governed by one phenomenon — a furious competition for all the most basic necessities of life.

Arriving in China you encounter a society that is the definition of economics taken to its extreme — vast, unlimited demands, severely limited resources. Leaving aside the implications that this has had through 5,000 or so years of Chinese history, it is more important to consider how this economic nightmare has been tackled over the past 40 years, and how the struggle stands today.

The communist revolution sought, among other things, to slay the economic dragon and rebuild, out of chaos and collapse, a new, prospering, self-governing and self-sufficient China. For all the mistakes, misguided idealism and subsequent chaos that are nowadays blamed on the Maoist era, some tremendous achievements were made. Simply figuring out how to feed the country's enormous population was an achievement. The industrial base and infrastructure — transport, public housing and communications — were rebuilt, lifting the nation out of the hope-

The Country and Its People

lessness and grinding poverty of the violent pre-revolutionary years. On top of that, discipline was imposed based on mass campaigns and a code of individual and group responsibility that is still expressed here and there today with the phrase "to be of service to the people." But then, something went wrong. While the people were encouraged to exist in a Utopian mood of cooperation and communal responsibility, power struggles erupted in the leadership; and in the most crucial high-level political struggle of all, on the direction in which the development of China should be guided, the embattled Chairman Mao unleashed the Great Proletarian Cultural Revolution. It got out of hand. The principle of self-sufficiency was taken to an idealistic extreme, the society turned in on itself and the clock of progress stopped while, for almost a decade, another wave of violence and chaos swept the land.

THE NEW CHINA

Today, it's hard to imagine the China of 15 years ago, a place whose infrastructure had fallen into disrepair. The Chinese modernization program has been

more successful than even its most optimistic backers could have hoped. The new China is booming, bringing high-class international hotels and modern travel services to the big cities — hotels with four- and five-star accommodation, IDD telephone services in all rooms, business centers and quality Chinese and international restaurants. The deluxe Palace Hotel and China World Trade Center in Beijing, the Hilton and Portman Ritz-Carlton in Shanghai and the Holiday Inn Downtown and Garden hotels in Guangzhou are among the new properties which reflect this general upgrading throughout China.

This top end boom has had the effect of inspiring mid-range and even budget hotels to refurbish and train their staff in the basics of the hotel industry. Still, improved though standards may be, it's likely that in the mid-range and certainly in the budget hotels you will still come across toilets and showers that don't work, hot water that never materializes, creaky plumbing, idiosyncratic heating, threadbare carpeting and all the other discomforts sent to plague the traveler.

TRANSPORTATION

Nothing better reflects China's giddy push for the future than the improvements that are taking place in the transportation infrastructure. Roads are being upgraded everywhere you look. New trains are being brought into service. And most air-routes these days are serviced by modern Airbus, Boeing, and McDonnell Douglas jets. Airports too are being upgraded, although more remote destinations are still subject to delays, cancellations and poor passenger service.

The rail system, like the rest of the infrastructure, is under tremendous people pressure. On any day most railway stations throughout China are

home to vast crowds of people and their baggage, some of them camped outside them waiting for tickets or trains. Others fill the booking halls, struggling and sometimes fighting to get to the ticket windows. The simple process of checking through the train gates to get to the trains can turn into a mob scramble, sometimes policed but sometimes uncontrolled, which can leave you breathless, angered and even bruised. The best way to avoid such scenes is to travel "soft sleeper," the Chinese equivalent of first class, which will not only provide you with a comfortable berth but should also provide you with a first-class waiting room away from the pandemonium elsewhere in the station.

Yet for all this, the trains do run strictly on time. They are also reasonably comfortable, and they can stir the imagination. Whenever time permits, choose the train for travel across China — few experiences compare with the sight of paddy fields flashing past, seen from the inside of a train.

There is little romance, however, about the public buses. Inner city buses are always cheap, but they are often ludicrously overcrowded and sometimes the haunt of pickpockets. Long-distance services are not much better. The trend these days is towards "sleeper buses." If there are two of you, this form of transport is fine for an overnight trip, but if you are on your own you will probably find yourself squeezed into the equivalent of a single bed with a complete stranger. On obscure long-distance routes the general practice is to cram as many passengers in as possible and then putter along at an average of around 25 km/h (15 mph) — though travel is much faster on the new highways that are being built around China.

Travel in China can be frustrating beyond words. Yet, like almost everything else in China, there's another side to the coin of discomfort. You may find yourself pressed against the inside wall of a bus, fighting claustrophobia, and someone will get up and offer you a seat and insist that you take it, despite your protests, because you are a foreign guest. Such gestures of comradeship and hospitality happen often in China, and they tend

to happen at the most crucial moments, when the three most vital qualities that every visitor to China must have — patience, understanding and peace of mind — are wearing dangerously thin. They prove, time and time again, the admirable strength of the ordinary Chinese people, their ability to put up with the most grueling, derelict conditions, day after day, and still retain a sense of humor and generosity. It's merciful that it does happen, because even the most equable Western temperament can reach breaking point in the pitfalls and surprises of this bewildering society.

THE MILLIONAIRE SYNDROME

China's long period of cultural isolation manifestly affects the way in which the Chinese regard foreigners. Many of them believe all Westerners are millionaires. Certainly, when you compare the standard of living that Western tourists exhibit in China with the level at which they live, particularly in the working-class districts of major cities and the poorer rural areas, foreigners look as though they've got money to burn. (Not all Chinese regard foreigners as rich. The rise of the Chinese capitalists, particularly the new wave of entrepreneurs and joint-venture factory czars of Shanghai and the burgeoning Pearl River Delta in Guangdong province, has already created an elite level of wealth beyond anything that the average Westerner can imagine.)

At some of the major tourist attractions, particularly the Great Wall at Badaling near Beijing, the terracotta army in Xi'an and the Stone Forest in Yunnan province, the hustle for tourist money has become so fierce that you encounter packs of souvenir hawkers more frenzied than any you're likely to see outside, say, Kuta Beach in Bali. At Xi'an they're so persistent that they've had to be confined to fixed areas outside the terracotta tomb because visitors were unable to view the soldiers for their sales clamor inside.

THE MAIN ATTRACTION

Back in the early days of China travel, the sudden appearance of a foreigner was enough to generate an instant crowd of captivated onlookers. This intense fascination has ebbed somewhat over the last decade, so that in the big cities most Chinese won't bat an eyelid at the sight of a foreign face. But leave for the provinces and when you walk the streets you are under constant public scrutiny. On the trains it sometimes reaches the point where you can hardly bear to move for the attention and excitement that it can generate up and down the carriage. Wherever you go, you become the main

China's national rail network is one of the last in the world to operate steam locomotives alongside modern diesels.

attraction; and while it is generally a nice thing to be, it can also be tiring.

But what you get in return is attention. The Chinese not only want to study you, they want to be involved in some way with you. So, if you lose your bearings in the streets someone will inevitably help. If you're at a loss in the railway booking halls, someone will show you where to get your ticket. People will invite you to eat with them, to take pictures of them and their children. With what little they have, they'll offer you cigarettes, fruit, sweets, biscuits, sunflower seeds, nuts and other modest but touching gifts aboard the trains and buses. On an individual tour, you'll feel at times as though the Chinese people are almost handing you from one to another right across China.

CAN I HELP YOU?

Even in the most fraught situations, when the language barrier threatens to overwhelm you, an angel will usually appear with the greeting, "Hello. Can I help you?" This is the opening gambit of another cultural exchange that foreign visitors are called upon to take part in throughout China. It comes from young students, and there are many millions of them, who are striving to learn English to "better ourselves" and who have very little opportunity to try out their vocabulary and pronunciation.

Some will seize upon any foreigner they see, and only the most insensitive can resent it. Most of the students are earnest and friendly and, in return for a little conversational practice, will go to great lengths to help with ticketing and other information. If their English is good enough you can also break through the official jargon of China and get some sense of the deeper impulses and attitudes of the society.

Although the English students are far more likely to be working part time jobs or busy in the classroom than lurking in the train station these days, it's still difficult at times not to feel that you are carrying an imaginary sign which says "teacher." Impromptu English-language sessions can be so frequent that some China travelers burn out and hide behind a few words of another language altogether when approached by the student of English. Just watch out that you don't end up becoming the recipient of an English lesson yourself if you do this.

THE CHANGING SCENE

China is changing at such breakneck speed that even the Chinese themselves find it difficult to keep up. Where just a decade ago there were exhortatory slogans, there are now billboards advertising Remy Martin, Marlboro and Coca-Cola.

Where everyone dressed in near-identical Mao suits, they now deck themselves out in fashionable outfits from chains like Giordano and Bossini. Where once the streets teemed with Flying Pigeon bicycles, they now buzz with Hondas.

This burgeoning affluence and the promise of riches to come is making China a more confident place. The hand-over of Hong Kong in 1997 and Macau in 1999 were grand events that ended what many Chinese consider a humiliating chapter in their history — the ceding of territory to opium-peddling foreigners. And while there has been much hand-wringing (often justified) about Hong Kong's legal integrity now that it is back in China's hands, astute observers have been heard to point out that influence is a two-way street: over the last decade China has become more like Hong Kong than the opposite.

Perhaps this new China is not quite the country many of us imagine before we go, but it is no less interesting for it. The familiar emblems of the modern world take on new nuances of meaning in a Chinese context. China can never lose its power to surprise and astound. And with a said 5,000 years of history behind it, how could it be any other way?

THE CHINESE PAST

THE CULTURAL SAFE-DEPOSIT

A short visit to China is a fleeting encounter with one of the most complex cultures on earth, touching the tiny tip of an immense and almost limitless cultural iceberg. An extensive tour is a route-march through the cultural heritage of 4,000 to 5,000 years of recorded Chinese history, and at the end of the march it is still as complex and elusive as ever. You come away feeling that for all you've seen, and all the distance you've traveled, you've done little more than lightly scratch the surface. In one respect this is all that anyone can do, for the vast bulk of China's history lies buried in the ground. It's estimated that its current array of temples and monasteries, grottoes and statues, relics and artifacts and great monuments is only about 10% to 20% of that which may some day be available to see — the rest of it languishing in a kind of cultural safe-deposit, awaiting the archaeologist's key.

The history that it represents covers such a long and tumultuous span of time and events that no guidebook could ever do it justice, and no visitor other than the lifelong China scholar could really set foot on Chinese soil with anything but the vaguest idea of what it's all about. The best that can be done in any one book, in fact, is to put it into a reasonably understandable perspective. As with its geography, Chinese history must be approached in its simplest form.

THE DISTANT DAWNING

The approach begins with the evidence that proto-human life existed in China at least 600,000 years ago. The most vivid testimonial lies in a museum and excavated cave at Zhoukoudian, about 50 km (31 miles) southwest of Beijing, where two teeth and a skull were discovered in the 1920s, providing the physical profile of one of the most celebrated archaeological finds of all time — the apelike Peking Man.

As long ago as 5000 BC, Peking Man's more human descendants were farming the rich alluvial valleys and plains of the Yellow, the Yangzi

Whether the Xia actually existed or not, it is now firmly established that by about 1700 BC the various tribal settlements of eastern China, between what are now Shanghai and Tianjin, had been pulled together under the rule of one monarch to form the state of Shang — China's first dynasty. The first steps were taken toward a sophisticated level of civilization during the subsequent six centuries of Shang rule. The first written records appeared, inscribed on bamboo strips and on oracle bones and tortoise shells used in the first stirrings of institutional religion, including the tradition of divine rule. Also, the huge pharmacopoeia of Chinese herbal medicine began to form. In the later stages of Shang rule the royal

and other river networks in China's southeast region. For evidence of this, go to the culturally strategic city of Xi'an where, 40 km (25 miles) to the east, you'll find the Banpo Museum, a tacky tourist attraction which has an old-fashioned museum section featuring bones, pottery, stone tools, a covered excavation of a settlement of that distant Neolithic period and an interesting reconstruction of the circular earthen-walled and mud-roofed dwellings of that age.

For the Chinese, history begins with Huangdi, the Yellow Emperor, who according to the ancient historian Sima Qian unified much of northern China and who was succeeded by a string of other emperors before the founding of the legendary Xia dynasty. Datings of the Xia dynasty vary depending on the source, but scholars generally agree that its founding was somewhere around 2000 BC.

capital was based at what is now Anyang in the far north of Henan province, where Shang tombs, ruins and writings have been excavated, and in the now strategic rail junction city of Zhengzhou.

The eventual collapse of the Shang reign in around 1027 BC weakened the tradition of centralized rule, and power was spread among independent regional warlords who jostled for supremacy but nonetheless owed allegiance to a titular ruler, the duke of Zhou. They were a wealthy, lavishly indulged bunch, as can be appreciated today in the small Hubei Provincial Museum in Wuhan, where you can view some of the 10,000 treasures and relics unearthed in 1978 from the tomb of one of the prominent nobles of that time, the Marquis Yi of Zeng. The exhibition is evidence not only of

LEFT: Cadre's son with toy gun in Shenyang.
RIGHT: One of 50,000 Buddha images in the
53 Yungang Grottoes west of Datong, Shanxi Province.

wealth and refinement but of another important step at that time along the road to civilization — it features a huge bronze musical bell chime, 65 bells in all and each with two different pitches. It is such a sophisticated instrument that its frequencies are close to those of today's modern music.

Inevitably these rival lords fell out with each other, and the society stumbled into more than two centuries of almost constant warfare known as the Warring States period. At this point, Chinese civilization came up against its first important crossroad. Wracked by intrigue and bloodshed, it could only hope for a supremely powerful state and an iron-fisted ruler to put it back on the civilized path and save it from continuing barbarism.

Curiously, however, although this era is usually regarded as one of battle and confusion, it was no benighted dark age. Intellectually, the period is known as one in which "100 schools of thought" contended. Many of the great classical writings that were to enter the Chinese literary cannon and become cornerstones of the Chinese scholar-bureaucrat system were written at this time. The most famous product of these times was Confucius (551–479 BC), who looked at the confusion about him and searched for a solution in an ordered world governed by reciprocity in relationships: "Let the ruler be a ruler and let the subject be subject," he said. Thus was Confucianism born. Daoism too owes its origins to the same period. The legendary sage Laozi, who probably lived and died before Confucius was born, and Zhuangzi (369–286 BC) espoused a philosophy that emphasized the individual in nature rather than the individual in society. Harmony with the Way was Taoism's essential message.

THE IRON EMPEROR

The immense power of the strongman who ultimately strode into the breach and saved the society at that crucial time, in 221 BC, can be imagined today when you stand and study one of China's most astonishing historic monuments — the eerie, half-excavated terracotta army of Qinshi Huangdi, the first emperor of Qin, outside Xi'an. This Darth Vader of Chinese history ruthlessly smashed and subjugated his rival warlords and then set about to impose his rule on much of the rest of China.

Although he paid posthumously for his iron reign, his "dynasty" collapsing in a vengeful popular uprising after his death, Emperor Qinshi Huangdi established two conventions which have dictated the impetus and attitude of Chinese society ever since: He gave the Chinese race its first real unity, and he began work on a magnificent protective barrier that would shield this unified civilization from outside threat, the Great Wall. He also re-established the Shang dynasty's pyramidal social structure, the peasant masses at the base and the various succeeding levels of merchants, military, scholars and aristocracy reaching upward to the divine authority of one supreme ruler; this structure of power not only stayed in place for many dynasties to come but was reaffirmed as recently as during the "reign" of Chairman Mao Zedong.

THE AGE OF THE HAN

After the brief 11-year reign of Qinshi Huangdi, the first of the great dynasties arose: the Han. During its epic 400-year rule it strengthened the political and social pillars that Emperor Qinshi Huangdi had set in place, and so much so that its name has since been synonymous with membership in the Chinese race, the vast bulk of society being referred to as Han Chinese. It also codified the teachings of a very learned, if ultra-

conservative, scholar of a previous age, Confucius (551–487 BC), to provide this society with a set of ethics and responsibilities by which all the different classes of people knew and appreciated their place.

The Han reign is remarkable, though, for its main preoccupation, protecting Chinese unity and civilization. While military expeditions were sent to the south to try to conquer resistant tribal groups and bring them into the Han "family," armies were also marched north to the harsh deserts of the northwest frontier, beyond the reach of Qinshi Huangdi's then-primitive Great Wall, to try to contain and crush the civilization's main enemies, the Xiongnu, or Huns; a fierce confederation of nomadic slave-trading tribes of Central Asia.

One campaign after another was waged against these northern "barbarians," the modern-day descendants of whom can be seen among the strangely alien Turkic-speaking minorities of northern Gansu province and the cities of Hami, Turpan, Ürümqi and Kashi (Kashgar) in the Xinjiang Uygur autonomous region. Under Han rule the die of the Chinese imperative was cast — it pitted membership of a select and civilized society against the barbarism that rode the wilds without. So vital was this imperative that the cost of constant warfare with the Xiongnu eventually exhausted the dynasty and, in the second century AD, brought it to its knees.

Blind Man's Bluff

But not before another imperative had been introduced to the Chinese experience — the cultural imperative. The wars against the Xiongnu were waged not only to keep the Han nation intact but also to keep open and free of Xiongnu harassment

The legacy of Qinshi Huangdi, the ruthless "father" of Chinese unity, his terracotta army stands vigil near Xi'an.

the society's main link with the outside world — or rather, its link with the mysterious lands that lay somewhere far beyond the barbarian domains.

This rather tenuous thread was the fabled Silk Road, the long and often perilous overland trading route that began near what is now the port of Sur in Lebanon and snaked across northern Persia and Afghanistan, northern India, and part of the rugged territory now known as Tajikistan and Kyrgyzstan, and entered China at a point near Kashgar on the western border of present-day Xinjiang. From there the trail split into two to skirt the Takla Makan Desert and Turpan Basin, to pass close to Dunhuang and then through the fortified trading city of Yumenguan (Jade Gate Pass) and

to continue southeast through Lanzhou to terminate at Chang'an, near present day Xi'an.

With middlemen handling the business, two great civilizations, the Roman and the Chinese, traded with each other via the Silk Road like blind men exchanging gifts, neither setting eyes on the other. Huge camel trains carried Chinese silks, pottery and medicines along the Silk Road to the west, and back the other way came exotic animals and birds, plants, precious metals, precious stones, and products and artifacts of the Roman Empire. Along with them, around the year AD 65, came an invading force that no Great Wall or mighty army could hope to stop — Buddhism, destined to flourish alongside Confucianism and another already established Chinese belief, Daoism, as one of the Three Teachings of Chinese society.

So while the Han dynasty kept faith with the essential conventions of Chinese society — unity,

protection of the civilization and the pyramidal social order — it introduced another convention which has dictated Chinese action and attitude ever since. Down through the centuries the Chinese response to foreign ideas or influence has tended to be an alternating pattern of acceptance or invitation followed in many cases by abrupt and even violent rejection when that influence has been deemed troublesome enough to threaten the three pillars of unity, civilization and social order. And this "open closing door" syndrome explains a great deal about the Chinese society that we are dealing with today.

Though Buddhism itself later had its own share of suppression and rejection, it was certainly invited into China in the Han reign. It is said that in AD 64 the Han emperor Ming had a dream in which a golden Buddha materialized before him. He saw this as a spiritual message and sent two emissaries to India to learn more about the religion. Two Indian monks were also invited to visit China. They traveled in along the Silk Road bringing volumes of sutras, or religious texts, packed on white horses.

The emperor ordered the construction of the White Horse Monastery to commemorate the event. You can stand and ponder the significance of Buddhism in China at this, the country's oldest Buddhist institution, set into a soaring hillside 13 km (eight miles) north of Luoyang, which at one point became the Han capital.

CHAOS AND THE CANAL

With the collapse of the Han dynasty in the year AD 220, the pillars of Chinese sovereignty tumbled. Confusion and warfare reigned as various triumphant northern tribes fought to take advantage of the power vacuum, and for more than 270 years, from AD 304 to 580, no fewer than 20 dynasties rose and fell. Most of them were non-Chinese, headed or manipulated by the Xiongnu, the Tibetans and other "barbarian" groups from beyond the northern and western frontiers.

Foreign influence, in the form of Buddhism, rushed to fill the void too. During the most successful dynasty of that time, headed by the Toba, a nomadic cattle-raising tribe, it was adopted as the official religion, and the emperor was declared the reincarnation of Buddha himself.

The Toba court was based first in Datong, west of what is now Beijing and close to the present Inner Mongolia border, and later Luoyang. Today we can thank this "barbarian" dynasty and its religious fervor for its three most magnificent artistic contributions to Chinese culture — the huge Buddhist grottoes and their many murals at Mogao

On the Grand Canal at Suzhou, patched and battened mainsail powers sampan ABOVE while OPPOSITE cargo barges snake along in convoy.

near Dunhuang in Gansu, Yungang near Datong and Longmen on the banks of the Yi River, 16 km (10 miles) south of Luoyang.

Significantly, it was the continuing barbarian threat from the north that enabled the Han Chinese to regain power for themselves. In the face of attacks by Turkic tribes in the northwest, the Chinese and their Toba masters joined forces to defend the state, and the Chinese were able to take advantage of the pact to eventually drive the weakening Toba dynasty from the throne.

The Sui grasped the reins of power, and although it a was very short-lived dynasty, lasting only 37 years from AD 581 to 618, it quickly rebuilt the pillars of Chinese civilization and sovereignty. Unity was restored and even strengthened, the Sui rulers conquering the south and starting work on the single most unifying link between the southern and northern provinces, the Grand Canal.

It's estimated that close to five million peasant laborers were put to work on the canal, which eventually connected four great river systems — the Yangzi, Huang (Yellow), Huai and Qiantang — and made it possible to ship merchandise, men and military supplies from Hangzhou to the Sui court in Luoyang and then west to Xi'an. Extended even further in later reigns, the canal has since been celebrated as the longest manmade waterway on earth, and its importance to Chinese society can be appreciated even today as you stand on the bridges of Suzhou and Wuxi, the most colorful canal cities, and watch flat-hulled cargo boats and long convoys of tethered, loaded barges plying their way along waterways teeming with launches, tugs, sampans and other small vessels.

While the Sui dynasty strengthened and reinvigorated the Han Chinese society it also poured more conscripted labor and costly materials into new work on the Great Wall to keep the society intact. This protection of the civilization again became the paramount task of the dynastic order that swept the Sui from power in the year 618 and ushered in the "golden age" of the Tang.

THE GOLDEN TANG

The Tang dynasty (AD 618–906) is noted for its grand cultural contribution to Chinese history. Under its auspices the arts flourished, poetry and literature reached celebrated levels of sophistication and the development of porcelain, to name but one innovation of that era, thrust the technology of China well ahead of anything else in the world.

But the Tang reign is also significant for the constant dilemma that it faced as regards the world beyond its borders. As in the age of Han rule, it

The awesome Grand Buddha of Leshan.

was cut off from all direct contact with the mysterious lands of the West, this time by the rise of Islam in the Middle East. But this was still an era of greatly expanded trade via the Silk Road and by sea, and the "open door" also allowed a growing stream of foreign influence to seep into the society — Nestorian Christianity from Syria and Persia; Manichaeism, also from Persia and driven east by Christian persecutors; Hinduism from India; Zoroastrians and even Jews, along with foreign merchants, mainly Moslem, whose Silk Road caravans were the vehicle of this new cultural invasion.

Buddhism also continued to spread throughout the society and in fact reached one of its artistic zeniths during the early Tang years. Huge monasteries, temples and stupas sprang up along the Silk Road and elsewhere, extravagant Buddhist festivals took their place in the Chinese peasantry's calendar of largely agricultural events and observances. Buddhism and the native "Chinese" Daoism — an older religious philosophy, with many deities, based on the relationship between man and nature — began a kind of cultural exchange in which the gods of one became the incarnates of the other. The Tang emperors themselves added their imperial splendor to the Buddhist grottoes at Dunhuang, Luoyang and Datong, commissioning the taller and more magnificent Buddha statues that make these cliff galleries and caves the tourist drawcard that they are today. The magnificent Grand Buddha of Leshan is another legacy of the Tang reign, along with a few dramatic hillside sculptures at Dazu in Sichuan province.

At the same time the Tang rulers had the continuing barbarian threat in the north to contend with. Large military campaigns were fought not only against the persistent Turks of the northwest but the Tibetans to the west. And then there were increasingly dangerous challenges by the "Golden Horde" Tartars, or Khitans, who rode the same arid steppes and desert basins as the Turkic tribes.

Tang armies were posted on permanent patrol of the frontier regions, operating from fortified garrisons, and at one point they managed to rout the Turkic warriors and bring what is now the Xinjiang autonomous region under Chinese control. In China today you can see all around you one of the most common symbols of the Tang dynasty's frontier wars — intricate ceramic, bronze and iron "Tang horses" which have been popular works of art for centuries. These powerful "heavenly" war horses originally from the wilds of Central Asia were obtained by force of arms in the Han dynasty's punitive expeditions to replace the smaller, weaker steeds that the Chinese cavalries rode up until that time. They proved so successful that Han and Tang sculptors and artists

immortalized them, and today some of the original sculptures and block prints can be found in the major museums of China — notably the Shaanxi Provincial Museum in Xi'an — and the National Palace Museum in Taiwan. Elsewhere, cheap mass-produced copies pack the shelves of souvenir shops and art and crafts centers.

But the constant struggle against the barbarians led to a great deal of damaging intrigue and power-play within the Tang hierarchy, weakening the dynasty. At the same time its authority came under growing challenge and pressure from Buddhism and other influences that had traveled with it down the Silk Road. The three pillars of Chinese civilization began to shake again, and in AD 845 the Tang emperor of the day launched a violent reprisal to put things right.

"In the cities, in the mountains, there are nothing but (Buddhist) priests of both sexes," his imperial edict raged. "The number of monasteries grows daily. A great deal of gold is wasted on embellishing them. People forget their traditional rulers in order to serve under a master priest. Could anything more pernicious be imagined?"

The "Open Closing Door"

In the ensuing crackdown, all foreign religions were banned from China and foreigners were barred from all ports. And in the case of Buddhism, more than 4,500 monasteries were destroyed, and a quarter of a million monks and priests thrown out into open society. Confucianism was restored as the omnipotent national belief. Although trade was allowed to continue along the Silk Road, the Chinese door was firmly closed for some time on all cultural influence from the West, and the pattern of the "open closing door" came into being.

Inevitably, the Tang dynasty collapsed into chaos, uprising and constant power struggles that saw no fewer than five northern "dynasties" and 10 southern kingdoms rise and fall between the years AD 906 and 960. China's social pillars swayed and crumbled, and the power and prosperity of the Silk Road disintegrated with them, beginning an era in which China was almost completely isolated from everything beyond its western borders.

THE AGE OF ART

The collapse continued even with the rise to power of another great dynasty, the Song (960–1279). Although the Song rulers fought to buttress the main conventions of the society — the Confucian ethics of natural order and hierarchy were rigidly imposed, for instance, to shore up the society's pyramidal authority — they had considerably less success with the defense of the Han realm. The Khitans finally broke through in the north to establish their own Liao dynasty based at Shenyang, only to be supplanted in turn by another barbar-

ian power, the Jurchens. An alliance of Turks and Tibetans established another dynastic power-base in the northwest — with the result that the Song dynasty was actually driven south where, for 150 years, it ruled from Hangzhou.

Nonetheless, the Song era is remembered as another great cultural benchmark in Chinese history. It was an age of refinement that added new luster to the arts with its particular developments in landscape painting, and it introduced the willowy green-glazed celadon ware to the growing showcase of Chinese ceramic techniques. It was also the age of the poet, one in which these romantic men and women of letters were elevated to the rank of social heroes — and none more so than the renowned Su Shi, better known as Su Dongpo, the product of a talented literary family who was also governor of Hangzhou for two years before it became the Southern Song capital.

You can see impressive statues of Su Dongpo, his father and brother, and study their literary works and stele rubbings of their calligraphy at the Temple of the Three Sus, built on the site of their family home at Meishan, 90 km (56 miles) west of Chengdu.

THE WRATH OF KHAN

Preoccupied as it was with the arts and civilized living, and confined within the southern-central region of China, the Song dynasty was in no shape or position to defend the territory or the integrity of the civilization when, around the year 1206, it faced the most terrible barbarian challenge of all time. In that year a huge confederation of nomadic tribes gathered in the wilderness beyond the northern frontiers and, under the banner of the ruthless warlord whose name has since been a byword for horrific violence and pillage, Genghis Khan's Mongol hordes thundered down through the boundless grasslands to put China to the sword.

The swift and brutal Mongol cavalries made short work of the Tibetan-Turkic stronghold to the west, and within a short time were ready to crush the Jin dynasty of the Jurchens ruling northern China from present-day Beijing. Only one thing stopped, or rather delayed them, the Great Wall, and it actually took Genghis Khan two years of procrastination beyond the immense barrier to arrive at the conclusion that it could be breached only by massive human-wave attack. He finally hurled the bulk of his armies at it, and despite a courageous stand by its Jin defenders and savage battles that left thousands dead on both sides, his warriors finally smashed their way through and descended upon Beijing in a flood-tide of murder and rapine.

When, after a short siege, the Mongols poured into the Jin capital, they went on a horrific month-long rampage in which almost the entire population was put to death and the city sacked of all its treasures. Then it was razed to the ground. From there, the Mongols turned their attention to the Song dynastic stronghold to the south.

At this, the most perilous point in Chinese history, it seemed as though the civilization faced complete destruction. The three pillars upon which it stood — unity, protection and social order — lay in ruins. Above the smoke and carnage stood a half-savage bandit chief whose lustful, simplistic outlook on life had been expressed in these bleak terms: "The greatest joy is to conquer one's enemies, to pursue them, to seize their property, to see their families in tears, to ride their horses, and to possess their daughters and wives."

began doing what no nomadic brigand had ever done before — he began to build. First he constructed an entirely new imperial capital from the ruins of the Jin court, now Beijing. From the ashes of mass pillage a new imperial tradition emerged, an empire greater than anything the Chinese had ever seen. And when the intrepid Venetian business explorer, Marco Polo, journeyed along the route of the Silk Road to spend some 20 years in the court of the Great Khan, arriving in the year of Kublai's ascension to the imperial throne, Chinese civilization was reaching toward the zenith of its power and prestige.

Its pyramidal structure had been restored, society ascending class upon class to the absolute

Khan the Builder

But then a kind of miracle happened. With the initial conquest achieved, it was left to Genghis Khan's grandson, Kublai, to rule northern China and defeat and subjugate the Southern Song. Kublai Khan happened to have intelligence and a certain vision—he saw himself as the supreme ruler of a vast Eurasian empire, and for that he needed the help of experienced administrators; and, obviously, the only skilled people capable of administering China were the Chinese themselves. So, at the very brink of ruin, the Chinese bureaucracy reassembled and thus survived, and the Chinese civilization set about civilizing its conqueror.

In 1271 Kublai Khan proclaimed himself emperor of China and established a new dynasty, the Yuan. Eight years later he completed the conquest of virtually the entire country and immediately

rule of the Great Khan, the new Son of Heaven. It was well protected, forming the lavish centerpiece of the vast Mongol empire and nothing less in Chinese eyes than the very "center of the universe." It was also technologically about 900 years ahead of the Western world, as Marco Polo himself recorded, marveling over such inventions as gunpowder, paper, printing, canal lock-gates, the compass and the great four-masted sailing junks that carried him home in 1292.

Chinese civilization had survived by absorbing and civilizing its conquerors, and after the death of Kublai Khan this process of absorption continued through the reigns of eight succeeding Mongol emperors. It was aided by the fact that, after the Great Khan, the Yuan leadership became

Decorated doorway opens onto courtyards and palace quarters and the distant vista of Coal Hill (Mei San) in the Forbidden City, Beijing.

inept, the settled Mongol armies became flaccid, the taste for lavish living of the succeeding Sons of Heaven forced increasingly heavy tax burdens onto the peasantry, with traditional consequences.

THE GLORY OF THE MING

With the Mongol authority weakening and the peasantry reaching breaking point, the Chinese rose up in open revolt in 1352 and within 16 years had wrested back the reins of power and sovereignty, establishing the glorious Ming dynasty. The dissipated remnants of the great Mongol empire were driven back into the wilds beyond China's northern frontier.

Chinese ethnic unity was restored, along with the two other essential social pillars; and, to make sure that they could never be shaken or toppled again, one of the first major tasks that the Ming dynasty undertook was a massive, complete restructuring and strengthening of the Great Wall — a project that took many millions of laborers no less than a whole century to complete.

The strengthening of the Great Wall was more than just a move to keep the retreating Mongols and other barbarians out, it was symbolic of the overriding Ming attitude to the rest of the world. While this era is noted as an age of Chinese exploration, with the eunuch admiral Zheng He leading large oceanic expeditions to parts of Asia, Arabia and Africa, it was also a time in which China again shut the door on contact with the West. The nation's vision of itself as the Middle Kingdom, the center of all things, became more entrenched. The lands beyond Admiral He's junks had nothing that China needed or did not already possess.

The Silk Road, already in decline since its heyday during the Tang dynasty, was completely abandoned, and by the fifteenth century Islam had replaced Buddhism as the driving spiritual force along the old silk routes as far east as the Takla Makan region of Xinjiang, brought there by Arab imperial ventures in the wake of the Mongol collapse. Today, Islam is as strong as ever in China's northwestern region, with large Moslem minorities living side-by-side with Han Chinese in an area ranging north from Xi'an and Lanzhou through the Ningxia autonomous region to the Inner Mongolia border and west as far as the boundary of Xinjiang.

Within the Wall

With the rest of the world shut out, the Chinese set about virtually reconstructing their nation during the Ming reign. Beijing, destroyed by Ming forces in the struggle to unseat the last Mongol ruler, was completely rebuilt and firmly established, for its strategic position guarding the north, as the nerve-center of Chinese rule; much of its present-day historic splendor, such as the Forbid-

den City and Temple of Heaven, is a legacy of the Ming architects and builders.

The Great Wall was transformed into the monolithic heavily defended structure that can be viewed today at places like Badaling, 75 km (46 miles) north of Beijing, and at Shanhaiguan at its eastern extremity, overlooking the Bo Sea. Ming engineers built double walls of massive stone blocks and filled the interior with packed earth and rock to form what is, in effect, an elevated roadway with defensive turrets on either side, along which troops and supplies could be rushed in event of an enemy threat. Some 25,000 fortified watchtowers and garrison towers were built along the huge barrier, linked by a communications system of fires, flags, drums and rockets. The Ming Tombs, another of today's cultural drawcards, dotting the plain of Shisanling, 50 km (31 miles) northwest of Beijing, testify to the living power and posthumous glory of the Ming emperors.

In many respects the Ming dynasty recalled the "golden age" of the Tang reign. It was an era of prosperity, and of population growth, both of which provided a fertile seed bed for new advances in the arts. Porcelain and ceramics reached their highest level of craftsmanship and creativity; intricate *cloisonné*, which can be seen in a myriad of latter-day forms all over China today, became a celebrated art form; novelists replaced poets as the society's literary lions. But in the midst of all this social fattening and refinement the Ming court began rotting at the core — and the Forbidden City bears testament to the failure of the dynasty.

While the Forbidden City represents the grandeur of the Ming reign it also symbolizes the hollowness of Ming authority. Within its heavily guarded walls and courts, beyond which the common people ventured only at pain of immediate death, the later Ming emperors became corrupt

pleasure-seeking imperial recluses, isolated completely from the society. Their power was usurped by conniving court eunuchs who virtually ruled the nation behind their backs and amassed huge personal fortunes at the expense of the people. Once again, the three social pillars began to sway.

The moral and political bankruptcy of the waning Ming dynasty was compounded by a famine spreading across the far northern provinces, triggering peasant uprisings. It was ultimately bankrupted altogether by betrayal — its eunuch overlords treacherously opening the gates of power to a rebel army backed and manipulated by a new invading force from beyond the Great Wall, the Manchus. The glorious age of the Ming finally ended in 1644 in an awful night of madness and murder: The last Ming emperor, besieged by rebels, hacked his closest family members to death and

Wide moat and watchtowers made the Forbidden City both sanctuary and virtual prison of the emperors.

then hanged himself on Coal Hill (Mei Shan, also known as Jing Shan), a mound built by his more illustrious predecessors out of earth excavated from the moat around the Forbidden City.

THE LAST DYNASTY

The Manchu Qing dynasty, formed from an alliance of tribes with no real cultural distinction to the north and northeast of the Great Wall, was the last to rule China. Although it remained in power from 1644 to 1911 it presided over the total disintegration of the three vital pillars of society — unity, protection of the civilization and strict pyramidal authority — and when it finally sank into oblivion it left China in the throes of something which, for all its turmoil and upheaval over so many centuries, it had never experienced before: revolution.

As with the preceding Ming, the early Qing emperors were vigorous builders, and many of China's monasteries, temples and cultural monuments owe their survival to renovations and expansion in their reigns.

These early rulers wielded enough personal authority to keep the social pyramid intact, and this gave China a new period of stability and prosperity. It also caused another upswing in the population, but this time the country's food production didn't keep pace, so famine and unrest broke out again. More significantly, China had not kept pace with the rising scientific and technological power of the Western world. Confronted with this power, the later Manchu rulers retreated into hidebound conservatism, clinging to an illusion of Chinese cultural supremacy, and in doing this they slammed the China door shut again behind them. It was this retreat that destroyed the 4,500-year-old dynastic order.

The Western Challenge

To be fair, the Manchu had inherited a society that the Ming dynasty had already allowed to slip far behind the technological development of the West. Whereas Chinese invention and science had been nearly a thousand years ahead of the West during the Yuan dynasty, by the time of the Manchu rule they were obsolete and virtually helpless in the face of modern Western naval firepower and maritime strength, military weaponry, and the corresponding fierce drive for trade and colonial expansion by the major European powers.

Instead of modernizing to counter this new threat, the Manchu response was the imperious dismissal of anything that it could have gained from the Western world; and nothing sums up the Qing dynasty's insular attitude more bluntly than the imperial reply to Britain's demand for a free two-way exchange of trade. "I set no value on strange or ingenious objects," the emperor informed Great Britain's King George III, "and have no use for your country's manufactures."

It was probably the most fateful declaration that any Chinese ruler had ever made, for it set into motion a trade struggle, which was followed by open armed conflict, and which ultimately tore apart Chinese sovereignty.

The British, following on the heels of the Portuguese and Dutch, had actually been trading with China for years, but their traders were strictly confined to segregated enclaves in Guangzhou (Canton) and Macau. And the trade itself was very much a one-way deal — the British could buy all the teas and silks they wanted but could not interest the Chinese in anything worthwhile in return. The British were forced to pay for their tea, in particular, with silver bullion, and they bought so much of the stuff—trying to keep pace with a growing national craving for it back home — that at one point the nation's silver reserves sank so low that the Exchequer was almost bankrupted. To try to wrest some of the bullion back, they cast about for anything they could find that would provoke a similar fierce demand in China. And they found the ideal commodity — opium from Bengal.

The Opium Wars

The struggle that followed the wholesale introduction of opium to China can be described in modern-day hindsight as one of the most sordid of history's episodes. In 1839, when opium smuggling and addiction had reached the point of crisis in China, the Qing administration blockaded the Guangzhou trading depot, confiscated the British traders' opium stocks and burnt it all in front of them. The British retaliated with naval attacks, and in a decisive battle off the southeast coast the advanced guns and rockets of an iron-hulled steam-paddle warship, the *Nemesis*, smashed and sank the Qing navy's main fleet of antique junks. And the pillars of society went down with them.

From that point on, China was at the mercy of the Europeans and the one rival Asian power that was modernizing rapidly to meet the Western challenge, Japan. China became the victim of its own imperial arrogance, ruthless Western expansion, and what seems today to be one of history's most bitter ironies — the spectacular Great Wall, costing many thousands of lives to build, standing in permanent vigil against the threat from the north, while the most perilous threat of all came from the south, from the seas and from the "round-eyes" of distant Europe.

In the ensuing Opium Wars, Britain grabbed Hong Kong as a colonial trading post and forced open the China door, establishing treaty ports such as Shanghai, Hankou, Amoy (Xiamen) and Nanjing. From that point on the Europeans (including Russians) and Japanese rushed to carve up the country into commercial "spheres of interest." In 1870 Japan took Taiwan, then annexed Korea and then, in 1895, secured parts of southern Manchuria. Much of the rest of Manchuria was acquired by Russia as a concession four years later. In 1905 the Japanese defeated the Russians in an historic naval battle, grabbed the Russian Manchurian concession as booty and began what was to become a progressive and bloody campaign to subjugate and colonize all of China. In the south, the French acquired the Indochina Peninsula — Vietnam, Laos and Cambodia. In the east, the Germans forced their way into Shandong province, establishing Qingdao (Tsingtao) as their own treaty port.

The Iron Empress

Apologists for this era of foreign intervention in China often point to the fact that the occupying powers did, after all, build China's first modern infrastructure — factories, roads, railways, telegraph systems. Those who condemn it point to the sole reason why that infrastructure was laid down — to extract the resources that the Europeans were after and distribute the export products from their own countries that they wanted the Chinese to buy.

No matter how one views it, the overall picture of that time is certainly not of a backward nation enjoying the white man's benefits. There were dreadful famines and just as dreadful uprisings — including the violent Taiping and Boxer rebellions, both of them ruthlessly crushed — against the alien rule and the impotence of the Manchu, against corruption, against injustice and against the Western presence.

When it finally became clear that only modernization, by the Chinese for the Chinese, could enable them to resist and possibly drive out the Europeans, another of the bitter ironies of Chinese history came to pass. The stubborn and scheming Empress Dowager, the last effective imperial ruler of China, turned around and fought to restore and strengthen the traditional pillars of autocracy and conservatism that had ruled Chinese society for 4,000 years before her. In doing so she quashed all attempts around her to reform and modernize society and its armed forces — even imprisoning the heir-apparent, Guangxu, when he came of age and ascended to the throne, for suggesting change.

Her last-ditch stand on behalf of the China of her imperial ancestors was not only imprudent but also in vain. In the south of China particularly, contact with the foreign communities and the growing practice of many "modern" Chinese families of sending their sons and daughters to study in Britain and other European countries had led to an upsurge of modern ideas. The seeds of revolution began sprouting, nurtured and closely

watched from exile in Japan and elsewhere by a fervent young reformist from Guangdong province, Sun Yatsen.

As the battle lines of conservatism and reform hardened, so China approached the second most crucial crossroads of its long history. But to give the Ci Xi her due, she held out to the end — even arranging the murder of her politically "wet" emperor charge just before she died in 1908.

Of all the evidence that remains of the Empress Dowager's bizarre but decisive reign, nothing alludes more to its style and character than the extravagant Summer Palace she built herself in 1888, about 12 km (seven and a half miles) northwest of Beijing. It cost a fortune, about 24 million

taels (42.3 million ounces) of silver — and she appropriated the money from funds set up to modernize the Chinese navy.

THE REPUBLICAN FAILURE

When the Empress Dowager died, the dynastic tradition died with her. She left another emperor on the throne, (Henry) Pu Yi, but he was eminently unqualified for the job: He was only two years old. A constitutional government, already established in the Iron Empress's fading years, moved swiftly to take the reins of power. In 1910 China's first National Assembly was held, and a year later Sun Yatsen returned from exile to become president of a provisional government based in Nanjing, where Sun Yatsen Tomb is now

Old Silk Road gateway near the Great Wall.

one of the main tourist landmarks. For the first time in its long history, China was having a taste of democracy. Largely for this reason, the Chinese Republic, the first of the nation's two great modern-day revolutions, was destined from the very beginning to fail.

From today's vantage point it is little wonder that a society structured for such a vast length of time on a strict autocratic pyramidal rule, and faithful for most of that time to the social order laid down by Confucianism, should find the principles of democracy alien and unworkable. As it was, the period from 1911 right up until the 1930s was one of social and political chaos, with regional warlords vying for power, Sun Yatsen unable to build enough personal authority to institute effective national rule, the government in Beiping (now Beijing) too weak to run the country properly and the Japanese and the European powers playing one rival faction off against the other to promote their own interests.

Again, there were devastating famines in the north, peasant revolts, trade union strikes and demonstrations that were dealt with violently by the authorities. Out of all this turmoil there emerged the rival, bitterly competing political movements that were to decide the future structure and course of the Chinese society — the nationalists led by Chiang Kaishek and the communists under a revolutionary leadership that was eventually dominated by Mao Zedong.

THE REVOLUTIONARY STRUGGLE

Backed by the European "allies" and the United States, Chiang Kaishek attempted to secure the mandate of the old emperors by establishing himself as the head of a fascist-style military dictatorship. Hardly a government, it nonetheless held power for 20 years, during which time Chiang concentrated his main energies on a campaign to purge the communists from society. He was so obsessed with this that his forces virtually stood by and allowed Japan to expand its occupation of the north.

By 1935 the Japanese had colonized Manchuria and set up the puppet state of Manzhouguo (Manchukuo) with the ousted Qing emperor, Henry Pu Yi, as its king. They had also occupied Hebei province and Inner Mongolia. Two years later, Japanese planes, tanks and infantry smashed their way down through the heart of China, occupying the country as far south as Guangzhou and forcing Chiang Kaishek and his nationalists to retreat to a western enclave in Chongqing.

The communists stayed in the hills and behind the Japanese lines in Shandong province and the northeast, and from there they conducted guerrilla warfare against the occupation army—aided by the local peasant population — that not only helped defeat the Japanese but also shaped the character and outcome of the communist struggle for power after World War II had ended.

To understand the immediate postwar cataclysm in China, it has to be simplified and placed again within the context of the three traditional pillars of Chinese society. In the choice of leadership that the Chinese had before them, there was Chiang Kaishek on the one hand, supported by foreign interests, a proven failure in the defense of the civilization and realm, and self-proclaimed ruler of a pyramid that had most of its essential lower masses looking elsewhere for leadership. On the other hand there were Mao Zedong's communists, comparative heroes for their guerrilla struggle against the Japanese, definitely not bankrolled nor bolstered by foreign governments (not even by the Soviet Union at that stage), and, as a result of Maoist political policy and the grassroots nature of their guerrilla operations, intimately linked with the vast bulk of the peasant masses and workers without whose support the abiding structure of Chinese society could not be complete.

The outcome was inevitable: full civil war in which the communist forces drove the nationalist hierarchy further and further south, followed by the communist victory in which Chiang Kaishek and his diehard followers fled to exile in Taiwan, followed in 1949 by the founding of the revolutionary People's Republic of China.

THE THREE MAOIST PILLARS

Much has been written about the tumultuous and yet largely misinterpreted 30 years of Maoist communism in China, and much of it has come from over-idealistic observers of the left or hysterical anti-Communists of the right. Only an occasional incisive study and coldly objective pen has attempted to place the emotionally charged events and implications of the revolutionary era against the far broader background of Chinese history. Only then have the three pillars of that history been applied to the Maoist experience, and only then has it been considered not so much how Chairman Mao changed the society but what he restored to it.

Mao Zedong restored the traditional ruling principles of the dynastic past to the new Chinese society. These principles were essential if he was to successfully harness it to the painfully burdensome plow of recovery and reconstruction. He restored unity and national self-respect after many decades of chaos and humiliation. He restored the full vitality of protection and defense, in ways that may have seemed bewildering to outsiders but were quite demonstrably satisfying to the Chinese in the very beginning.

Foreign presence and influence was removed entirely from Chinese soil. It was also swiftly countered whenever and wherever it threatened. (The Chinese response to the American-backed United Nations intervention in neighboring Korea in 1950, and India's military border incursion in 1962, are good examples of this protectionism.) Even in its close but short-lived 12-year cultural and technical pact with the Soviet Union, the Maoist government kept faith with the dynastic tradition. When Moscow's influence was seen as a threat (its insistence, for one thing, that revolutionary socialism should be achieved through the industrial proletariat, not Mao's peasant masses), the bond was severed, the Soviets charged with revisionism and their technicians and advisors sent packing. With that, the Chinese effectively shut the door once again on the outside world.

The basic character of Mao's society was a straight copy of that of imperial times. The pyramid was rearranged and restored, the various classes of Chinese society reaching upward once again from the vast, shifting peasant seas to the authoritative hand of the Great Helmsman. Mao's authority and popularity rivaled that of the emperors, not by unquestioned divine rule but by the constantly promoted "cult of the personality" that made him, nonetheless, a living god.

Mao's political base amongst the peasantry and his lifelong promotion of the peasant class came not just from his own modest rural beginnings but from an understanding of the lesson that all emperors before him had been forced to learn and heed. "The prince is the boat, the common people are the water," an old Chinese proverb had cautioned them. "The water can support the boat, or it can capsize it."

Mao's policy of industrial and agricultural self-sufficiency, manifested in the controversial Great Leap Forward, and its collapse in 1962, echoed the attitudes of the Ming, Yuan and latter Qing rulers toward foreign "manufactures." Mao even resurrected and harnessed the tradition of the mass campaign, only now the huge work brigades dug mammoth canals and constructed hydroelectric dams and power stations instead of imperial palaces, Great Walls and elaborate tombs.

THE RED GUARDS

Mao's most fateful mass campaign, the violent Cultural Revolution beginning in 1966, was launched against the growing power of moderates within the hierarchy whose ideas deviated in one crucial respect from the Maoist dream — they believed, and probably quite rightly so, that China could not modernize and develop behind closed doors, by its own sweat alone. It is tempting, as unlikely as it may seem, to recall the wan-

ing days of the Qing dynasty in the subsequent rampage by Mao's Red Guards and the events that took place next — the crackdown on "bourgeois revisionist" elements who were apparently willing to risk the sovereignty and integrity of China once again with "foreign" modernization and reform.

So fierce was the struggle between the Maoist and "revisionist" factions that the Cultural Revolution almost became an outright cultural civil war, and eventually the Red Guards had to be forcibly reined and disbanded to prevent the conflict tearing the society completely apart. But for more than a decade the struggle continued, with moderate leaders such as Zhou Enlai and Deng Xiaoping

attempting to promote Western-style modernization and Mao's opposing revolutionary line taken to the point of harsh and unacceptable social experiment by the so-called Gang of Four led by Mao's radical wife, the former actress Jiang Qing.

It was during this long struggle that the clock of progress virtually stopped in China, and society at large, weary of all the infighting, suddenly faced the cold and disturbing reality of its position in the global society with the twenty-first century rapidly bearing down upon it. It was technically, scientifically and militarily backward, even with its nuclear and aerospace programs, at a time when the other great powers of the world, the United States, Japan and especially the Soviet Union, were stepping into an age that was getting far beyond China's reach.

Mao Zedong, now regarded as "70% right and 30% wrong."

THE FOUR MODERNIZATIONS

When Mao Zedong died in September 1976, the moderates, now renamed "pragmatists," moved swiftly to prosecute and imprison the Gang of Four. In their place came the Four Modernizations, aimed at repairing and developing the country's infrastructure and sciences and boosting agriculture, industry, national defense and technology to the "front ranks of the world" by the year 2000. Deng Xiaoping emerged as the new Chinese leader, heading the campaign to steer China away from revolutionary socialism and into the economic fast lane of controlled free enterprise, expanded

international trade and joint investment with foreign interests. In a moment that delighted the Western world, whatever it may have done to the diehard socialists back home, Deng even appeared at a rodeo on a tour of the United States wearing a Texan 10-gallon hat.

TIANANMEN SQUARE MASSACRE

On the night of June 3, 1989, the Chinese leadership stunned the world by sending armed People's Liberation Army troops into Tiananmen Square to brutally crush a huge carnival-like demonstration by students and young workers which was perceived as a major threat to Communist Party rule.

It's still not known exactly how many demonstrators and bystanders were killed in the square and adjacent streets that night. The government

has since insisted that only a handful of "enemies of the state" perished in the night-long terror of gunfire and tanks, but foreign doctors who were on duty in Beijing that night reported the toll to be between 2,500 and 3,000. In any case, the bodies were spirited away and secretly disposed of, and in the aftermath the party chiefs launched a full-scale purge, with much-publicized show trials, of "dissident" elements in Beijing, Shanghai and other major cities.

The Tiananmen Square Massacre, as it has since been known, caused worldwide revulsion, transforming China overnight from the great business and travel opportunity of Asia to an international pariah. American and European tourism slumped,

Western and Japanese investment and economic aid took a similar nosedive; and in Hong Kong, upwards of a million people flooded into the streets in mass demonstrations against the killings and in support of the student pro-democracy movement — a show of popular and political feeling never before seen in this British colony. What came next was hardly surprising — a clamor by Hong Kong Chinese, suddenly fearful for their future in China's takeover of Hong Kong in 1997, to emigrate and obtain foreign citizenship.

The ruthlessness and violence of the crackdown reflected China's age-old imperatives: the perceived need for powerful central rule and national cohesion, and an ingrained fear at the highest levels of government of anything that could trigger disintegration. On top of that, the Communist Party, having opened the economic door to the world with a beaming promise of friendship and cooperation, made it patently clear that economic liberalization would not be matched with political reform. The jailing of dissidents, continued widespread execution of "criminal elements" — many of them convicted of crimes that would rate a minor jail term in the West — violent suppression of dissent in Tibet and hard-line opposition to pre-1997 democratic development in Hong Kong only emphasized the Communist Party's determination to stay in power, apparently whatever the cost.

DENG'S LEGACY

Despite the bloodletting of the Tiananmen incident — or *liu-si* (June 4), as it's now known baldly in Chinese — when Deng Xiaoping died in 1997 he left behind a China barely recognizable from the China Mao had presided over. Indeed, his so-called "open-door" policy to the West and pragmatic economic policies ("I don't care whether the cat is black or white as long as it catches mice," he famously once said) were major factors in creating the climate of dissent that led to Tiananmen. Nevertheless, few will deny that Deng significantly loosened China's ideological straitjacket, allowing the country to pursue an economic agenda aimed at making China a force on the world stage.

Deng decentralized production, allowing market forces to come into play. On the agricultural front, the collectivized economy was ushered out and a household system that allowed producers to sell surpluses on the free market brought in. On the east coast, Special Economic Zones (SEZs) were established, encouraging foreign investment. The results speak for themselves. China is freer and more affluent than it has been in more than half a century.

CHINA IN THE NEW MILLENNIUM

With the turning of the new millennium, "whither China?" remains as popular a question for the pundits and China watchers as it ever has in the past. After all, the closing decades of the twentieth century provided so much drama to feed speculation: the Tiananmen massacre, the dramatic collapse of Soviet and East European communism in 1991, the mounting tensions over the "renegade province" of Taiwan, the death of patriarch Deng, the Hong Kong hand-over in 1997, the Macau hand-over in 1999. If one thing is certain, it's that China-watching hasn't gotten any simpler.

Governing China hasn't got any simpler either. Despite the enormous boosts to national pride that came with the hand-overs of Hong Kong and Macau, huge problems remain in China, and many wonder whether the Chinese Communist Party is able to adapt fast enough to keep up with the massive changes sweeping through the country.

In the two decades since China first opened its doors to the West, it has transformed itself into an entrepreneurial powerhouse, racking up massive foreign reserves and a trade surplus that makes the United States as nervous as Japan did in the late 1980s. But for all that, economic growth has slowed from a giddy 11% annually through most of the late 1990s to a projected — some say optimistic — seven percent in 2000. Such slowdowns are frightening for the Chinese Communist Party, which, ideologically bereft, derives most of its legitimacy and hold on power from its ability to keep delivering on a nationwide desire for ever-increasing prosperity. The Chinese government keeps as watchful an eye as ever on emerging dissent, cracking down on popular movements like the Falungong, a nationwide *qi gong* movement with as many followers, some say, as the Chinese Communist Party itself, for fear that they emerge as political forces.

The other thorn in China's side is Taiwan, a small island of 23 million off the southeast coast of China. With Hong Kong and Macau back in the fold, China would like nothing more than to have reunification with Taiwan. The problem is that Taiwan has evolved a long way from the days when it was ruled by Chiang Kaishek's Nationalists. In theory, both China and Taiwan agree on the principal of reunification, but disagree on the terms. In practice, there is little support in democratic Taiwan for reunification with China, a point that was proved in Taiwan's March 2000 presidential elections, which swept the long-serving Nationalist party from power and elected a former pro-independence president, Chen Shui-bian. China has repeatedly threatened that it is prepared to resort to military action if Taiwan does not eventually come to the table, and the issue remains one of Asia's potentially most destabilizing flashpoints.

THE CULTURAL LEGACY

PERFECT OBSOLESCENCE

The craft and artistry of Chinese culture owes much of its inspiration to animist beliefs and Daoist nature worship that originated in the nation's distant past; and it can thank the divine power and patronage of the various imperial dynasties for the creative heights that it aspired to and achieved over the centuries.

As for the extent to which it has survived, virtually unchanged for almost 5,000 years, that can be marked down to a fairly rigid discipline that has ruled most artistic and technological creation

LEFT: An enthusiastic young stallholder displays his wares in a small clothes market in Beijing.
RIGHT: A reminder of a now distant era, Fuzhou's massive Mao statue is one of China's most imposing.

in China from the mists of prehistory. It's a simple discipline, but one that both preserved and, ironically, led to the eventual downfall of the Chinese cultural tradition. In a nutshell, the principle was this: if an art or craft has been brought to perfection, leave it alone. Don't fiddle with it. This explains many mysteries about Chinese art and technology — why ancient architectural styles, especially those of temples and pavilions, have basically survived to this day; why most of the Chinese painting, embroidery, ceramics, sculpture, *cloisonné*, lacquerware and other artistic products offered in today's souvenir shops are almost exact modern-day copies of those of the past. It explains why the key principle of traditional painting

As oceangoing craft, huge four-masted junks struck out across the vast Indian Ocean on several great expeditions under the flag of the Ming dynasty nautical hero, Admiral Zheng He, reaching the coast of East Africa and, as some historians have claimed, perhaps even rounding the Cape of Good Hope. At that time, Western vessels had barely reached the stage where they could confidently venture beyond the sight of land.

Yet while the junk was developed in myriad forms to suit various tasks and conditions on China's lakes, rivers and coastal waters, its basic principles, once considered perfected, were deemed to be just that — perfect. No further improvement or experimentation was really

and calligraphy, for example, is an established and strict discipline of brushwork, hand-motion, color, light and shade, composition and even mental control, the rule being to achieve excellence or even brilliance within a perfection dictated by the masters of the past — this discipline certainly discouraging experimentation for its own sake.

Perhaps the best illustration of this discipline, and its consequences, is the traditional Chinese sailing craft, the junk. Evolving first from bamboo and inflated-skin river rafts, the development of the junk raced centuries ahead of all nautical technology in the West. It incorporated the principles of the watertight compartment, battened and easily maneuverable sails and the stern-post rudder and then undertook far-ranging expeditions and trading voyages throughout Southeast Asia while Western man was still paddling about in shallow waters in goat-skin coracles.

attempted. By the nineteenth century, when Western nautical technology had now far outstripped that of the Chinese, the "perfect" junk — rendered even more obsolete by the conservatism of the latter stage of the Manchu Qing dynasty — sailed bravely into the guns and Congreve rockets of the British ironclad, steam-powered warship, the *Nemesis*, and was literally blown out of the water.

What's left of the junk, the tattered sailing barges and fishing boats occasionally sighted on China's major lakes, on some of the rivers and in the fishing grounds off the coast, is a virtual replica, even today, of the craft that ruled the waves a thousand or more years ago. It is also a testament to the fundamental gulf between Chinese and Western cultures — discipline and tradition on the one hand, a constant drive for improvement and its inherent "planned obsolescence" on the other; and it is a cultural difference that must be considered in any study of Chinese arts and ingenuity.

THE ARTISTIC EXPLOSION

Chinese arts, both "art for art's sake" and the applied variety, are said to date back as distantly as around 4500 BC, during the reign of Huangdi, the Yellow Emperor, one of the three mythical fathers of Chinese civilization. It's said that sericulture, or silk-making, originated during his reign, his empress teaching others how to spin it from the silkworm cocoons and weave it into the elegant, diaphanous, fiercely strong material that has ruled fashion tastes worldwide ever since.

that ruled the hand, the eye and, indeed, the state of mind that existed, or should exist, for each stroke of the brush. Different calligraphic styles were perfected, some of them branching again into carved stone tablets, or steles, others joining the illustrative arts in the ensuing crucial development of engraving and wood-block printing.

Pottery and decorative firing techniques appeared in Chinese art and craft as early as the Neolithic period, but during the Shang dynasty (1600–1100 BC) bronze was discovered and causing yet another crucial artistic leap. Stylized cast bronze *tings*, or cooking cauldrons, were among the first applications of this art form, excellent examples of which can be seen in museums all over China.

Silk not only fostered a vast and innovative range of fashion and intricate embroidery over the ensuing centuries, it also formed the backdrop to the distinctive and variously acclaimed tradition of Chinese painting. Most early painting was done on silk and, as with many Chinese creative pursuits, what began as a technical expedient was later elevated into the realm of pure art.

During the time of that distant "Camelot" of Chinese history, the first written script was developed, with agricultural records, herbal medicine remedies and spiritual prophesies inscribed on tortoise shell, bones and bamboo strips. A quantum leap took place around AD 106 with the invention of paper, and from that point on the Chinese visual arts branched into the celebrated tradition of calligraphy — a combination of art and literature. Brushes of pig-bristle and inks of soot and glue were developed. A discipline evolved

In architecture, squat mud-brick huts of the Neolithic period gave way to increasingly palatial columned, glazed-roof buildings and pavilions as the dynastic tradition set in with the reign of the Shang rulers. Almost all early Chinese construction was of wood, and the constant risk and ravages of fire have naturally wiped out almost all trace of ancient architectural styles. However, because of the abiding philosophy of "perfect obsolescence" — the preservation of a design once it has been perfected — fire-ruined homes, temples and palace buildings were often rebuilt on their original sites and quite close to their original design; so that while most of the present-day architectural monuments in China date back no

OPPOSITE: Businessmen meet in the eighth floor café of a commercial tower in Shenzhen's rapidly developing Special Economic Zone. ABOVE: Youth sporting Western fashions in Beijing.

further than the Ming dynasty, they remain fairly faithful to the styles of the more distant centuries.

Early roofs were thatched, but later clad with ceramic tiles which, in themselves, became an increasingly elaborate form of art. As the weight of all this tiling increased with each new architectural ambition, more and more complicated engineering techniques had to be developed to support it, and a study of any palace building or old temple will show the almost incredible system of brackets, columns, beams and levers designed to hold everything up. The distinctive curved or winged roofs are believed to have been adapted from Indian Buddhist architecture, and became popular and increasingly flamboyant from the

time of the Song dynasty (960–1279). The Ming and Qing dynasties saw the same flamboyance extended to ridge ornaments — sculptured animals, people, plants and other motifs — mounted at each end of the roof to repel evil influences.

The arrival of Buddhism in the first century gave Chinese art and crafts considerable new inspiration and impetus, especially in the fields of sculpture and rock carving, wall painting and bas-relief, silk painting, calligraphy and printing. Other than that, the irresistible demands and patronage of the various great dynasties added new artistic drive as they paraded, one after the other, down the annals of Chinese history.

ABOVE: In China "retro" really means "retro": here two models pose in Tang dynasty inspired fashions. RIGHT: The onlookers are as colorful as the performers at the Butter Festival, which takes place at Ta'Er Monastery, a short distance south of Xining.

THE DYNASTIC LEGACY

The Han dynasty (206 BC–AD 220) is noted as a major artistic period in which advanced silk weaving was developed, glaze was used on pottery, relief sculpture appeared and the early traditions of Chinese painting and portraiture were laid down. In the later "golden age" of the Tang rulers (618–906), sculpture and rock carving reached their "perfection," painting achieved almost unparalleled sophistication and porcelain made its debut on the vast artistic stage.

The Song period is regarded as possibly the most accomplished and elegant era of Chinese art, when poets — among them the acclaimed Su Dongpo — were established as literary heroes, when the field of landscape painting flourished with new color and composition. Boosted by the establishment of an Academy of Art, painters developed new perspectives in their work in which depth and elevation were illustrated with various subtle levels and shades of light and color. It was during the Song reign that the full discipline of brushstrokes was established. Elsewhere, the Song era became famous for the introduction of the almost translucent celadon ware, and for the simple elegance of all arts ranging from ceramics to carved ivory and lacquerware.

But it was the Ming reign (1368–1644) that gave China much of the artistic tradition that is still widely evident today. It was a time of hot patriotism — the reins of power returned to Han Chinese control after the short but bloody subjugation under the Mongols — and this was reflected in huge civil engineering feats like the reconstruction of the defensive Great Wall and in the boldness, brilliant color and general exuberance of painting. This burst of color was reflected in other arts — ceramics, sculpture and embroidery — and it also found its way into a new technique of multicolored wood-block printing. Porcelain became even finer and more elegant in design, and the distinctive blue and white porcelain that we see today originated in the Ming kilns. *Cloisonné* — strikingly colored enamels fired onto intricate metal designs — developed in Beijing.

If there is a point in the history of Chinese arts where the principle of "perfect obsolescence" is turned upside down, it is in the ensuing Manchu Qing reign. Ironically, and unfortunately, the elegance and taste that had been achieved up to and during the Ming dynasty in almost all art and crafts deteriorated into a largely gaudy flamboyance and extravagance from then on — and in any study of existing Chinese traditional art and architecture today, the eyes and instincts search for that almost elusive simplicity of the past in a broad canvas of what can often be described as comparative kitsch.

Hong Kong, Macau, and the South

HONG KONG

On July 1, 1997, 156 years of colonial rule came to an end, and the tiny enclave of capitalism known as Hong Kong rejoined the communist "motherland." It rained through much of the lead-up to the hand-over, and, despite celebrity concerts, processions, parades and an extravagant fireworks show over Victoria Harbour, when the clock struck midnight the crowds seemed puzzled about what to do next. Only one thing was certain, an era had come to an end.

A few years later, Hong Kong, at least to the visitor's eye, seems little changed. To be sure, Mandarin can be heard spoken on the streets a lot more than before, but Hong Kong remains the busy enclave of capitalist endeavor that it always was. Hong Kong may belong to China now, but it's a separate world from the big China over the border.

BACKGROUND

The Chinese — who have a slogan for everything — say that Hong Kong and China equal "one country, two systems." The former colony is now the Hong Kong Special Administrative Region (HKSAR), and has been promised a high degree of autonomy and the freedom to continue its capitalist lifestyle for 50 years after 1997.

It's easy to forget that historically Hong Kong was part of China. After all, when the British annexed it in 1841, it was famously nothing but a "barren rock." And since then the colonial status of the island has reduced it in popular Western imagination to a kind of Chinatown writ large. If China is the Great Wall, the Forbidden City, Mao and his adoring hordes armed with little red books, then Hong Kong is altogether more homey: junks in the harbor, joss smoldering in back-street temples, tiffin on the peak. If for British "expats" Hong Kong was a home away from home, China was that place "over the border."

Nevertheless, Hong Kong *is* Chinese. The British got it as spoils of the first Opium War with China, an insult that has never been forgotten. From the beginning Chinese flooded in. They came first from Guangzhou (Canton) and the southern provinces fleeing famine and the harsh rule of the Manchu Qing dynasty, most of them with nothing to lose and thus, with thrift and hard toil, everything to gain. The colony's second major attribute, its nineteenth-century British and European venture capitalists, were always a small minority. But what a combination those armies of

The new Hong Kong Special Administrative Region bauhinia-flower flag and the national flag of China replace the Union Jack and Hong Kong colonial flags over the Legislative Building in Central Hong Kong.

MASS TRANSIT RAILWAY

TSUEN WAN LINE	KWUN TONG LINE	ISLAND LINE	KOWLOON, CANTON RAILWAY
CENTRAL	QUARRY BAY	SHEUNG WAN	
ADMIRALTY	LAM TIN	CENTRAL	LO WU
TSIM SHA TSUI	KWUN TONG	ADMIRALTY	SHEUNG SHUI
JORDAN	NGAU TAU KOK	WAN CHAI	FANLING
YAU MA TEI	KOWLOON BAY	CAUSEWAY BAY	TAI WO
MONG KOK	CHOI HUNG	TIN HAU	TAI PO MARKET
PRINCE EDWARD	DIAMOND HILL	FORTRESS HILL	UNIVERSITY
SHAM SHUI PO	WONG TAI SAN	NORTH POINT	FO TAN
CHEUNG SHA WAN	LOK FU	QUARRY BAY	RACECOURSE
LAI CHI KOK	KOWLOON TONG	TAI KOO	SHA TIN
MEI FOO	SHEK KIP MEI	SAI WAN HO	TAI WAI
LAI KING	PRINCE EDWARD	SHAUKEI WAN	KOWLOON TONG
KWAI FONG	MONG KOK	HENG FA CHUEN	MONG KOK
KWAI HING	YAU MA TEI	CHAI WAN	KOWLOON
TAI WO HAU			
TSUEN WAN			

opportunity-grabbing Chinese and dour, ledger-worshipping inheritors of an empire made. Hong Kong couldn't help but make money.

It has never stopped making money. It probably does it better than anywhere else in the world. When the communist revolutionaries marched into Shanghai, the textile barons took their money and even their manufacturing equipment to Hong Kong, and the colony retooled, fattened and diversified. By 1966, Hong Kong was not only the main Southeast Asian trans-shipment point for

Vietnam war materials — its harbor packed with freighters — but it was also one of the most popular R&R venues for the American troops.

By the mid-1970s Hong Kong was moving from trade in textiles and toys to international banking and finance and electronics, and vastly improving its housing and public transportation infrastructure. By the early 1980s it was obvious that a new China was emerging, a more pragmatic China that was prepared to leave ideology simmering on the back burner while it got its moribund

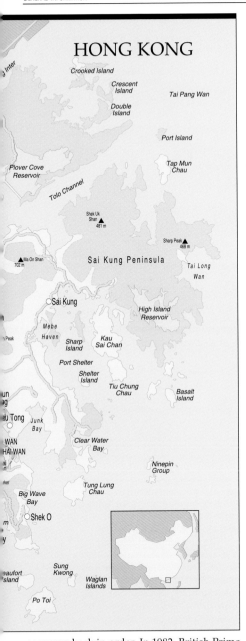

HONG KONG

Crooked Island

Crescent
Island
Tai Pang Wan

Double
Island

Port Island

Plover Cove
Reservoir

Tap Mun
Chau

Tolo Channel

Shek Uk
Shan ▲
481 m

Sharp Peak ▲
468 m

▲ Ma On Shan
702 m

Sai Kung Peninsula

Tai Long
Wan

○ Sai Kung

High Island
Reservoir

Mebe

Peak   Haven   Sharp   Kau
Island Sai Chan

Port Shelter

Shelter
Island
Tiu Chung
Chau
Basalt
Island

un
ng

au Tong   Junk
○   Bay

WAN
HAI WAN

ai
n

Clear Water
Bay

Ninepin
Group

ker

Tung Lung
Chau

Big Wave
Bay

○ Shek O

m

y

Sung
eaufort Kwong
sland   Waglan
Islands

Po Toi

which includes Macau and southern Guangdong
— one of the front-runners of the new wave of
Asian economic "tigers." It welcomes around
11 million visitors a year, including over two million business travelers and package tourists from
mainland China. The "barren rock" of 150 years
ago is now one the world's great cities.

GENERAL INFORMATION

The **Hong Kong Tourist Association (HKTA)**
WEBSITE www.hkta.org provides advice and books
on shopping, sightseeing, culture, dining and
entertainment. Offices are at: Star Ferry Concourse,
Tsimshatsui (open 8 AM to 6 PM, daily); Hong Kong
International Airport (arrivals terminal, buffer
hall; 24 hours, daily); GF, The Center, 99 Queen's
Road, Central, Hong Kong (open 8 AM to 6 PM,
daily, tourist literature and cyberlink 24 hours).
For **multilingual tourist information** ((852)
2508-1234 (daily; 8 AM to 6 PM).

All Hong Kong clinics and hospitals have
English-speaking staff. In an **emergency** dial (999.

The local **telephone system** is excellent, and
local calls are free if they're made from a private
phone; public phones cost HK$1 a call. Most hotels
have international direct dialing (IDD). Card-
phones for both local and IDD calls are located at
some 500 sites and operate on stored-value
phonecards available at most Telecom CSL shops,
Hong Kong Telecom Service Centres and HKTA.
For directory inquiries (1081.

Try to avoid **changing money** at Hong Kong's
bureaux de change, particularly at the airport,
where rates are nothing short of extortionary.
Change large amounts at the banks: the Hong Kong
Bank has good rates (it charges HK$50 per trans-
action); the Bank of America is the best place to
exchange United States dollars.

Most countries have a consular office in Hong
Kong. The main ones are:
Australia ((852) 2827-8881 FAX (852) 2585-4121;
Belgium ((852) 2524-3111 FAX (852) 2868-5997;
Canada ((852) 2810-4321 FAX (852) 2810-6736;
Denmark ((852) 2827-8101 FAX (852) 2827-4555;
Finland ((852) 2525-5385 FAX (852) 2810-1232;
France ((852) 2529-4351 FAX (852) 2866-9693; **Germany** ((852) 2529-8855 FAX (852) 2865-2033; **Greece**
((852) 2774-1682 FAX (852) 2334-2738; **Italy** ((852)
2522-0033 FAX (852) 2845-9678; **Luxembourg** ((852)
2877-1018 FAX (852) 2869-6623; **Netherlands** ((852)
2522-5127 FAX (852) 2868-5388; **New Zealand**
((852) 2877-4488 FAX (852) 2845-2915; **Portugal**
((852) 2802-2587 FAX (852) 845-7944; **Singapore**
((852) 2527-2212 FAX (852) 2861-3595; **Spain** ((852)
2525-3041 FAX (852) 2877-2407; **Sweden** ((852)
2521-1212 FAX (852) 2596-0308; **Switzerland** ((852)
2522-7147 FAX (852) 2845-2619; **United Kingdom**
((852) 2901-3000 FAX (852) 2901-3066; **United
States** ((852) 2523-9011 FAX (852) 2845-1598.

economy back in order. In 1982, British Prime
Minister Margaret Thatcher visited Hong Kong
for the first talks on the hand-over of the New
Territories, whose lease was due to expire in
1997. In the event, Britain agreed to hand the
whole lot back.

Although it's still in its early days, one thing is
obvious: The much-feared Anglo-Chinese agree-
ment didn't sink the territory at all. If anything,
Hong Kong gets more prosperous by the day. It is
the jewel in the crown of the Pearl River Delta —

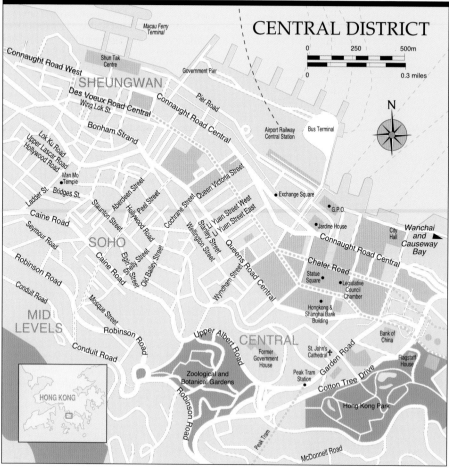

CENTRAL DISTRICT

GETTING AROUND

Hong Kong can be slightly confusing to the newcomer, simply because the region's namesake is a small island, amounting to just seven percent of the total area — the majority of "Hong Kong" is actually elsewhere.

Hong Kong divides into Hong Kong Island, Kowloon, the New Territories and the Outlying Islands. Hong Kong and Kowloon are where most of the action is, and these areas are easily accessible by Mass Transit Railway (MTR). The MTR runs under the harbor, but for visitors the Star Ferry is an obligatory rite of passage. The New Territories are serviced by the Kowloon–Canton Railway (KCR), while the Outlying Islands have fleets of ferries connecting them to terminals in Central.

The **Mass Transit Railway** (MTR) operates four lines that connect Hong Kong with Kowloon, the New Territories and now, on the new Tung Chung Line, Lantau Island. Fares are inexpensive and the system is easy to use. MTR trains run from 6 AM

to 1 AM, every two minutes during rush hour. The Airport Express links Hong Kong's international airport at Chek Lap Kok, Lantau, with Kowloon and Hong Kong Island.

The **Kowloon–Canton Railway** (KCR) runs through Kowloon and the New Territories to Lowu at the Chinese border. The **Light Rail Transit** (LRT) operates in the western New Territories between Tuen Mun ferry pier and Yuen Long. The LRT has a number of lines, which can be a bit confusing, so be sure to study the route map before getting on any train.

Taxis are plentiful and reasonably cheap on both sides of the harbor, with urban taxis operating on a HK$15 flagfall for the first two kilometers (a bit more than a mile) and HK$1.40 for each 200 m (220 yards) thereafter and rural taxis on a HK$12.50 flagfall and HK$1.20 for each 200 m (220 yards) thereafter. If you cross the harbor you must pay an extra HK$20 for the Cross Harbour Tunnel fee — it's actually HK$10 each way; the driver gets to keep the extra HK$10 for his return toll. The toll for the new Lantau Link is HK$30.

The HKTA provides bus timetables and information on routes. The main bus terminals are just west of Exchange Square on the island and the Star Ferry in Tsimshatsui. Fares are cheap, but you must have exact change.

For nostalgia on a budget, it's hard to beat the near-century-old (started in 1904) tram service that runs from Kennedy Town in Western District right through the heart of Central, Wanchai and Causeway Bay and then into the North Point, Quarry Bay and Shaukeiwan. The fare is a flat HK$2 (HK$1 for children), but at that price don't expect to get anywhere in a hurry.

The Star Ferry shuttles back and forth between Central District and Tsimshatsui for HK$2.20 first class from 6:30 AM to 11:30 PM. The Hong Kong Ferry Company ((852) 2542-3081 operates ferries from piers in Central district, just west of the General Post Office.

WHAT TO SEE AND DO

Central District and the Peak

Central is the Manhattan of Hong Kong. The best way to approach it is via the Star Ferry from Tsimshatsui — a first-class trip still costs only HK$2.20, making it probably the cheapest scenic cruise in the world (see also ANYONE FOR THE PEAK?, page 29 in TOP SPOTS).

Attractions in the immediate vicinity of the Central Star Ferry terminal are mostly of the neck-craning variety. Stroll directly ahead to Statue Square for a striking contrast of tradition and the twenty-first century — the Legislative Council Chamber and the Hongkong and Shanghai Bank respectively. British architect Norman Foster designed the latter, the most expensive building in the world on completion in 1985. The vast atrium has a soaring escalator ride that basks in natural light beamed in by a computer-controlled bank of 480 mirrors. The massive building next door is the Bank of China Tower, designed by Chinese-American, I.M. Pei. Behind the bank is Hong Kong Park, where you'll find Flagstaff House, home to some unassuming Chinese teaware.

Back near the pier, Li Yuen Street East and Li Yuen Street West are back alley survivors, narrow streets closed to traffic, hedged in between the department stores and office blocks of Central, and crowded with stalls selling everything from newspapers to key rings.

The Hillside Escalator Link is the world's longest outdoor escalator (800 m or 880 yards), running above street level up Cochrane Street, across Hollywood Road, up Shelley Street to Robinson Road in the Mid-levels, then making its final ascent to Conduit Road. It only runs one-way, going down until around 10 AM, then up until 1 AM. Travel time is around 20 minutes.

Man Mo Temple, with its ornate green tiled roof, bell tower, smoke tower and main hall of prayer, is dedicated to the God of Civil Servants (often translated as "literature"), Man Cheong, and a famous second-century warrior, Kwan Kung, or Mo, since deified as the God of War and guardian deity of businessmen (due to his skills with the abacus). The temple dates back to the 1840s and is at the corner of Hollywood Road and Ladder Street. After visiting Man Mo Temple, a stroll around this area is recommended for its hole-in-the-wall shops and temples.

The cable-operated Peak Tram is, like the Star Ferry, an obligatory Hong Kong experience. (Free, open-roofed, double-decker buses are also avail-

able from the Star Ferry.) Climbing smoothly up a disturbingly sheer series of hillsides, so sheer in some places that you have to stand at a 45-degree angle to move from your seat, the tram trundles 373 m (1,224 ft) up the 554-m (1,817 ft) Victoria Peak, which dominates Hong Kong Island.

In the colonial past there was a direct corollary between residential altitude and status in Hong Kong's snooty social circles. Times have changed very little. The mansions up here command dizzying prices. Ogle them along with the view — one of the most breathtaking anywhere in the world.

For an even higher view from the peak, the Peak Tower has lookouts, while the Peak Galleria next door is touted as Hong Kong's loftiest

Garish pavilions, sculptures and other attractions at Aw Boon Haw (formerly Tiger Balm) Gardens in Causeway Bay.

shop-filled plaza. Most of the restaurants and cafés have terraces that exploit the view of the harbor glittering far below.

Wanchai and Causeway Bay

Wanchai and Causeway are best seen from one of Hong Kong's rattling double-decker trams.

Apart from the tram journey itself, however, Wanchai and Causeway Bay don't have a lot to offer the visitor. The world of Suzie Wong, much celebrated, long gone, is Wanchai's main claim to fame, but most of the bars are tired and overpriced these days. On the harbor front, the dramatic new extension of the Hong Kong Convention Centre out into the harbor is worth a look. Inspired by

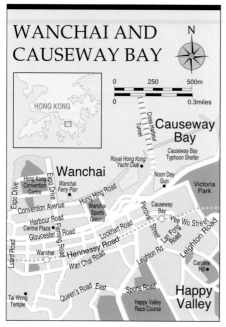

WANCHAI AND
CAUSEWAY BAY

N

0   250   500m

0   0.3miles

HONG KONG

Cross Harbour Tunnel

Causeway Bay

Royal Hong Kong Yacht Club

Causeway Bay Typhoon Shelter

Wanchai

Noon Day Gun

Victoria Park

Hong Kong Convention Centre

Expo Drive

Wanchai Ferry Pier

Hung Hing Road

Convention Avenue

Wanchai Sports Ground

Causeway Bay

Harbour Road

Central Plaza

Gloucester Road

Fleming Road

Lockhart Road

Yee Wo Street

Lan Fong Road

Leighton Road

Luard Road

Wanchai

Hennessy Road

Percival Street

Leighton Rd.

Caroline Hill

Wan Chai Road

Tai Wong Temple

Queen's Road East

Sports Road

Happy Valley Race Course

Happy Valley

the image of a seabird soaring into the sky, it was finished just in time to host the Change of Sovereignty Ceremony on June 30, 1997. The 155,000-sq-m (1.67-million-sq-ft) extension is purpose-built for meetings, conventions and special events and has a grand foyer whose 30-m-tall (100-ft) "glass curtain" gives spectacular 180-degree panoramic views of the harbor.

Opposite the Convention Center is **Central Plaza**, Hong Kong's highest building. For those who don't have time for the Peak, the viewing podium on the forty-sixth floor offers bird's-eye views of Hong Kong's inner-city sprawl.

The main reason for going to Causeway Bay is, of course, to shop, both day and night, in the boutiques and giant Japanese department stores. But, there are a few other attractions — on the waterfront in a small garden opposite the Excelsior Hotel and World Trade Centre, you can actu-

ally watch the firing of the famous **Noon Day Gun**, whose origin to this day is still in dispute. Access is via a small tunnel to the west of the Excelsior Hotel in front of the World Trade Centre. Nearby, the Causeway Bay Typhoon Shelter houses junks and sampans alongside the luxury craft of the Royal Hong Kong Yacht Club.

Also nearby, the **Happy Valley Racecourse**, founded in 1846, is, like its bigger and more modern sister track over in Shatin, the site of some of the world's most frenzied gambling.

On Tai Hang Road you'll see a large white pagoda standing in the shadow of monolithic housing estates. This is the famed Tiger Balm Gardens, now renovated and renamed **Aw Boon Haw Gardens** in memory of its 1935 founder, a flamboyant Chinese multimillionaire who came up with the recipe for the renowned balm that cures everything from a headache to a rattlesnake bite. Grotesque but fascinating is the best description of this cornucopia of grottoes, pagodas and statuary of figures from Chinese mythology.

The Island Trail

From Central District, the main tourist route leads over or through the island's central mountain spine to Aberdeen, Repulse Bay and Stanley. Take the No. 6 bus from the Central Terminal at Exchange Square to Repulse Bay and Stanley, or the more scenic route on the No. 70 air-conditioned express bus, also from Exchange Square, via the Aberdeen Tunnel and Deep Water Bay.

Thousands of fisherfolk still live on a small clutter of junks and their successors, new-style bullet-nosed trawlers, in **Aberdeen**. A sampan tour through the junks and to the floating restaurants should cost HK$50 per person (for about half an hour's ride), depending on your bargaining skills.

Just south of Aberdeen are **Ocean Park** and **Middle Kingdom** ℂ (852) 2552-0291 and **Water World** ℂ (852) 2555-6055, a huge playground and marine entertainment complex. All three are easily reached from Central by a special Citybus from Admiralty MTR station or by a No. 6 minibus from the Hong Kong Star Ferry terminal, but unless you have children with you they are of minimal interest.

Kowloon

A short hop across the harbor and you're in another world; not that this will be apparent immediately. Next to the Star Ferry terminal is **Harbour City**, a vast mall complex, and this — combined with the boulevard feel of Salisbury Road, the venerable Peninsula Hotel on one side and the modern **Hong Kong Cultural Centre** on the other — makes first impressions deceiving. Duck north into the tourist strip of Tsimshatsui's Nathan Road,

A junk passes Exchange Square, providing a contrast to Central District's stark architectural wonders.

and you'll soon discover that Kowloon is far more boisterously Cantonese than cosmopolitan Hong Kong island.

Next to Star Ferry is the old Kowloon-Canton Railway Station's **Clock Tower**, and beside it the Hong Kong Cultural Centre. Within the complex there's the world-class **Hong Kong Museum of Art** ((852) 2734-2167, which has a superb collection of oil paintings, lithographs of old Hong Kong along with other exhibitions of Chinese fine art and historical pictures. The museum is also host to changing exhibits of international art. The museum is closed Thursdays. Next door is the domed **Space Museum** ((852) 2734-2722. Call ahead to check times for shows in English.

are on display, and the **Kowloon Mosque** ((852) 2724-0095. Guided tours can be arranged for the latter, but by appointment only.

The **Hong Kong Science Museum** ((852) 2732-3232 is in Tsimshatsui East. It has around 500 exhibits, more than half of them "hands-on."

In Yaumatei, **Temple Street** is a tourist fixture not only for bargain shopping but to watch the street theater of Chinese opera, fortunetellers and street dentists. Close by, on the corner of Nathan Road and Public Square Street, but best visited during the day, is **Tin Hau Temple**, a complex of four temples originally built in the late 1870s but refurbished in 1972 after a fire destroyed the roof and rafters. Two blocks west, **Jade Market** sprawls

Built in 1928, the **Peninsula Hotel** was the glittering crown of Hong Kong high society through to the late 1970s, and even had the dubious distinction of being the headquarters of the Japanese military administration during the occupation in World War II. It's seen some of the most distinguished and most flamboyant names of the twentieth century come and go, and even today it's a place where you can play "Place the Face" in its ornate and renowned lobby.

Enter Nathan Road from here, and you're on the **Golden Mile**. By night this area probably packs in more neon per square meter than anywhere else in the world. If any spot gives itself over unrepentantly to that most beloved of Hong Kong pastimes — pursuit of a quick buck — it's this strip of Nathan Road. Amidst the boutiques, electronics stores and jewelry shops is the **Museum of History** ((852) 2367-1124, where relics of Hong Kong

its precious wares right across the sidewalks everyday from 10 AM until around 3:30 PM — expensive purchases should be left to discerning jade shoppers.

Close to the Diamond Hill MTR station, Kowloon's latest attraction is also perhaps its most impressive. The **Chi Lin Nunnery** may not be a historical attraction (it was opened in early 2000), but the wooden buildings were constructed in faithful Tang dynasty style, using wooden pegs instead of nails. Take the C2 exit from Diamond Hill MTR station. The nunnery is closed on Wednesdays.

The New Territories

The New Territories, serviced by the KCR, sprawl over a large area, defying brief summary. But a good place to start is Shatin, home to the **New Town Plaza**, a multilevel mall development of vast proportions. More worthy is the remarkable **10,000 Buddhas Monastery** behind Shatin Railway Station. The climb up 431 steps is enough to wind even the fittest of sightseers, but it's worth the effort. In the main hall, the walls are line not with 10,000 but 12,800 Buddha images.

In Tsuen Wan, the northernmost stop on the MTR, is the **Chuk Lam Shim Yuen Monastery**, also known as the "Bamboo Forest Monastery." Now an ornate, sprawling temple with a sweeping, curved and tiled roof, it houses three of Hong Kong's largest Buddha images. Also of interest is the **Sam Tung Uk Museum** ((852) 2411-2001, on Kwu Uk Kane, which recreates a traditional Hakka village.

Territories tour, you'll find relative tranquillity, windsurfing and other water sports, blazing sunsets, interesting fishing communities and wonderful hiking in the country parks. To get to Sai Kung, take the MTR to Choi Hung and then take a bus No. 92 or minibus No. 1.

The HKTA and some private tour operators offer a number of New Territories tours. The HKTA Land Between Tour, for example, takes in such attractions as the Bamboo Forest Monastery, Tai Mo Shan mountain, the fish and duck farms of Shek Kong, the golf club at Fanling, Luen Wo market, the bird sanctuary at Luk Keng, Plover Cove Reservoir, a fishing village in Tolo Harbour, Tai Po, the Chinese University and Shatin. All this

From Tsuen Wan, take a No. 60M or No. 68M bus to Tuen Mun, from whence it's a short Light Rail Transit (LRT) ride to **Ching Chung Koon Temple**, a Taoist temple, also known as the "Temple of Green Pines," and packed with garish images and altar guardians that were carved in Beijing 300 years ago. Nearby, not far from the Lam Tai Light Rail (LR) station, is **Miu Fat Monastery**, a huge, multistory temple, packed on most days with worshippers and visitors and virtually lined throughout with thousands of small Buddha images and niches paid for by the faithful.

Another area of interest is **Sai Kung**, where a cluster of old villages around the shallow bay are being transformed into marine resorts. If you feel like taking a rest from the shopping plazas and packed streets of the urban tourist districts, or feel the need to put your feet up after your New

for HK$385 for adults and HK$335 for children and senior citizens.

The Outlying Islands

With so many things to see in Hong Kong and Kowloon, few short-term visitors get to see Hong Kong's outlying islands. Those who do are usually surprised at just how relaxed the pace of life is in these islands, which actually are not that far from Hong Kong at all.

Ferries and hoverferries to Lantau, Peng Chau, Lamma and Cheung Chau leave from Pier 5, 6 and 7 in Central, west of Star Ferry.

Nearly twice the size of Hong Kong Island, **Lantau** is the site of the new Chek Lap Kok International Airport. Nevertheless, the island remains

OPPOSITE: Scenic gondolas glide past an ornamental pagoda at Ocean Park. ABOVE: Pedder Street and the old clock tower in the late 1860s.

surprisingly undeveloped. Hiking, camping, fishing and other recreational pursuits are popular. It also features a colossal Buddha statue, monasteries, temples, a fort and even has a small tea plantation.

The prime reason for visiting Lantau is **Po Lin (Precious Lotus) Buddhist Monastery**, which lies on the high Ngong Ping Plateau close to Lantau Peak. To get there, take a No. 2 bus from Mui Wo ferry pier on Lantau or a bus No. 23 from Tung Chung MTR station.

First established in 1905, the present temple complex dates back to 1927. The main temple features three magnificent bronze Buddha images — including Sakyamuni, the Healing Buddha and the Lord of the Western Paradise; and an even more spectacular one, the "world's largest" outdoor bronze Buddha statue (34 m or 111 ft tall and weighing 250 tons). It's the latter which attracts the crowds. Don't be mistaken, there are bigger Buddhas around, but this is the biggest "outdoor bronze Buddha." It's an impressive sight.

The village of **Tai O**, which can also be reached from the Mui Wo ferry pier by No. 1 bus, is famous for its seafood restaurants, which cluster along the waterfront, and several restored temples, including the beautiful eighteenth-century **Kwan Tai Temple**.

Lamma Island is the closest of Hong Kong's other islands and, apart from an ugly electric power station, is otherwise a rustic retreat from city life. Ferries go to two destinations, **Yung Shue Wan** (which has a large expatriate community) in the north near the power plant, and **Sok Kwu Wan** which lies in the island's narrow central spine.

Lamma features several good beaches, many countryside walks, including a strenuous climb up its main peak, Mount Stenhouse, interesting village life and two Tin Hau temples, one in each major town. But it's famous above all for its seafood restaurants, which line the waterfront in both Yung Shue Wan and Sok Kwu Wan.

There's another crowded and popular huddle of seafood restaurants on the main waterfront, or Praya, of **Cheung Chau**, an island that lies close to Lantau. A huge fishing and trading fleet, including many junks, sits off the promenade. At the boat-building yard you'll see as you enter the harbor, traditional fishing junks as well as elegant teak and yakal pleasure junks were once constructed, in a confusion of crowded slipways. Nowadays, the yard mostly does repairs and the occasional building of a new fishing trawler.

Cheung Chau was once a thriving port, watering place and market town for junks plying the South China Coast to and from Macau, and had a busy, well-developed society long before Hong Kong itself was settled. Much of that society remains — clans and trade guilds still dominate the island's industrious but carefully paced fishing

and business life. The island comes to life in the week-long **Bun Festival**, in April or early May, held to appease the spirits of victims of a plague which swept Cheung Chau in the later 1880s. The island has several interesting temples, notably **Pak Tai Temple**, built in 1783, and enshrining images of the Spirit of the North, also known as the Supreme Emperor of the Dark Heaven and Protector of all Seafarers, along with the attendant gods Thousand Mile Eye and Favorable Wind Ear.

SHOPPING

Hong Kong has become the great Oriental emporium that the early China traders dreamed of. Local television advertisements parade Swiss watches, French perfumes, high-class jewelry and upmarket Japanese electronic consumer products. Huge self-contained, climate-controlled, luxury-packed shopping malls litter the landscape, making Hong Kong the ultimate shopper's theme park.

Before you leap into the fray, grab a copy of the HKTA's *Official Shopping Guide* (see SHOP TILL YOU DROP, page 48 in YOUR CHOICE). Remember, especially in prime tourist territory (like Nathan Road, Tsimshatsui), there are some unscrupulous operators. Ascertain that you're getting the standard warranty and accessories on electrical goods; find out whether paying by credit card will make the purchase more expensive; bargain by all means but not too heatedly; and lastly, don't allow yourself to be lured into shops by touts.

Hong Kong's reputation as an electronics bargain basement needs some qualification nowadays. Always come armed with prices from back home, for comparison's sake, and shop around. The electronics shops of Tsimshatsui, for example, are generally at least 10% more expensive than their rivals just a mile up Nathan Road in Yaumatei and Mongkok — where, incidentally, prices are always labeled and not subject to the whim of an aggressive sales clerk.

Computer equipment can be reasonably priced, and you'll find everything from mainstream dealers to hole-in-the-wall outlets selling everything from cables to Windows 2001.

For Chinese items and antiques there's really only one place to go: the area in Central starting from the upper end of Wyndham Street, continuing all the way along Hollywood Road until you reach "Cat Street," just by the Man Mo Temple.

Temple Street is Hong Kong's most popular night market and can be reached by MTR, alighting at Jordan station. From the Jordan Road entrance you make your way through block after block of stalls and shops selling fake Rolex, and Cartier watches and designer clothes, more cheap watches, sunglasses, silk ties, trousers, shirts,

Looking out across the marine club at Aberdeen and its famous floating restaurant.

sweaters, jackets, suits, men's underpants at about HK$20 for three pairs and T-shirts for HK$15 to HK$20. You can pick up electronic key rings that beep, solar calculators the size of credit cards (which also double as FM radios), or FM radios the size of cigarette lighters, or cigarette lighters that double as FM radios. You'll find Nepalese hawkers sitting on the sidewalk selling Nepalese jewelry, masks and colorful bags. You'll see street dentists, Chinese opera, and for HK$50 to HK$80 you can have some of your fortune told — the full story will cost more. For more on shopping in Hong Kong, see SHOP TILL YOU DROP, page 48 in YOUR CHOICE.

WHERE TO STAY

Living space in Hong Kong is highly sought after, and this is reflected in local room rates, which are among the highest in Asia. Nevertheless, the situation has improved over the last few years, with many hotels offering substantial discounts for those who book ahead or who book at the airport before going into town. For those in the mood to splurge, Hong Kong has some of the best hotels in Asia.

Luxury

Luxury hotels in Hong Kong charge rates that start at between HK$2,200 and HK$3,000. Typically there's a service charge of 10% and a government tax of five percent.

The **Peninsula** ((852) 2920-2888 FAX (852) 2722-4170, Salisbury Road, Tsimshatsui, Kowloon, is Hong Kong's most venerable hotel. The doors swung open in 1928 and the rich and famous have been arriving ever since. High standards are affirmed in countless tiny details, the classic look of the rooms, complete with marble bathrooms, fax machines and CD players. The hotel's restaurants are among the best in Hong Kong, notably Gaddi's and Felix, designed by avant-garde French designer Philippe Starck.

The **Mandarin Oriental** ((852) 2522-0111 FAX (852) 2810-6190, 5 Connaught Road Central, Hong Kong, is the Peninsula's rival over the water. Like the Peninsula, it is considered one of the world's best, and along with all the facilities one would expect — babysitting, health center, sauna, nonsmoking rooms, indoor swimming pool, hotel doctor — it also has arguably the best hotel location in all Hong Kong.

Back on Kowloon side, the **Regent** ((852) 2721-1211 FAX (852) 2739-4546, 18 Salisbury Road, Tsimshatsui, Kowloon, is more oriented to the needs of the business traveler, but it commands a loyal following, and makes for a less expensive, though undoubtedly five-star, alternative to the Peninsula and Mandarin. Facilities are comparable to Hong Kong's best, and include

a heated outdoor pool, a gymnasium, solarium and disabled facilities.

Mid-range

Finding a room in Hong Kong for under US$100 is much easier now than it was a couple of years ago. If you fly in, check with the Hotel Reservations desk at the airport — a large array of surprisingly generous discounts are available.

The **Garden View International House** (HKYWCA) ((852) 2877-3737 FAX (852) 2845-6263, 1 MacDonnell Road Central, Hong Kong, is that most miraculous of things: an affordable hotel a brief stroll from the peak tram terminus. It overlooks the zoological gardens, and has business and health centers, babysitting services, an outdoor swimming pool, and even provides classes on Chinese arts.

Harbour View International House ((852) 2802-0111 FAX (852) 2802-9063, 4 Harbour Road,

Wanchai, is similar to the Garden View. Wanchai is perhaps not such a fabulous setting, but a harbor view is hard to beat, and the hotel has all the facilities you would expect of a good mid-range hotel.

The **Guangdong Hotel** ((852) 2739-3311 FAX (852) 2721-1137, 18 Prat Avenue, Tsimshatsui, Kowloon, has an excellent location in the heart of bustling Tsimshatsui. The **Kowloon Hotel** ((852) 2929-2888 FAX (852) 2739-9811, 19-21 Nathan Road, Tsimshatsui, is behind the Peninsula Hotel, and for a third of the price of staying at the Peninsula itself you can stay here and use the Peninsula's swimming pool and other facilities.

The **Salisbury YMCA** ((852) 2268-7000 FAX (852) 2739-9315, 41 Salisbury Road, Tsimshatsui, has long been a favorite of repeat visitors to Hong Kong. The health club is widely celebrated, the rooms are spacious and service standards are very high. It's wise to book well in advance.

Hong Kong, Macau, and the South

Inexpensive

The most infamous blot on Hong Kong's accommodation landscape is Chungking Mansions in Tsimshatsui. This 17-story complex of five blocks at 30 Nathan Road has the cheapest accommodation in town — around HK$200 for a single room or HK$300 to $400 for a double (usually with private bath), and some guesthouses have dorm beds. Most of the cheaper guesthouses are on the upper floors of Block A and B.

The majority of Chungking's offerings are not for the fainthearted. One exception is **Chungking House** ((852) 2366-5362 FAX 2721-3570, Block A, 4/F. A superior guesthouse, Chungking House has a coffee shop, laundry service, a dining area, tour desk and a total of 75 rooms. Those who can

You can still enjoy fresh air and open spaces on Hong Kong's outlying islands — this one is Lamma — before such peaceful spots catch the eye of developers.

bring themselves to join the A-block elevator queue will find themselves pleasantly surprised once they reach the Chungking House foyer.

For those on a rock-bottom budget, the dorm accommodation at both the **Golden Crown Guesthouse** ((852) 2369-1782, 66–70 Nathan Road, and the **Victoria Hostel** ((852) 2376-1182, 33 Hankow Road, are similarly priced, more pleasant alternatives to Chungking Mansions.

Hong Kong has seven youth hostels, though none are conveniently situated. Only one, **Ma Wui Hall** ((852) 2817-5715, on Hong Kong Island's Mount Davis, has anything approaching a central location. If you've got heavy luggage, you'd be best advised to take a taxi. Bus No. 54 from the Outlying Islands Ferry Terminal in Central or No. 47A from Admiralty pass close by, but you're still faced with a stiff 45-minute walk from the bus stop at Victoria Road and Mount Davis Path.

Moving up several notches in the price and comfort bracket, the **Star Guesthouse** ((852) 2723-8951, Flat B, Sixth Floor, 21 Cameron Road, Tsimshatsui, is recommended due to the fact that, unlike many budget digs in Hong Kong, it's kept clean and some of the rooms even have windows that let in light.

WHERE TO EAT

Hong Kong may be part of China now, but on the cuisine front its offerings are more cosmopolitan than ever. To be sure, when it comes to Chinese, Hong Kong is rivaled only by Taipei as a place to sample the best the cuisine can offer; but it is also worth exploring some of the city's international restaurants, which have enjoying something of a boom in recent years.

Dining out in Hong Kong is subject to huge variations in expense. It's possible to grab a bowl of noodles or a quick meal at one of the fast-food chains for as little at US$4 to US$5, but at most of the sit-down restaurants recommended below, lunch will start at around US$10 and dinner from US$20 per person. Of course, at Hong Kong's best restaurants, expect to pay a lot more — US$50 per head is more the norm at top hotel restaurants around town.

Central District

Among Hong Kong's best is the **Summer Palace** ((852) 2820-8553, 5/F Island Shangri-La, Pacific Place, Supreme Court Road, Central, where dim-sum lunches give way to evening à la carte dining in a Song dynasty setting.

The imperial courts of Chinese cuisine in Central are the **Yung Kee Restaurant** ((852) 2522-1624, a multistory gaudily decorated Cantonese eating place in Wellington Street, and the famous **Luk Yu Tea House** ((852) 2523-5464, in nearby Stanley Street, which is such a popular *dim sum*

establishment and restaurant that you virtually need to camp outside overnight to get a table.

Another *dim sum* standard is the **Diamond Restaurant** ((852) 2544-4921, 271-273 Des Vœux Road Central. It's best to avoid peak hours, when the restaurant gets very busy, and to encourage diners to partake at nonstandard times, the restaurant offers off-peak discounts. Just as popular, and lauded by many as Hong Kong's best *dim sum* experience, is the unimaginatively named **Chinese Restaurant at City Hall** ((852) 2521-1303, 2F, City Hall, Central. It's best to avoid weekends, when the queues have to be seen to be believed.

A perfect place for an inexpensive lunchtime Chinese meal is **Noodle Box** ((852) 2536-0571, Shop 3, 30–32 Wyndham Street, Central, a spotlessly clean restaurant that serves nothing but noodles.

On the international front, a current favorite is **El Pomposo** ((852) 2869-7679, 4 Tun Wo Lane,

Central, a Spanish restaurant that is celebrated for its *tapas*. Reservations are recommended for evening meals.

In Lan Kwai Fong, Central's popular bar and nightclub enclave just below Wyndham Street and off D'Angillar Street, is **Tokio Joe** ((852) 2525-1889, an upscale sushi restaurant that tugs in the beautiful people, usually as a prelude to a night of fun. This is Japanese cuisine at its best, and prices reflect the quality.

Lan Kwai Fong and the SoHo (South of Hollywood Road) area — an old-fashioned residential neighborhood that has become a sophisticated alternative to the more boisterous Lan Kwai Fong — abound with superb restaurants.

A recommended venue for sampling the SoHo experience is **Soho Soho** ((852) 2147-2618, 9 Old Bailey Street, an upscale eatery that serves that most unexpected of things — "modern British" cuisine. And if you associate British with fish and

chips, Soho Soho's English standards served with a nouvelle twist will come as a pleasant — in some cases almost revelatory — surprise. The restaurant is closed on Sundays.

For an ambient Gallic experience, SoHo's **2 Sardines** ((852) 2973-6618, 43 Elgin Street, was one of SoHo's pioneers and is going as strong as ever. The perfect place for an intimate dinner, the restaurant serves far more than just sardines — the stuffed quail is recommended. Meanwhile, bucking tradition, which dictates Hong Kong Chinese restaurants be a glare of neon and Formica, **Bistro Manchu** ((852) 2536-9218, 33 Elgin Street, Mid-levels, serves northern style Chinese cuisine in an atmosphere that rivals even the most stylish international restaurants in the area.

Old World grace and charm at afternoon tea in the lobby of the renowned Peninsula.

Finally, a treat less for the taste buds — though they will not be disappointed — and more for the eyes is the **Peak Café** ℂ (852) 2849-7868, 121 Peak Road. The cuisine is dubbed "pan Asian," but by popular consent it is the Indian dishes that come up tops. The real reason to head up here, however, is the superlative views. Be sure to book ahead in order to get an alfresco dining spot.

For a quick food fix on the run, all the major fast-food chains have branches scattered around the city, if your tastes or budget run in that direction. For fast food with a gourmet twist look out for **Delifrance** in Queensway Plaza and World-Wide Plaza. **Oliver's Super Sandwiches** are another excellent chain, and branches abound not only in Central but throughout Hong Kong.

Wanchai and Causeway Bay

Among the best of Hong Kong's Cantonese restaurants is the Grand Hyatt's **One Harbour Road** ℂ (852) 2588-1234, extension 7338, 8/F Grand Hyatt, 1 Harbour Road, Wanchai. The restaurant is lauded, not only for the excellence of its Cantonese cuisine, but also for its sophisticated ambiance — a welcome quality in a city where the best in dining is so often marred by crowded and garish surroundings.

An outstanding Chinese restaurant is this area is **Szechuan Lau** ℂ (852) 2891-9027, 466 Lockhart Road, Causeway Bay, which as the name suggests specializes in Sichuan fare, and is commonly regarded as one of the most authentic in town. House favorites include spiced perfumed chicken, chili and camphor-flavored tea-smoked duck and kumquat beef, but it's also a good place to try Sichuan standards such as *gongbao jiding* (diced chicken with chili and peanuts) and *huiguorou* (double-cooked pork).

Another recommended Sichuan restaurant in the area is the family-run **Red Pepper** ℂ (852) 2577-3811, 7 Lan Fong Road. Favorites include "strange taste" spiced shredded chicken and the sizzling prawns, though the *mapo doufu* (chili, pork and mashed tofu) probably gets ordered more than any other dish here. Success, as is often the case in Hong Kong, has made this restaurant less friendly than it once was, but the food is still superb.

Experiment with a little known Chinese cuisine at the **Forever-Green Taiwanese Restaurant** ℂ (852) 2890-3448, 93 Sun Wui Road, Causeway Bay. The first of several branches, it's a good place to experience the seafood based, and often very spicy, cuisine of Taiwan, which evolved from the Min cuisine of Fujian province.

Because of the big multistory Japanese department stores in Causeway Bay, the area abounds with Japanese restaurants. At the top of the range you'll find expensive places such as **Kanetanaka** ℂ (852) 2833-6018, 22/F East Point Centre, 545–563 Hennessy Road.

Wanchai has several celebrated Thai restaurants, in particular the cheap and cheerful **Thai Delicacy** ℂ (852) 2527-2598, 44 Hennessy Road, and the **Chili Club** ℂ (852) 2527-2872, 1/F 88 Lockhart Road, which has been doing a roaring business for as long as most residents can remember. Causeway Bay is also home to one of Hong Kong's only Indonesian restaurants, a place that has been in business so long it is surprising it has not spawned more imitators. The simply named **Indonesian** ℂ (852) 2577-9811, 28 Leighton Road, Causeway Bay, is an unpretentious place that serves inexpensive dishes from around the archipelago. The beef *rendang* is particularly recommended.

For Mexican specialties, American steaks and seafood, margaritas and nightly entertainment, **Casa Mexicana** ℂ (852) 2566-5560, G/F Victoria Centre, 15 Watson Road, North Point is a lively venue — not the place for quiet night out.

Homesick Brits should head over to **Harry Ramsden's** ℂ (852) 2832-9626, 213 Queen's Road East, next to the Hopewell Centre, where they'll find authentic, though pricey, English fish and chips.

Tsimshatsui

For superb Cantonese cuisine in sumptuous surroundings, the **Spring Moon** ℂ (852) 2315-3160, 1/F, Peninsula Hotel, has few peers. Prices, as to be expected, are far from inexpensive, but given the quality of the service and the food are extremely reasonable. The restaurants *dim sum* menu concentrates more on quality than on variety, but rate amongst the best in town.

For those not watching their budgets, two excellent restaurants for shark's fin soup, other seafood and game dishes are **Sun Tung Lok Shark's Fin Restaurant** ℂ (852) 2730-0288, G/F Harbour City, 17–19 Canton Road, and **Fook Lam Moon** ℂ (852) 2366-0286, 1/F 53–59 Kimberley Road.

Tsimshatsui is a good place to sample Chinese vegetarian cuisine: **Bodhi** ℂ (852) 2366-8283, 1/F 32–34 Lock Road, has a wonderful selection of bean-curd, fungi and bamboo-shoot dishes.

Tsimshatsui also has a surprisingly good range of international cuisine. The longest running of them all is **Jimmy's Kitchen** ℂ (852) 2376-0327, 1/F, Kowloon Center, 29 Ashley Road (also a branch in the basement of the South China Building, Wyndham Road, Central), whose pedigree dates back to the 1920s. Jimmy's has, however, kept up with the times and is an immensely popular place for steak meals (some Asian dishes are also available) amongst expats and locals alike.

For more steak, served in gargantuan portions, **Morton's of Chicago** ℂ (852) 2732-2343, 4/F Sheraton Hong Kong Hotel & Towers, gets the nod from hungry carnivores. Don't go here unless you have

Like an apparition from the movie *Ghostbusters*, the 78-story monolithic Central Plaza streaks upward out of the harborfront business district of Wanchai.

a *big* appetite. Patrons who manage the Key Lime Pie after one of Morton's steaks probably deserve a prize of some kind.

For years **Au Trou Normand** ((852) 2366-8754, 6 Carnarvon Road, has been rated the finest French restaurant in town, and its classic recipes, its variety of wines and decor are still five-star. Its main competition is at the Peninsula Hotel ((852) 2366-6251, which has excellent European restaurants in **Gaddi's** and the extraordinary East-meets-West **Felix** ((852) 2366-8521. The latter specializes in "fusion" cuisine, but while the food here is an experience in itself, it is the restaurants interior decor, and in particular its space-age men's room, that astounds first-time visitors.

alfresco tables on the pavement are at a premium (book ahead).

NIGHTLIFE

As in all great cities, Hong Kong's nightlife scene caters to all tastes and is constantly evolving. Unless, however, you are a businessperson on an expense account, **Lan Kwai Fong** in Central, near the Pedder Street exit of the Central MTR station, is probably the best place to sample the city's vibrant nightlife. If you're in town on a Friday or a Saturday night, it is worth wandering through this area simply to soak up its ambiance — of course, you might stop off for a drink while you're at it.

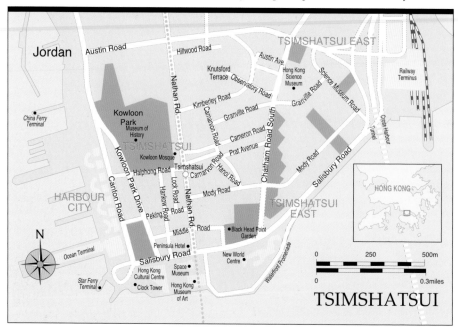

TSIMSHATSUI

A more recent arrival is the **Maman Wine Bar & Restaurant** ((852) 2722-1818, 71 Mody Road, Tsimshatsui East, which has created such a buzz about its wine list (more than 50 varieties by the glass) that it is easy to forget that the restaurant's food disappoints no-one. Another winning quality of Maman is its spacious seating — a rarity in Hong Kong. Regulars swear by the lobster bisque.

Sabatini ((852) 2721-5215, 3/F Royal Garden Hotel, 69 Mody Road, is considered one of Hong Kong's top Italian restaurants with good reason. Everything from the decor to the unobtrusive live music (nightly) is just right, and the desserts almost outshine the pasta mains, which is saying something.

A less expensive alternative to Sabatini is the trendy **Tutto Bene** ((852) 2316-2116, 7 Knutsford Terrace, an extremely popular place where the

Club 64 ((852) 2523-2801, Wing Wah Lane, has long been a favorite first stop, and the crowd often spills out onto the lane; the alfresco seating here is provided by the restaurants. Going upmarket — Club 64 is famously low-life, which in Hong Kong means drinkers loosen their ties — **La Dolce Vita** ((852) 2810-8098, 9 Lan Kwai Fong, remains one of the places to see and be seen in Hong Kong after a surprisingly long run of success. Across the road, the **Jazz Club** ((852) 2845-8477, 2/F California Entertainment Building, frequently features top international performers, along with their regular, first-rate house band.

For the latest club sounds, one of the coolest places in Hong Kong is **Phi-b** ((852) 2869-4469, Lower Basement, Harileta House, 79 Wyndham Street, Central. It's a different show every night of the week, so it's a good idea to check ahead for what's on before heading down.

Wanchai may have once been the **Suzy Wong** bar, brothel and nightclub district of Hong Kong, but it has now become a respectable business and restaurant area, though the expensive and somewhat tame (compared to Bangkok and Manila) girlie bars linger on.

A good place to start an evening in this part of town is **Coyote** ((852) 2861-2221, 114–120 Lockhart Road, Wanchai, though only if you are in the mood for Mexican-themed decor. The bar is famed locally for its happy-hour specials, mostly involving — inevitably — margaritas.

Joe Bananas ((852) 2529-1811, 23 Luard Road, is a Hong Kong institution and is known universally — there's no point pulling punches — as a

For late-night dancing in Tsimshatsui, **Someplace Else** ((852) 2369-1111, Basement, Sheraton Hotel, 20 Nathan Road, Tsimshatsui, is not the hippest place in town but can be a fun night on a Friday or Saturday — the music tends to be fairly eclectic.

HOW TO GET THERE

All international flights arrive at Chek Lap Kok International Airport, an architecturally impressive and recent addition to the territory. The fastest way into town is by train, which connects with Hong Kong's MTR rail service in Central.

"meat market." Not a place to bring a date, but perhaps a place to find one. On the edge of Wanchai, **JJ's** ((852) 2588-1234, Grand Hyatt Hotel, 1 Harbour Road, comes a close second to Joe Banana's as a place for singles to mingle, but in grander surroundings.

Tsimshatsui is littered with hole-in-the-wall bars, but most of them are unexciting places. An exception is **Delaney's TST** ((852) 2301-3980, Basement, Mary Building, 71–77 Peking Road. The pub makes a good stab at reproducing Irish ambiance on Hong Kong soil, and there is also a good selection of pub food (including breakfast from 8:30 AM if you're in the area).

Also in Tsimshatsui, you don't have to be dining out to take a trip to **Felix** (see WHERE TO EAT, above) and soak up the ambiance of Philippe Starck's minimalist interior design. The bar area is the perfect place for a drink and a quiet conversation.

From Hong Kong flights fan out into all corners of the world. Flights are also available to most major destinations in China.

MACAU

China's latest addition to the family is the former Portuguese colony of Macau. The hand-over took place on December 20, 1999, and while it was a far more muted affair than the Hong Kong hand-over two years earlier, in China it was a significant event. At last the final reminder of China's colonial humiliations was once again Chinese soil.

In Macau, China inherited a place very different from neighboring Hong Kong. Under Portuguese administration, Macau had evolved into a

The laser-lashed dancefloor of Club Bboss, one of the biggest and most astonishing entertainment centers in the world.

territory that was at once a Latin-influence siesta zone and at the same time a freewheeling city in which casinos were the major source of wealth. For travelers and tourists it was a place to both to have a whirl with the dice and to enjoy the city's equally impressive architecture and food.

Little has changed. The casinos are doing better business than ever, the city may be modernizing but many of its charms linger on, and the food is as good as it ever was. Macau is even home to a nightlife scene that seems healthier today than it ever was under the Portuguese.

All the more reason to visit. Accessible from Hong Kong, and with an international airport and easy access to China, Macau is even worth considering as a China entry point.

Macau arose as a trading port for foreigners on the South China Coast long before Hong Kong, and was established by Portuguese traders and missionaries in 1557. Its trading power gave way to that of Canton (Guangzhou) and the other treaty ports opened up by the British in China, and was eventually eclipsed by the phenomenal growth of Hong Kong, leaving this tiny mainland enclave with a lot to show in the way of culture, especially its Roman Catholic churches and cathedrals, but not much else.

Nowadays it's a fascinating blend of Cantonese joss and often crumbling Portuguese architecture — along with the annual roar and high-octane odors of its most celebrated European contribution, the Macau Grand Prix (mid-November). It's fascinating to visit, and for those who linger a day or two, it offers superb dining and luxurious accommodation.

GENERAL INFORMATION

Macau's visa regulations are similar to those of Hong Kong. In other words United States, Australian, New Zealand and most European citizens are entitled to a visa-free entry for a specified period of time — more than enough to see the sights.

The local currency is the pacata, but Hong Kong dollars are accepted throughout the territory — their values are nearly identical, though the pacata is worth fractionally less. Chinese yuan are not accepted.

The **Macau Tourist Information Bureau** ((853) 340-390 is at 9 Largo do Senado, Macau. They have an office in Hong Kong ((852) 2549-8884 at Room 1303, Macau Ferry Terminal, Shun Tak Centre, 200 Connaught Road.

GETTING AROUND

Macau is three distinct entities. The old city is on a peninsula, which is linked by a bridge to the island of Taipa, which is in turn linked by bridge to a second island of Coloane. It's a small place,

and the city itself is easily explored on foot. For longer trips, taxis are easily flagged down and are very inexpensive.

WHAT TO SEE AND DO

Macau is fascinating to explore, mostly as an example of how two alien cultures have managed to live fairly peacefully alongside each other for centuries. It can be seen in the intriguing contrast of Buddhist temples and Roman Catholic churches, and in how much more laidback the Cantonese character is here than in nearby bustling Hong Kong. The comparisons with "Hong Kong 20 years ago" are inevitable, but they're becoming less and less applicable as Macau rebuilds itself. Nevertheless, Macau remains a far less hectic destination than Hong Kong, and it's still possible to stumble across backstreet scenes that are long gone in all but the most remote backwaters of the New Territories in Hong Kong.

A good place to start exploring the city is at its very center, where the remains of Macau's emblematic church of **São Paulo** stands. Built in the seventeenth century and destroyed by fire in 1835, all that remains today of the church that was once Christianity's greatest monument in the East is its façade (carved by Japanese Christians). Still, it's quite a stunning sight and is Macau's most popular postcard image.

Overlooking the church is the **Fortaleza do Monte**, a 200-year-old fort that in its day was used to fire on Dutch ships that strayed too close to Portuguese waters. It's in ruins nowadays, but it's a pleasant place to poke around, and there's a museum that documents the fort's history.

It's a pleasant walk a couple of hundred meters northwest of here to the **Luís de Camões Museum** and the **Camões Grotto and Gardens**. The museum, named after the sixteenth-century Portuguese poet, is notable mostly for the structure it is housed in, a beautiful eighteenth-century villa, but it also has some interesting local history in display. The park is a favorite local gathering place, and a good spot to rest up and watch Macanese doing the same.

While you are in central Macau, be sure to visit the **Old Protestant Cemetery**, whose gravestones have been restored and whose epitaphs make fascinating, often touching reading.

East of the central district are a couple of interesting attractions. At the **Lou Lim Loc Gardens**, a leafy glade in the middle of the city, old men while away the hours playing mahjong and walking their birds. Above here is the **Guia Fortress and Lighthouse**. The whitewashed lighthouse is very photogenic and, built in 1865, is the oldest on the entire Chinese coastline. It can be reached by cable car, or on foot in around an hour.

122

Beneath the lighthouse is the Macau Ferry Terminal, where you can find the **Grand Prix Museum** and the **Wine Museum**. Unless you happen to be a keen racing fan, the former is likely to be of less interest than the latter, which is enlivened by free tastings. Both are open daily from 10 AM to 6 PM.

South of the center is the **A-Ma Temple**, at Barra Point, from which Macau derives its name, A-Ma Gau or Bay of A-Ma. It's dedicated to a peasant girl who miraculously survived a violent storm on her way to Guangzhou in the early sixteenth century, and subsequently reappeared in Macau as a goddess. The monastery features several images of her, along with Buddhist and Taoist statues, and a model of an ancient war-junk.

Of more interest is the nearby **Taipa Village** and **Taipa House Museum**. Bikes are available for rent in the village, but it's chief draw is its shorefront restaurants, some of which are superb and make the perfect place for a leisurely lunch. The museum is minor but interesting in the way it contrasts the turn of the century living styles of the Macau Chinese and Portuguese residents.

On the considerably larger Coloane Island, the **Chapel of St. Francis Xavier** rates a special visit because of its baroque cream and white, oval-windowed architecture and its relics of the disastrous attempt to Christianize Japan — a crusade which ended with the massacre of hundreds of foreign and Japanese missionaries, priests and

Opposite A-Ma Temple is the **Macau Maritime Museum**, which concentrates on Portuguese and Chinese maritime links past and present. Excellently presented, the exhibits are a treat, and it's even possible to take a boat tour of the harbor. It's open from 10 AM to 5:30 PM daily except Tuesday.

The chief attraction north of the center, a mostly residential district, is the **Kuan Iam Tong Temple**, on the Avenida do Coronel Mesquita. It is dedicated to the Goddess of Mercy (Guanyin) and features the deity herself costumed in embroidered silk and flanked by 18 Buddha images. There are also images of the Three Precious Buddhas in pavilions and halls placed among elaborately landscaped gardens and fountains.

Macau's two islands are not rich in sights, but worth exploring all the same. On Taipa Island, the **Macau Jockey Club** has room for 15,000 spectators, but will be deserted unless it is a race day.

followers in 1597 and 1637. Bikes can be rented at **Coloane Village**, and are a good way to explore the island further.

WHERE TO STAY

Travelers get much better value for their money in Macau than they do in nearby Hong Kong. Granted, the best in Macau does not rival the best in Hong Kong, but they are close enough to satisfy all but the pickiest Sybarites. Bear in mind that prices for Macau hotels rocket on weekends, when pleasure-seekers from Taiwan and Hong Kong flock there.

Luxury
The **Hotel Lisboa (** (853) 377-666 FAX (853) 567-193, 2–4 Avenida da Lisboa, simply has to head any list of luxury hotels in Macau, but not necessarily

for the obvious reasons. For a start, this faintly ludicrous orange-colored cylinder is Macau's major architectural landmark, with more than 900 rooms, it's Macau's largest hotel, and then there are the scarlet carpets, the chandeliers, the bell boys and the "ladies with rooms." Blame it on the casino, but whatever the detractors say, there's no denying that the Lisboa is an experience like no other in China. The standard rooms, which go for nearly mid-range rates, have little going for them beyond their price, but the suites make a luxurious retreat from the "Crazy Paris Show" and the push and shove of the casino.

A much classier downtown place to stay is the **Mandarin Oriental (** (853) 567-888 FAX (853) 594-859, 956–1110 Avenida da Amizade, which basically packs in all the luxury and extras that are possible for a five-star hotel. Its waterside location is a winner, as is its alfresco dining, but other less expected treats include a children's club (if you happen to have them) and rock climbing. The heated outdoor pool is another nice touch.

A favorite for Hong Kong residents looking for a romantic weekend is the **Pousada de São Tiago (** (853) 378-111 FAX (853) 552-170, Avenida da República. It's the only hotel in all of China in which guests get to stay in a seventeenth-century fort. The rooms are beautiful, and the hotel itself is tremendously atmospheric place. Attached to it is the São Tiago Cathedral, an eighteenth-century addition.

Mid-range and Inexpensive

A recommended mid-range hotel is the **East Asia Hotel (** (853) 922-433 FAX (853) 922-430, 1 Rua da Madeira. One of Macau's oldest, it has undergone a thorough overhaul and is now a modern, smart and conveniently located place to be situated. Ask for a room on the upper floors, where there are great views to be had.

The **Hotel Métropole (** (853) 388-166 FAX (853) 330-890, 493-501 Avenida da Praia Grande, is another reliable hotel with a good location. Close to the Lisboa, it offers luxurious standards at prices slightly cheaper than the lowest of those at the former.

Moving down in price is the excellent **Vila Universal (** (853) 573-247, 73 Rua de Felicidade. The less expensive rooms come at budget prices (around US$10), but in all price brackets the Universal gives off a spacious, breezy air that makes it a pleasure to stay in. Friendly staff keep the place spotlessly clean.

Similarly priced, the **Hotel London (** (853) 937-761, 4 Praça Ponte e Horta, is not quite as winning a place to stay as the Universal, but it has very reasonably priced rooms that are infinitely better value than anything it's possible to find in Hong Kong.

WHERE TO EAT

Many Hong Kong residents pop over to Macau for the food alone. The reason they do so is not for the Chinese food — which is better in Hong Kong — but for the combination of small-city ambiance with the great flavors of Macanese cuisine, a curious mixture of Portuguese, Cantonese and African influences.

The famous place for the total Macau dining experience is **Fernando's (** (853) 882-531, 9 Hac Sa Beach, Coloane. Chances are, if someone from Hong Kong says they're going to Macau for dinner, this is where they're going. At this beachside bistro with oodles of character and some of the best Portuguese food in the territory — everybody raves about the salads — reservations are essential on the weekends.

Also on Coloane and far less famous (which means more room) is **Cacarola (** (853) 882-226, 8 Rua de Gaivotas, Coloane, which earns countless repeat visitors for its friendly service and excellent food. Try the squid with black bean salad. The beef with garlic and bacon is also recommended.

In Macau itself, another institution is **Alfonso III (** (853) 586-272, 11A Rua Central. Reservations are essential at this intimate place serving famously authentic Portuguese fare. Restaurateur Alfonso's three daily specials are chosen according to whatever is freshest at the market, and are thus, for obvious reasons, recommended.

Restaurante Nova Caravela ((853) 356-888, 205 Avenida de Almeido Ribeiro, is a good place to escape to if the crowds are hogging Macau's more famous eating houses. Situated in a restored colonial building, it's the perfect place to sample that Macanese classic — African chicken.

NIGHTLIFE

For many Hong Kong and Taiwanese visitors, there is just one reason to descend on Macau: casinos. It goes without saying that all those who enter do so at their own risk. The odds are stacked in the house's favor. But providing you know exactly how much you have to lose, a quick whirl can be a lot of fun, and who knows…

The **Lisboa** is the biggest, most popular and busiest casino, and the only place in Macau where roulette is still played. There are eight other casinos, including the **Macau Palace** floating casino, the **Kam Pek**, the **Jai Alai** (near the Yaohan Department Store and ferry terminal) and deluxe casinos in the **Mandarin Oriental** and **Hyatt Regency**.

You'll find the main Chinese games are roulette, fan tan, blackjack and big and small (dai-siu).

The traditional Chinese hotpot is commonly served in cold weather.

The rows of slot machines are left to the bread-and-butter punters, Japanese tour groups and other visiting foreigners. The Chinese games are only for experienced gamblers. Best to stay out of it and just watch. Watching Chinese gamble is a fascinating, if not scary, experience — the atmosphere can be very tense.

Macau's most venerable nightlife experience is the **Crazy Paris Show** ((853) 377-666 at the Hotel Lisboa. How it has lasted as long as it has is anyone's guess. Tacky in the extreme, the "naughty" semi-nude dancing modeled on a Parisian cabaret is at moments almost embarrassing, but it never fails to pull the punters in.

The waterfront area on Avenida Marginal Baia Nova has emerged as Macau's new nightlife area over the last couple of years. It's not as sophisticated as Lan Kwai Fong in Hong Kong, but the "docks," as local expats have taken to calling the area, does have some interesting spots for a drink. Oddest of them is the **MGM Café** ((853) 753-161, which is the only bar in all of China — if not the world — to have chosen to theme its decor around the superhero Batman.

For something a little more sedate, expats gather for convivial drinking sessions at a number of back-home-style pubs near the race course on Taipa island. The most popular is the **Irish Pub** ((853) 820-708, Shop C-D, Block 6, Edifício Nam San, 116 Avenida Kwong Tung, Taipa. It's a good place to toss darts and knock back a couple of ales.

HOW TO GET THERE

From Hong Kong's Shun Tak Center in Central, jetfoils, high-speed catamarans and ferries cross the Pearl River Estuary to Macau 24 hours a day. Jetfoils are fastest, taking just under an hour and costing around US$20. All tickets include a government departure tax.

From Macau there are also daily ferries to Guangzhou. The land crossing to Zhuhai is virtually a hop, skip and a jump from the Macau Ferry Terminal — a five-minute taxi ride.

An increasingly large number of flights are landing at Macau's international airport, though most of them are from regional destinations.

SHENZHEN

BACKGROUND

Old China hands remember Shenzhen, in the days before the Open Door policy was launched in 1979, as nothing but rice fields, a hamlet and a border river — a popular place for tourists who were bussed to the Hong Kong side of the border for their first glimpse of the forbidden PRC. Today, Shenzhen is China's capitalist showplace, a city that sprang up overnight, taking mighty Hong Kong by surprise. It's easily China's most successful, most freewheeling Special Economic Zone (SEZ). You don't go there today to catch a glimpse of China, you go to take a look at the future — the combination of high-tech, joint-venture manufacturing and processing and rapid urban development that is being repeated, at a somewhat slower pace, in cities right across the country. Many of these Chinese have the same idea in mind, and Shenzhen has become the target of so many domestic "migrants" — people from poorer areas seeking work, especially the higher-than-average wages it offers — that the city has had to throw an electric fence around its export processing zone to keep unauthorized people out. As for Hong Kong, Shenzhen has become both a major business opportunity and something of a pain in the neck. While it's the center of massive cross-border investment and trade, with many Hong Kong Chinese middle-management now moving there to live closer to their factories, it's also a den of corruption and a haven for large-scale smuggling of everything from black market cigarettes to stolen luxury cars — Mercedes Benzes, and others — from Hong Kong.

Shenzhen is also set to take some of the infrastructural strain off Hong Kong. The city has its own international airport, which lies around 40 minutes by taxi from the Hong Kong border — flights from here to other China destinations can be as little as half the price of flights bought overseas. It's also developing a major new deep-water port and container terminal at Yantian, aimed at providing a new southern conduit for China's trade.

GETTING AROUND

Shenzhen has arguably the best public transportation system in China. The bus network is cheap and less crowded than elsewhere. The minibuses are privately operated and cheap but the signs are only in Chinese so you may need help. Taxis are ubiquitous and are required to use their meters, though for long distances you will need to bargain a fare.

WHAT TO SEE AND DO

There's very little to do in central Shenzhen but stroll around and gawk at the highrise hotels and prosperous shopping complexes. The western part of the Special Economic Zone is Shekou port, where you can get a hoverferry to Hong Kong, and where you will find Shenzhen's mind-boggling vacation resorts and Shenzhen University.

Nothing but ricefields, a hamlet, and a border river in 1979, Shenzhen today is a burgeoning city, the center of the nation's most successful, most freewheeling Special Economic Zone.

Two sprawling attractions at the western end of the Special Economic Zone, near Shenzhen Bay, **Splendid China** and **Window of the World**, are extremely popular with Chinese tourists but will seem tacky to most Westerners. Splendid China reproduces the historical sights of China in miniature; Window of the World does the same on a global scale. Minibuses run frequently from the Hong Kong border, or you might take a taxi. CTS and CITS have one-day tours here from Hong Kong which also call at a traditional Hakka village (see TAKING A TOUR, page 60 in YOUR CHOICE).

Close by and similar in concept, you can see 20 **recreations of the villages** of China's minorities, this time in original size, complete with dancing and daily enactment of minority festivals. Tacky in the extreme.

WHERE TO STAY

Shenzhen has a good range of accommodation, though whether the city is worth an overnight stay is debatable.

Luxury

There are a number of luxury hotels in Shenzhen nowadays. The best of them is the **Landmark Hotel** ((755) 217-2288 FAX (755) 229-0473, which, unlike most of its rivals, actually conjures up some atmosphere in its foyer and restaurants. Slightly cheaper alternatives can be found in the **Century Plaza Hotel** ((755) 232-0888 FAX (755) 233-4060, the **Hotel Oriental Regent** ((755) 224-7000 FAX (755) 224-7290, and the **Shangri-La** ((755) 233-0888 FAX (755) 233-9878.

Mid-range

If you are looking for bargains, try Hong Kong travel agents (including CTS), which often have special package deals that would otherwise be difficult to find.

A good place, should you choose to do it yourself, is the **Nanyang Hotel** ((755) 222-4968 FAX (755) 223-8927, Jianshe Lu. The staff may not be particularly accommodating, but the rooms are large and well maintained.

Also recommended, and possibly the most convenient mid-range hotel in town given that it's planted on top of the railway station — look for the massive structure with red Chinese characters down its side — is the **Dragon Hotel** ((755) 232-9228 FAX (755) 233-7564.

WHERE TO EAT

Dim sum breakfast and lunch is widely available and tends to be found on the second and third floors rather than the lobby. Prices are slightly lower than in Hong Kong; you'll probably have to pay in Hong Kong dollars. One recommended place that is popular with Hong Kong visitors is the Dragon Hotel's *dim sum* restaurant, located above the railway station.

The **Banxi Restaurant** ((755) 223-8076, on Jianshe Lu, has long been rated as one of Shenzhen's top places for a seafood meal.

Food Street is a small lane off Renmin Nanlu specializing in seafood and freshwater fish. Make sure you find out the price before you order even though prices are generally low. Old-timers will remember this street as the location of China's first McDonald's — today the hallowed site is occupied by a **KFC**.

HOW TO GET THERE

Shenzhen airport is around 40 minutes by taxi or an hour by minibus from the Hong Kong border. Direct hoverferry services run to the airport from the China Ferry Terminal (China Hong Kong City Building) ((852) 2736-1387, Canton Road, Tsimshatsui, Hong Kong, six times daily. The trip takes around one hour. Citybus ((852) 2736-3888 runs to Dongguan five times daily, leaving from the basement of the China Ferry Terminal, and stopping at Shenzhen airport.

The Kowloon–Canton Railway (KCR) has the fastest and most convenient transport to Shenzhen from Hong Kong. Take a train to Kowloon Tong station and change there for Lo Wu. It's possible to get a one-day visa at the border, providing you stay in the Shenzhen SEZ. Citybus (see above) have eight departures daily to Shenzhen.

There are four hoverferries running daily from the China Ferry Terminal in Tsimshatsui (see above) to Shekou, a port on the west side of Shenzhen. The trip takes around 50 minutes.

GUANGZHOU (CANTON)

The capital of Guangdong province, Guangzhou is also the nation's preeminent southern gateway and a radial tour center from which you can strike out for major cities and cultural destinations in Guangdong, Fujian, Guizhou and Yunnan provinces, Guangxi Zhuangzu autonomous region and Hainan Island. Its air and rail links cover virtually all of China. The Pearl River (Zhu Jiang), a major waterway, brings ocean shipping into the city's waterfront from the South China Sea and provides access right across the hinterland as far as Guangxi Zhuangzu autonomous region and Yunnan province.

Guangzhou's climate, along with that of most of the southern region, is subtropical: hot and humid in summer (July and August average 29°C or 84°F), and from July to September the area is prey to heavy monsoon rains and fierce typhoons that boil up out of the Pacific south of the Philippines and dash themselves, virtually one after the other, on the China coast. The most comfortable time to visit is between October and March, though you should be prepared for cold weather in the height of winter.

BACKGROUND

Along with Shanghai and Beijing, Guangzhou is China's most modern and progressive city. For one, its Cantonese-speaking population of (unofficially) around eight million live on the doorstep of one of the world's most prosperous cities — Hong Kong is just 111 km (69 miles) away. For two, as locals like to point out, Guangzhou has some

sons and daughters of Chinese merchants and reformists in Guangzhou and the south — some who had been educated overseas, some of them influenced by local foreign missionaries, all of them hungry for modernization and reform — who led the first major rebellions against the Manchu rule. Sun Yatsen, the exiled "spiritual" leader of the reformist movement and the first republican president, was born in Huaxian to the northwest of Guangzhou. In 1923, Guangzhou was where he gave the nationalist Guomindang Party its final form, the movement that later formed the military backbone of Chiang Kaishek's brutal campaign to exterminate the Chinese communists.

1,500 years history of foreign contact, starting with Arab merchant seafarers and then later with Portuguese Jesuits in Macau during the Ming dynasty, and the guns of the British "merchant princes" opening up Guangzhou itself as a trading port in the seventeenth century.

In the early nineteenth century Guangzhou was the main arena of the fierce test of strength between the British traders and the Qing throne over the alarming rate at which British opium exports were pouring into the society. In the two Opium Wars that followed, British warships and troops broke the back of the obsolete Qing defenses, grabbed Hong Kong as a colonial trading haven and triggered an international carve-up of Chinese territory and sovereignty that eventually caused the complete collapse of the 4,500-year-old dynastic order. As that collapse approached at the turn of this century, it was the

GENERAL INFORMATION

American Express ((20) 8331-1611 is in room 816 of the Guangdong International Hotel (see WHERE TO STAY, page 133).

Airlines represented in Guangzhou include **Air China** ((20) 8668-1319, **China Eastern Airlines** ((20) 8668-1688, **China Northwest** ((20) 8330-8058, **China Southern** ((20) 8668-1818, **Malaysia Airlines** ((20) 8335-8828 and **Singapore Airlines** ((20) 8335-8999. **Garuda Airlines** and **Thai International** both have offices at the Garden Hotel on Huanshi East Road.

Consular offices include **Australia** ((20) 8335-0909, in the GITIC Plaza building, and the **United States** ((20) 8188-8911, on Shamian Nanjie, Shamian Island.

A Shenzhen seafood restaurant, where a large selection of live fish and crustaceans are displayed in front of the restaurant for customers to choose from.

GETTING AROUND

Guangzhou is a flat, sprawling city, crossed from east to west by a main artery **Zhongshan Lu** that is all of 15 km (nine miles) in length, and from north to south by two main roads, **Renmin Lu** and **Jiefang Lu**. Circling the central city area is **Huanshi Lu**; the northeast section, Huanshi Donglu, is where many of the best hotels can be found.

If Guangzhou seems at first to be too vast and populous to make sense of, these three major thoroughfares help simplify it by linking up the three principal districts that are of interest to tourists — the **waterfront and Shamian Island**, site of the

For destinations not served by the metro, taxi is the best alternative. Finding one is never a problem — the streets are teeming with them. Fares start at Y8 — reckon on around Y20 for trips around town, Y40 to the airport. The only problem is communication: Few drivers speak much English; some of them, mutter locals, don't even speak Cantonese.

Bicycles are available for rent on the street close to the rear entrance of the White Swan (see WHERE TO STAY, page 133). There's also a good trolley-bus service running between the three districts, but like public buses all over China they're overcrowded, slow-moving and distinctly uncomfortable in the Guangzhou humidity and heat. There's

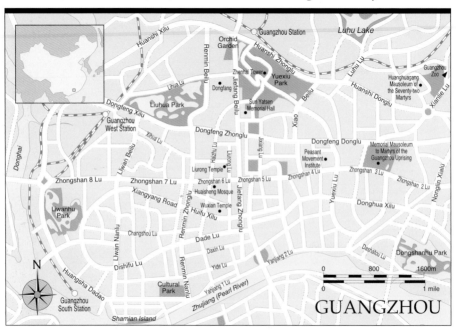

International Settlement in the treaty port days; the **northern commercial and tourist district** which includes the main railway station, Dongfang and China Hotels, Trade Center and Yuexiu Park; and the **cultural district**, running to the east along Zhongshan Lu, featuring the main temples and mosques and monuments to Guangzhou's more recent revolutionary history.

The easiest way to get around Guangzhou is by the impressively twenty-first century metro line, which after more than six years of digging now has an 18-km (11-mile) east–west line in operation. It won't connect you with the main train station, but for trips around central Guangzhou and connections with Shamian Island it's a convenient way to get around. Essentially, it travels north from Shamian Island before traveling east along Zhongshan Lu, taking in many of the city's prime attractions. Magnetic tickets are fixed at Y6.

a good English-language tourist map in circulation that can be found at the desks of any of the top hotels.

WHAT TO SEE AND DO

Guangzhou and most of the entire south of China were isolated for many centuries from the imperial seats of power, and therefore are not exactly overloaded with great cultural attractions. However, Guangzhou does have the Guangxiao Temple, dating back to the third century BC, and to this it has added the relics of its foreign trading contacts, its monuments to latter-day rebellion and its special present-day social character to offer itself as a city well worth strolling about and touring.

Being as big and spread out as it is, covering about 60 sq km (36 sq miles), it's also difficult to get around in the space of a few days unless you approach it from the point of view of its three distinct tourist districts — Shamian Island and environs; the northern commercial area around the train station; and the tourist district that includes Yuexiu Park and the complex of temples, and monuments spreading to the east off Zhongshan Lu.

Shamian Island and Environs

Flat and partly reclaimed, Shamian Island is linked by two bridges to the Pearl River waterfront, and is where the "foreign devil" British and French traders and taipans built their warehouses, homes, banks and business headquarters after the British

victory in the Opium Wars. The buildings are still there, providing a time warp of sedate, sometimes slightly pompous Victorian architecture. Efforts have been made to renovate some of the old buildings, and some boutiques and cafés have arrived, giving the area something of a facelift. Gentrification continues to proceed at a snail's pace, though, and for the moment Shamian remains a winning mix of new and old, cafés and bars rubbing shoulders with busy *dim sum* restaurants.

With the entirety of Guangzhou bustling so prosperously it's difficult to believe now how "revolutionary" this area was back when market reforms were tentatively introduced at the tail end of the 1970s. Back then tourists were advised that **Qingping Market**, on Qingping Lu just to the north of Shamian Island, heralded a new era as they gawked at the caged animals and piles of vegetable produce. Nowadays it's just another market,

though a particularly busy one. To the east, across the bridge and along the waterfront, **Renmin Nanlu** was another pioneering commercial district. It has retained that emphasis and is a fascinating district to explore on foot.

Qingping Market in particular is a raucous, friendly, crowded bazaar in which every step and turn of the head is living proof of the Cantonese taste for all things bright and beautiful, all creatures great and small: sugarcane, vegetables and fruit (look for succulent lychee in June and pineapples in October); live catfish and carp; eels, snakes and tortoises in netted bowls and big fishtanks sprayed continuously from hoses to keep the water aerated; baskets full of chickens and

pigeons; caged monkeys, dogs and raccoons; racks hanging with roast dog and a confusing array of butchered furry flesh and offal, all of it bound for the cooking wok. Of course, some animals end up here that shouldn't, and locals can sometimes get irate with shutter-happy tourists. The Guangdong government is stepping up its efforts to stop locals eating endangered species but is finding it very difficult to enforce. Monkeys are seen less often in Qingping Market, but all this means is that prospective customers now have to ask for "behind the counter" service.

Directly north of the market, along Dishipu Lu, is the **Yuexiu District**, a newly restored collection of old store fronts that now house family restaurants and souvenir operations.

LEFT: Guangzhou street scene and mural, circa 1986.
RIGHT: The main entrance to Huaisheng Mosque, Guangzhou.

From the market area you can wander north along Haizhu Zhonglu which runs parallel to Renmin Lu, turn right on Huifu Xilu and find the Daoist **Wuxian (Five Immortals) Temple**. It's said to be the spot where more than 2,000 years ago five rams appeared carrying ears of rice in their mouths and ridden by five gods. The gods vanished, but the rams stayed and turned to stone, whereupon the local people began planting rice.

The Wuxian Temple has a large rock in its courtyard bearing a hollow that is said to be the footprint of one of the gods. It also sports a huge Ming dynasty bell, three meters (10 ft) high and weighing five tons. The bell has no clapper and is believed would warn of impending disaster for the city should it ever make a sound.

North of Wuxian Temple on Guangta Lu, the **Huaisheng Mosque** represents the centuries of Islamic culture brought to Guangzhou by Arab traders. Like most Islamic places of worship it's quite severely free of ornamentation and idolatry, but its arched gateways and main hall of prayer are an interesting contrast of Moslem and Chinese architecture. It has a minaret that looms over the sweeping, tiled Chinese-style roofs and looks as though it's been rendered with concrete; but it's said to take its name, Guangta (Smooth Minaret) from this apparently unique surfacing. The mosque dates back to the year AD 627 in the Tang dynasty and commemorates the Arab missionary Saud Ibn Abu Waggas who was the first to bring the Koran to China.

Further north on the other side of the main east–west artery Zhongshan Lu, stand the two most interesting temples in Guangzhou, the **Guangxiao Temple** and the **Liurong (Six Ban-yan Trees) Temple** with its towering nine-story **Hua Ta (Flower Pagoda)**. You can't miss the pagoda, and can reach it by walking north along either Haizhu Beilu or Liurong Lu from Zhongshan Lu.

The Liurong Temple was given its name by the renowned poet Su Dongpo who visited it some seven centuries ago and was captivated by the banyan trees (since gone) in its grounds. Both Liurong and the nearby Guangxiao Temple were built in honor of Hui Neng, the sixth patriarch of Chan (Zen) Buddhism, and in the grounds of the Guangxiao complex there's an open pavilion featuring frescoes of Hui Neng preaching to the monks and of the Indian monk, Bodhidharma, who is said to have visited Liurong at one stage.

Both temples attract large crowds of Cantonese sightseers and worshipers. Religion is coming back in Guangzhou, and none are happier about it than the elderly women who can be seen teaching their grandchildren how to light the joss stick, place it in the incense altars and kowtow to the images.

These two temples are about as far as you can comfortably go in one day's walking, and mark

the boundary of Shamian Island and environs exploration.

At night, there's another treat in the Shamian Island district which definitely should not be missed — the **Cultural Park**. This large playground off Liu'ersan Lu and Renmin Nanlu just north of Shamian Island is where the Cantonese go at night to have fun. It's just as much fun watching them enjoying themselves. In the eerie, ill-lit tropical darkness you come across a fairground and Ferris wheel, a roller-skating rink packed with teenagers, an early Buck Rogers rocket ship space simulator, a shooting gallery with pneumatic "bazookas" that fire tennis balls, a pool hall and the very latest in modernized leisure in Guangzhou — a video arcade.

Meanwhile, at an auditorium near the stage, the high-pitched singsong shriek and clash of gongs announces another act in the continuing story of Cantonese Opera, with its regal and lavishly-costumed princesses, kings and mandarins gliding and flapping about the stage.

Pet Birds and Pagodas

The district from the Dongfang to the China Hotel between Renmin Beilu and Jiefang Beilu places you within close strolling proximity of a number of scenic and cultural attractions. To the north, heading toward the railway station, there's the **Orchid Garden** where, in a landscaped setting, you can view more than 10,000 orchids from 100 species, and visit the seventh-century **Mohammedan Tomb**, claimed to be the burial place of the same Moslem missionary Waggas to whom the Huaisheng Mosque is dedicated.

Directly south of the Mohammedan Tomb, and far more worthy of an hour or so of your time, is the **Nanyue Tomb**. Discovered in 1983, this 2,000-year-old archeological site is home to the tomb of Zhao Mo, the grandson of Zhao Tuo, a Qin dynasty general sent to subjugate the southern tribes and who, on hearing of the collapse of the Qin dynasty, promptly established his own independent southern kingdom here in Guangzhou.

Liuhua Park, to the west of the Dongfang Hotel, is a pleasant garden set among artificial lakes, but the much larger **Yuexiu Park** on the eastern side of Jiefang Beilu is of more interest for its cultural and social attractions. Take a stroll through the park and inevitably you will find yourself at the **Zhenhai Tower**, the solitary remnant of the old city wall of Guangzhou, and now home to the **Municipal Museum**, which provides a fascinating journey through 2,000 years of local history culminating in a top-floor tea shop with views over the city. West of the tower is the **Five Rams** statue, remarkable only insofar as they celebrate the founding of Guangzhou (nicknamed in Chinese *yangcheng* — "the city of the rams"), which according to legend is owed to the arrival of five immortals riding rams.

Close to Zhenhai Tower there's a monument to Guangzhou's favorite son, Sun Yatsen, but it's a drab concrete monstrosity and could well be given a miss — except on Sundays, when it's a venue for hundreds of bird lovers showing off their caged warblers. A more interesting park diversion is the **Journey to the West Theme Park (Xiyouji Leyuan)**, a tacky but enjoyable tribute to one of China's best loved tales.

For candid photography in which you run little risk of offending anyone's sensibilities, the **Children's Park** to the southeast of the Sun Yatsen Memorial Hall is a good place to go. You get there

Guangzhou City Museum. Don't be put off by the first-floor exhibition of Guangzhou's industrial products; head upstairs to a fine natural history exhibit and some good selections of Chinese fine arts.

Farther to the northeast along Xi'anlie Nanlu, you can view the **Huanghuagang Mausoleum of the 72 Martyrs**, the monument to a similar, earlier uprising — and similar reprisal — in April 1911 in the last days of the Manchu Qing rule. Beyond that there's only one major attraction left, **Guangzhou Zoo**, which like most Chinese zoos is best passed up unless you're keen on watching pandas and other wildlife in old-fashioned, dank and quite dispirited captivity.

by going directly south from the memorial on Jixiang Lu and turning left on Zhongshan Lu.

The Revolutionary Tour

The third main tourist venue of Guangzhou begins roughly at the Children's Park and continues east along Zhongshan Lu. There you'll find the city's contemporary monuments, the **Original Site of the Peasant Movement Institute (Nongmin Yundong Jiangxisuo)**, where in 1926 Mao Zedong trained cadres, including Zhou Enlai, who were to spearhead his communist revolution. Nearby is the **Memorial Mausoleum to the Martyrs of the Guangzhou Uprising (Qishier Lieshi Mu)**, where, a year later, these same cadres headed a communist takeover of most of Guangzhou, only to be crushed by the ruling Guomindang forces.

To the south of here, and close to the Nongjing Suo metro stop, set back from Yuexiu Lu, is the

WHERE TO STAY

Guangzhou has a good range of accommodation. However, watch out for the Guangzhou Trade Fair, which is held for a week twice annually, in mid-April and in mid-October. During these periods rooms are almost impossible to secure, and it's not unusual for rates to double.

Luxury

By Chinese standards, Guangzhou has a large number of luxury hotels, and you get better value here than in Hong Kong. Expect to pay from US$170 upwards for a double in the luxury bracket.

Religion re-emerges in the post-revolutionary age — joss and towering pagoda RIGHT and worshiper LEFT at Liurong (Six Banyan Trees) Temple, Guangzhou.

The **White Swan Hotel** ((20) 8188-6968 FAX (20) 8186-1188, with 843 rooms, was one of China's earliest luxury hotels, and it remains top-class by any standards. Its tastefully decorated riverside coffee lounge and vast atrium features a traditionally styled pavilion and waterfall and a viewing deck on to which visiting Chinese groups are allowed each day to take photos of each other. But the White Swan's main selling point is its location on Shamian Island, the peaceful former foreign concession.

Most of Guangzhou's other luxury hotels are in the northeast of town, on the bustling commercial strip of Huanshi Donglu. The **Guangdong International Hotel** ((20) 8331-1888 FAX (20) 8331-1666, 339 Huanshi Donglu, a soaring glass tower, is a good option for business travelers, offering a selection of restaurants, highly rated business facilities, and tennis courts, a swimming pool and sauna. Also in this area is the first-class **Garden Hotel** ((20) 8333-8989 FAX (20) 8335-0467, with its elaborate chandeliered lobby, bowling alley, swimming pool, roof restaurants, disco, coffee lounge, sun decks, bars, boutiques and beauty salons. Some travelers claim it is the best in Guangzhou. The **China Hotel** ((20) 8666-6888 FAX (20) 8667-7014, Liuhua Lu, with over 1,000 rooms, has an outdoor swimming pool, tennis court, bowling alley, an impressive health center on the fourth floor, and a Hong Kong-style basement Food Street. Most impressive of all, it is home to a branch of the Hard Rock Café.

Mid-range

One of Guangzhou's outstanding mid-range options is the renovated **Guangdong Victory Hotel** ((20) 8186-2622 FAX (20) 8186-2413, 53 Shamian Beijie. The location, on charming Shamian Island, is a great plus, but the tastefully appointed rooms with rates from around US$60 are also hard to beat. There's an excellent Cantonese-style restaurant with *dim sum* breakfasts on the ground floor.

The **Aiqun Hotel** ((20) 8186-6668 FAX (20) 8188-3519, 113 Yanjiang Xilu, (the name means "love the masses") is a massive, refurbished structure that overlooks the Pearl River. Foreign guests rarely stay here, and beyond the front desk English is rarely spoken, but rooms are reasonably priced and a discount of around 20% is generally available upon request. Not far from here, the **Guangzhou Hotel** ((20) 8333-8168 FAX (20) 8333-0791, Haizhu Square, is a more upmarket option, where English is spoken and the hotel amenities include shopping, hairdressers, restaurants and so on.

Inexpensive

For as long as anyone can remember the **Guangzhou Youth Hostel** ((20) 8188-4298, on Shamian Island, has had a monopoly on Guangzhou's foreign budget travelers. In the past it was a grim place, where the staff were known to steal from the guests. It has cleaned up its act, renovated, and now has rooms (complete with satellite television) from around US$15.

Nowadays, however, the Shamian Island youth hostel has a rival — a real youth hostel that is recognized by the World Youth Hostel Federation. The **Guangzhou City Youth Hostel** ((20) 8666-6889, extension 3812 FAX (20) 8667-0787, 179 Huanshi Xilu, has basic but clean rooms with private bathrooms for less than US$10 — a bargain in Guangzhou.

If you don't mind spending slightly more, a superb choice is the **Guangdong Shamian Hotel**

((20) 8188-8359 FAX (20) 8191-1628, 52 Shamian Nanjie, just around the corner. It may have little in the way of the amenities available in better hotels, but the rooms are clean and the staff are friendly. The hotel's one drawback is that so many of the cheaper rooms lack windows — ask to see your room before you check in.

WHERE TO EAT

For the Chinese, a visit to Guangzhou is a culinary pilgrimage. Some of the famous "old houses" have been serving customers for over 100 years. As was the case elsewhere in China, the fortunes of many of Guangzhou's best restaurants took a turn for a worse during the dark days of the Cultural Revolution, but nowadays Guangzhou's reputation as one of the best cities in China to eat out in is back on track.

Starting with the best, *dim sum* aficionados should head over to the **Taotaoju Restaurant (** (20) 8181-6111, 20 Dishipu Lu, an atmospheric place that was an academy of learning in the seventeenth century and is now on Guangzhou's most celebrated restaurants.

The **North Garden Restaurant (Beiyuan Fanguan) (** (20) 8333-0087, 202 Xiaobei Road, is a series of rooms laid out around a Chinese garden where fish swim in a miniature lake crossed by a miniature bridge. Prices are close to those of Hong Kong. It gets packed early in the evening and has an extensive menu. The new annex next door is something of an eyesore, but business is business, and few Chinese guests are likely to complain.

ucts like tofu to ingeniously duplicate the tastes and textures of various meats. The **Tsai Ken Hsiang Restaurant (** (20) 8334-4363, 167 Zhongshan 6-Lu, is a famous vegetarian restaurant, sometimes spelled in the tourist literature Caigenxiang.

Ask a local where to eat and chances are they'll direct you to the Dashatou wharf on Yanjiang Lu, next to the Pearl River. A string of neon-strung seafood restaurants have sprung up here, catering to the Cantonese passion for expensive seafood. If you can get a group of people together — with preferably one Chinese speaker — they can be a lot of fun.

With so many top-notch hotels around town, as you might expect there are also countless hotel

West of the city, the **Panxi Restaurant (** (20) 8181-5718, 151 Longjing Xilu, is Guangzhou's busiest restaurant, and its pavilions and dining rooms are scattered through a romantic landscape of gardens, pools and ornamental bridges. Like the North Garden its menu is upmarket and gourmet — stewed turtle in pottery, swallow's nest and crabmeat soup, white fungus (from stone) and bamboo pith with chicken slices in consommé, fried sea slug with chicken, perch, kidney, shrimp and vegetables. But it also offers fried prawns, fried frog and chicken slices, chicken with spicy sauce, fried noodles, and chicken slices in soup, with beer, at quite a reasonable price for a one-night blowout in a restaurant that, more than any other in contemporary China, recalls the splendor of the dynastic past.

It's worth sampling some Chinese vegetarian dishes, which are Buddhist in origin and use prod-

restaurants to choose from. A couple of favorites are **Le Grill (** (20) 8331-1888, at the Guangdong International Hotel, and **La Casa (** (20) 8333-8989, at the Garden Hotel. In the China Hotel is the **Hard Rock Café (** (20) 8666-6888, where you can find that internationally tried and tested formula of loud rock music and overpriced treats such as hamburgers and french fries — don't forget to buy the T-shirt.

For inexpensive dining there are any number of choices around town. Guangzhou has the full complement of fast-food barns these days — **KFC**, **McDonald's** and **Pizza Hut** are just a few of the big names that have set up shop here. Popular Hong Kong chains like **Café de Coral** have also had considerable success. For inexpensive local

The Peasant Movement Institute LEFT, and its shrine-like setting ABOVE where Mao Zedong's communist lieutenants were first trained.

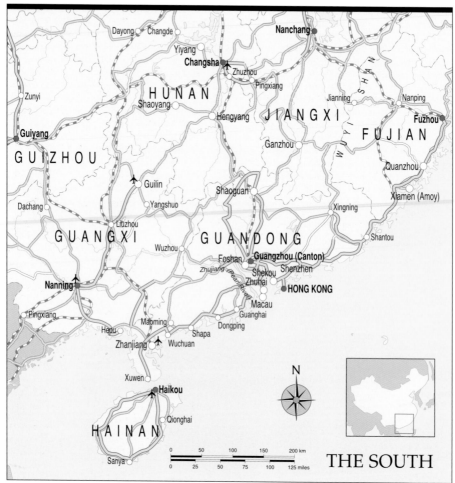

THE SOUTH

dining, take a stroll around Shamian Island, where almost all the restaurants (including the excellent *dim sum* restaurant in the **Victory Hotel**) sport English menus these days.

NIGHTLIFE

Guangzhou has a lively nightlife, but like many other Chinese cities places come and go in popularity much faster than the life-span of a guidebook. The best place to get an idea of where is currently in is the free magazine *Clueless in Guangzhou*, which is available in most big hotels.

A reliable place for some pub food and a few casual drinks is the **Elephant and Castle** ((20) 8359-3309, 363 Huanshi Donglu, which seems to have taken over from the nearby and once popular **Hill Bar** ((20) 8333-3998, extension 3913, 367 Huanshi Donglu, as the place for Guangzhou's expatriate community to rub shoulders.

The more adventurous might want to try and late-night excursion to **L'Africain**, on the junction of Dongfeng Donglu and Nonglinxia Lu, a rave venue that packs in sweaty bodies on Friday and Saturday nights.

HOW TO GET THERE

You can get to Guangzhou from just about anywhere in China, and you can do it by air, rail, bus or river craft. There are daily express trains from Beijing and Shanghai, and there is also a direct train service from Kunming.

AROUND GUANGZHOU: FOSHAN AND SHUNDE

Getting to the sights around Guangzhou under your own steam can be tiresome, especially in the hot summer months. A good alternative is to take a tour. The tour offices in the major hotels run coach tours to cultural locations around the city, and their itineraries include visits to carving and other crafts factories. They also operate tours of Foshan, the famous ceramics and crafts city 28 km (17 miles) southwest of Guangzhou, where you have the opportunity to watch artists at the **Foshan Folk Art Research Society** making traditional lanterns, paper-cuttings and brick carvings, weavers producing silk in the city's mills and ceramic miniatures being painted in their thousands at the **Shiwan Artistic Pottery and Porcelain Factory**.

Tours of Foshan also include a visit to the 900-year-old Song dynasty **Ancestral Temple**, whose remarkable architecture features dozens of ceramic figures and animals lining the crests of its roofs. It's possible to go on your own from the Guangzhou–Foshan (Guangfo) Bus Terminal, which you will find just off Daxin Zhonglu to the east of Shamian Island. It's a one-hour bus ride to Foshan, and once there, you can find reasonably-priced accommodation at the relatively upmarket **Golden City Hotel ℂ** (757) 335-7228 FAX (757) 335-3924, 48 Fengjiang Nanlu, or the cheaper **Foshan Huaqiao Hotel ℂ** (757) 222-3828 FAX (757) 222-7702, 14 Zumiao Lu, if you want to stay overnight.

Shunde is a small town — approximately 45 km (27 miles) away — famous among gourmets as the home of Cantonese cuisine. The place to sample the cuisine is the **Qinghui Yuan**, a two-in-one treat — a Qing dynasty garden and a restaurant that is rated as one of the best Cantonese restaurants in the province. Should you want to savor the flavors a little longer, opposite the garden and restaurant is the 384-room **Courtyard New World Hotel ℂ** (765) 221-8333 FAX (765) 221-4773, a top-notch member of the Marriott chain. Shunde can be reached by train from Guangzhou.

SOUTHERN CHINA: THE RADIAL ROUTE

North of Guangdong province there are two key junctions that open up the east–west rail routes — at Hengyang in Hunan province you change to the daily Shanghai–Kunming express trains for the dog-leg run west to Guilin and Kunming, and at Zhengzhou in Henan province you can connect with expresses from Beijing, Qingdao and Shanghai which will take you west to Chengdu, Lanzhou and Xi'an.

Buses leave the Long Distance Bus Terminal on the south side of Huanshi Xilu a short distance to the west of the Guangzhou railway station for upcountry destinations in Guangdong province and beyond. Travel times are constantly being reduced by improvements to the roads. The new expressway between Shenzhen and Shantou means that a journey that once took 12 hours or more can now be covered in around four hours. You might stay overnight in Shantou on the east coast (perhaps making a side trip to the historically more interesting Chaozhou, just an hour away by bus), and carry on the next day to Xiamen

(Amoy) in Fujian province. There's also a daily 10-hour bus service to Zhanjiang, the southern coastal jumping off point for Haikou on Hainan Island. For Guilin direct bus services are available (around 20 hours), but the better option (if you're not flying) is to take a high-speed ferry to Wuzhou (around four hours) and then take a second bus straight to Guilin, or go first to the beautiful Li River township of Yangshuo and carry on to Guilin by river ferry.

Ferries and hovercraft to Hong Kong, Macau and Haikou on Hainan Island leave from the Zhoutouzui Wharf on the south side of the Pearl River. To get to it you go across the Renmin Bridge and west along the extension of Tongfu Xilu to

the waterfront. For boats to Wuzhou you go to the Dashatou Pier on Yanjiang Donglu.

Before you attempt to organize bookings yourself (always a headache in China), ask at the front desk of your hotel. In most cases your hotel reception can handle bookings, or at least refer you to a reliable nearby agent.

XIAMEN (AMOY) AND FUJIAN PROVINCE

The southeastern coastal city of Xiamen and the whole province, with its capital Fuzhou, are famous for their long-standing trade contacts with the rest of the world. Great Chinese fleets sailed from here during the Yuan and Ming dynasties to explore and establish trade through-

A Hengyang infant in bright New Year's costume.

out Southeast Asia, and waves of emigrants left these shores for all parts of the world in the last century. Yet for all this, Fujian languishes off the beaten tourist track and has yet to be fully explored by foreign visitors.

Compared with western areas of the southern region, Fujian's value as a mainstream tourist destination is debatable. But for the individual traveler looking for a relatively untrodden trail to follow, it offers some physical and cultural rewards.

A rugged mountainous province, Fujian is bounded on the west by the **Wuyi Mountains**, a 250-km (155-mile) range that's been a popular Buddhist retreat since Fujian was taken under the wing of imperial rule in the Tang dynasty. More than 100 monasteries were built among the heavily wooded slopes, and a wealth of surviving architecture and relics awaits the modern-day visitor. The mountains are also renowned for their

Dahongpao tea, just one of the many Fujian brands that have made the province one of China's leading producers of the "lusty leaf."

The easiest access to the Wuyi range is from **Yingtan** in Jiangxi province, the railway junction that links the Guangzhou–Shanghai line with Xiamen. There are hotels in Yingtan and a long-distance bus station where you can get transportation to either **Huanggang Shan**, one of the major Wuyi peaks, or to **Jianning** or **Nanping**, stopping off in the mountains along the way.

XIAMEN

Xiamen, which is actually an island linked to the mainland by a long causeway of railway and road, is, like Shenzhen, a Special Economic Zone. But while Shenzhen was piggybacked by booming Hong Kong, Xiamen is flush with Taiwanese investment. The local dialect, known as

138

minnanyu, is nearly identical to the dialect spoken in Taiwan, and the nearest Taiwanese-controlled islands — Matsu and Quemoy (Jinmen) — are just a couple of kilometers (a mile or so) offshore from Xiamen.

Background

Historically, Xiamen was established as a major seaport in the Ming reign and returned the compliment by becoming a notorious pirate lair and the launching base for an ill-fated campaign in the seventeenth century to stem the southward influence of the Manchu Qing dynasty and restore the Ming rule. The campaign was led by one of the pirate chiefs Zheng Chenggong, better known as Koxinga. He didn't get far in his bid to drive the Manchus from China, but turned around and instead kicked the Dutch out of what is now the island of Taiwan.

Xiamen was also an unofficial trading depot, doing a thriving under-the-counter business in silks with the Portuguese, Spanish and Dutch, until a British naval force stormed ashore after their victory in the first Opium War in 1841 and opened it up as a full treaty port. There is evidence today of its role as an international settlement in the surviving colonial architecture of parts of its skyline.

General Information

American Express ((592) 212-0268 is in Room 212 of the Holiday Inn Crowne Plaza Harbour View Hotel (see below).

Airlines represented in Xiamen include **Air China** ((592) 508-4376, **China Eastern Airlines** ((592) 202-8936, **Dragonair** ((592) 202-5389, **SilkAir** ((592) 205-3275, and **Xiamen Airlines** ((592) 602-2961.

What to See and Do

Although Nanputuo Temple is officially Xiamen's main attraction, most foreigners agree that Xiamen's charm reposes mostly in the small island of **Gulangyu**, which lies just off the city's waterfront and is linked to it by ferries that run with Star Ferry-like efficiency through the day and into the night.

Foreigners started settling on Gulangyu in the 1840s, and in 1903 the island was declared a Foreign Settlement. The villas, churches and civic buildings you see today on streets blissfully free of motorized traffic are all that remain of the settlement. It's reminiscent of Shamian Island in Guangzhou, except on a grander and better preserved scale.

Apart from strolling around the island, admiring the architecture and work of cottage craftspeople (Gulangyu is one of the few places in the world where you can still buy masterfully executed oil portraits of Stalin, though who buys them is a

mystery), Gulangyu also has two average beaches, the **Zheng Chenggong (Koxinga) Memorial Hall**, commemorating the pirate patriot of the Ming reign, and a viewing platform on top of **Sunlight Rock**. Below the rock is **Shuzhuang Garden**, which features a maze and one of the finest landscaped rockeries in southern China.

South of Xiamen is Xiamen University, which has an interesting **Museum of Anthropology**. Next door to the university is the remarkable Tang dynasty **Nanputuo Temple**. Although built during the Tang reign it was renovated under the Manchu Qing dynasty and features exquisite architecture and an impressive array of Buddhist statuary, including images of the

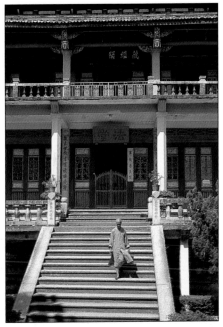

Maitreya, or Future Buddha (also depicted as the rotund Laughing Buddha or Milefo), several guardian deities, three images of Sakyamuni Buddha, four Bodhisattvas and other guardian figures.

An unusual tourist attraction, but one the town is particularly proud of, is the **Jimei High School**. Set in a picturesque park beside the sea around 15 km (nine miles) north of Xiamen, the school is the result of donations provided by Chen Jiageng, who made his fortune in Malaya and returned to do good works in China before passing away in 1961. It's only worth the visit if you're completely stuck for something to do.

OPPOSITE: Nanputuo Temple in Xiamen features an impressive array of Buddhist statuary and relics. ABOVE: A lone monk descends the stairs at Nanputuo Temple, one of China's most important Buddhist centers.

Where to Stay

Xiamen has a good selection of hotels to suit all budgets.

LUXURY

Holiday Inn Crowne Plaza Harbourview ((592) 202-3333 FAX (592) 203-6666, 12–8 Zhenhai Lu, is one of Xiamen's top hotels. It has international restaurants and facilities, but its winning feature is its location in the heart of old Xiamen (other luxury hotels are out in the suburbs), near the harbor. For travelers looking for some luxury, it is easily the best choice.

The **Marco Polo Xiamen** ((592) 509-1888 FAX (592) 509-2888, 8 Jianye Lu, Hubin Bei, is the

FAX (592) 202-5950, 113–121 Xi'an Lu. It's a typical mid-range Chinese hotel, with a restaurant and basic amenities.

For very reasonably priced accommodation with some character, try the **Xin Qiao Hotel** ((592) 203-8883 FAX (592) 203-8765, 444 Zhongshan Lu, a rambling, restored structure that once served as a guesthouse for cadres.

INEXPENSIVE

You can save money and relax in beautiful surroundings at the **Gulangyu Guesthouse** ((592) 206-3856 FAX (592) 206-6060, 25 Huangyan Lu, Gulangyu, on Gulangyu Island. This is a rare opportunity to retreat from the honk of traffic in

Holiday Inn's main rival, but its location is better suited to businesspeople reaching out to Xiamen's industrial hinterland than to tourists. The **Xiamen Mandarin Hotel** ((592) 602-3333 FAX (592) 602-1431, 101 Xinglong Lu, Huli, is a slightly less luxurious option; it's aimed mostly at business travelers.

MID-RANGE

Few foreign travelers stay there, but it's hard to beat the **Lujiang Hotel** ((592) 202-2212 FAX (592) 202-4813, 54 Lujiang Dao, for both its location and general ambiance — it's in a restored old colonial structure right next to the Gulangyu ferry pier, in the heart of old Xiamen. The hotel is popular with Taiwanese tourists and business people.

Less conveniently located but cheaper and affording splendid views over Zhongshan Park, is the **Xiamen Singapore Hotel** ((592) 202-6668

coastal China. The hotel's only real disadvantage is that it's around a 15-minute walk from the ferry terminal — there's no public transport on Gulangyu Island.

Back in Xiamen itself, the **Donghai Hotel** ((592) 202-1111 FAX (592) 203-3264, Zhongshan Lu, has some well-maintained budget rooms and an excellent location in the heart of town.

The long-running backpacker standby is the **Xiaxi Hotel** ((592) 202-4859, Xiaxi Lu, on a small alley that runs off Zhongshan Lu in the center of town. It offers little in the way of comforts, but room rates are rock-bottom.

Where to Eat

The local specialty is seafood, and locals claim Xiamen is home to more than 200 restaurants specializing in it. Gulangyu Island has the highest density of seafood restaurants — order from the seafood on ice out front — but it's a good idea to keep a tab on prices as you order to avoid being presented with a horrifying bill when you finish.

Back in town, in the Jianye Building, **Lucky Full City Seafood** ((592) 505-8688, is one of Xiamen's most highly rated seafood restaurants —Chaozhou style, which for many Chinese gourmets is the most subtle of the many Chinese regional cuisines.

Xiamen is also renowned for its snacks. One place to sample these is the **Huanzhehe Restaurant** ((592) 212-5825 on Zhongshan Lu. The sweet peanut soup served here is a local delicacy.

For *dim sum*, try the very popular restaurant at the **Lujiang Hotel** (see above), and don't forget that the rooftop is also home to a restaurant that is the perfect place for an evening meal with a view. The **Donghai Hotel** (see above) also has a highly rated seafood restaurant.

How to Get There

Xiamen has an international airport, with direct access from Singapore, Hong Kong, Manila, Macau, Kuala Lumpur, Penang and Jakarta. Flights to local Chinese destinations are plentiful. There's access by train from either Shanghai or Guangzhou by changing at Yingtan and traveling south on the Xiamen branch line, but land travel out of Xiamen is mostly by bus.

QUANZHOU

Quanzhou, three hours up the coast by bus from Xiamen, is believed to have flourished long before Xiamen came into its own as a trading center, the site of ancient Zaiton, the "great resort of ships and merchandise" that Marco Polo wrote about after his epic travels during Kublai Khan's reign. An astonishing relic of that grand mercantile era can be seen in the grounds of the **Kaiyuan Monastery**.

Originally called the Lotus Monastery, Kaiyuan Monastery was built in AD 686 under the Tang reign and was renovated during the Ming dynasty. It not only features another impressive collection of Buddha images but also 72 panels of bas-relief carved with figures of human-headed lions that are reminiscent of Egyptian Pharaonic art. But that's just the monastery. Behind it you'll find the **Exhibition Hall**, which deserves a close look; you'll find a magnificent relic of the power and glory of ancient Zaiton — the excavated hull of a huge oceangoing junk, dating back to the Song dynasty, and maps of the great oceanic expeditions that the eunuch admiral Zheng He commanded in the Ming reign to the distant shores of East Africa and Madagascar.

Quanzhou's only other notable attraction is the **Qingjing Mosque**, which built around 1,000 years ago is one of China's oldest. Perhaps of more interest than the mosque itself, is the small museum on the grounds that includes a potted history of Quanzhou's Muslim community complete with English translations.

Where to Stay

Nearby Xiamen is a much more pleasant place to be based than Quanzhou, which has little in the way of luxury accommodation. The **Quanzhou Hotel** ((595) 228-9969 FAX (595) 218-2128, 22 Zhuangfu Lu, is the best of the city's hotels, though standards are far from international.

Slightly cheaper but similar in standard is the **Golden Fountain Hotel** ((595) 228-5078 FAX (595) 228-4388, Baiyuan Lu, a remodeled wing of the old Overseas Chinese Hotel.

HAINAN ISLAND

If you were a mandarin, or government official, in the days of dynastic rule in China and you were transferred to the island of Hainan, you would have dragged yourself down there feeling quite thankful that you still had a head on your shoulders. Hainan was, and still is, the far southern limit of the Chinese civilization, a place of exile for any bureaucrat or court official who had incurred the emperor's displeasure. There's a beach with two big boulders on the island's extreme southern tip that's called Tianya Haijiao, or literally "Edge of the Heavens, Corner of the Seas," and if you stand there in the sands and gaze out across the seas you can imagine the ghosts of the past standing there with you, still wondering how it all went wrong for them.

Hainan is a large tropical island, covering an area of 32,000 sq km (12,355 sq miles), much of it clothed in lush forests, rice fields and fruit-growing plantations, low-lying in the north and mountainous in the central region and south. Its tallest hills, the Wuzhi Shan (Five-Fingered) Mountains, rise to nearly 1,900 m (6,234 ft) and can clearly be seen from the mainland 18 km (11 miles) away. Aside from forested slopes and balmy beaches, there are fertile valleys where a mixed population of Li and Miao minorities and Han Chinese settlers cultivate rice, sugarcane, rubber, tropical fruits, coffee, tobacco, pepper and cocoa.

The island has attracted overseas Chinese investment as one of the Special Economic Zones. It is also strategically important — much of its west coast is a burgeoning naval, air and military base facing Vietnam. The west also happens to have the main concentration of Li minority villages, and while you can get to them quite freely nowadays you must keep in mind that this is a sensitive

In spring the rape fields of northern Guangxi wash the landscape with yellow hues.

military zone. On the island's east coast you can find the Danjia boat people, who operate a fishing and pearling industry.

HAIKOU

Haikou has its charm — the old part of town south of the Haidian River is reminiscent of Macau or Malacca — but for most travelers it's a whistlestop on the road to better places.

General Information

The main branch of the **Bank of China** is at 33 Datong Lu, with its own ground floor entrance in the huge Haikou International Commercial

need to stay in Haikou. All the same, the city does have a good range of accommodation.

The **Mandarin Hotel** ((898) 845-8888 FAX (898) 855-0311, 18 Wenhua Lu, is Haikou's most luxurious accommodation. Featuring Chinese, Southeast Asian and Italian restaurants and a resort-style swimming pool, it's easily the best choice for those looking for some comfort.

The Hong Kong-managed **Huandao Tide Hotel** ((898) 626-8888 FAX (898) 626-5588, Heping Dadao, Haidian Island, a gleaming glass tower with a riverside location, is a close runner-up. Indeed, with tennis courts, a swimming pool, shops, restaurants, a food court, and a grand atrium lobby, it's more a self-contained city than a hotel.

Center. **Dragonair** ((898) 854-8888, extension 6123-5 has an office in the Mandarin Hotel on Wenhua Lu. Most hotels around town sell domestic air tickets.

What to See and Do

In the center of Haikou is **Haikou Park**, a calm retreat from the traffic and a busy venue for teams of tai chi exponents in the early hours of the day. Just north of here **Donghu** and **Xihu** lakes mark the southern extent of the **Old Quarter**, a busy commercial district that teems with interesting architecture and fascinating street scenes. The Haidian River waterfront remains shabby despite efforts to spruce it up.

Where to Stay

Given that luxury buses whiz through to Sanya in just three hours these days, there's probably no

For quality mid-range accommodation, the **Hainan Overseas Hotel** ((898) 677-2623 FAX (898) 677-2094, 17 Datong Lu, combines a superb location in the central business district, friendly service and well-appointed rooms. The **Seaview International Hotel** ((898) 677-3381 FAX (898) 677-3101, 6 Haixiu Lu, is an older establishment where the rooms look slightly the worse for wear, but sizeable discounts are available on request, making this a reasonably priced, central hotel.

How to Get There

Making travel arrangements in Haikou is easy. Luxury buses go to Sanya and Wenchang every half hour or so from the corner of Daying Houlu and Jichang Lu (next to the Haikou Hotel).

The airport is in the middle of town, just five minutes from most hotels. Taxis are inexpensive, though little English is spoken.

SANYA (YA XIAN)

Sanya has the best beaches in all China, along with good seafood and comfortable beach-style accommodation. As a result it's developing rapidly, with twice-weekly air connections from Hong Kong with Dragonair and a host of charter flights from around the region touching down at the nearby Phoenix airport.

What to See and Do

Dadonghai, the best of the beaches, is lined with resort-style hotels these days, but those fearing the worst are in for a surprise. The foreshore has

Where to Stay

Dadonghai is the place to stay. It has a good range of accommodation, countless restaurants, and good swimming.

The best of Sanya's hotels is the new **Mountain-Sea-Sky Hotel ℂ** (899) 821-1688 FAX (899) 821-1988, which overlooks Dadonghai. With two swimming pools (one freshwater, one salt), no fewer than five bars, Chinese, Japanese and Western restaurants, and splendid views of Dadonghai beach it's easily the first choice for anyone looking to splurge on somewhere to stay.

On the beachfront, the **South China Hotel ℂ** (899) 821-3888 FAX (899) 821-3888 is the most comfortable, with gym, swimming pool, first-class

been landscaped, with lawns and shady palms and firs, and the beach is free of litter.

Chinese tourists head up to **Luhuitou** to see a statue that immortalizes a local folktale about a hunter who, after pursuing a deer to the top of this steep peninsula, was surprised to see the deer turn its head back to look at him and turn into a beautiful maiden (the two promptly settled into domestic bliss and lived happily ever after). The statue is a nonevent, but the views of Sanya and the surrounding coast are a treat.

Tianya Haijiao is the southernmost tip of Hainan, and the site of famous rocks carved with the legend: "End of the World" in Chinese. This area is something of a tourist trap nowadays, with restaurants, an aquarium, ethnic traders selling pearls, and professional photographers. It's still worth making the 24-km (15-mile) trip out there.

dining (providing you stick to Chinese cuisine) and business facilities. Also recommended is the **Pearl River Garden Hotel ℂ** (899) 821-1888 FAX (899) 821-1999, which has similar facilities and a beachside location. The **Gloria Resort Sanya ℂ** (899) 856-8855 FAX (899) 856-8533 is a luxury hotel at nearby Yalong Bay, and is the preferred place to stay for most tour groups that come through.

For those in search of more modest comforts, the **Seaside Holiday Inn Resort ℂ** (899) 821-3898 FAX (899) 821-2018 combines a certain charm with budget rates. It has well maintained doubles and cottages in delightful landscaped grounds. Rates are highly negotiable, particularly when business is slow.

OPPOSITE: A tourist ferry glides through the fairyland setting of karst pinnacles and hills along Li River from Guilin. ABOVE: Rounded karst hills beyond Guilin.

HOW TO GET THERE

From the tourist's point of view, Hainan has three immediate destinations: the capital Haikou on the north coast, just across the Qiongzhou Strait from mainland Hai'an; the port and beach resort of Sanya (Ya Xian) on the south coast; and the mountains and colorful mountain folk in between.

From Hong Kong, Dragonair has flights to Haikou — tied in with vacation packages to Haikou–Sanya–Haikou — daily. You can also fly to Haikou and Sanya from Guangzhou. From Zhanjiang you can take a daily direct flight to Haikou.

Boats leave daily from Hong Kong, Beihai, Zhanjiang, Guangzhou and Hai'an to Haikou and (less frequently) Sanya. Zhanjiang, a three-hour hop by ferry from Haikou, has three departures daily to and from Haikou, and is the most popular option for overlanding travelers.

If you want to do some sightseeing en-route, take a train from Guangzhou to Guilin, then travel by rail again to Zhanjiang, continue by bus and ferry across to Haikou and then travel right down the island by bus to Sanya.

CITS (see TAKING A TOUR, page 60 in YOUR CHOICE) in Hong Kong handles all bookings.

GUANGXI–ZHUANGZU AUTONOMOUS REGION

THE KARST HILLS

Chinese culture abounds with literary superlatives, paintings, embroidery, murals, sculpture and other artwork that all attempt to express the beauty of Guilin and its Li River scenery. Even the very meticulous and businesslike *Official Guide to China* produced by the Imperial Japanese Government Railways in 1915 had to cast about for a little poetic inspiration. "The neighborhood (of Guilin) is rich in picturesque scenery," it observed. "The mountains are singular in that the peaks all rise immediately from the plains, each by itself, so that they have been fitly compared by the poet Fan Shih-hu to young bamboos sprouting out of the ground, apparently without any connection with each other. On the river banks there are innumerable grotesque and singular rocks which form objects of interest and attraction to poets."

In fact and in legend, these hill rocks have been littered over the centuries with the wine-flasks of inebriated poets, one of whom, Han Yu, got as far as describing the Li River (Lijiang) as "a turquoise gauze belt, the mountains like a jade clasp." Another managed to start a poem but couldn't finish it and promptly turned to stone. Yet another gave up trying to express himself altogether and simply drank himself to death.

What they were struggling to capture in prose was a geological phenomenon called karst — the erosive action of rivers and drainage over many millions of years on a belt of limestone that extends right across the southern provinces, carving away the softer rock to produce abrupt and fanciful hills and extensive underground caves.

GUILIN

This sprawling city of 680,000 attracts so many visitors for its famous Li River scenery and surrounding necklace of karst hills that it's tempting to dismiss the place as a tourist trap these days. Guilin is certainly highly industrious in its pur-

suit of the tourist dollar, and there is much industrial ugliness to bemoan around town, but it remains one of the most fascinating travel destinations in China. And when the rat race in downtown Guilin becomes too much for you, remember that rural Yangshuo is just an hour or so downstream.

General Information

The main **Bank of China** ((773) 282-4810 is at 5 Shanhu Beilu, but you can change money at most of the major hotels too.

Dragonair ((773) 282-3950, extension 1150 has an office in the Guilin Bravo Hotel, 14 Ronghu Nanlu.

CITS ((773) 282-8304 is at 41 Binjiang Lu. It has a useful English service that can help you book hotels and transportation.

Getting Around

Guilin's Qifeng Airport is 28 km (17 miles) from the city center, and the best way to get to or from it is by the minibuses (US$3) that depart from the CAAC office on Shanghai Lu. A taxi will cost around US$15.

Taxis are ubiquitous around town, and in theory there's a fixed fare of around US$2 per trip, but Guilin taxi drivers are not unknown to sting tourists for extortionate amounts of money. If you arrive at either the airport or the train station, check at the free English information counters there for the latest city taxi fares before flagging one down.

While it's still possible to rent a bicycle in Guilin for the day, the city traffic makes cycling around

for instance — but you'll require a great deal of imagination to transform these stalactites and stalagmites into such fanciful images.

The same richly descriptive names have been given to all the karst landmarks in and around Guilin — **Duxiu Feng** (Solitary Beauty Hill) north of the Lijiang Hotel and the Liberation Bridge over the Li River, **Diecai Shan** (Piled Silk Hill) on the city's northern outskirts, **Xiangbi Shan** (Elephant Trunk Hill) to the south, **Laoren Shan** (Old Man Hill) to the northwest. While they look interesting from a distance they offer little more than a grueling climb and more often than not grimy views of the city when you reach them. But again, there's a great deal of interesting street-

the city a far less pleasurable experience than it once was. You'll see bicycle rental shops and stands all around town. The going rates are around Y20 daily — don't leave your passport as a deposit; negotiate to leave cash (around Y200) instead.

Minibuses to Yangshuo leave from in front of the train station.

What to See and Do

Guilin's main attractions are all in town. **Qixing Gongyuan** (Seven Star Park) is a well-landscaped strolling spot with gardens and traditional hump-backed stone bridges over streams and pools, a precipitous climb that takes you up through viewing pavilions and restaurants to the top of its craggy karst hill, an interesting Ming dynasty bridge called Hua Qiao (Flower Bridge) and six caves with rock formations that have been given evocative names by the Chinese — Monkey Picking Peaches,

life to be seen on the way, particularly if you're adventurous enough to travel out to them on a rented bicycle.

Choose the formations that have more than city views to offer. For example, at **Fubo Hill** on the river bank east of Duxiu Feng you'll find the **Qianfo Dong** (Thousand Buddha Cave) with many Tang and Song dynasty Buddha images carved into its rock faces. Further north at Diecai Shan you'll find more Buddha carvings in its Wind Cave. But the most fascinating cave by far is in **Ludi Yan** (Reed Flute Cave) which lies about 15 km (nine miles) to the northwest of the city and is best reached these days by the No. 3 bus, which terminates at the cave.

Reed Flute Cave is a tour of the underworld as seen through a Disney cartoonist's fantasies —

Trained cormorants are a fisherman's best friend in Guilin, Guangxi Province.

it's an extensive network of beautiful and bizarre natural grottoes, galleries and vast caverns such as the Dragon King's Crystal Palace, which was a local secret for several centuries and used as a place of refuge in times of civil war. Visitors are taken through in groups and the whole attraction is well presented, with imaginative lighting effects adding a touch of magic at each turn of the narrow, winding stone stairways. As you pass through each area the lighting dies to pitch blackness behind you, so be careful to keep up with the group.

Where to Stay

As one of China's premiere tourist attractions, it's small surprise that Guilin has hotels to meet almost every budget. But if it's solitude and backpacker prices you want, head down to Yangshuo, just over an hour away by minibus.

LUXURY

The **Sheraton Guilin Hotel** ((773) 282-5588 FAX (773) 282-5598, Binjiang Nanlu, is the best of Guilin's international luxury hotels. With features like an outdoor swimming pool, Jacuzzi, gym, special rooms with access for the disabled, it stands out from most of the other hotels around town. Ask for a room with a view of the Li River when you book.

The **Holiday Inn Guilin** ((773) 282-3950 FAX (773) 282-2101, 14 Ronghu Nanlu, opened in 1987, was the first of Guilin's international hotels, and it's still an attractive place to base yourself in Guilin, with a central but quiet location overlooking the small Banyan Lake. All rooms come with international direct-dial phones, satellite television and minibar, and for those who want to get local the hotel even supplies mahjong rooms.

The **Guilin Royal Garden Hotel** ((773) 581-2411 FAX (773) 581-2744, Yanjiang Lu, is in the north of town, on the far side of the Li River looking out across the Wave Subduing Hill. The rooms are may not be quite as well appointed as those at the Sheraton and the Holiday, but nobody could complain about their size—each comes complete with two queen-size double beds. The Royal Garden is a good place to stay if you want to escape from the push and shove of downtown Guilin.

MID-RANGE

Once Guilin's top hotel, the **Lijiang Hotel** ((773) 282-2881 FAX (773) 282-2891, 1 Shanhu Beilu, still puts on a good show even if it looks distinctly unpromising from outside, with the full complement of services, and rooms with views that rival those of the Sheraton and the Holiday Inn. It's right in the center of town, overlooking Fir Lake.

The **Guilin Osmanthus Hotel** ((773) 383-4300 FAX (773) 383-5316, 451 Zhongshan Nanlu, is not in the same league as the Lijiang, but if it's mid-range value for money you're looking for, the

Osmanthus is probably the best bet in town. It's an older establishment, and the bargains are in the slightly down-at-heel east wing, where you should be able to secure an acceptable air-conditioned double for around US$40.

Not far from the Holiday Inn, and also overlooking the small Banyan Lake, is the **Ronghu Hotel** ((773) 282-3811 FAX 282-5456, 17 Ronghu Beilu, another long-runner and one that does a good business with budget tour groups. It's a reliable mid-range hotel, with rates slightly higher than the Osmanthus. It's centrally located and the extensive grounds are a leafy retreat from the honking traffic of Guilin.

INEXPENSIVE

There's hardly any budget accommodation in Guilin nowadays, with nearby Yangshuo having established itself as the preferred place to stay for the backpacker crowd. The only option, for those watching their money and who need to overnight here is the **South Stream Hotel** ((773) 383-2257, 84 Zhongshan Nanlu, opposite the railway station and next to the bus station. Clean singles and doubles are available here from around US$10.

Where to Eat

The north-south Zhongshan Lu is packed with eating places, enough to fill an entire chapter. You'll find that they offer mainly Cantonese cuisine with local specialties and local variations. They appear to have mushroomed in such numbers to cash in on the seasonal droves of visiting Hong Kong Chinese. There are a couple that also offer exotic game dishes — monkey, civet cat, raccoon and the like—which are also aimed at the Hong Kong Chinese palate.

All the major hotels have restaurants, the best of them being in the **Sheraton** and the **Holiday Inn**. For good Chinese fare at very affordable prices, the **Hong Kong Hotel** ((773) 383-3889, 8 Xihuan Yi Lu, has a revolving restaurant on its nineteenth floor.

At night **Zhongshan Lu** transforms into a long strip of alfresco food stalls offering a better range of cuisine than even the hotels. The section near the Guilin Hotel, is the best. It's one big tumultuous open-air food market, lit by hissing gas lamps and doing a roaring trade in fresh meat and vegetable hotpots, noodles and soups. Elsewhere you can find little sidewalk snack stalls—knee-high tables and tiny bamboo stools — which do a delicious and very cheap sweet bean soup with eggs. Overcharging has long been a problem here; it's best to clarify prices when you order.

The Thousand Buddha Cave in Guilin vies with the Wind Cave for rock sculptures dating back to Buddhism's grand age in China.

How to Get There

To get to Guilin you can fly directly from Hong Kong on Dragonair and CAAC, or by CAAC from Guangzhou. There are also daily flights from Kunming. The Shanghai–Kumning railway pauses in Guilin, which means that you can jump on a train to either of those destinations — subject to ticket availability, and there can often be long waits on this busy line.

The popular route from Guangzhou for budget travelers is to take a ferry to Wuzhou and change there to a direct bus to either Guilin or Yangshuo. Slow ferries take around 24 hours, but the express services from both Hong Kong and Guangzhou power upriver to Wuzhou in around six hours. The bus from Wuzhou to Guilin takes around six hours.

YANGSHUO

"The rivers and hills of Guilin are the most beautiful in China," says one of the many historic tributes to this karst region, "and those of Yangshuo's surpass Guilin." One of the great surprises of Yangshuo is that, despite having been an obligatory stop on the backpacker trail for nearly two decades now, and having been more recently discovered by domestic tourism, it is still a captivating retreat from the big-city push and shove of nearby Guilin.

Nevertheless, many travelers get only a quick look at the place as part of the six-hour, 80-km (50-mile) boat cruise from Guilin, which passes through a fairyland of mounds, towers, cones and craggy pinnacles soaring sharply out of a silken swathe of flat rice land. Budget travelers, on the other hand, usually avoid the somewhat overpriced boat cruise and take a minibus from Guilin to Yangshuo, where they are free to explore the area's stunning karst scenery at leisure by bicycle or by foot. Among the area's many charms are the evenings, when fleets of lantern-lit bamboo fishing rafts spread down the placid waters, the fishermen using tame cormorants to dive for the fish.

Getting Around

Yangshuo is small enough to stroll around, but for longer jaunts, bicycle is the only way to go. Bicycles (usually mountain bikes nowadays) can be rented for next to nothing, and there are plenty of viewpoints outside the town where you can sit for hours with a picnic lunch and beer or wine and do what the poets of old did — contemplate the karst skyscrapers thrusting up out of the rice paddies and try to put it all into words.

What to See and Do

Yangshuo has enough to see and do to keep you busy for three or four days at least. Many travelers

become so bewitched by the place that they linger for a week or more. Yangshuo's pulling power derives not in small part from its small village atmosphere. How many places in China give you the opportunity to stay in a small community, rent a bicycle and explore the surrounding countryside, with its patchwork paddy fields and stunning karst peaks?

Yangshuo village itself has little to see, though the harbor area on the Li River is charming, and it's easy to while away an afternoon shopping for crafts. **Yangshuo Park** is a pleasant spot for a stroll if you don't mind paying the overpriced gate charge.

High on every visitor's agenda is **Moon Hill**, a one-hour bicycle trip out of Yangshuo. It's a steep walk up the hill, which earns its name from the massive moon-shaped hole near the summit, but the views are ample reward for the effort of the climb. Not far away, enterprising locals will take

you on tours of cave systems with names such as **Black Buddha Caves** and **Dragon Cave**.

The village of **Xingping** is another popular bike excursion. The village is on the bank of the Li River three hours downstream with even more impressive mountain scenery than Yangshuo. Xingping's **market** is the same day as Yangshuo's, but it's larger and worth a special trip to see (see CORMORANTS, CAVES AND LIMESTONE PEAKS, page 18 in TOP SPOTS).

Where to Stay and Eat

Yangshuo has long been a Mecca for backpackers, and is one of the few places in the country where budget travelers get some choice for their money. But, while budget accommodation still abounds, Yangshuo is starting to tentatively reach out to travelers who demand a bit more comfort.

Yangshuo's best hotel is the **Paradise Yangshuo** ((773) 882-2109 FAX (773) 882-2106,

116 Xi Jie. The air-conditioned rooms all have satellite television, international direct-dial phone, and the best of them sport superb views (of the kind Guilin hoteliers would die for) of Yangshuo's legendary nearby hills. Room rates start at around US$100 — good value given rates for similar standards of accommodation in Guilin.

Most of Yangshuo's other accommodation options cater almost exclusively to the backpacker crowd, but some of them also have inexpensive mid-range rooms that are quite agreeable if you like the feeling of roughing it a little.

Far and away, Yangshuo's most popular budget hotel is the **Hotel California** ((773) 882-5559 FAX (773) 882-5959, 35 Xianqian Jie, Yangshuo, which along with budget rooms also has some surprisingly well-appointed luxury rooms.

A punter navigates the river Li at Yangshuo.

The newly opened **Explorer Hotel** ((773) 882-8116 FAX (773) 882-7816, on a side-alley just off Xi Jie, in the center of "town," is a far cry from the Yangshuo Paradise, but it exudes a family-run charm that makes it a pleasant place to stay. Amenities are basic, but all rooms at least have 24-hour hot water.

On the food front, Yangshuo is brimming with cafés that are not afraid to attempt anything. Don't be surprised to find *chow mein* rubbing shoulders with pizza on the menu. Ever-popular standbys such as banana pancakes and müsli feature on everyone's breakfast menus. Making recommendations is difficult, as competition is fierce and places come and go in popularity very quickly.

Kong) to Yangshuo and take around five to six hours. From Guilin minibuses run all day (every 15 to 20 minutes) and take around an hour. Buses also run direct to Guangzhou and Shenzhen, but it's a grueling 15-hour trip to either. For onward train travel from Guilin, most of the cafés and hotels in Yangshuo these days can make ticket reservations.

NANNING

Once a poor nondescript port on the Yong River, Nanning has grown and flourished over the years to become the cultural and administrative capital of Guangxi-Zhuangzu autonomous region. De-

The best advice is to take a stroll along Xi Jie and duck into whatever haunt takes your fancy.

Lisa's deserves a mention for the fact that it's been running longer than virtually anywhere else and still manages to pull in the crowds.

Under the Moon, also on Xi Jie, is characteristic of the new generation of Yangshuo eatery, slightly swish, with a pleasant upstairs balcony, and surprisingly good Western food.

Be adventurous, duck into restaurants for afternoon tea and mid-morning snacks (everything is very inexpensive) and plan your evening meals accordingly. The only grounds for complaint is that almost all the restaurants screen Hollywood movies, sometimes a bit too loudly, in the evenings.

How to Get There
Direct buses run from the Wuzhou ferry terminal (which has connections to Guangzhou and Hong

velopment continues, with a high-tech park nowadays and increasing number of international air connections to cities around the region.

There's very little to see or do in town, and most travelers who turn up here are on route to Pingxiang, the Vietnam border town. The Zhuang and Dong minorities inhabit Nanning in great numbers, but you're not likely to recognize them on the streets — they dress and look almost identical to Han Chinese.

Background
Nanning has revived one of the most exciting of all the cultural events in southern China, the **Dragonboat Festival**, staged on the fifth day of the fifth lunar month (usually June), which commemorates a statesman named Qu Yuan who drowned himself in a river in 295 BC as a protest against government corruption. He was

so admired and respected for his fidelity and virtue, the story goes, that the villagers rowed out to where he'd disappeared and beat gongs and drums and dropped rice cakes to keep the fish away from his corpse.

Nowadays, slim shallow-draft "dragonboats," 40 m (130 ft) long and manned by up to 60 rowers, race up and down the rivers on Dragonboat Day with gongs and tom-toms beating the rhythm, spectators screaming encouragement and water exploding and cascading everywhere.

General Information

To change travelers' checks, the **Bank of China** has a foreign exchange service at Minzu Dadao. **CITS (** (771) 281-6197 is at 40 Xinmin Lu. Go to CITS if you want to visit Vietnam but don't have a Vietnam visa.

What to See and Do

Nanning is a good walking and bicycling city with a lot of activity in its streets, especially in the cool of the evenings when the farmers and open-air market vendors move into the side-streets with their stalls. The main cultural attraction is the **Guangxi Provincial Museum**, east of the Yongjiang Hotel (see below) on Minzu Dadao, which features, among other relics and artifacts, more than 300 ancient bronze drums, the largest collection of its type in China. The drums are products of the Dongson, a people who traded with Burma and Thailand around 2,000 years ago. Take some time also to explore the museum grounds, which have some fine examples of Dong and Zhuang traditional architecture.

Bailong Park, also known as Renmin Park, is an unassuming spot, but worth a short visit if you are in Nanning for a day. The ruins in the park are remnants of a fort built in the early twentieth century.

Twenty kilometers (12.5 miles) northwest of the city are the **Yiling Caves**, a karst formation as interesting as Guilin's Reed Flute Cave with splendid stalactites and stalagmites. It winds for about one kilometer (around half a mile) under ground.

Where to Stay

LUXURY

Nanning's top luxury hotel is the **Mingyuan Xindu Hotel (** (771) 283-0808 FAX (771) 283-0811, 38 Xinmin Lu, which is rated with four stars and lists its room rates in Hong Kong dollars. There is nothing particularly distinguished about this hotel, and unless you are the fastidious type, you will be better off going down market and saving yourself some money.

Slightly less expensive and better value for money is the **Nanning International Hotel (** (771) 585-1818 FAX (771) 588-6789, 88 Minzu Dadao,

which has a good location in the center of town and comes with standard four-star amenities. Rates start at around US$80.

MID-RANGE

The **Yongjiang Hotel (** (771) 280-8123 FAX (771) 280-0535, 48 Jiangbin Lu, in the south of town, near the Yongjiang Bridge, has had a face lift in recent years, and offers some of the best accommodation in town these days. For mid-range travelers, however, there are also cheaper rooms in the old wing of the hotel.

The **Yongzhou Hotel (** (771) 280-2338 FAX (771) 281-0951, 59 Xinmin Lu, is in a pleasant part of town, not far from Bailong Park. Room rates are slightly cheaper than those at the Yongjiang.

INEXPENSIVE

The best budget option for travelers in Nanning is the **Civil Aviation Hotel** (no phone), which is on Chaoyang Lu, next door to the CAAC office, just a short walk from the railway station. Those looking to really save money should ask about the dorm rooms, but comfortable singles and doubles are also available at reasonable rates. Discounts can be had on request.

How to Get There

Nanning now has an international airport with direct flights to Vietnam. It's around 35 km (22 miles) from town, and taxis to the airport cost around Y100. Airport buses leave from the CAAC office on Chaoyang Lu. Domestic flights leave from the same airport, fanning out to destinations all over China.

In 1997 Nanning's rail connection with Kunming was completed, which enables travelers to connect directly with Yunnan province. There are also special express train links with Beijing, and trains south to Zhanjiang, the mainland access point for Hainan Island.

ONWARD TO VIETNAM

From Nanning it is possible to go to the Chinese border town of Pingxiang either by train or by bus. Minibuses run to a point close to the Friendship Gate (the customs post designated for foreigners), from which it is necessary to take a motorcycle taxi (not much fun if you have a lot of luggage) to customs. The Friendship Gate is not far from the Vietnamese town of Lang Son, though the town immediately over the border is called Dong Dang. Providing you set out early from Nanning there's no reason why you shouldn't be in Hanoi enjoying a cheap bottle of east European plonk and a fairly decent *coq-au-vin* by evening.

Smiles light the faces of a group of young Dong minority women in northern Guangxi.

The West

KUNMING AND YUNNAN PROVINCE can be regarded as another radial tour center interlocking with the southern tour route from Guangzhou and, at the same time, opening up the western tour trail that runs north to Chongqing and Chengdu in Sichuan province, and to the capital of Tibet, Lhasa.

YUNNAN PROVINCE

Yunnan, which translates into "South of the Clouds," is a mountainous subtropical province and a kind of Chinese Golden Triangle, bordering Myanmar (Burma), Laos and Vietnam. It shares four main rivers with these neighboring states,

including the mighty Mekong, and has a certain cultural intercourse too through its minority hill tribes. The most prominent of these, the Dai, have their own tribal homeland, the Xishuangbanna autonomous district to the south of the province. There are also Lisu, Lahu and Yao clans whose tribal domains spread as far as the northern border region of Thailand.

Originally part of a southern kingdom called Nanzhou, Yunnan was conquered by the Yuan Mongols in the thirteenth century and brought under imperial rule. It was the scene of a violent Moslem rebellion and an equally bloody government reprisal in the nineteenth century and then became a foothold for French incursions into China from their colonial bases in Laos and Vietnam.

ABOVE: The Abbot of Bamboo Monastery, Kunming. RIGHT: A winged roof hangs over Kunming watchtower and canal bridge.

A legacy of the French presence is a narrow-gauge railway linking Kunming with Hanoi, which is now back in operation and is a popular overland route with backpackers.

In World War II Kunming became one of the bases of Chiang Kaishek's beleaguered nationalist government and swelled with refugees from the east, who were fleeing Japanese forces. The British and Americans kept the city alive with vast shipments of supplies from Burma, bringing them in along the famous Burma Road and by airlift from India.

KUNMING

Kunming is unique amongst China's provincial capitals. It's not just the year-round balmy weather, it's that life is slower, and despite the inevitable modernization, the city still manages to afford the occasional snatch of color in its back streets.

On a less positive note, almost all of the narrow older streets lined with traditional prewar "bamboo"-tiled and lattice-windowed homes and shops have been cleared away over the last five years. These remnants of the city's once charming back streets received their final death knell in the lead-up to the World Horticultural Expo in 1999.

If you rent a bicycle or set off on a long walk, however, it is still possible to enjoy the city's busy street life, its grand parks, open markets and nighttime food stalls. Kunming also has several interesting temples, and there are more in the Western Hills overlooking the vast, freshwater Lake Dian. It is also the access point for bus tours of the Stone Forest and air and bus transport to Dali and the tribal minorities of the Xishuangbanna region.

General Information

The **Bank of China** is at 444 Beijing Lu, but money can also be changed at any of the larger hotels around town.

Kunming has some overseas air connections, and foreign airlines represented in town include **Dragonair (** (871) 313-8592, Golden Dragon Hotel, 575 Beijing Lu, **SilkAir (** (871) 316-5888, extension 6223, Holiday Inn Hotel, 25 Dongfeng Lu, and **Thai Airways (** (871) 313-3315, King World Hotel, 28 Beijing Lu. For domestic flights contact **China Southern (** (871) 310-1831, or **China Southwest (** (871) 353-9696.

For tourist information and tours, the best place to go is the **Yunnan Overseas Tourist Corporation (** (817) 316-3018, 154 East Dongfeng Road.

Getting Around

Bicycle is the best vehicle for sightseeing in Kunming. Both the Kunming and Camellia hotels (see WHERE TO STAY, below) rent them.

What to See and Do

Green Lake Park (Cuihu Park) is a landscaped cultural park and leisure area with attractive gardens and traditional halls and pavilions set around ornamental pools. It's a good place to meet locals and watch them rowing on the lake, roller-skating and photographing each other. There are often art and crafts exhibitions on the grounds and outside, and on weekends the adjacent street is full of market stalls, ice cream vendors, and "sugar sculptors" — who fashion elaborate filigrees of butterflies, dragons and other subjects out of thin strands of hot toffee. You'll also find shooting galleries, paper silhouette artists and even old fairground "Test Your Strength" machines.

Southwest of the park at the main traffic circle at **Dongfeng Xilu**, **Daguan Jie** and **Renmin Xilu**, you can watch minority tribespeople arriving in town to sell their produce; at night, alongside the Yunnan Arts and Crafts Store, the street turns into one of the most colorful and clamorous open-air eating places to be encountered anywhere in China.

East of the Green Lake Hotel, on Yuantong Jie, you'll find the **Yuantong Monastery**, constructed in the Yuan dynasty between 1301 and 1320 and featuring a huge, ornately sculptured gateway, an elegant triple-arched stone bridge, an eight-sided pavilion and spectacular Buddha images in the main hall. It's another excellent place to study the religious liberalization that's occurring now in China — the brisk back-to-business reverence with which the older matrons plant their joss sticks and kowtow to the images and altars. Another easily accessible cultural attraction is the **Golden Temple (Jindian)**, which lies about seven kilometers (four miles) northeast of Kunming and can be reached by bicycle or the No. 10 bus. It was built during the Ming dynasty and became the summer residence of a Manchu military turncoat, General Wu Sangui, who was sent south in 1659 to put down a rebellion and set himself up as a rebel warlord instead.

THE BAMBOO TEMPLE

Kunming's most fascinating temple is the Qiongzhu Si (Bamboo Temple), about 12 km (seven and a half miles) northwest of Kunming. It's recognized as the first Chan (or Zen) monastery to be built in Yunnan province, but the original Tang dynasty buildings burned down and were replaced in the fifteenth century. During another facelift between 1883 and 1889 the Sichuan sculptor Li Guangxiu was commissioned to decorate one of the halls with images of the 500 *arhats*, or immortal beings commanded to remain on earth and protect the laws of Buddhism.

Li and five assistants produced a lifelike but bizarre and even Boschian human tableau, filling the walls of the hall, that was later condemned

as a sick caricature of some of the important personalities of the time. Thankfully, no one doubted the artistry enough to have it destroyed, and today it ranks amongst China's most impressive cultural relics.

To get to the Bamboo Monastery you take a bus from outside the Yunnan Hotel on Dongfeng Lu. The journey takes around 30 minutes.

LAKE DIAN

For a rewarding full day's excursion from Kunming, and one that combines physical exercise, fresh air and cultural interest, take a No. 6 bus from the Xiaoximen bus depot near the traffic circus just down from the Green Lake Hotel (see WHERE TO STAY, below) and head out to the **Western Hills** and Lake Dian. You can also take bus No. 4 from the **Yuantong Temple** to **Daguan Park** at the lake's northernmost point and from there take a boat cruise, departing at 8 AM, to Haikou, passing under

the sharply rising hillsides called Sleeping Beauty, because their contours are said to resemble a maiden at rest.

From the No. 6 bus terminal the road winds upward through forested slopes to provide panoramic views of Lake Dian — the second largest freshwater lake in China — with its spreading thickets of fish traps and elegant square-sailed cargo junks that flutter lazily like white moths down its main channel. The road winds higher and higher, and there are several interesting temples and grottoes along the way — eleventh-century **Huating Temple**, the biggest around Kunming; the Ming dynasty **Taihua Temple** with its magnificently grotesque door gods; and the **Sanqingge Temple**, a temple pavilion and former country villa built during the Yuan dynasty and later turned into a Daoist place of worship.

At the top of the climb you'll find the **Longmen (Dragon Gate)** complex of grottoes and pavilions

set high in a cliff face and commanding another panoramic view of the lake. Dragon Gate was built some two centuries ago in the reign of the Qing emperor Qianlong. The paths and caves took 72 years to hack out of the rock, and then a sculptor named Zhu Jiage spent another eight years fashioning the various images that adorn the main cave, including a large statue of the god of literature. One day, so the story goes Zhu was shaping a pen-brush in the statue's hand when it snapped off. He was so mortified that he hurled himself from the precipice to his death.

You can finish off your tour of the Western Hills by climbing down to the lake itself. Below Dragon Gate there's a steep pathway that zigzags down to a sleepy fishing village right at the water's edge. From there you can stroll out along a causeway to a narrow channel and rest a while watching the

Lanterns and pavilions at eventide in Green Lake Park.

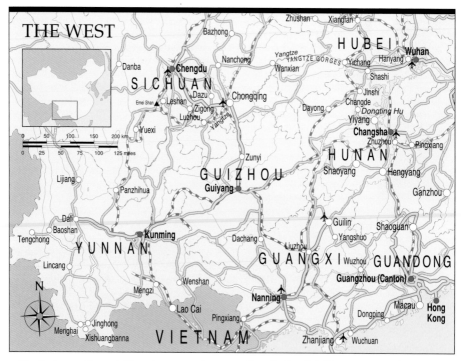

THE WEST

sailing junks pass through. There's a sampan ferry there that is usually packed with day trippers and their bicycles being poled across the narrow neck of water. On the other side you can walk about a kilometer (just over half a mile) to Haigeng Beach and climb on board a No. 44 bus for your trip back to Kunming.

THE STONE FOREST

Everyone who goes to Kunming goes to the Stone Forest (Shilin), a bizarre mushroom-patch of fungus-shaped gray rocks that are believed to have been formed and sculpted by two natural forces — the earth's crust pushing upward and the wind and rain eroding the bared limestone outcrops. They are quite a remarkable spectacle, and what is also remarkable about a visit there is the tenacity with which hordes of colorfully costumed souvenir hawkers, mostly women and girls of the Sanyi, a clan of the Yi minority tribe, will try to sell you ornately embroidered "hill tribe" bags, purses and other items.

Although the Stone Forest is interesting, there's a truly fascinating attraction around the small lake at the forest's entrance — the **Five Tree Village** with rustic old mud-brick homes featuring "horned" roofs and traditional doorways, wandering pigs, goats, donkeys and other livestock and, in the autumn and winter, huge bunches of corn hanging high in the trees above the homes to dry.

There are various ways to get to the Stone Forest, but the easiest is to take any of the day tours

offered by hotels in Kunming. Providing there are not too many stops at souvenir shops en-route, the journey should take around two hours.

The old French narrow-gauge line, which runs all the way to Hanoi, provides access to the Stone Forest via Yiliang. Buses from Yiliang to the Stone Forest take just 45 minutes but are infrequent, making this combination of train and bus an inconvenient travel option.

Where to Stay

LUXURY

Kunming's premiere luxury hotel is the **Holiday Inn Kunming (** (871) 316-5888 FAX (871) 313-5189, 25 Dongfeng Donglu. Along with six restaurants and bars, the hotel houses a bowling center.

The Holiday Inn's main competition is the newly renovated **Green Lake Hotel (** (871) 515-5788 FAX (871) 515-3286, 6 Cuihu Nanlu, now under the management of the Hilton group. The hotel has a superb location overlooking Green Lake Park and has some of the best Chinese restaurants in town. Formerly a government guesthouse, it has now been upgraded to five-star international standards.

The **King World Hotel (** (871) 313-8888 FAX (871) 313-1910, 28 Beijing Lu, is popular with business travelers — many of them these days from Thailand — and deservedly so. It's an efficient and well-maintained operation with a good business center and good-value, well-appointed rooms. The location, too, in the heart of town is hard to beat.

MID-RANGE

The **Kunming Hotel** ((871) 316-2063 FAX (871) 318-8220, 145 Dongfeng Donglu, is a sprawling place with a wide variety of rooms to choose from. The north wing sports luxury prices, but rooms in the South Wing are very good value at around US$50. This is one of those hotels that guests rarely have to leave, with shops, amusement arcades, travel agents and restaurants.

The **Camellia Hotel** ((871) 316-8000 FAX (871) 314-7033, also on Dongfeng Donglu, has some reasonably priced mid-range rooms, with air-conditioning and attached bathroom.

INEXPENSIVE

The **Camellia Hotel** (see above) has been the favorite of backpacking travelers for more than a decade, and continues to pack the budget-conscious into its dormitories. The other popular budget option is the **Kunhu Hotel** ((871) 313-3737, 44 Beijing Lu, which is slightly cheaper than the Camellia but much less friendly and poorly maintained. It is recommended only if the Camellia happens to be full.

Where to Eat

Most of the good hotels have excellent Chinese restaurants, and prices that are surprisingly cheap. Elsewhere, there's a wide range of restaurants and cuisine to choose from. The Chinese Restaurant at the Holiday Inn hotel is an excellent place to sample Yunnan specialties, such as "across the bridge noodles (*guoqiao mian*).

The **Cooking School**, directly opposite the Camellia Hotel, deserves a mention less for its decor and service — both of which leave much to be desired — than for the fact that it has for many years been giving travelers an opportunity to sample some of Yunnan's regional specialties.

The great advantage of the **King Dragon Regional Cuisine Village**, on Tuodong Lu, is that it brings together a large number of restaurants under one roof. While, Yunnan cuisine is a highlight, there are also restaurants offering everything from spicy Sichuan fare to Beijing duck. Head upstairs for a good sit-down meal — the ground floor restaurants are mostly rough and ready.

The busy commercial district around Dongfeng Xilu is a good hunting ground for restaurants. Look for Xiangyun Jie, where the long-running **Beijing Restaurant**, at No. 77, does fabulous northern-style cuisine at reasonable prices. The Sichuan-style **Chuanwei** is on the same street, as are a host of other snack vendors and small restaurants. Not much English is spoken here, but if you're willing to be adventurous, you'll undoubtedly come up with some delicious rewards.

Not far from here, on Nantong Jie, is the **Yunnan Across the Bridge Noodle Restaurant**. "Across the bridge noodles" (*guoqiaomian*) is

Kunming's most famous local dish and you'll find it served with much pomp and ceremony at all the major hotels in town. But for the real thing, in down-to-earth plebeian surroundings (and at rock-bottom prices), this restaurant is the place to go. The noodle dish itself is a winter dish in which a thin film of oil over a bowl of broth keeps the heat in and allows condiments to cook — you will hear the story of how it came into being countless times if you visit Kunming.

Popular with well-off locals and visiting foreigners alike is the ranch-style **Billy Niupai Steakhouse** ((817) 331-1748, 47 Tianyuan Road. The beef is imported from the United States, and the steaks are surprisingly good.

How to Get There

Kunming is connected with frequent flights from all the major Chinese cities. Dragonair flies from Hong Kong, SilkAir from Singapore, and Thai from Bangkok. Daily trains run there from Guilin and Chongqing via the junction of Guiyang. Getting a sleeper on the Shanghai–Kunming Express will usually require at least three-days advance booking.

Onward to Vietnam

With the proper paperwork — you will need a Vietnam visa with Lao Cai indicated as the port of entry — it is possible to travel by train from Kunming to Hanoi. Trains running on this narrow-gauge, French-constructed railway take around 18 hours either way.

DALI

The old walled city of Dali lies around seven to eight hours by bus to the west of Kunming, and has become one of the most popular destinations in all of Yunnan. There's no denying the beauty of the place. Nestled between the turquoise Erhai Lake and snowcapped Cangshan mountain range, Dali is one of the most picturesque corners of China.

Dali was originally the capital of a kingdom ruled by the Bai minority tribe until it was conquered by the Yuan Mongols in the thirteenth century and absorbed into their empire. In many respects, this town still rests somewhere in the Middle Ages, trapped in a time warp of traditional winged-roof and neatly whitewashed homes, an encompassing wall and old town gates that are still the main access for a daily parade of farmers from the surrounding countryside with their horses and carts. Bird cages hang in the narrow streets and alleys, householders can actually be seen scrubbing the outsides of their homes. Things are changing fast here, however. New hotels are springing up, and the construction of an airport has turned this formerly sleepy town into a major tourist destination.

When to Go

The best time to go to Dali is in April, when Bai tribespeople from all over the region flock to the **Third Moon Fair**. Next best is June, when the town stages a spectacular **Dragonboat Festival**. At other times the Bai pour into Dali every Saturday for the open-air markets, and another market is held every Monday at **Shaping**, two kilometers (one and a quarter miles) away.

What to See and Do

It's easy to while away a day wandering the back streets of Dali, shopping for souvenirs and ducking into the travelers cafés that line Huguo Lu, the street locals refer to as "Foreigner's Street."

Most of the attractions are out of town. If you rent a bicycle (as always, recommended), you can ride down to the **Erhai Lake** in about 10 minutes, where you will find the small village of Caicun. From here ferries go to the villages of Wase and Haidong (check with locals for times in Dali before setting out).

Dali is the sort of place that if you sit around in a café for a short while you will meet people who are doing interesting things, such as heading off on hikes or extended trips into the country. A popular hike is up to **Zhonghe Temple**, to the west of Dali. It's not an easy walk, but when you get up there you are rewarded with stunning views.

Where to Stay and Eat

There are actually two Dalis, a point which causes some confusion. Old Dali is the place to stay, not Dali city, which is a sprawling, uninteresting place, also known as Xiaguan.

The top hotel in Old Dali is the **Jinhua Hotel** ((872) 267-3343 FAX (872) 267-3846, which is right on the corner of Huguo Lu and Fuxing Lu, in the center of town. Although the hotel has some budget rooms, it is the air-conditioned suites, which come at around US$50, that are the best value. The hotel has shopping, dining, a business center and even an art gallery.

Most of Dali's other accommodation options are unfortunately rather uninspiring. The **Red Camellia Hotel** ((872) 267-0423, 32 Huguo Lu, also known as No. 4 Guest House, is just up the road, close to all the restaurants and has a wide range of rooms, from dormitories to basic singles and doubles. The **Old Dali Inn** ((872) 267-0382, Boai Lu, also known as the No. 5 Guesthouse, tends to take the overflow from the Red Camellia. Rooms vary immensely, so it's wise to look before committing to anything. Its most winning feature is its courtyard flower garden, and if you can get one of the doubles with attached bathroom facing onto the garden this is quite a pleasant place to stay.

As in Yangshuo, that other backpackers' haven, it's difficult to make recommendations for restaurants in Dali. Almost all the popular restaurants can be found on Huguo Lu, and the best advice is to take a stroll and pop into wherever takes your fancy.

Marley's Café is one of the longest runners, and occasionally hosts Bai banquets, which are well worth sampling. **Café de Jacks**, which once went by the less ostentatious name, Jack's Café, is another long runner, though the food is a little more dubious. It's popular after-hours, when it becomes a bar. For authentic Chinese food, **Old Place**, on Boai Lu, comes complete with an English menu, and is popular in winter for its hotpots. Its only drawback is that it is occasionally invaded by drunken karaoke singers.

How to Get There

Dali has its own airport, and flights turn up four times a week from Kunming. Bus transport fans out from Dali to Baoshan and Dehong, a minority region on the Myanmar border, and to Lijiang. To get to Xishuangbanna, you will need to go to Baoshan first.

LIJIANG

If you've visited Dali it may be hard to believe, but Lijiang is equally, if not more, beautiful. The new town is just what the name suggests, but the old quarter is a fascinating maze of canals and old buildings.

On February 2, 1996 an earthquake measuring around seven on the Richter scale struck Lijiang, killing approximately 300 people. The town has bounced back, and today there is no sign whatsoever of the disaster.

The surrounding valley is a treat to explore, with many Tibetan monasteries, some beautiful frescoes, and, presiding over it all, Jade Dragon Snow Mountain (Yulongxue Shan).

Lijiang is famous above all as the home of the Naxi minority. Much has been made of the fact that the Naxi were (perhaps in some remote areas still are) a matriarchal society. You will see very little evidence of this in Lijiang and its surrounding villages, but for those willing to go farther afield the Naxi are still a matriarchal tribe by all accounts. In the Naxi world, women own all property and they choose their mates. Their written language is, like Chinese, pictographic.

Good books on the area include *The Ancient Nakhi Kingdom of Southwest China* by Joseph Rock, a pioneering anthropologist who lived in the area from the early 1920s until 1949, and who is still remembered by some locals. Easier reading, and giving an insight into the man himself and the Naxi is *In China's Border Provinces: The Turbulent Career of Joseph Rock, Botanist-Explorer* by J.B. Sutton — essential reading for anyone who has an interest in the region.

What to See and Do

Travelers use Lijiang as a base from which to do treks and make day trips into the surrounding countryside. The immediate attractions are Lijiang's monasteries, which belong to the *kagyupa* (red hat) sect of Tibetan Buddhism. You won't see many monks nowadays, but the monasteries are often scenically located and command stunning views. **Yufeng Monastery**, at the foot of **Yulongxue Shan** (Jade Dragon Snow Mountain), about 20 km (12.4 miles) north of Lijiang, is particularly worth a visit and can be combined with a trip to **Baisha**.

Baisha is such a small village, it's hard to believe that it was once capital of the Naxi kingdom, before Kublai Khan made it part of his Yuan empire

a small village that somehow has ended up with the name Walnut Grove. Check in the cafés of Lijiang on the latest details about doing the trek. Don't do the trek alone — a number of individual trekkers have gone missing over the years. Unfortunately a road now cuts through the gorge.

Back in Lijiang itself, evenings are enlivened by performances of the local **Naxi orchestra**, conducted by Mr. Xuan Ke. His explanations tend to ramble, but the performances themselves are captivating.

Where to Stay and Eat

Lijiang's best hotel, and a sign of the changing times and fortunes of this once off-the-beaten-track

in the fourteenth century. Baisha's main attractions are its frescoes executed in Tibetan style with Tibetan Buddhist, Muslim, Taoist and Dongba elements. They illustrate well the mixed lines along which Naxi religion developed as a result of its situation as a crossroads for Mongols from the north, Tibetans from the west, Turko-Mongols from the northwest and Chinese from the south and east. The frescoes can be seen at the **Dading Pavilion**, **Dabaoji Palace** and **Liuli Temple**. Baisha's other attraction is Dr. Ho, a local herbal doctor who has been made famous by visiting travel writers such as Bruce Chatwin. He will no doubt hail you on the street and sell you some of his miraculous herbal tea.

Tiger Leaping Gorge is one of the world's deepest, and the two-day trek through it has passed into backpacker legend. Overnight accommodation — extremely basic — is available midway at

destination, is the 23-story **Guan Fang Hotel** ((888) 518-8888 FAX (888) 512-8335, a four-star hotel with indoor tennis, a swimming pool and a revolving restaurant.

The **Lijiang Grand Hotel** ((888) 512-2431, a Chinese–Thai joint venture, is also recommended, not just for its excellent location close to the old quarter of Lijiang, but for its excellent, air-conditioned rooms. The hotel has a good business center, and its Jade River Restaurant is highly recommended.

Budget travelers usually opt to stay in one of the converted guesthouses in the old Naxi section of town, an experience, if you don't mind roughing it a little, that is hard to beat. The best of the old-town hotels is the **Ancient City Inn** ((888) 512-0891, where heated rooms with 24-hour hot

Natural limestone pillars form the formidable Stone Forest (Shilin) near Kunming.

water are available in a charming traditional Naxi home built around a courtyard.

The **Inn of the First Bend** ((888) 518-1688 FAX (888) 518-1688, 43 Mishi Alley, Xinyi Street, is the most popular of the Naxi-style budget inns, and along with dorm beds it also has some inexpensive single and double rooms. The hotel's restaurant offers some of the best traditional Yunnan cuisine in town.

Lijiang's most interesting dining experiences are to be had in the old Naxi quarter, where the *Naxi mixian* (rice noodles cooked in a clay pot) is the local specialty. Restaurants serving this dish abound, and it is testimony to Lijiang's increasing popularity as a tourist destination that many of them have English menus.

The long-running **Mama Fu's**, also in the old quarter, remains as popular as ever, serving up a mixture of Western, Chinese and Naxi favorites. Also recommended is **Lamu's Café** in the Ancient City Inn (see above).

Yinjiu has a 500-year history and has a lychee-based wine tasting like a medium sweet sherry. Try it.

How to Get There

Lijiang has its own airport around 20 km (just over 12 miles) south of town, and numerous flights connect it with Kunming daily.

A new highway means that buses (many daily) make the run between Lijiang and Dali in around three hours. Minibuses do the trip slightly quicker. Buses to Kunming can take up to 15 hours, a marathon trip. For onward travel to Sichuan, buses run between Lijiang and Jinjiang, a town on the Kunming–Chengdu rail route. It can take up to nine hours to get to Jinjiang, an uninspiring town just over the Sichuan border, by bus.

XISHUANGBANNA

This special autonomous prefecture, in the south of Yunnan province bordering Myanmar (Burma) and Laos, is the heartland of the Dai minority. They are Buddhists and are famous for their elaborate Burmese-style temples and their homes, which are built on stilts, leaving room underneath for boats and livestock, and their traditional dress — the women wearing an exotic combination of colorful turbans, silver bracelets and necklaces and long slim ankle-length sarongs.

The Dai are also renowned for their spectacular rites and festivals, and there's hardly a tourism documentary on Chinese television that doesn't promote their tribal dances, with their blaze of strange animist costumes and headdresses — particularly their ceremonial Peacock Dance. The best time to see this ritual performed is in April, at the time of the **Dai New Year**, when it's presented along with Dragonboat races and the Water Festival. In this day-long Mardi Gras — also a feature of the festive calendar in Thailand — the revelers drench each other with water in a very enjoyable "wringing in" of the New Year.

Xishuangbanna is not only popular with Western travelers, it has also become a mini-Thailand for Chinese tourists, who find the combination of tropical heat, colorful minorities and spicy food every bit as exciting as Westerners do.

JINGHONG

Jinghong lies on the Lancang Jiang, or Mekong River, about 29 km (18 miles) from the Burmese border, and acts as the gateway to the rest of Xishuangbanna. There's little to do around town, except enjoy long lazy meals and watch some local Dai dancing in the evenings.

Those with time should make a side-trip to **Menghan** (also known as Ganlanba), a village just two hours by bicycle from Jinghong with some splendid nearby *wats* (temples). Menghan has some basic Dai-style accommodation.

Where to Stay and Eat

Jinghong's best hotel is the **Dai Garden Hotel** ((691) 212-3888 FAX (691) 212-6060, 8 Nongling Nanlu, a luxury option that tries hard — and mostly succeeds — to create some traditional Dai atmosphere. The **Xinmin International** ((691) 212-6888 FAX (691) 213-2880, on Jingde Donglu, offers similar standards, but by contrast has little character.

For mid-range accommodation no other hotel can match the pedigree or the character of the **Banna Hotel** ((691) 212-3679, 12 Gelanzhong Lu. Renovations and additions have stripped it of some its charm, but for around US$20 to US$30 you can get a comfortable air-conditioned double with views of the Mekong.

The **Banna Mansion Hotel** ((691) 212-5100, corner of Jinghong Nanlu and Jinghong Xilu, right in the center of town, is another mid-range to luxury hotel.

Budget travelers all head to Manting Lu, in the south of Jinghong, where a string of very basic Dai-run hostels provide beds for rates as low as US$5 per night, and offer home-cooked meals that many remember for years afterwards as among the most delicious on their entire China trip. One of the most popular places to stay here is the **Dai Building Inn**, a rustic stilt-house.

BEYOND JINGHONG

Trips to other destinations such as **Menghai**, **Menghun**, **Jingzhen**, **Nannuoshan**, **Damenglong** and **Mengyang** can be arranged through almost

A ferryman on Erhai Lake, Dali.

any of the hotels or guesthouses in Jinghong, although it is also possible to get around the region by local bus. Distances are not great in Xishuangbanna, which means that most towns and villages can be reached in two or three hours of traveling. Most villages have basic accommodation.

A highly recommended trip is to Mengyang, home to the Huayao tribe, and from there a further 10 km (six miles) on to the village of **Mannanan**, where villagers still dress in traditional Dai attire, the women in turbans. It's best to join a tour in Jinghong, as access is difficult by public transportation.

Around 25 km (15.5 miles) west of Jinghong, the small, nondescript town of Menghun has a colorful **Sunday market** that starts at daybreak and runs through until around midday. Although, it's preferable to spend the previous evening in Menghun, accommodation there is only for the stoic.

SICHUAN PROVINCE

CHONGQING

Chongqing, one of China's four administered municipalities, is a grimy, hilly industrial city at the confluence of the Jialing and Yangzi rivers that is smog-bound for more than 100 days of the year and in the summer is so fiercely hot that it is known as one of the Three Furnaces of the Yangzi. Having said that, there are three good reasons why it should be included in any western travel itinerary.

First, it has one of the most architecturally stunning hotels in China, the Renmin Hotel, with its magnificent triple-eaved "Temple of Heaven" domed auditorium and huge columns along its two residential wings. Secondly, the city is the western starting point for the Yangzi River ferry services that cut right across the heart of China. Thirdly, you go to Chongqing to get to Dazu (see below), one of the four most famous centers of Buddhist cave sculpture in China.

Although it has a long past, Chongqing's contemporary history is much more relevant to its current appeal. It was the headquarters of Chiang Kaishek and his Guomindang forces during Japan's relentless drive to occupy all of China in the 1930s and suffered devastating Japanese bombing as a result. A legacy of that violent period is a network of tunnels and shelters cut into its many hillsides, some of which have since been turned into small factories. At one point the city was a command post for both nationalist and communist forces in their brief military pact against the Japanese. The communists based their command at Red Crag Village on the Jialing River 10 km (six miles) from the city center, and

Zhou Enlai and his wife lived in house No. 13 and also at 50 Zengjiayan in the city itself.

General Information

Dragonair ℂ (23) 6280-3380 is in the Holiday Inn Yangzi Chongqing Hotel (see below). **CAAC ℂ** (23) 6386-2970 is on the corner of Zhongshan Lu and Renmin Lu.

The main branch of the **Bank of China** is on Minzu Lu in the city center, but as usual in China nowadays it's possible to change money at any of the major hotels.

What to See and Do

Being hilly, Chongqing isn't the sort of city you want to bicycle around. The buses are also particularly crowded. Thankfully, most of the city's attractions lay within the narrow peninsula that make up central Chongqing and are easily reached on foot. A stroll along the southern bank of the **Jialing River**, past the main bridge, will take you over clusters of European-style rooftops and homes that date back to Chongqing's days as a treaty port. If you head down Minzu Lu toward Chaotianmen Dock at the eastern end of the peninsula, you'll find the **Liberation Monument**, which is a huge clock tower, and, close to there, the interesting and very ancient (over 1,000 years, it is said) **Luohan Temple**, which has an impressive collection of 500 terracotta *arhats* and an imposing seated golden Buddha. The temple also has an inexpensive vegetarian restaurant of a very high standard. The Liberation Monument is also the center of the city's main commercial and tourist district, and around it you'll find department stores, crafts shops, several restaurants and the Xinhua Bookstore, where you can buy a good English-language city map.

Taking Zhourong Lu southwest toward the Yangzi River, you climb steps toward one of the city's urban ridges and, on the other side, you'll find a small recreational area where the city's old-timers gather to gamble in the afternoons and show off their caged birds. Below the park there's a big roller-skating rink where you can watch the youngsters enjoying themselves. Another interesting strolling spot is a bustling open-air market that tumbles down a steep "ladder street" toward the railway station, and which you can reach by going south on Zhongshan Lu from the Renmin Hotel and crossing over to it from the giant Shancheng Cinema. On the way down Zhongshan Lu you might call into **Pipashan Park**. On a clear day (not very common in Chongqing), the pagoda at the summit of the park affords good views of the city. The park is also home to the **Chongqing Museum**, which is not one of China's best but does have an interesting natural history section with dinosaur bones unearthed at the Sichuan city of Zigong.

YANGZI RIVER FERRIES

The most popular Yangzi trip is to go downriver from Chongqing to Wuhan. The three-day deluxe cruises offered by CITS and CTS (see TAKING A TOUR, page 60 in YOUR CHOICE) take in the three gorges — Qutang, Wuxia and Xiling — with several scenic and historical stops along the way. The Three Gorges Dam project, a controversial undertaking that will displace more than a million people, is likely over the next decade to cause the three gorges to disappear from sight. Given that once you get beyond the gorges to the town of Yichang (Hubei province), the Yangzi becomes a wide dun-colored sweep of river with little to see, it's likely that the dam

For true luxury standards the **Holiday Inn Yangzi Chongqing** ((23) 6280-3380 FAX (23) 6280-0884, 15 Nanping Beilu, is Chongqing's best, though its location on the southern bank of the Yangzi River leaves you a long way from the hustle and bustle of downtown Chongqing. Facilities include an indoor putting green and a twenty-first floor Western Restaurant, the Sunset Grill, which provides superb views of grimy Chongqing city.

MID-RANGE

The **Chung King Hotel** ((23) 6384-9301 FAX (23) 6384-3085, 41–43 Xinhua Lu, is a joint-venture operation near Chaotianmen Dock. Unlike many other mid- to top-end hotels around town, the

project will end the Yangzi's days as a tourist attraction.

Steamers go as far as Shanghai, a six-day journey, and tickets can be obtained in Chongqing and Wuhan through CITS or directly from the booking office on the dock (see also WUHAN, page 247).

Where to Stay

LUXURY

The remarkable **Chongqing Renmin (People's) Hotel** ((23) 6385-1377 FAX (23) 6385-2076, 173 Renmin Lu, despite impressive renovations, is still not quite five-star, but there's a grandeur about it that no other hotel in China can rival. Housed in the wings of the People's Concert Hall, rooms range from modest and inexpensive to luxury and surprisingly reasonably priced. The amenities have a distinctly Old China feel about them but then that, arguably, is part of the hotel's charm.

1930s-era building the hotel is housed in exudes some charm. The facilities include post and telecommunications, clinic, taxis, foreign exchange and a small gift shop. Popular with Hong Kong business people, the hotel also has a very good Sichuan restaurant.

The **Chongqing Guesthouse** ((23) 6384-5888 FAX (23) 6383-0643, 235 Minsheng Lu, is another good mid-range choice. It has a wide-range of rooms and prices and also has a couple of very good Chinese restaurants.

INEXPENSIVE

Huixianlou Hotel ((23) 6383-7495, close to the Liberation Monument, has long been the only hotel in Chongqing with rooms that budget travelers

Modeled on temple architecture, the ceiling of the People's Assembly Hall in Chongqing is classical Chinese design at its best.

can afford. Remarkably, the hotel still provides dormitory accommodation in seven-bed rooms, but it is the standard doubles that are best value in this clean and well-maintained hotel. The dormitory rooms and some of the doubles have panoramic views of the city.

Where to Eat

Chongqing is famed for its super-hot (as in spicy) hot pot. The chances are, even if you think you like spicy food, the hot pot served in Chongqing restaurants frequented by locals will leave you gasping. One place that serves hot pot cooked for tender Western palates is the Holiday Inn's **Chongqing Hot Pot**.

For a huge range of restaurants call into the **Metropolitan Tower Chongqing**, 68 Zhourong Lu, next to the Liberation Monument, which is said to be China's biggest shopping mall.

For excellent Chinese vegetarian cuisine the restaurant attached to the Luohan Temple is inexpensive and a good place to soak up the local atmosphere.

How to Get There

Being a junction city, Chongqing is accessible directly by air from virtually every airport in China. There are direct trains to Beijing and Chengdu, and if you're approaching on the clockwise route from the south you travel directly on a dog-leg route via Guiyang.

DAZU

From the tourist's point of view, Dazu is Chongqing's *raison d'être*. Along with remote Dunhuang, this small town has China's most impressive collection of Buddhist cave sculptures.

Dazu Buddhist Caves

To get to the **Dazu Grottoes** go up the main street and continue on out of town, climbing toward **Bei Shan (North Hill)** which has a pagoda set dramatically on top of it. If you climb directly on up to the pagoda you'll find something of immediate interest — three beautiful Song dynasty Buddha images sitting side-by-side in the courtyard of a farmhouse. The cave sculptures themselves — among some 50,000 of them dating back to the Tang and Song reigns and found at 45 sites scattered throughout this region — are back down the hill from the pagoda; but while they're interesting, and while Bei Shan offers stunning aerial views of the surrounding ricelands, this is really not what you've come to Dazu to see.

Baoding Shan (Treasure Peak Mountain) is what you've come here for. It lies 15 km (nine miles) northeast of Dazu and you can get a bus there from the town's main square. Baoding is a huge horseshoe-shaped grotto, something like an amphitheater, lined with more than 15,000 statues, engravings and bas-relief images. They were started during the Southern Song reign and took from 1179 to 1249 to complete. Most of the sculptures refer to epic Buddhist stories, and many depict animals and rural life and the stages of childhood, but they are dominated by two magnificent examples of Buddhist art — the ornate **Thousand-Hands-Thousand-Eyes Bodhisattva**, which you'll find in one of the pavilions, and a huge 31-m (102-ft) recumbent **Sakyamuni Buddha (The Sleeping Buddha)**, which fills one entire wall of the grotto. This one dramatic and inspiring sculpture explains why Baoding is rated with Datong, Luoyang and Dunhuang in the immense legacy of Buddhist art.

Where to Stay

Dazu has only limited accommodation, and for budget travelers it is expensive. The **Dazu Guesthouse** is a plush mid-range place that has been renovated to meet the needs of affluent tour group travelers. The **Beishan Hotel** is cheaper, though a night here is unlikely to rate high on your list of memorable China experiences afterwards.

How to Get There

Dazu lies 160 km (100 miles) northwest of Chongqing. Buses run approximately every half hour from the Chongqing long-distance bus station (next door to the railway station), and take around three hours.

CHENGDU

Chengdu, the Sichuan provincial capital, has had many names in the past. During the Han dynasty it was called the City of Brocade for the beautiful silks that it produced. In the tenth century it was the City of Hibiscus for the flowers planted along its main wall. Nowadays its name translates into Perfect Metropolis and it is an important industrial city that has somehow managed to retain an atmosphere of clean, well-ordered and expansive leisure, with wide boulevards, interesting monuments and temples and fine parks.

Chengdu is also another vital access city for tourists, it is the most convenient departure point for the exciting new frontier of travel in China, Lhasa and Tibet, and the gateway to one of the nation's most extraordinary Buddhist relics, the Grand Buddha at Leshan.

The city itself features another remarkable but more contemporary relic, a towering, centrally located statue of the Great Helmsman of the Chinese Revolution, Mao Zedong. Chengdu also has a somewhat important link with the post-Maoist society as well: Its province was the birthplace of Deng Xiaoping, who steered China to its current prosperity after the death of Mao.

General Information

Dragonair ((28) 675-5555 is in the lobby of the Sichuan Hotel (see below). **China Southwest Airlines (** (28) 666-5911 is opposite the Jinjiang Hotel on Renmin Nanlu.

The best branch of the **Bank of China** for changing money is next to the Jinjiang Hotel.

There is a **Consulate General of the United States (** (28) 558-3992 at 4 Lingshiguan Lu, which is on the fourth sector of Renmin Nanlu.

Getting Around

Chengdu is flat, spaciously laid out and thus a good bicycling town. Unlike many Chinese cities today, where motorcycles are rapidly replacing bicycles, antipollution laws in Chengdu mean that the majority of people still get around by pedal-power. Bicycles can be rented at a number of places close to the Traffic Hotel (see below). Taxis are easy to flag down, though not much English is spoken by drivers.

What to See and Do

The first stop on any sightseeing tour around Chengdu is the five-story **Exhibition Hall**, a giant department store, and the towering **statue of Mao Zedong** that looms over the city's busiest traffic circus at the junction of Renmin Nanlu and Renmin Xilu/Renmin Donglu north of the Jinjiang Hotel. From there you can bicycle over to the **Wuhou Temple**, which is in the southern suburb of Nanjiao across the Jinjiang River (or Nanhe as this part of the river is also called) to the southwest of the Jinjiang Hotel. Built in honor of Zhuge Liang, a brilliant military strategist and advisor to Emperor Liu Bei of the Three Kingdoms Period (AD 220–265), the temple features the tombs of both men, several shrine halls built in the much more recent Qing dynasty and a nearby lake and parkland with pavilions and a pleasant tea house.

Another pleasant temple park is **Wanjiang Lou (River Viewing Pavilion)**, which is dedicated to the Tang dynasty poetess Xue Tao and lies to the southeast near Sichuan University. Five kilometers (three miles) to the west of the city center, following the road from Xinximen, you can reach the famed **Thatched Cottage of Du Fu**, where one of the most illustrious poets of the Tang reign retired after serving in various official posts and wrote some 240 melancholic works that summed up his most vivid impression of all those years of official duties — the suffering of the people.

If you venture beyond Chengdu's western gate, heading north to the Ximen Bus Station, cross a creek and then turn left into the back streets, you'll find the **Temple of Wang Jian**, a Tang dynasty general who proclaimed himself emperor of Shu in the tenth century. The central coffin chamber has interesting wall carvings of female musicians,

dancers and musical instruments of that era, along with jade tablets, imperial seals and a carved stone portrait of Wang Jian himself.

Another popular spot is the **Wenshu (God of Wisdom) Monastery** which was built in the Tang reign and reconstructed in the seventeenth century and features a striking Tibetan Buddha image. Wenshu is worth a visit not only for its architecture and relics but also for a busy tea house within the grounds and the religious street life that goes on around its gates, with stalls loaded with devotional joss sticks, candles and fireworks.

If you have time to make a day of it, you could also bicycle about 18 km (11 miles) to the northeast of the city, out along Jiefang Beilu to the

Baoguang Si (Temple of Divine Light). It's a big monastery, founded in the ninth century and featuring a Qing dynasty Arhat Hall housing 500 clay sculptures of Buddhist immortals, including the Qing emperors Kangxi and Qianlong. Among the other treasures and relics there you'll find a Burmese white jade Buddha, paintings and calligraphy from the Ming and Qing reigns and a stone tablet engraved with hundreds of Buddha images.

Most of these cultural attractions — and others such as the ancient **Dujiangyan Irrigation System** (from the third century BC), 50 km (31 miles) northwest of Chengdu — are included in one- and two-day organized tours offered by CITS at the Jinjiang Hotel. Their tours also cover three popular destinations outside Chengdu: the **Su Dongpo Mansion** in Meishan, the mountain **Emeishan**,

A mechanical dragon breathes "fire" at Chongqing New Year fair.

and one of China's most remarkable sights — the monolithic **Grand Buddha** at Leshan.

About an hour north of Chengdu (minibuses leave from in front of Chengdu railway station) is the town of Guanghan, home to the **Sanxingdui Museum** (9 AM to 5 PM, daily) . Covering an area of 4,000 sq m (4,780 sq yards), the museum exhibits the somewhat mysterious yields of a discovery first made in 1929 of an ancient burial pit loaded with ancient bronzes. The creators of these artifacts — most of them quite unlike those of other archeological finds in China — have been identified as the Shu Kingdom, which is thought to have flourished in Sichuan from around 1600 to 1000 BC. Of particular interest are the jade and bronze

masks, grimly frowning visages some of which have an almost Egyptian appearance. Some controversy has arisen around the finds in the Chinese world, regarding the extent to which they can be claimed as part of the Han historical legacy, though you will find no hint of this at the museum itself.

Where to Stay

LUXURY

The **Holiday Inn Crowne Plaza** ((28) 678-6666 FAX (28) 678-9789, 31 Zongfu Jie, is Chengdu's most luxurious hotel, and not only features the full complement of Holiday Inn amenities but also has a superb location in the center of town. Also recommended is the **Sheraton Chengdu Lido** ((28) 676-8999 FAX (28) 676-8888, 15 Renmin Zhonglu, Section 1, a new 402-room hotel with a spa, fitness center, indoor heated pool and business center.

Chengdu's oldest luxury hotel, the **Jinjiang Hotel** ((28) 558-2222 FAX (28) 558-1849, 36 Renmin Nanlu, Section 2, is not quite up to the standards offered at the Holiday Inn and the Sheraton, but it has a good location and some history, having hosted foreign guests since the pioneering days of China's open-door policy. The drawback of this vast, modern complex with Chinese, Western, and Korean restaurants, a business center, nightclub, and swimming pool, is that it lacks a personal touch.

MID-RANGE

The **Sichuan Hotel** ((28) 675-5555 FAX (28) 678-5741, 31 Zongfu Jie, is a good mid-range hotel with a good location. It's popular with business travelers, but also offers tours and other travelers' services. For something less expensive, the **Jing Rong Hotel** ((28) 333-4472 FAX (28) 333-2285, 108 Erhuan Beilu, up near the railway station, manages to provide reasonably comfortable doubles from around US$40. Amenities are limited to a business center and a restaurant, but the spacious doubles more than compensate for the lack of other conveniences.

INEXPENSIVE

Like the nearby Jinjiang Hotel, in the luxury bracket, the **Traffic Hotel** ((28) 555-1017 FAX (28) 558-2777, 77 Jinjiang Road, is something of an institution. Amazingly, the hotel has not renovated and transformed itself into a business-class hotel. Rather it offers spotless rooms and friendly service at rates that keep budget travelers happy — the doubles with attached bathrooms and satellite television are a bargain.

Where to Eat

Like Guangzhou, Chengdu is celebrated China-wide for its restaurants. Indeed, it is the best place in China — and thus the world — to sample Sichuan's justly celebrated cuisine.

Sichuan food is known mostly as the spicy arm of Chinese cuisine, but this is only part of the story. It is in fact a diverse cuisine, and has a whole armory of delicious (and occasionally mouth-numbing) sauces with which it converts the edible into the delectable. One special treat is Sichuan duck, which in many ways is more sophisticated than its Beijing counterpart. Sichuanese chefs have developed dozens of ways of preparing duck without the fat and grease of the Beijing variety, a famous recipe being Zhangcha duck (*zhangcha ya*), the masterpiece of a Qing dynasty chef, in which tea, camphor leaves and cypress twigs are used to flavor the skin and flesh. Another popular recipe is roast duck with a jelly made from the root of a taro. Yet another is savory and crisp duck in which the bird is first soaked in salt water, then smoked, steamed and fried and seasoned with prickly ash.

One of Chengdu's great attractions is the fact that the streets teem with snack shops and hole-in-the-wall restaurants that serve up the best of Sichuan cuisine at budget prices. Not much — if any — English is spoken in such places, however, and if you are only just finding your way into Chinese cuisine, it's probably a good idea to stick with the hotel restaurants initially. All the top hotels in town have outstanding Chinese restaurants, but the place to go is the twenty-first floor **Skyline Terrace** ((28) 558-3333 at the Minshan Hotel, 53 Renmin Nanlu. Combining a terrific view with dishes prepared by some of Sichuan's best chefs, the terrace is popular with both visitors to Chengdu and well-off locals.

Chengdu's most famous restaurant is the **Chengdu Restaurant** at 134 Shandong Dajie. In the comfortable dining area upstairs, you'll find an English menu that guides you through most of the Sichuan repertoire. Some favorites you might consider trying include *gongbao jiding* (chicken, chilies and peanuts), *guoba roupian* ("crispy rice" and pork), *mapo doufu* (bean curd, chilies and pork — the quintessential Sichuan dish, say some), *yuxiang qiezi* (fish-flavored eggplant) and of course the aforementioned duck.

Sichuan is also renowned for its snacks — though this reputation is eclipsed in the West by Cantonese *dim sum*. **Long Chao Shou Special Restaurant** ((28) 667-6345, 8 Chunxi Nanlu, is the best place in town to sample Sichuan snacks. Established in 1940, the restaurant has three floors and seating for up to 1,500 people. The sampler courses, which allow you to graze at random through the Elysian fields of Sichuan budget snack heaven, are a filling bargain at around US$2.

Another famous restaurant is **Chen Mapo Doufu** ((28) 776-9737, opposite Culture Park (Wenhua Gongyuan) on the corner of Xiyi Huanlu and Qingyang Zhengjie, which is said to be the home of *mapo doufu*, perhaps Sichuan's most famous dish. The restaurant has been running since Qing dynasty times and if its claims are to be believed the recipe for its *mapo doufu* is unchanged. The third floor is less rowdy than the lower floors.

For excellent Peking duck, the aptly named **Beijing Roast Duck** ((28) 665-0482, 20 Zongfu Lu, opposite the Holiday Inn, is highly recommended. Strong on ambiance, the serving staff dress in Qing dynasty robes. Reservations are recommended, as the restaurant is very popular with local diners.

Lastly, no trip to Chengdu is complete without a visit to a Sichuan tea house, as much an institution here as the pub is in Britain. Known as *chadian*, you will see them all over Chengdu, but mostly in parks. Just look for the tatty bamboo furniture and the clusters of animatedly gesticulating oldies. The **Renmin Teahouse** in the middle of Renmin Park is the biggest in town and a treat. Tea comes in bottomless pots and costs next to nothing.

Nightlife

The fourth section of Renmin Nanlu is the place to take a look at Chengdu's lively nightlife scene. The **Racing Club** ((28) 553-9772, 12-1 Renmin Nanlu, Section 4, is the most popular on the strip, and usually has an interesting mix of expats and locals. The nearby **Santa Barbara** ((28) 557-2632 is also popular, and a good place to rub shoulders with locals.

The **Jinjiang Theater** on Huaxing Zhengjie provides visitors with a fabulous opportunity to see Sichuan opera, or *chuanju*. Some hotel tours will even arrange a backstage visit, an opportunity not to be passed up on any account.

How to Get There

You can reach Chengdu from all directions by air, with direct flights from Beijing, Guangzhou, Chongqing, Kunming, Guilin, Nanjing, Shanghai, Wuhan, Xi'an and Lhasa and Hong Kong. You can get there directly by train from Xi'an, Lanzhou and Beijing, and from Chongqing. (See LIJIANG, page 160, for information on the overland route between Sichuan and Yunnan provinces.)

LESHAN

Once a sleepy little town with a long history, Leshan has joined China's go-go race to economic reform and is now a small modern city graced with office blocks and traffic problems. Who can blame it? After all, Leshan has one of the world's most impressive man-made sights, and with all those visitors — domestic and foreign alike — flocking in, one likes to look one's best.

Leshan dates back to the Tang reign and is set alongside sweeping river flats at the confluence of the Min, Qingyi and Dadu rivers about 165 km (102 miles) south of Chengdu. In the eighth century it was decided that something had to be done to

OPPOSITE: A huge sleeping Buddha dominates the cave sculptures at Baoding, near Dazu. ABOVE: The Grand Buddha at Leshan — "so immense that 100 people can congregate on his head."

control the dangerous torrents at this river meeting place and a monk named Haitong suggested that only a monumental spiritual force could possibly tame the waters. The result is the awesome 71-m (233-ft) sitting Buddha carved into the face of Mount Lingyun, right across the waters from Leshan.

The Grand Buddha

The Dafo (Grand Buddha) is so immense that 100 people can congregate on his head. You could fit a couple of football teams on his toes. When first built he was painted and gilded with gold leaf and a 13-story pavilion, or "Buddha House," protected him from the elements. That shelter was destroyed during the Ming dynasty, and since then the monolith has been totally exposed—but saved from serious erosion by an ingenious internal drainage system. You can climb all over the statue, view it from the Grand Buddha Temple along-

side its head, or take a ferry trip from the Leshan Pier which will give you astonishing perspectives of its size from the river.

Much work has been carried to ensure that Dafo does not collapse due to soil erosion. An accumulation of water on his left side caused him to begin to "bloat" in the 1990s. Entered into the UNESCO heritage listing in 1996, Chinese and foreign experts have been working to make sure he does not "bloat" any further (or worse still, take a tumble into the river at his feet). It seems that work has done its job, and it's unlikely that views of the immense Buddha will be marred by unsightly scaffolding as they were often in the late 1990s.

Two-day package tours are widely available in Chengdu. These allow you an hour and a half at the Grand Buddha before rushing you on to the Su Mansion at Meishan followed a lot of hiking an overnight stop and at Mount Emei. You'd be better off doing the trip on your own and

overnighting at Leshan. With more time on your hands you can study one of the world's greatest religious monuments from all angles, in your own good time.

Where to Stay

In town, top of the range is the **Jiazhou Hotel** ((833) 213-9888, 8 Baita Jie, a smart hotel with pleasant river views. The **Taoyuan Hotel** ((833) 213-1811, Bijiang Lu, is the most popular spot with budget travelers.

How to Get There

Buses do the trip from Chengdu to Leshan in as little as three hours, leaving from Chengdu's Xinnanmen bus station, next to the Traffic Hotel. Trains take around four hours. Buses to Chongqing take around 10 hours — you would probably be better off to go back to Chengdu and travel to Chongqing from there.

EMEISHAN

Emeishan is one of China's four Buddhist sacred mountains, and has been a pilgrimage destination for well over a millennium. For those with the endurance for a couple of days of steep climbing, this is an exciting opportunity to join thousands of Chinese in a celebration of old myths about the sacredness of mountains and the aesthetic of the views they offer. Some 30 (reduced from an original of 150) temples and monasteries provide simple accommodation along the way.

Come prepared with warm clothes and sturdy boots if you're planning to climb Emei, particularly between October and April, when temperatures can plummet. Even in summer, it can be very cold on the summit, which is close to 3,000 m (9,850 ft).

Access is via **Emei Town**, and true pilgrims begin their ascent from the nearby **Baoguo Temple**. Given that this route involves a demanding three-day round trip, most foreign visitors start with a minibus to **Qingyin Pavilion**, from where you are looking at 10 hours of climbing to get to the **10,000 Buddha Summit**, via **Wannian Temple**, **Xixiang Pond**, **Jieyin Hall** and the **Golden Summit**. At Jieyin Hall you can cheat by taking a short cable-car ride up to the summit, saving yourself two hours of hard slog. This is what you may have to do if you want to get up to the summit in one day. Dedicated cheaters can take a minibus all the way to Jieyin Hall, jump into the cable-car and arrive at the summit refreshed and ready for the descent.

The popular descent route is identical to the ascent as far as Xixiang Pond, making the cable-car option a sensible one for at least one leg. After the pond, the descent veers west to **Xi'anfeng Temple**, from where it's around four hours to Qingyin Pavilion. At Jieyin Hall, you have the option of taking a minibus back down to Emei Town if you have run out of puff.

How to Get There

Emei Town is just 30 km (19 miles) from Leshan, and minibuses between the two are frequent. Both also have railway stations, which means that it is possible to catch a train to one, bus on to the other and catch another train back to Chengdu. Note, though, that buses run between Chengdu and Leshan in just three hours.

At Leshan, visitors flock to the feet of the astounding 71-meter-tall (230-ft) Grand Buddha that towers over the Min River.

Tibet

TO PAY A VISIT TO TIBET is to step through a portal from the materialism of the modern age into a society which is still, to a large extent, ruled by deep medieval spiritual impulses. Tibet is transcendental — even the main route to Lhasa by air from Chengdu is a journey toward the heavens, soaring upward over the vast and awesome snow-tipped ranges of the Tibet–Qinghai Plateau to touch down in a dusty valley three kilometers (two miles) above sea level.

Tibet is also vividly hued compared with the far more mundane revolutionary character of the Chinese "lowlands" — a sudden blaze of tribal costume, coral and turquoise beadwork, gilded temple roofs, garish gods and demons, fluttering

by China, India, Nepal, Myanmar (Burma), Sikkim and Bhutan, and it is mostly mountainous, very sparsely inhabited, has few serviceable roads and no railway. And it has a climate in which the temperature can fall to freezing point on mountainsides even at the height of summer and plunge to minus 40°C (minus 40°F) in winter, bringing heavy snowfalls that block the mountain passes and make many areas more isolated than ever.

Its main travel artery is the bumpy highway that runs west from Lhasa to Shigatse and then cuts south to the border with Nepal. Another key mountain road carries on from Shigatse and skirts the Himalayas, following the western border, around the holy mountain of Kailash,

prayer-flags, spinning prayer-drums, silver and brass and rich golden yak butter, priests in flowing crimson robes, lamas in deep maroon, saffron and yellow — and through the seemingly incessant whirl of color, the mournful squeal and rumbling bellow of temple pipes and horns.

For centuries, Tibet was isolated, almost inaccessible, a forbidden citadel hidden in the eaves of the very roof of the world. Today it is the most coveted of all the tourist destinations in China, the place where just about every China traveler wants to go.

THE LAND AND THE PEOPLE

There is a striking incongruity about Tibet — that its people are so warm and welcoming and yet its geography so inhospitable. It covers an area of close to 750,000 sq km (290,000 sq miles) bordered

before pausing in Ali and heading north to Yecheng and Kashgar in the Xinjiang Uygur autonomous region. Lhasa is also linked with the "lowland" by a road that runs to Golmud in Qinghai province.

The Tibetan people are believed to be of mixed Mongoloid-Turkic lineage. Before the arrival of Buddhism, Tibetan armies rampaged through Turkestan, Pakistan, Nepal and even China, at one time overrunning the Tang dynasty capital of Chang'an (contemporary Xi'an). But when Buddhism arrived it took hold with a vengeance, so that by the tenth century the Tibetans had gone from being a warlike, much-feared race to being a nation of monasteries, a people ruled by monks.

OPPOSITE: Bon Animism and Buddhist refinement are combined in a Potala Palace wall hanging.
ABOVE LEFT: A beaded market woman.
RIGHT: A tribeswoman prays at Lhasa temple.

The evolution of the various Buddhist sects that contend (mostly peacefully) in Tibet is very complex. It's enough to say that by the seventeenth century the Dalai Lamas of the Gelugpa order had become the most revered incarnate lamas in all Tibet. Today's Dalai Lama is the fourteenth, and he is adored by his people as a God King. He fled Tibet in 1959, during an unsuccessful uprising by the Tibetan people in protest at the Chinese occupation of their country. The Chinese had marched into Tibet and "liberated" it in October 1950, shortly after the Communist Party finally came to power.

Under Chinese military rule most of the country's 4,000 monasteries were shut down and the monkhood disbanded. Nowadays,

life, and death rites, from all other Buddhist schools of thought.

For more than two decades after the Chinese takeover, Tibetan religion was virtually driven underground. But in the current liberalization it is beginning to flourish again, and starting from early 1986 the regular "summonses" of the various sects and temple festivals have been restored in Lhasa and throughout the mountain domain. There is still a running rivalry between the occupying Chinese and Tibetan independence groups, though, as the riots in 1988 violently proved, and travelers are warned that this tension could close the region to visitors at various times.

monasteries are reopening the length and breadth of the land. The Beijing government would even like to see the Dalai Lama return, and have in fact renovated his private apartments in the Potala Palace in Lhasa, but there appears to be little chance of this former religious monarch regaining any real measure of power.

BUDDHISM AND BON

Tibetan Buddhism, or lamaism, was bonded onto a form of animism called Bon, which ruled Tibetan spiritual life in ancient times. Some of its imagery and ritual have been absorbed quite comfortably into the Buddhist practices — spirit and demon worship, prayer-flags and offerings to the guardian spirits of mountain passes, for instance — adding the color, reverence and mystique that distinguish its ceremony and monastic

GETTING TO TIBET

There have never been any easy answers when it comes to travel around Tibet. In theory, of course, the Chinese government is much in favor of tourism up on the high plateau, but on the other hand, they take a dim view of individual travelers spending long periods of time in Tibet, particularly when there's the risk that they'll make disaffected Tibetan friends and come away sympathizing with the Tibetan plight, which is just the opposite of what the Chinese government wants tourists to do. The idea, essentially, is to cash in on Tibet's ethnic appeal and show tourists Tibetans who look happy about life in the New Tibet. Obviously, when protests occur on the streets of Lhasa, Tibet-bound tours can end up stranded in Chengdu and Kathmandu.

As for tours versus individual travel, the official position is "no individual travelers." For all that, individual travelers have been going to Tibet for over 10 years, and will probably continue to do so. The catch is, no matter where you enter from these days, you will probably have to join a "tour" if you want to get a ticket into Tibet. In both Chengdu and Kathmandu (the two most popular access points for Lhasa), it's not possible to buy an air ticket unless you are on a tour. Adventurous travelers departing for Lhasa from Kathmandu can get around this problem by getting a China visa before they arrive in Nepal. Armed with a Chinese visa, it's possible to march up to the border at Kodari and walk over into Tibet.

HEALTH

Attractive and challenging as Tibet is, any plan to visit the country must take health into account. Because of the high altitude it is definitely no place for anyone with a heart condition, anemia or any other form of chronic ill-health. Elderly people, particularly, should think twice about risking it. Even young, healthy visitors are affected by the 4,000-m (13,100-ft) altitude, the most immediate symptoms being a slight shortness of breath, an initial sense of lightheadedness and a gradually consuming lethargy. On a long bicycle ride or a trudge up the endless stone stairways leading into the Potala, all these symptoms come together in panting exhaustion and headaches if frequent rest stops are not made along the way.

Some people, young or old, suffer a more severe form of altitude sickness, with headaches

and chronic nausea caused by an insufficient supply of oxygen to the brain. Altitude sickness strikes at random, and whether you come down with it or not will depend on your own metabolism. It can often be eased with aspirin and a period of complete rest, but if it persists and is extremely debilitating there's only one cure — get a plane back down to the "lowlands."

Otherwise, the simplest way to cope with it is to always take things easy, attempt only one major excursion or errand a day, drink plenty of tea, and if you wake up gasping for breath in the middle of the night don't panic — it's just your brain changing your pattern of breathing to suit the high-level conditions. Just go back to sleep and await the sun's nine o'clock alarm call.

LHASA

A visit to the sacred Tibetan city of Lhasa is a highlight of any China tour. Lhasa is so utterly different from anything you will have experienced before that its sights and smells will stay with you for the rest of your life. It is very easy to spend a week, acclimatizing to the altitude and slowly taking in Lhasa's many sights.

GENERAL INFORMATION

The **Bank of China** is at 13 Linkor Lu. Air tickets are sold at **CAAC (** (891) 683-3446 on Nyangrain Lu. For overland travel bookings, small, privately run travel agents are legion in the old quarter of Lhasa, and are the best places to make bookings.

GETTING AROUND

You'll find that the street map of Lhasa is dominated by two main arteries. **Beijing Lu** runs east–west right through the heart of the new and old sections of the city, linking the Potala with the newer tourist hotels and, five kilometers (three miles) to the west of the city, the famed Drepung Monastery. To the east it links the post office with the main bazaar and pilgrim's path, the Barkhor, the holiest of all Tibet's temples, the Jokhang, and, beyond them, the most popular low-priced Tibetan guesthouses and restaurants.

To the north, starting from the rear of the bus station, **Jiefang Beilu** runs into dusty wastelands beyond the Sports Complex toward another huge religious center, the Sera Monastery. South of the city, the Lhasa River trickles and bubbles east to west over wide, flat pebbled beds and sand banks. Beyond the river, further south, the city is guarded by a high, sharply sculptured mountain range which acts as a kind of natural clock, or regulator of the rhythm of tourist life. In winter, for example,

A tribesman carries dried mutton for sale in Lhasa bazaar.

when the night air is absolutely frigid, only the brave or most brazen visitor stirs and moves from the bedcovers before the dot of 9 AM, when the sun blasts over the range and begins softening the bitter chill.

Unless you're staying in one of the high-priced tourist hotels east of the Potala, there's only one readily available form of transport in Lhasa — a bicycle. The city is flat and, despite the fact that there is a lot more traffic on the roads today than there was a few years ago, it is easy to get around once you have acclimatized to the altitude.

WHAT TO SEE AND DO

Lhasa's main cultural attractions are involved with its religious life, so agenda planning often begins with finding out about "events" at the local temples and monasteries. Because of the long suppression of religious activity, the full religious calendar is only now being slowly restored, and "events" can often be announced only days before they are about to happen. But if a temple is opening up for a day of worship by pilgrims, or if new lamas are being chosen or inducted, or if a new *thangka*, or sacred tapestry, is being unveiled, word quickly buzzes around the tourist community (see ALL ROADS LEAD TO LHASA, page 26 in TOP SPOTS).

First, though, any new arrival needs an immediate immersion course in the Tibetan social and cultural character, and the place to get this is in the **Barkhor**, where you find the main bazaar and a bustling and picturesque rabbit warren of streets that form a sacred pilgrim's path around the Jokhang Temple. The **bazaar** is a crowded, kaleidoscopic whirl of friendly faces, the stunned expressions of out-of-towners, "Honest Joe" bead and artifact traders and colorful costumed tribespeople from all over the country — their mahogany faces so hauntingly reminiscent of another time and another culture that the entire pageant looks like a massive gathering of the North American Indian nations.

The Jokhang

As for the Jokhang Temple, it is the sacred spot around which everything else revolves. Built in the seventh century by King Songsten Gampo, a fierce military campaigner and the founding father of Buddhism in Tibet, it is the nation's holiest shrine and contains its most revered religious relic, a gilded and bejeweled image of Sakyamuni Buddha. The Jokhang is beautiful and fascinating, its roof laden with gilded bells, birds, beasts, dragons and two deer holding the Buddhist Wheel of Dharma. Its forecourt is usually packed with worshipers either prostrating before the doors or lighting fragrant juniper in a tall hearth to please the gods. Inside,

among its shrine halls and relics, a vast gallery of brass prayer-drums spin in unison as the lines of faithful file through.

The area in front of the Jokhang was once part of the walled precincts of the Old City. Now it's been cleared and turned into a wide pedestrian square, flanked by crafts and provisions stores, and is the city's main social hub. Several cafés with rooftop seating have set up shop on the square, and there can be few more pleasurable ways to while away a late afternoon than sitting in one of these places, sipping tea and gazing out across the square at the Jokhang.

The Potala

The Potala Palace dominates all cultural sightseeing in Lhasa. It's such a magnificent structure that you could spend days studying it from all angles and in all weather and lighting before actually going inside. In the morning it blazes with gold in

the first rays of the sun, and then, as the sun climbs higher, it settles back into white and ocher. If there's an early morning mist or dust storm about, it seems to float on a bed of clouds.

The Potala was built by the Great Fifth Dalai Lama, a military and religious strongman who ruled from 1617 to 1682. He brought the Tibetans together as one sovereign people, established the ruling supremacy of the Yellow Hats — one of the three main Buddhist sects in Tibet — and provided the Potala as the seat of Tibetan government and both palace and tomb of the Dalai Lamas for centuries to come. The section that the Great Fifth built is known as the **White Palace**, the administrative and residential section, entered from the soaring eastern stairways and huge doors above the village of **Sho** at the foot of the temple-fort.

The western half of the Potala is the **Red Palace**, the religious center, and it is packed with chapels

and shrines, golden stupas, the tombs of eight Dalai Lamas and vast libraries full of Buddhist scriptures. The entrance to this section is a massive ornate gateway at the western end of the Potala with heavy medieval wooden doors decorated with knotted yak hair left as devotional offerings by pilgrims.

The Potala is subject to irregular opening hours. Check locally on the latest hours before heading out to explore it. It would be a pity to make the long climb to the entrance in vain.

Behind the Potala you'll find **Chingdrol Chilling Park** with a pavilion called the Lukhang set in the middle of it. This was a trysting spot built by one of the black sheep of the dynasty, the Sixth Dalai Lama (1683–1706), who became so debauched that he was kidnapped and murdered by his subjects.

The magnificent Potala Palace.

The Summer Palace

Three kilometers (two miles) to the west of the Potala, you'll find **Norbulingka (Jewel Park)**, the Summer Palace. It was laid out by the Seventh Dalai Lama (1708–1757) who ascended to the throne with the backing of China's Qing dynasty and whose reign brought Tibet under Chinese control.

The park features woods and gardens, pavilions, a small zoo and palace buildings erected by several rulers, including a new palace constructed by the present Dalai Lama before he fled Tibet. The whole complex is worth a full day's visit, and is less exhausting than the Potala. One interesting section that should not be missed is the **Kasang Temple**, where you can study some 70 magnificent hanging *thangkas* depicting Buddhist stories and mandalas. A number of these fantastic weavings, some of them so big that they're draped right down the central façade of the Potala Palace during special religious events, are so treasured and revered that they're often unveiled only once every 20, 30 or even 50 years.

Drepung Monastery

Drepung (Rice Heap) Monastery, about five kilometers (three miles) west of Lhasa city, or an hour's sedate travel by bicycle, was where the powerful Great Fifth Dalai Lama resided and ruled while the Potala Palace was being built. It's a huge monastery — in its heyday it had rich estates, held sway over about 700 subsidiary monasteries, and was staffed by no fewer than 10,000 monks. Most of its high lamas fled to India with the Dalai Lama in the Chinese military crackdown.

Nowadays only a few hundred monks and novices are left there, and part of the northwestern section, the Gwoma, is in ruins. A striking aspect of any visit is the vehemence with which some of the lamas will sometimes speak of the Chinese — the monastery fared badly in the Cultural Revolution. Wandering through Drepung is like stepping through a medieval town, with narrow stone alleyways rising and winding between the monastery's main temples, colleges and chanting halls. It is rich in relics, religious and historical, and as you move from one building to another you can find huge *thangkas* and murals, gold stupas, the tombs of three Dalai Lamas, yak butter sculptures, ancient weapons and armor, garish oracle dolls and the monastery's holiest treasure, a huge gilded Buddha.

In the hills to the west of the monastery you may stumble across young lamas practicing temple pipes and long bronze trumpets that are sounded in religious rites. One of the hills, **Mount Gyengbuwudze**, is a sacred spot where on certain occasions in the summer pilgrims flock to spend the night chanting and dancing.

Again, you need to keep an ear to the ground to learn when these devotional sing-alongs are to take place.

Sera Monastery

North of Lhasa, Sera (Merciful Hail) Monastery is an easier distance to ride. It takes about half an hour to get there along Jiefang Beilu, turning off to the right before you reach the Regional Military Hospital. Founded in the fifteenth century, Sera has a reputation for rebellious behavior, and in 1947 its high lamas actually plotted to overthrow the Dalai Lama and put their own man in the Potala.

The monastery features three interesting chanting halls and a wealth of religious artwork including an image of Ayaguriba, a horse-headed demon that typifies the blending of animist Bon and Buddhist beliefs, along with a huge image of the Maitreya Buddha, rock paintings, a magnificent array of murals in its Drezame chanting hall and its holiest relic, an image of the many-handed, many-eyed Bodhisattva Chenrezi — Tibet's version of the Avalokitesvara of India and China's goddess of mercy, Guanyin.

In the hills to the west of Sera the maps pinpoint a spot called the **Sky Burial Site**, a place upon which fierce debate is centered among the traveling community in Lhasa. It's where the traditional Tibetan funerals take place, the bodies broken up and cast among vultures and other scavengers to be picked clean. This practice, gruesome as it may seem to outsiders, is necessary because the frozen ground won't allow normal burial and fuel is too scarce for elaborate cremations. It has taken on a spiritual significance over the centuries, representing a fundamental principle of the Tibetan death ceremonies — that the spirit is sacrosanct and the earthly body means nothing.

The debate is whether it should be regarded as a tourist attraction or not. If the answer is not immediately obvious, the *domdens*, or body breakers, settle the matter quite effectively: Unwanted visitors are chased off in no time.

Street Sights

Aside from the color and splendor of its monasteries, Lhasa offers a few cultural sideshows that should not be missed — the **Moslem Mosque** in the heart of the Islamic Old Quarter south of the Banak Shol, for instance, and the **Lhasa Carpet Factory**, the biggest rug weaving center in Tibet, to the southeast of the city near the University of Tibet.

ABOVE and BELOW: Rooftop apartments of the Potala Palace, the former stronghold of the Dalai Lamas, now a vast museum of palace treasures, chapels and shrines, libraries and tombs of eight supreme rulers.

If you're interested in medicine, go along to the **Tibetan Traditional Hospital**, on Renmin Lu just west of the Jokhang Temple, which practices the complex folk-science of Tibetan medicine based on herbal treatments, astrology, acupuncture, moxibustion and even the Buddhist sutras. One interesting fact is that it forbids surgery: It was banned "forever" in the ninth century when the mother of the ruler of that time died during what must have been a primitive and agonizing operation.

WHERE TO STAY

Luxury

Formerly managed by the Holiday Inn group, the **Lhasa Hotel** ((891) 632-4509 FAX (891) 633-5796, 1 Minzu Lu, is still Lhasa's top hotel, and seemingly little changed from the Holiday Inn days. The management here do a remarkable job with very limited resources. The hotel has over 480 rooms and suites, all of them fitted with satellite television, air-conditioning, international dial-direct phones and, of course, essentials such as 24-hour hot water and even oxygen.

The only other hotel in Lhasa where it's possible to stay with some degree of luxury is the **Tibet Hotel** ((891) 633-6784 FAX (891) 633-6787, 221 Beijing Xilu, which is close to the Lhasa Hotel. It is a poor second to the Lhasa Hotel, however, and has for many years been the source of complaints about faltering service standards and other problems.

Mid-range

Lhasa scarcely has any mid-range hotels. The only places in town that qualify are soulless, drafty places, and most travelers who aren't in the Holiday Inn or the Tibet Hotel opt to go downmarket and stay in one of the more hospitable and atmospheric Tibetan-run hotels, notably the Yak Hotel (see below), which has some excellent value mid-range rooms done in Tibetan style.

The **Genguan (Gang-Gyan) Hotel** ((891) 633-7666 FAX (891) 633-5365, 81 Beijing Donglu, is not exactly a shining exception to this rule, but it does have an excellent location close to Barkhor Square, and the air-conditioned standard doubles are tastefully appointed. The hotel's major drawback is that it lacks character.

Inexpensive

If you're young at heart, the only place to be is in one of budget hotels in the old Tibetan quarter of Lhasa.

For many years now, the most popular hotel in Lhasa has been the **Yak Hotel** ((891) 632-3496 on Beijing Donglu, not far from the Barkhor. It has a wide range of rooms, from inexpensive dorms to "luxury" rooms with attached bathrooms (the supply of water here is erratic, particularly once

winter arrives). The main attraction is not so much the rooms — decorated with Tibetan motifs — as the big courtyards lined with sofas, where young travelers sun themselves by day and chat and strum guitars during the evenings.

The **Banak Shol** ((891) 632-3829, on Beijing Donglu just down the road from the Yak, has been catering to Westerners' Tibetan fantasies nearly as long as individual travelers have been making their way to Tibet — old-timers reminisce about it and sigh that it isn't what it once was, but the Banak Shol is still an atmospheric warren of courtyards and corridors, wobbly flights of stairs and precarious ladders. It even has some mid-range rooms with attached bathroom these days.

The **Snowlands** ((891) 632-3687 has been surviving on the same formula for more than a decade — cheap rooms, dinghy shared toilets, not always reliable water supply, but always beaming smiles from the staff. Some repeat visitors to Lhasa would stay nowhere else. The views of the Jokhang from the upper floors of the hotel are delightful.

WHERE TO EAT

Traditional Tibetan cuisine is very bland: salted tea mixed with yak butter and *tsampa* (a barley flour), dried yak meat and mutton, cheese and yogurt were long the staples of these hardy mountain people. Tourism and the arrival of large numbers of Han Chinese have changed all that, and Lhasa nowadays has plenty of good food.

The best restaurants in town are all at the **Lhasa Hotel**. The evening buffet featuring Indian and Tibetan cuisine at the **Gya Sey Kang Restaurant** is not to be missed. The decor is sumptuous, and the musical show is a rare opportunity to hear Tibetan performers. Full marks are reserved too for the **Hard Yak Café**, where yak burgers and French fries are featured on a menu that does commendable job of satisfying Western cravings with the resources at hand.

Some of the best authentic Tibetan cuisine in town can be found at the **Lhasa Kitchen**, a restaurant that tries perhaps a little too hard on the decor front but is consistently popular for its meals. It's next door to the Yak Hotel on Beijing Donglu.

and Lhasa. Nothing about getting to Tibet is easy, and if you've made it this far the bumpy two-hour bus journey will seem a fitting final hurdle.

The only viable overland routes to Lhasa are by bus from Golmud or Kathmandu. Alternative routes from Yunnan and Sichuan are strictly forbidden by the authorities, and travelers who attempt either of them will be turned back and possibly fined.

THE TIBETAN TRAIL

Beyond Lhasa, one of the world's most forbidding and yet exciting landscapes awaits the intrepid visitor to Tibet. The hinterland offers rug-

Not far away, **Tashi's**, on the corner of Beijing Donglu and Mentsikheng Lu (which leads to Barkhor Square), has long been popular with travelers. The menu is simple — most people order the chepati-like *bobi*, which comes either with meat or vegetables, or the dumpling-like *momos*. Tashi's cheesecakes are the stuff of legends.

On Barkhor Square is the **Barkhor Café**, a rooftop terrace that is better recommended for its views than its meals. It is, however, the perfect spot for a sundowner or a late afternoon milkshake.

HOW TO GET THERE

There are just a handful of points from which you can fly to Lhasa. Regular flights are available from Chengdu, Chongqing, Beijing and Kathmandu.

After arriving by air from Chengdu there's a two-hour bus ride between the Gonggar airstrip

ged adventure, breathtaking views of the Himalayas and Mount Everest and a gem-string of relatively undisturbed Buddhist wonders. Travel is arduous, accommodation and living conditions are primitive, but the rewards are well worth the struggle.

The standard overland trail from Lhasa is the Lhasa–Nepal overland route via Shigatse, Sakya, Gyantse, Tinggri, Everest Base Camp (an exciting optional extra) and Zhangmu (Kasa) on the Nepalese border.

Few travelers bother with the official CITS tour services. Clustered around the Yak and Banak Shol hotels in the Tibetan quarter of Lhasa are a growing number of private operators who can offer reasonably priced tours. The noticeboards at both

OPPOSITE: Rug seller. ABOVE: Three Tibetan pilgrim women sport spring hats and ornately silvered costumes.

of these hotels are always bristling with requests for travel companions to help share the costs on trips to dozens of destinations.

GYANTSE

Since the construction of the Lhasa–Shigatse Highway, Gyantse has become of a backwater, but that's no reason to leave it off your agenda. The old Shigatse highway, which goes via Gyantse, might be slow and potholed but it follows the edge of Yamdrok Lake, surely one of the world's most stunning sheets of turquoise water.

Gyantse itself is the closest thing you'll see to a true Tibetan town, short of traveling the

SHIGATSE

Shigatse is Tibet's second largest city and the junction for the route south to the Nepal border. It's also the traditional seat of power of the Panchen Lamas, the divine "prime ministers" of the Tibetan Buddhist hierarchy, appointed from within the city's huge **Tashilhunpo Monastery**.

One of the four greatest Buddhist monasteries in Tibet, Tashilhunpo was founded in the fifteenth century, sacked and looted by an invading army of Nepalese Gurkhas in 1791, stormed and closed down by the People's Liberation Army in 1960, yet survives today as one of the most

arduous road out west towards Mount Kailash. It also has one of Tibet's premiere attractions in the magnificent stupa temple, the **Kumbum**. Equally impressive is **Palkhor Monastery**, which has an interesting array of Buddha images. Presiding over the town is the **Gyantse Fort**, a crumbling structure on a hill top that was the site of fierce fighting between the British and Tibetans during the Younghusband Expedition of 1903.

Gyantse's dismal accommodation situation has improved little, if at all, over the years. There is only one place that can even come close to deserving a recommendation, and even then only by default — the **Gyantse Hotel** ((892) 817-2222. It does at least have 24-hour hot water, but expect little else in the way of comfort. The alternatives to the Gyantse Hotel are grim and best avoided. The best restaurants are in the newer Chinese quarter.

splendid of all Tibet's religious centers. It is famed for its immense nine-story *thangka* wall from which huge Buddhist tapestries are displayed during festivals, its 26-m-tall (85-ft) Maitreya Buddha, and the Panchen Lama's Palace, the main treasure of which is a priceless gold and silver stupa studded with precious gems. It also has its own exhibition of grotesque demons to recall the psychic horrors of Bon animism.

There are two other interesting Buddhist monasteries close to Shigatse, both built in the Mongolian style. **Shalu Monastery**, 22 km (13.6 miles) south of the city, was a center for psychic training in which lamas are said to have developed incredible paranormal powers, and some of the feats that they allegedly performed are depicted in a series of murals. **Narthang (Ladang) Monastery**, 15 km (9.3 miles) west of Shigatse, built in the twelfth century, was a leading theological center and printing house. It was almost completely destroyed by the Red Guards in the 1960s.

One other interesting center of culture is still flourishing in Shigatse, the **Silver Crafts Factory** where visitors can watch craftsmen and their young apprentices fashion traditional cups, bowls and yak-butter lamps from copper, silver and gold, working over charcoal furnaces and yak-skin bellows.

The top hotel in town is the **Shigatse Hotel** ((892) 882-2556 FAX (892) 882-1900, Jiefang Zhonglu, a cavernous place where most tour groups put up. It is a far cry from the best Lhasa has to offer, but it does at least manage to provide basic comforts for travel-weary guests.

Monastery, a Mongolian temple-fortress 26 km (16 miles) off the main highway from the Sakya River Bridge, which is 128 km (79 miles) from Shigatse. **Rongbuk Monastery**, near New Tinggri, at 5,000 m (16,404 ft) is probably the highest in the world and offers a clear view of Mount Everest; it is just six kilometers (almost four miles) below the Everest Base Camp. As for New Tinggri itself, there is a reasonably comfortable guesthouse with three-to-a-room beds and a restaurant.

Beyond New Tinggri the road climbs up through the high Lalung Leh pass and breaks through the Himalayan barrier — and from there it plunges 3,000 m (9,842 ft) over a mere

Elsewhere in Shigatse there is nowhere that is really worth recommending. The **Tenzin Hotel**, across from the market, has superb rooftop views of the Shigatse Fort, but a stay here is only for the more adventurous. Most of the rooms are dormitories and hot water is only intermittently available.

HIMALAYAN GRANDEUR

The 530-km (320-mile) stretch to the border town of Zhangmu crosses three high mountain passes, the third of which, Lalung Leh (at 5,214 m or 17,106 ft), beyond the town of **New Tinggri**, offers the grand physical and spiritual spectacle that draws almost every foreign pilgrim to Tibet — a panoramic view of the majestic snowcapped peaks of the Himalayas. On the way there are other fantastic sights, the monolithic **Sakya**

90 km (56 miles) down to the Zhangmu border crossing and the warm, lush "lowlands" of Nepal. It's a fabulous journey. If you start out early enough in the morning from New Tinggri, you will be enjoying your evening dinner in Kathmandu with memories of one of the world's most awe-inspiring journeys swimming around your head.

OPPOSITE: Jokhang Temple prayer wheels.
ABOVE: Sky Burial Site.

The Northwest

WITH THE EXCEPTION OF XI'AN, the northwest sees far fewer foreign travelers than either the southwest or coastal China, though Xinjiang has become a popular destination for backpackers. Travel in this part of China involves covering vast distances, and while flights are available for major destinations, at some point or another travelers in the northwest find themselves engaged on a gruelling bus journey. Nevertheless, for those who make the effort, the rewards are plentiful. Life is slower paced, there are far fewer people, and the northwest also provides some of China's most stunning landscapes — deserts, mountains and pristine lakes.

XI'AN

Xi'an is one of China's oldest and most illustrious cities — the capital of Shaanxi province, cultural hub of north-central China and the principal gateway to the remarkable oasis towns and cities, Islamic minorities, and Buddhist treasures of the arid northwest. It is the north-central crossroads of China, providing access by train between east and west and linking the northern and southern provinces.

The city has played a strategic role in Chinese history for more than 3,000 years. Known as Chang'an, it served as the capital for 11 dynasties covering a period of 1,100 years up to the reign of the Tang (AD 618–907). It was also the eastern terminus of the Silk Road and, lying in the path of the main Central Asian conduit into the heart of China, was a heavily fortified frontier post for several centuries.

In 1374, engineers of the Ming rule, already strengthening the Great Wall, bolstered Xi'an's defenses by tearing down and reconstructing the wall that had encircled the city since ancient times. The massive structure, 12 m (39 ft) high and 14 to 18 m (46 to 59 ft) thick and running for about 12 km (7.4 miles) around the city, still stands today and is the first vivid impression of Xi'an's historic importance that visitors get as they arrive by train.

Its historic prominence has endowed modern Xi'an with one of the greatest treasure-troves of ancient culture to be found anywhere in China, and it's given the city a new strategic role as the nation's number one tourist Mecca. In the high summer season it is packed with tour groups and, unfortunately, it is also a clamoring beehive of frantically persistent souvenir hawkers, especially at the most renowned and astonishing of all its cultural attractions — the life-size terracotta "army" of the iron man of Chinese history, Qinshi Huangdi.

A verdant riverbed contrasts with the sunbaked slopes of Turpan's Huoyan Shan (Flaming Mountains).

GENERAL INFORMATION

Northwest Airlines ((29) 426-4026 is the local arm of CAAC. Dragonair ((29) 426-2988 has an office in the lobby of the Sheraton Xi'an Hotel (see WHERE TO STAY, below).

There is a branch of the **Bank of China** at 318 Dong Dajie, but most hotels can change money.

The head office of **CITS** ((29) 526-2066 is at 32 Chang'an Beilu.

GETTING AROUND

Xi'an, flat and fairly compact (at least the section within the walls), is another city ideally suited to the bicycle. They can be rented at most of the budget hotels popular with travelers such as the Flats of Renmin Hotel on Fenghe Lu (see below).

Taxis are easy to flag down, they use meters and are inexpensive. The bus system is chronically overcrowded and best avoided if you have much luggage.

Xi'an's Xiguan airport is a long, 40-km (25-mile) drive from central Xi'an. It's best to take a CAAC bus. The taxi drivers out at the airport are a rapacious crew.

WHAT TO SEE AND DO

Xi'an is of interest in itself and for the cultural attractions that lie around its ancient walls, such as the Qinshi Huangdi Mausoleum. In Xi'an, the **City Wall** is worth more than a casual inspection, especially at its four main gates to the north, south, east and west, over which the Ming engineers built small multistory forts with firing points from which teams of archers and sappers could shower hostile forces with arrows, gunpowder bombs and blazing oil and naptha.

As for the **Bell Tower**, transplanted to the hub of the city from an earlier fourteenth-century site during the Qing dynasty, it's such a central landmark and so festooned with trolley-bus cables that you can't help but notice it every day. Before the 1949 revolution it was used as a garrison and prison by the Kuomintang nationalists. There's a smaller and more interesting **Drum Tower** just slightly to the west of it, and beyond that the fascinating **Qingzhen Si (Grand Mosque)**, one of the biggest Islamic places of worship in China. Once you've visited the mosque don't neglect to take some time out and explore the neighboring Muslim Quarter, where you'll see storeholders roasting kebabs and flat breads, and where sheep heads jostle with sweetmeats for your attention.

The **Xi'an Beilin Museum**, lying close to the old city's South Gate, is part of an old Confucian temple with exhibition halls rebuilt in the 1960s

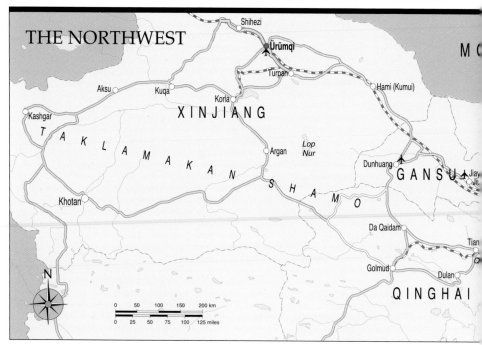

THE NORTHWEST

to the Ming and Qing architectural styles. Its three main halls are packed with relics covering the period from prehistory to the Tang dynasty, and they include terracotta horses from the Qin reign, gilded Sui dynasty Buddha images, carvings from the Warring States period and Tang pottery, figures, horses and camels.

The museum's most prized exhibit is the extraordinary Forest of Steles — 2,300 large stone tablets engraved with imperial edicts, commentaries on the classics, celebrated styles of calligraphy and other records of the ages back to Han times. One stele dated AD 781 records the appearance of the Syrian Christian school of thought, Nestorianism, which found its way to ancient Chang'an via the Silk Road.

South of the city wall there are two Tang dynasty pagodas, **Dayan (Big Wild Goose)** and **Xiaoyan (Small Wild Goose)**, the larger one built to honor the Buddhist monk Xuan Zang, who first brought the Buddhist scriptures from India to China, and to house the 1,335 volumes of translations that he spent virtually the rest of his life producing.

Farther south again is Xi'an's other important museum, the **Shaanxi History Museum**, which opened its doors in 1992. The ground floor traces the evolution of Chinese civilization from its Shang dynasty beginnings through the upstairs collections from the Zhou and Han to the side room collections from the Tang, which being the most recent are the best preserved and most interesting to the nonspecialist.

Geming (Revolutionary) Park and the nearby **Memorial Museum of the Eighth Route Army**, in the north of the city near the railway station, commemorate the communist revolutionary drive against the nationalists and the Japanese in the 1930s. It's a place of special interest to Canadians, because Norman Bethune, the Montreal medic who joined Mao's forces and became one of the most beloved foreign heroes of the communist cause, lived and worked here with Zhou Enlai and Deng Xiaoping at one stage of the campaign.

The Terracotta Warriors

The plains surrounding Xi'an are dotted with tombs, pagodas and temples, but there's really only one great attraction to make every effort to see — the **Qinshi Huangdi Mausoleum** and its terracotta army. There's also **Banpo Museum**, where you can view an interesting reconstruction of a Neolithic mud-hut hamlet and relics of that distant age — including clay jars in which children were buried — and the **Huaqing Hot Springs Resort**, a complex of baths, temples and halls in which the Qin, Han and Tang rulers languished and bathed.

The **Tomb of Qinshi Huangdi** is nothing short of awe-inspiring — the packed rows of some 1,000 life-size fully armed and armored warriors, each of them bearing the distinctive features of the men they were modeled on, standing with their horses under the sweeping roof of a protective exhibition hall. Of all the historic landmarks of the great China pilgrimage, this is perhaps the

place of deepest sanctity (see AN ARMY IN STONE, page 24 in TOP SPOTS).

SHOPPING

Xi'an is the perfect place for souvenir shopping. The vast hordes of tourists passing through ensure variety and a good turnover. Some of the tourist sights (the **Small Goose Pagoda**, for example) have selections of high quality souvenirs. The **Grand Mosque** is a good place to shop for bargains, though you must be prepared to haggle. Just east of the South Gate is an area called **Shuyuanmen**, where the shops have been given a facelift to make them resemble a scene from a Hong Kong drama set in Qing dynasty China. The result is a little tacky, but it's a good area to browse for souvenirs all the same.

The **Friendship Store**, on the corner of Nanxin Jie and Dong Dajie, is a good place to survey Xi'an's souvenir plenitude, though many of the items here can be found elsewhere around town — notably Shuyuanmen — at cheaper prices.

WHERE TO STAY

Luxury
Xi'an is an important tourist destination where you will have no problem finding luxury accommodation.

The **Hyatt Regency Xi'an** ((29) 723-1234 FAX (29) 721-6799, 158 Dong Dajie, is one of the city's best, a gleaming citadel a world apart from the rest of Xi'an. Bill Clinton chose to make the Hyatt his home while visiting Xi'an in 1998, something the hotel is a little too keen to remind guests about, but it's difficult to fault the hotel on any other count. With five top-notch restaurants, gymnasium, sauna, aerobics center, shopping and tastefully appointed rooms, it's the perfect place to wallow in luxury after a long day of sightseeing.

The **Sheraton Xi'an Hotel** ((29) 426-1888 FAX (29) 426-2188, 12 Feng Hao Lu, has 438 rooms and 16 suites. Apartments with kitchenettes are also available. Along with restaurants it has a cocktail lounge and disco, and there's an indoor heated pool and a gym.

The **Shangri-La Golden Flower Hotel** ((29) 323-2981 FAX (29) 323-5477, 8 Changle Xilu, is recommended for its spacious rooms. Doubles come with two queen-size beds, while deluxe doubles have the same, with the addition of a sofa and large writing desk.

The Holiday Inn-managed **Bell Tower Hotel Xi'an** ((29) 727-9200 FAX (29) 721-8970, on the southwest corner of the Bell Tower, is a modest affair by Holiday Inn standards, but it has the best location of any luxury hotel in town.

Mid-range
If you're staying in a mid-range or budget hotel, make it one that's inside or at least not too far outside the city walls — though you may find this advice difficult to adhere to as choices are limited. Three options are worth considering.

The **Xi'an People's Hotel** (also referred to by its Chinese name, the **Renmin**) ((29) 721-5111 FAX (29) 721-8152, 319 Dongxin Jie, is one of those sprawling Soviet-inspired guesthouses, which like most others around China these days has been blandly renovated. Rooms here are good value, though it pays to take a look at a few before making a choice — rates and standards vary according to how recently rooms have been given a facelift.

The **Jiefang Hotel** ((29) 721-2927 FAX (29) 721-2617, Railway Station Square, only just creeps in as an "inside the walls" hotel, being part of the walls. Don't expect it to be a medieval keep; it's another big Chinese hotel, but the price is right and the location directly opposite the railway station is a godsend for those early morning starts.

The **Wuyi (May Fifth) Hotel** ((29) 721-0804 FAX (29) 721-0824, 351 Dong Dajie, may not be the best hotel in town, but the location is second only to that of the Bell Tower Hotel (above), the staff are friendly, and there's a good restaurant downstairs. It's easily one of Xi'an's best bargains, though it is often full as a result — book ahead.

Inexpensive
There are just two popular budget hotels: the **Flats of Renmin Hotel** ((29) 622-7644, 9 Fenghe Lu,

which is in an isolated but not unpleasant area just west of the city walls; and the long-running **Victory Hotel** ((29) 789-3040, on the corner of Huancheng Nanlu and Yanta Lu, just south of the city walls.

The Victory has the advantage of being closer to the sights than the Renmin, but the Renmin is far and away the more popular of the two, largely due to lackadaisical service at the Victory. The popularity of the Renmin Flats, which offers both dormitory accommodation and budget singles and doubles, is also helped by the two popular restaurants across the road. Between them, they provide bicycle rental and travel advice, decent breakfasts and a constant stream of companionship.

WHERE TO EAT

Obviously, with all those four- and five-star hotels around, there's no shortage of excellent hotel restaurants. But after you've eaten your fill at the Hyatt or the Sheraton, don't forget there are some very good and reasonably priced restaurants out on the streets too.

A highly recommended evening of food and entertainment is **Tang Le Gong (Tang Dynasty)** ((29) 526-1620, Chang'an Lu, where all the dishes are based on imperial Tang dynasty recipes. To accompany the food, performances of Tang dynasty dance and music are held nightly. Reservations — essential — can be made through most hotels in town or by calling the restaurant directly.

Laosunjia ((29) 721-6828, 364 Dong Dajie, can't be recommended too highly. For those who are not spending much time in the west of China, it represents a rare opportunity to try Chinese Moslem cuisine at its best. The house specialty is the *yangrou paomo*, in which a couple of cakes of bread are laboriously "crumbed" (by you, with your fingers) into a big soup bowl, to which a broth with noodles, lamb and sauces is added, producing a delicious meal.

The huge **Xi'an Restaurant** ((29) 727-3185, 298 Dong Dajie, a short walk east of the Bell Tower,

offers cuisine ranging from Beijing duck to steak and fries in its 14 dining rooms containing 300 tables and capable of seating a total 1,800 diners. Unless you're in the market for a splash out meal, it's best to stick to the downstairs area, where they throw together tasty Chinese meals in plebeian surroundings.

The **Wuyi Restaurant**, 351 Dong Dajie, is part of the hotel of the same name. Again the downstairs section is best, but for a sit-down meal the upstairs area, specializing in the cuisine of Jiangsu, is not a bad choice.

The **Dongya (East Asia) Restaurant** ((29) 721 8410, 46 Luoma Shi, just south of the Bell Tower, is something of an institution, having been founded in 1916 in Shanghai, and brought to Xi'an in the 1950s. It has some of the best Chinese food in Xi'an. Try the *wuxi paigu* — spare ribs cooked in sweetened soy sauce.

An excellent choice for a meal is the **Sichuan Restaurant**, 151 Jiefang Lu, east of the Renmin Hotel. It doesn't look promising, but if you have an interest in China's spiciest cuisine, you will enjoy a meal here.

The locals' favorite eating places can be found in the two Muslim food quarters in the Drum Tower district. Food stalls in the **Damaishi Jie** and **Majia Shazi** open until midnight. They offer snacks like soup dumplings, fried persimmon cakes and barbecued lamb and beef.

Backpackers gather at **Mum's Home Cooking** and **Dad's Home Cooking**. Both of them are on Fenghe Lu, opposite the Flats of Renmin Hotel, next door to each other. Dad's was the pioneer, Mum's followed shortly after: Both offer tasty, inexpensive Chinese and Western food, cheap beers and useful travel information.

HOW TO GET THERE

Xi'an can be reached by air from almost any airport in China. There are also direct trains from Beijing, Shanghai, Chengdu, Qingdao and Wuhan and direct rail services in turn to Xining and Ürümqi, opening up the "wild west" of Qinghai and Xinjiang, and the route of the old Silk Road. Dragonair flies from Hong Kong.

MAIJISHAN GROTTOES

If you are traveling between Xi'an and Lanzhou by train, an extremely worthwhile diversion is the Maijishan Grottoes. The grottoes are around 35 km (22 miles) south of Tianshui, which in turn is around half way between Lanzhou and Xi'an .

Tianshui itself is an uninspiring urban sprawl that divides into the two centers: Beidao (which is where the train stops) and Qincheng (which is where buses arrive). If you time things right, there should be no need to stay overnight in either district, but there is accommodation if you need it.

Maijishan (Wheat Stack Mountain) is China's fourth largest Buddhist cave complex, built from AD 384–417. The others are at Luoyang, Datong and Dunhuang. One of the main attractions is a 16-m-tall (52-ft) Buddha, which announces itself from quite a distance before you reach the spectacular site.

The central section of the cliffs was damaged by an earthquake in AD 734, but the east and west sections (particularly the latter) contain some fine sculptures and murals. Since many of the caves are locked up, in order to get the most out of your tour you need a guide with keys. To organize an English-speaking guide, contact CITS ((938) 213-621, at the Xibing Hotel in the Qincheng district of Tianshui.

The best place to stay is in the Qincheng district rather than in the Beidao railway station area. The **Tianshui Hotel** ((938) 821-2611, on Yingbin Lu, has comfortable and good-value doubles, though it is hardly the lap of luxury. Budget travelers generally stay in the **Xihuang Hotel** ((938) 273-4700, next to next door to the railway station in Beidao. There's a choice of dormitory beds and rooms, both of which are very inexpensive, though the hotel is a fairly grotty establishment.

LANZHOU

If Xi'an is the crossroads of central China, Lanzhou, the capital of Gansu province, is its radial right arm. From this former Han dynasty garrison and frontier post there is access by rail to the heart of Qinghai province, and from there by road to Tibet. Another rail route runs directly to the old Silk Road oasis towns of the northwest, and yet another sweeps across the northern reaches of China, across the vast grasslands of Inner Mongolia, toward Beijing.

A key industrial city, Lanzhou is modern, well laid out with wide streets and boulevards, and has good hotels and department stores. It also sports a huge Beijing-style central city square (Dongfanghong, or East is Red, Square), about 10-minutes' walk west of the Lanzhou Hotel. Thousands of people meet here every day to fly kites and balloons and climb a strange and novel sightseeing tower which looks like a Moslem minaret with a children's slide winding around it.

The city's Moslem community is quite large, and it is really the first major center heading into the northwest where you can recognize the distinctive, surprisingly Middle Eastern features of the region's Turkic lineage. It also has a number of historic and cultural attractions, including an interesting set of Buddhist cave sculptures dating from the Tang dynasty.

WHAT TO SEE AND DO

Lanzhou lies on the south bank of the Yellow River. On the north bank is **Baita Shan (White Pagoda Hill)**, a hilly park with Ming and Qing dynasty pavilions and a Buddhist pagoda. A cable-car swings over there (across the river) from just west of the Zhongshan bridge.

The **Gansu Provincial Museum**, opposite the Friendship Hotel, has the skeleton of a prehistoric mammoth dug up in 1973 and an interesting array of Neolithic and Han era pottery, murals, clay and bronze figures and the revered "Flying horses" that gave the Han and Tang cavalries

the speed, mobility and endurance they needed to fight the nomadic Huns and the Turkic tribes. This is one provincial museum that is worth visiting, and English labeling is even thoughtfully provided.

The city's prime attraction is the **Bingling Si Caves**, near the hamlet of **Yongjing** on the Yellow River in Dasi Valley, a beautiful area of mountains, sheer cliffs and deep ravines. From Lanzhou the journey by bus and boat takes about six hours, but during the summer months access may not be possible because of flooding.

First dug about 1,500 years ago, one of the grottoes has an inscription that is recognized as the oldest example of cave writing in China.

OPPOSITE: Boisterous, colorful souvenirs and hawkers at the tomb of the terracotta soldiers. ABOVE: Muslims gather for prayer at Xi'an's Grand Mosque.

In the year AD 420, Buddhist monks extended the grottoes and began work on an impressive parade of carved Buddhas and other devotional art. More were added over the centuries until there were 183 caves crammed with art and relics by the time of the thirteenth-century Mongol rule. They contain nearly 700 Buddha images, including a 27-m-tall (88.5-ft) Maitreya sculpture, more than 80 clay figures and a big display of Qin and Tang dynasty murals.

WHERE TO STAY

The **Lanzhou Legend Hotel** ((931) 888-2876 FAX (931) 888-7876, 599 Tianshui Lu, is right on the Xiguan traffic circle and the best of Lanzhou's hotels. It proudly touts itself as Lanzhou's "only four-star hotel," and to be fair it does a very good job of offering upmarket comforts, though in a more Chinese than international way, its amenities including ping pong, snooker and karaoke among the usuals. The hotel's Zen Cantonese restaurant is recommended for *dim sum*.

The **Ningwozhuang Hotel** ((931) 841-6301 FAX (931) 841-7639, 365 Tianshui Lu, is that rambling institutional style of guesthouse much beloved by tea-sipping cadres back in the 1950s. Its winning feature is its extensive and leafy grounds. The rooms on the other hand vary in value for money, some of them seeming overpriced given their state of repair.

Just across from the Lanzhou Legend, and also on the Xiguan traffic circle is the **Lanzhou Hotel** ((931) 841-6321 FAX (931) 841-8608, 434 Donggang Xilu. It's probably the best overall choice of all Lanzhou's hotels for both mid-range and budget travelers, having a wide range of rooms to choose from—everything from dormitories to quite plush and excellent value doubles.

Lanzhou Mansions ((931) 841-7210, the huge block on your left as you exit the station, is another hotel that offers both budget and mid-range accommodation. The three-bed dorms with attached bathroom are good value for money, and there is also a wide selection of singles and doubles, most of which are serviceable for an overnight stay.

HOW TO GET THERE

There are direct air services to Lanzhou from most major Chinese cities and also from more minor regional destinations such as Dunhuang. There are two alternative train routes linking the city with Beijing, one sweeping over Inner Mongolia via Baotou, Hohhot and Datong, and the other cutting across the center of China via Xi'an and Zhengzhou. Direct trains to and from Shanghai also take the Xi'an-Zhengzhou route.

Which came first? A trader in Lanzhou ponders an age-old question.

XIAHE

Nine hours south of Lanzhou is the enchanting town of Xiahe with its famous **Labrang Monastery**. Often called "Little Tibet," for those who don't have time to get up to the high plateau a visit to Xiahe is a perfect second-best. Like Tibet, be prepared for some acclimatization problems: Xiahe is 2,920 m (9,580 ft) above sea level, which is more than enough to leave you short of breath and slightly insomniac for a few days.

Labrang, one of the great Gelugpa, or Yellow Hat, monasteries, is very active, even by Tibetan standards. Although the erstwhile monk population of 4,000 has been reduced by half, the monastery still has more monks than any monastery in Tibet has. They come from all over the Tibetan regions of western China — Sichuan, Qinghai, Gansu and Tibet itself. There are daily debates, and quite often you can see performances of traditional Tibetan music (which, incidentally, is unmelodic to Western ears, consisting mostly of chants and tortured blasts from enormous horns).

Don't expect luxury accommodation in Xiahe, which is quite an off-the-beaten track destination. The **Labrang Hotel** ((9412) 21849, several kilometers to the west of town, past a small Tibetan village, is furnished in Tibetan style and has a wide range of rooms, from dormitories to delightful doubles with attached bath. It has long been the most popular hotel in Xiahe with foreigners, and deservedly so.

XINING

There are daily trains from Lanzhou to Xining, the capital of Qinghai province, and the trip is short enough to take a first-class soft-seat or even venture into the hard-seat section. You'll roll along through green-swathed terraced loess landscape in summer — the ancient sculpture of the Yellow River — or, in midwinter, witness bleak scenes of dun-colored terraced mounds and hills, looming over frozen rivers and streams, mud-bricked walled compounds and villages huddle in the loess fields, the only sign of life an occasional donkey kicking its heels in the morning sun and dust, following its master out into the neat flat farming plots.

Xining started its days as a military garrison and trading center in the sixteenth century. Like the rest of Qinghai it has long been a place of exile, and even today some sources calculate that one in 10 residents of the province are either prisoners or released prisoners who cannot return to their home provinces.

Despite such grim statistics, Xining today is a fairly modern industrial city populated by an interesting mix of Han Chinese, Moslem Huis and Tibetans. Its eastern inner-city district is where you'll find the Moslem Quarter, a crowded market enclave around the picturesque Grand Mosque.

The city has long played a frontier role as a supply and provisions depot for the vast and largely inhospitable Tibet–Qinghai Plateau, which sweeps away to the west and south right to the foothills of the Himalayas. Little has changed, and today Xining is bustling city in which commerce seems to crackle in the air.

What to See and Do

Xining is not brimming with sights, but for those who have traveled here across China, the unique character of the place will be apparent immediately. There's more space here, the light is harder, the air crisper, and if you feel yourself slightly out of breath as you stroll around town, it's because you're at an altitude of 2,200 m (7,000 ft).

The chief attraction in town is the **Moslem Quarter**, with its impressive **Grand Mosque**, dating back to the fourteenth century. If you're feeling particularly energetic, you might consider climbing for about an hour up into the hills north of the Huangshui River to visit **Beishan Temple**. With around 1,400 years of history, this is an ancient place of worship, and the views of Xining from up here are fabulous. Be warned, however, it's an extremely steep climb to the temple up hundreds of stairs, and for those recently arrived to Xining's higher elevations it will be hard work. From the railway station, a No. 11 bus will take you to the foot of the hills.

Huangzhong, about 25 km (15.5 miles) to the southwest of Xining, is where you'll find the magnificent Tibetan-style **Ta'er Monastery**, one of the six greatest lamaseries of the Gelugpa, or Yellow Hat Sect (Labrang at Xiahe, above, is another). This is a good taste of what is to come in Tibet, if that is where you are headed. Note the beautiful Hall of Meditation, with its silk *thangkas*. Ta'er was built in 1560 in memory of the founder of the sect, Tsongkapa, and is famous for its ornate yak-butter sculptures of human figures, animals and landscapes.

If you can, pay a visit to the monastery early in the day. There's plenty here to keep you busy for a full day, wandering through the many halls of the monastery, hiking up around the surrounding hills for a stupendous panoramic view, and finally enjoying a hearty bowl of inexpensive noodles at one of the stalls that surround Ta'er. Buses leave from the long distance bus station across from the railway station, while minibuses leave throughout the day from the Ximen bus station in town next to the gymnasium (*tiyuguan*). The trip takes around an hour.

Where to Stay and Eat

Xining's finest is the **Qinghai Hotel** ((971) 614-4888. It's aimed mostly at business people and tour groups, and inconveniently located 10 km (six miles) from the railway station.

For a basic but clean and friendly stopover, the most popular hotel with foreigners is the **Yongfu Hotel** ((971) 814-0236, directly opposite the railway station.

Some of Xining's best dining takes place on the streets (not that you'd want to do this in the winter months, when temperatures plummet). Look out for sizzling kebabs and simmering pots of noodle broth. Around the Yongfu Hotel are several Moslem restaurants.

TO LHASA

From Lanzhou you can travel by train and bus all the way to Lhasa, crossing one of the most rugged, least-explored tourist areas of China, Qinghai province.

There are two trains a day from Xining to **Golmud** in the center of Qinghai province, where you face the bus journey from hell: anywhere from 25 to 35 hours nonstop and much of it along precipitous mountain roads. Buses also run from Golmud to Dunhuang in Gansu province, home of the Mogao Buddhist Grottoes, the most famous surviving treasures of the old Silk Road.

Golmud has just one hotel that is open to foreigners, and it's a fairly grim place where the best rooms are grotty doubles. The **Golmud Hotel** ((979) 412-066 is also home to **CITS** ((979) 412-764, which all travelers going on to Tibet are forced to do business with.

THE NEW SILK ROAD

From Lanzhou, a northwest rail route opens the door to the great garrisons, oasis towns, cities and Buddhist relics that were among the wonders of the Silk Road and have survived the ravages of time since its death. Jiayuguan is the first convenient radial point on the Lanzhou–Ürümqi railway, providing access by bus to Jiuquan, a similar outpost that was prominent in the Han dynasty's expeditions against the Xiongnu, and to Dunhuang and its fabulous Mogao Caves.

Jiayuguan

Jiayuguan was also an important Han military outpost, but it was not until the Ming dynasty that its strategic position, guarding the Jiayuguan Pass, was considered critical to the defense of the northwest frontier. The Ming emperor Hongwu bolstered the garrison by building the **Tianxia**

Xiongguan, a huge stronghold which from that point on served as the western extremity of the Great Wall. The Ming engineers were so meticulous, and their specifications so exact, that when this "Impregnable Defile Under the Heavens" was completed, only a single brick was left over. It is now proudly displayed in one of the fort's halls.

The fort is one of northwest China's most impressive sights. Be sure, too, to visit the **Overhanging Great Wall**, a reconstructed stretch of the wall. It provides wonderful views of Jiayuguan, the fort and the snowcapped mountains in the distance.

Jiayuguan's top hotel is the **Changcheng Hotel** ((937) 622-6306. It has a variety of rooms ranging from around US$30 and up. The popular **Jiayuguan Guesthouse** ((937) 622-6983 also has some "luxury" rooms that are serviceable for an overnight stay, along with inexpensive dorms budget rooms. It has a good central location opposite CAAC and the post office, and is home to CITS, which offers tours of the area's attractions.

DUNHUANG

The reason to visit this hot and dusty oasis town is its nearby **Mogao Buddhist Grottoes**, 25 km (15.5 miles) to the southeast. In these caves, all 492 of them, you can see China's best preserved cave art (over 45,000 murals) and some of the most impressive Buddhist statuary (over 2,000 items) in the whole country.

More than 1,000 caves were originally excavated here and filled with carvings, murals, clay sculptures and other artwork. The work began in the fourth century AD and continued for several centuries. The surviving grottoes are crammed with treasures: murals covering a total of 4.5 hectares (11 acres), 3,400 bas-relief and three-dimensional wall sculptures, several thousand pillars with the lotus motif and floral floor tiles, and five ornate Tang-era wooden shrines. At the turn of the twentieth century a Daoist priest broke through to a sealed grotto and came upon another 50,000 relics dating from the Jin to Song period.

This massive endeavor was started by the Turkic-speaking Toba rulers of the Northern Wei dynasty (AD 386–594) and added to in the ensuing Sui, Tang, Five Dynasties and Song reigns — each dynasty stamping its own artistic style on this amazing exhibition. The aesthetic high point was reached in the Tang reign, and the sculptures, and murals of that time reflect the dynasty's three thumb-rules to acceptable art — richness, exuberance and opulence. The Buddha images are made of clay and painted, and range in height from a few centimeters to a towering 33 m (108 ft). Among them is a huge sculpture of the Maitreya Buddha executed by Ma Sizhong between the years AD 713 and AD 741.

The Northwest

Be sure not to miss out on the Japanese-financed **Research and Exhibition Center**, which is next to the Mogao Caves parking lot. The center exhibits murals from seven different caves in lighting that makes it possible to fully appreciate the artists' work.

The Chinese are very sensitive about the Mogao Grottoes, and photography is strictly forbidden. Over a period of years from the late 1800s to the 1930s, several Western scholar-adventurers, notably the Swede Sven Hedin, the German Albert Von Le Coq, the Frenchman Paul Pelliot and Great Britain's Aurel Stein, infiltrated the paths of the Silk Road from the west and virtually ransacked its "lost" and barely surviving oasis centers,

including Dunhuang, of some of the most splendid Buddhist artwork, manuscripts and relics — an act for which the Chinese have never really forgiven the West. Read *Foreign Devils on the Silk Road* by Peter Hopkirk for a racy account of the West's plundering expeditions in what was then called Chinese Turkestan.

Dunhuang's other tourist attraction is its nearby sand dunes. **Mingsha Shan**, the "Singing Sand Dune" is almost a tourist trap nowadays, with activities such as "sand tobogganing" and paragliding taking place on its slopes. Nevertheless, the more than 200-m (655-ft) dunes here, which are said to thrum in windy weather, are an impressive sight. **Yueya Quan**, an improbable lake in the middle of the desert, is a more dubious excursion but it is close to the dunes and worth a

A Tibetan worshiper at Ta'Er Monastery near Xining.

look — historical records show it to have existed for thousands of years despite the lack of rainfall.

Where to Stay and Eat

Dunhuang's cave art has turned into such a magnet for tourism that the former dusty oasis has virtually become a resort town these days. For travelers this is surprisingly good news, in that it provides a wide range of accommodation choices.

Dunhuang's best is the **International Hotel** ((937) 882-8638 FAX (937) 882-1821, 28 Mingshan Lu, a new three-star arrival that is extremely good value. Similar in standards is the older **Dunhuang Hotel** ((937) 882-2008 FAX (937) 882-2309, 14 Yuangang Donglu. It's a sprawling affair built around a courtyard, and rooms vary slightly from wing to wing but are generally well maintained and come with international direct-dial phones.

Currently the favorite with budget travelers is the **Five Rings Hotel** ((937) 882-2620, a tidy and friendly operation next door to the bus station on Mingshan Lu. Beds are available in either spotless dormitories or in inexpensive singles and doubles with attached bathrooms.

The increasing numbers of tourists and travelers making their way to Dunhuang has led to an inevitable explosion of travelers' style cafés. While the most fun place to eat is the **Night Market** opposite Dunhuang Museum on Yangguan Donglu, where roadside stands will cook up a meal on the spot, the backpacker cafés are also good places to meet people and some offer quite tasty creations. Try **Shirley's**, next door to the Five Rings Hotel, for travelers' favorites like shakes and banana pancakes.

How to Get There

Daily flights are available all through the summer season from Xi'an and Lanzhou, and on a less frequent basis the rest of the year.

To get back on to the main Lanzhou–Ürümqi railway line, there are buses from Dunhuang to the station at Liuyuan, about three and a half hours away. From there, the path is open to the second great frontier of modern travel in China — the barren, but fascinating "wild west" of Xinjiang.

It's also possible, with permission from the local Public Security Bureau, to take a bus from Dunhuang through to Lhasa. The journey involves a change of bus in Golmud, and is a grueling expedition not to be undertaken by the fainthearted. The cost, with a permit, is around US$200.

XINJIANG–UYGUR AUTONOMOUS REGION

This is classic "great game" country, with politics, espionage, disguise, murder, mystery and intrigue. Read another of Peter Hopkirk's books, *The Great Game*, which tells with immense

readability and historic detail the importance of these desolate but strategic locations.

The Uygurs are the most numerous and most prominent of some 13 Moslem Turkic-speaking or Mongol minorities that inhabit this harsh, sun-baked region. The others include ethnic Russians, Tartars, Uzbeks, Tajiks, Xibes, Dours, Khalkhas, Kazakhs, Kalmucks (Kalmyks) and Hui in this huge melting pot of previously fierce nomadic tribal groups of Central Asia. The region itself has had a variety of names over the centuries, including High Tartary, Chinese Turkestan, Kashgaria and Serinder (the Silk Route).

Divided by the Tian Mountains into two vast desert basins, Xinjiang is one of the most

geographically hostile places on earth. In the south lies the dreaded Takla Makan — an 800,000-sq-km (308,880-sq-mile) inferno with 100-m-tall (67-ft) shifting dunes and fierce sandstorms — which in the Turkic tongue is known as the place where travelers "go in (and) don't come out." To the north lies the Gobi, which stretches up into Mongolia and, to the southwest, is another waterless sea of dunes known as the Land of Death. In the central region the desert sinks 154 m (505 ft) below sea-level to form the pitilessly hot Turpan Depression.

TURPAN

At the heart of the furnace, Turpan is the first major tourist destination on the northwest trail. This oasis town was an important link in the Silk Road, and a jewel in the Buddhist crown, until the eighth century when Islam spread from the West, its forces destroying much of the region's Buddhist statuary as they went. The town now presents an interesting contrast of the two religious influences, a key center of the Moslem Uygur culture and an access point for some of the surviving Silk Road Buddhist relics.

Turpan, though a major tourist destination these days, has one of China's harshest climates. Situated in a depression approximately 80 m (262 ft) below sea-level, the summers are blisteringly hot, frequently recording the highest temperatures in the whole country, while in the winters the thermometer often dips below zero. Locals have made an interesting effort to make the summer heat more bearable by planting nearly the whole town with vine trellises that turn the streets into a series of shady green tunnels.

Getting Around

Turpan, though flat, is one place where few feel inclined to leap onto a bicycle; the heat is soporific. For short jaunts around town, a donkey and cart is a perfect way to jolt to your destination. For longer trips, get together with a group of other travelers (there are always plenty in town) and rent a minibus for a day of sightseeing. Figure on spending around US$50 to US$60 for a minibus.

What to See and Do

The eighteenth-century Afghan-style **Emin Minaret** is a couple of kilometers (a mile and a quarter) southeast of town and is easily Turpan's most impressive sight.

Most of Turpan's other attractions lay quite a distance out of town. Notable are two ruined cities that once played prominent roles on the old Silk Road. **Gaochang**, about 46 km (28 miles) to the east of Turpan, was the capital of the Uygur state established by the Uygurs when they migrated into Xinjiang from Mongolia in the ninth century. While **Jiaohe**, 20 km (12.4 miles) west, was a Tang dynasty garrison in the wars against the Turkic tribes.

Both towns are derelict but give a clear impression of the mud-brick and rammed earth architecture of that age, and the thoroughfares and lanes, official halls, monasteries and pagodas, homes and courtyards, corridors and underground passages and thick earthen walls of what were, in fact, relatively sophisticated settlements. Underground chambers were dug below each dwelling to give shelter from the fierce daytime heat. At Gaochang you'll find the remains of a monastery with some parts of it still reasonably intact. To the northwest of Gaochang there's an ancient burial complex, the **Hastana Tombs**, with murals of some of the dead.

North of Turpan, right in the central pan of the Turpan Depression, the **Huoyan Shan (Flaming Mountains)** offer a vivid experience of the intense heat of the region. The daytime temperature on the slopes often reaches 70°C (158°F). The rock and red soil flare into shimmering "fire" when the sun strikes, hence the name. One Ming dynasty novel describes how a famous monk and his disciples were caught in the raging "fires" on the range and were saved by the Monkey King, Sun Wukong, who put out the flames with a fan so that they could continue on their way.

BEZEKLIK GROTTOES

The Turpan region's most famous attraction, the Bezeklik Grottoes about 50 km (31 miles) northwest of town are, for almost everyone who visits, a disappointment. They were cut into the western slope of Huoyan Shan in the Northern Wei period just before the rise of the Tang dynasty — 64 grottoes excavated or built of mud-brick, featuring Buddhist shrines and chambers. Nowadays they look worn, and besides, most of the finest artwork was swiped by the German Silk Road explorer, Albert Von Le Coq. The murals were shipped to the Berlin Museum, where they were destroyed by Allied bombing in World War II.

Where to Stay and Eat

The **Turpan Guesthouse** ((995) 852-2301 has been the choice abode of foreigners in Turpan for as long as anyone can remember. Backpackers crowd into the dorms, while the well-heeled cool off in the air-conditioned rooms, which start at around US$25. Best of all are the vine-covered verandahs where you can sit in the cool of the evening, dining, nibbling on Turpan's justly famous grapes, and wondering if you'll ever feel the chill of winter again. In the evenings, all through the summer months, Uygur song and dance performances are held in the hotel grounds.

The other popular lodging in Turpan is the **Oasis Hotel** ((995) 852-2478, with spacious grounds and a host of useful amenities. Like the Turpan Guesthouse it has both dorms and more upmarket tourist rooms. In actual fact, it has the edge on the Turpan Guesthouse in terms of the quality of rooms, but its relative distance from the bus station means that it loses a lot of business, particularly during the soporific summer months.

John's Information & Café, an essential stop on the Turpan dining circuit and a mine of useful information on the area, is just across the road from the Turpan Guesthouse. The best restaurants in town are in the Oasis Hotel.

How to Get There

The only way to get to Turpan (known in Chinese as Tulufan) is by bus. The nearest train station, which is sometimes called Turpan station, is at Daheyuan, a 35-km (22-mile) bus journey away.

A packed crowd at the Ta'Er Butter Festival, one of the main spiritual observances of Lamaism.

There are frequent bus services between Turpan and Ürümqi, a five-hour journey.

ÜRÜMQI

This, the Xinjiang capital and the next stop along the northwest railway line, is a disappointingly drab city at first glance. Certainly it lacks the small town oasis atmosphere of Turpan. But as you explore the place, stumble across a Uygur bazaar, visit a museum or two, and chance upon the mosques of Jiegang Nanlu, you begin to realize that below the familiar Han exterior of this city run some fascinating Middle Eastern undercurrents.

General Information

The **CAAC** booking office ((991) 264-1826 is at 62 Youhao Nanlu, in the northwest of town.

The **Bank of China** has its main branch at 343 Jiefang Nanlu. **CITS** ((991) 282-1427 is at 51 Xinhua Beilu.

For onward travel to Central Asia, the **Kazakhstan Consulate** ((991) 382-5564 is at 31 Kunming Lu. It also sells air tickets.

Getting Around

Oddly, Ürümqi is one city where bicycles are not for rent. Taxis, however, remain very cheap, and are a welcome alternative to the horribly crowded city buses.

What to See and Do

Among Ürümqi's parks, **Renmin Park** and **Hongshan Park** are worth visiting. The Renmin Park lies near the center of town, and is superb early in the morning when locals come out in force to do their daily calisthenics. Hongshan Park is a hilly area in the north of town. At the summit is a pagoda, and from here you get stunning views of Ürümqi, the desert and the faraway mountains.

The **Xinjiang Regional Museum**, as the name suggests, is the best in the region. The museum could be better organized, more English labeling is needed, but overall it's an interesting insight into Xinjiang and the old Silk Road that once crossed it. In particular look for the four 3,000-year-old bodies, which were mummified in the scorching desert sands and are now on public display. One of the females is reckoned quite a beauty.

For a closer look at the minorities and their lifestyles there's a pastureland called **Baiyanggou (White Poplar Gully)**, about 60 km (37 miles) south of Ürümqi and accessible by bus or taxi. It's a traditional gathering place for the Kazakh herders. Visitors can watch them tending their sheep, horses and cattle and, for a fee, can spend the night in their yurts feasting on mutton and rice and being entertained with Kazakh song and dance.

But the area's most splendid attraction lies 115 km (72 miles) east of Ürümqi — **Tian Chi (Heaven Lake)**, 2,000 m (6,400 ft) up, on the slopes of Mount Bogda, the 5,445-m-tall (17,860-ft) principal peak of the Tian Mountains. This towering range rises in central Xinjiang and marches 2,500 km (1,550 miles) into the heart of Central Asia, presenting a stunning contrast of soaring snowcapped peaks set amidst the fiery flat desert wastes. The marauding Xiongnu regarded the Tian range as heaven. It has an astounding number of glaciers — 6,896 of them — forming an enormous reservoir of ice which, as it melts, feeds six great rivers in Xinjiang, as well as the region's vital subterranean cisterns.

Heaven Lake is alpine in its beauty, unspeakably refreshing after the desert lowlands. Heavily wooded slopes roll down to the edge of the turquoise water. In the warmer summer months (it gets bitterly cold through the winter, and may even be inaccessible at this time), it's possible to rent horses for less than US$10 a day and trek up into other valleys, where you can stay in yurts with the local Kazakh herders.

Buses to Heaven Lake leave at around 9 AM from the north end of Renmin Park in Ürümqi. It is a good idea to purchase your ticket the day before departure from the Hongshan Hotel (see below).

Where to Stay

Top of the range is the **Holiday Inn Ürümqi** ((991) 281-8788 FAX (991) 281-7422, 168 Xinhua Beilu, which given its remoteness does a remarkable job of catering to the luxury needs of its guests. You'll find a good health club, a disco, excellent restaurants and a top-floor lounge.

The Holiday Inn's main rival is the newer **Yindu Hotel** ((991) 453-6688 FAX (991) 451-7166, 39 Xibei Lu, a flash establishment whose amenities match the Holiday Inn's but with not quite the degree of international panache that the latter has.

The **Laiyuan Hotel** ((991) 282-8368 FAX (991) 282-5109, 3 Jianshe Lu, not far from the Holiday Inn, is comfortable mid-range hotel, where extremely good value rooms are available for those who ask for a discount.

The most popular budget hotel in town is the **Hongshan Hotel** ((991) 282-4973, on the corner of Xinhua Beilu and Guangming Lu. It has a fine central location close to the shops, restaurants and buses for Heaven Lake, and the hotel itself is seemingly home to every travel agent in town, making it the best place to organize onward travel. The hotel has both dorms and inexpensive doubles.

The classic lines of Islamic architecture TOP contrast with the ornate Islamic decoration on the new Turpan mosque BOTTOM.

Where to Eat

Save breakfasts (and lunch too if you like) for the **Holiday Inn** buffet, which is an unimaginable treat after pulling into town from the rigors of the northwestern trail. If breakfast and lunch leave you hungry for more, the Holiday Inn has a good selection of restaurants, including **Kashgaris**, which does *haute cuisine* Moslem-style.

Opposite the Hongshan Hotel is **John's Information & Café**, which is run by the same John who has cafés in Turpan and Kashgar. By common consent, however, the Ürümqi branch is the pick of the pack, and it's an excellent place to choose from a selection of Western and Chinese travelers' favorites on the menu and to meet other travelers. As the name suggests, "information" is also a mainstay of the café's business.

Elsewhere, be adventurous and try some local Uygur street food. The area around and in **Erdaoqiao Market** is a good place to sample kebabs and flat breads. Pop into a noodle shop, too, and try the local noodle soup — just ask for *lamian*.

How to Get There

Ürümqi is well connected with the rest of China by air. Daily rail services run to Lanzhou, Xi'an, Zhengzhou, Nanjing and on to other parts of China. For travel farther west, however, you have just two choices: bus or air.

On to Central Asia

An adventurous route out of China is from Ürümqi into Kazakhstan. It is now possible to walk into the Ürümqi railway station and buy a train ticket for less than US$100 to Almaty. If you're game to fly Kazakh Airlines, you can fly to Almaty for around US$120 (the booking office is in the Kazakhstan consulate, see above); CAAC will fly you there too, but at nearly double the price. Buses are the cheapest way to get to Almaty, but few travelers relish the thought of a 24-hour bus journey into the unknown. You *will* need a visa; they are available from the Kazakh Consulate in Ürümqi.

ÜRÜMQI TO KASHGAR

The road from Ürümqi to Kashgar is the ancient Silk Road proper, and while the overland journey remains grueling, for those who can countenance the rigors of long-distance Chinese bus travel, it remains a fascinating trip. Essentially there are two routes, both of which were used in ancient times. The northern route travels north of the Takla Makan Desert, stopping at the ancient city of Kuqa, while the southern route skirts the Takla Makan to the south, taking in the city of Khotan. Today, neither Kuqa nor Khotan are significant cities, but despite their dusty poverty they are both interesting places to break the long journey between Ürümqi and Kashgar.

Kuqa, during the early Tang dynasty, was a major center for Buddhism in China. Today there is very little evidence that remains of these glory days, and the town is a dusty outpost that divides into a Uygur old city and a mostly Chinese new city.

The highlight of a trip to Kuqa is the **Friday Market**, a colorful bazaar that packs in Uygur traders from afar. The **Kuqa Mosque**, in the heart of the old city, is also worth taking some time to visit.

While it's the old city that makes for the most interesting exploring — a Central Asian huddle of mosques and bazaars — the place to stay is in the new city. The **Qiuci Hotel (** (997) 712-2005 is a quiet place with comfortable doubles with attached bathrooms.

Khotan, on the southern route to Kashgar, though exceedingly remote, is more accessible from Ürümqi as it has its own airport. The small

town's most interesting attraction is its **Silk Factory**, which can be visited through tours offered at Khotan's hotels. Such tours usually also take in the town's **Jade Factory** and **Carpet Factory**, at both of which items are for sale.

The place to stay is the **Khotan Guesthouse** ((903) 202-3564, a sprawling affair on the edge of town that has some comfortable double rooms with attached bathroom. The hotel's lobby restaurant has the best food in town.

KASHGAR

If anywhere is the heart of old Chinese Turkestan, it is this faraway place called Kashgar (in Chinese, Kashi). The name has a ring to it. It speaks of caravan routes snaking through desert, of the long-dreamed-of shade of palms, the splash of water, of pomegranates and dates. Of course, Kashgar nowadays evokes little of such romance, but it still

provides a fascinating glimpse into the rhythms of Uygur urban life as it must have been a century or more ago.

Kashgar is in a sense the only true surviving Silk Road watering hole. Merchant camel caravans, Buddhist pilgrims and the occasional explorer like Marco Polo — they all passed through here. They passed through a lot of other places too; but, most of these have fallen into neglect. Only Kashgar continues to prosper.

Back in the nineteenth century it was a great bazaar in which Indian, Afghan and Russian traders rubbed elbows with Moslem and Mongolian tribesmen, Chinese settlers and exiles, bandits, brigands, corsairs, tomb and temple robbers and some of the scurviest, most dangerous human flotsam of Central Asia. It had its spies too — agents of a Russian intrigue centered on

The weathered ruins of ancient Jiaohe.

Afghanistan that the British took so seriously that they established a consulate and dispatched the redoubtable George and Lady McCartney there for 28 years to keep an eye on things. From their official residence, a fine colonial mansion called Chini-bagh, they kept tabs on the Russian consul and offered hospitality to archaeologists such as Hedin and Stein as they trekked through to ransack the crumbling ruins of the Silk Road. Both Chini-bagh and the Russian consulate are now hotels.

Kashgar today continues to function as a watering hole. Since May 1986, the border for travel to and from Pakistan via the Friendship Highway, which runs to the southwest and crosses the Karakorum Mountains, has been open. It's not unusual to see Pakistani and Indian traders in town.

Getting Around

The best way to get around is by bicycle. These are available from John's Information & Café or from outside the Qiniwak Hotel.

What to See and Do

Kashgar is an ethnic microcosm of the northwest, with a population that mixes Kazakhs, Mongols and Uygurs. Its central bazaar (the best in China) and nearby Id Kah Mosque and main square are where all the daily pageantry and trading take place. The mosque is designed in the typical Moslem, rather than Chinese, style with a huge arched main entrance and doors, elegantly tiled minarets and a domed prayer hall, and there are others in the backstreets around it including a large one that has fallen into quite colorful ruin.

Travelers lucky enough to be in Kashgar on a Sunday can visit Xinjiang's most colorful and boisterous Sunday market. It's on the eastern edge of town. Just follow the crowds — on a good Sunday as many as 100,000 people from near and far congregate here to buy and sell.

But the main attraction of Kashgar is the stunning Moslem architecture of the Abakh Hoja Tomb on the eastern outskirts of the town, a seventeenth-century family mausoleum that grew in the ensuing centuries into a major burial spot for the Moslem aristocracy of the region. Today it presents a contrast of both the severe simplicity and ornate architecture of Islam — it is surrounded by cone-shaped graves the color of baked clay, and out of the center of them rises the principal grave chamber with its splendid domed roof, decorated with green and amber tiles. Minaret-style towers stand at its four corners.

This main tomb contains 72 burial places, most of them decorated with mosaic tiles and draped with colorfully patterned shrouds. It's said that the tomb became a popular spot for wealthy

Moslems because they wanted to lie in rest beside the central sarcophagus which, as legend has it, contains the costumes of Xiangfei (Fragrant Concubine), a renowned beauty of the region who was kidnapped by a Qing dynasty ruler and taken to the Forbidden City in Beijing.

Kashgar's other big attraction is its access via the Friendship Highway and forbidding Karakorum Mountains to Pakistan. CITS are the people to go to for information about exit visas and buses for the cross-border journey.

Where to Stay and Eat

Kashgar's best hotel is nominally the Kashgar Guesthouse ((998) 261-2367, it has long been in need of a facelift and a change of management, neither of which looks likely happen. The location too, three or four kilometers (one or two miles) out on the western edge of the town, is not a major selling point.

A better choice is the Qiniwak (Chini-bagh) Hotel ((998) 282-0544 FAX 282-3842, the former McCartney residence and British consulate. It has an excellent location near the central market, and accommodation ranges from inexpensive dorms to quite plush singles and doubles in the hotel's new wing.

The most popular budget hotel in town is the Seman Hotel ((998) 282-2129, which is housed in the former Russian consulate. The rooms range from noisy dorms to comfortable and inexpensive singles and doubles with attached bathrooms. Another reason for its popularity is the proximity of a number of small restaurants serving delicious food via that most important of media, the English menu. And in case you were wondering, John's Information & Café is across the road doling out that client-winning combination of food and facts.

How to Get There

For the brave and the impecunious Kashgar is a two- or three-day bus journey from Ürümqi. Slow buses stop overnight in towns along the way. There are no more Holiday Inns out there on the northern edge of the Takla Makan Desert (think of those poor Silk Road merchants huddled up with their camels if the conditions get depressing). Daily flights between Kashgar and Ürümqi are a civilized addition to Xinjiang's travel network. CAAC ((998) 283-6444 is at 106 Jiefang Nanlu.

ONWARD TO PAKISTAN AND KIRGYZISTAN

The Karakorum Highway spans 1,300 km (800 miles), over the Khunjerab Pass to Rawalpindi in northern Pakistan, from whence you can travel on to Islamabad. You need at least four days to

ABOVE: The aptly named Heavenly Lake near Urumqi. BELOW: Mongolian yurts on the shores of Sky Lake.

reach Islamabad, and you will also need a Pakistan visa — arrange one in Beijing or in Hong Kong. From the beginning of May until the end of October, which is when the pass is open, there should be daily departures from Kashgar.

Theoretically it is possible to travel from Kashgar to Kirgyzistan providing you have a visa, but it's a rough journey that involves hiring a vehicle for the four-hour journey to the border and then hitchhiking on the Kirgyzistan side.

ACROSS THE NORTH

If you are entering China along the Friendship Highway, Ürümqi is the railhead for the swing

right across the north of the country, through the boundless grasslands of Inner Mongolia to Beijing. If you've cut up into the northwest from Lanzhou there's no alternative, other than an expensive plane flight (Ürümqi–Kashgar), to retracing your route by rail back to this key junction for access across the north.

There are, in fact, two rail routes to the north from Lanzhou, and care must be taken when booking tickets not to be stuck aboard the wrong one. One direct service heads to Beijing via Baotou and Hohhot in Inner Mongolia, then Datong, the third of the four greatest centers of Buddhist cave art in China. The other cuts back southeast to Xi'an, then across the heartland of China through Luoyang, the site of the Longmen Grottoes, and Zhengzhou, the access point for the Shaolin Monastery, after which it heads north to Beijing through Shijiazhuang in Hebei province.

Luoyang and Zhengzhou can be approached just as easily from the east, from Guangzhou, Shanghai and Beijing, leaving the trip across the northern plateau the most exciting route from Lanzhou.

THE GRASSLANDS

The grasslands route takes you through the panoramic flat green seas of Gobi scrubland and lusher pastureland that stretch from horizon to horizon across Nei Menggu (Inner Mongolia), broken only by occasional settlements of yurts, the animal-skin tents of the nomadic sheep and cattle herders. Until the railway line was pushed across the plains, the

Dahingan Range, a thickly wooded stretch of hills running northeast to southwest across the plateau, effectively isolated the Mongolian tribes, or "banners," from the rest of the world, and for the most part kept the rest of the world out of Mongolia.

As for the Mongolians themselves, they were a warring, fragmented and greatly feared "barbarian" race ruled by khans, or tribal chiefs, until one man turned their solitary, idyllic existence upside down for them — Genghis Khan. In one of the most incredible, explosive events of history these sheep and cattle herders — brilliant horsemen and cavalry tacticians, to be sure — suddenly banded together under this savage warlord's command and thundered out of the wilderness to conquer China and carve an empire that stretched beyond the western borders of Russia and Persia. And, just as swiftly as they pillaged and subjugated much of the vast Eurasian landmass, so their terrible adventure ended: Within less than a century they had been crushed in China by the Ming, pushed back out of the territories to the west and were straggling and limping back into the grassy wilds far beyond the Great Wall.

From that time of retreat and withdrawal, the Mongolian "nation" was divided between the tribes of the north and the remnants of the China "expedition" in the south — a division that the Manchu Qing dynasty was happy to maintain for its own sake when it brought the entire region under Chinese control in the seventeenth century. By the turn of the twentieth century the Russians were competing for control of the region, and in 1924 the Soviet Red Army moved in and promoted the establishment of the autonomous People's Republic of (Outer) Mongolia in the north, leaving the southern Nei Menggu or Inner Mongolia to Beijing. The region is now heavily settled with Han Chinese, who vastly outnumber the estimated two million Mongols, many of whom have returned to their greener but far less ambitious pastures with little to show for their historic glory but two spiritual legacies — Tibetan-style Buddhism and Islam.

BAOTOU

The first major stop on the journey to the east is Baotou, the autonomous region's largest city, and an ugly industrial center supported by iron and coal mining. It is, however, the site of one of the main centers of lamaist Buddhism in China, the magnificent **Wudang (Willow Tree) Monastery** which lies on a hillside 70 km (43 miles) northeast of the city.

Wudang is one of the finest surviving lamaseries in Inner Mongolia, and its size alone testifies to its importance — it contains more than 2,500 living units, classrooms, temples and prayer halls. Its origins are similarly illustrious. It was built in 1749 by the then-reigning Dalai Lama himself and has since been a temporary residence for at least seven Tibetan rulers. Its architecture is flat, whitewashed and Tibetan on the outside with blazes of color inside in its temples and schools. Ornately woven pillar rugs, beautiful Tibetan carpeting and huge murals decorate the main hall, Suguqindu, where the lamas pray and chant the scriptures. Other halls are filled with images of Sakyamuni Buddha, including one bronze statue that's 10 m (33 ft) tall.

Baotou itself, however, is not a particularly pleasant place to find yourself in need of lodging. If you get stuck there, try to make sure you're stuck in East Baotou (Donghe), where you will find the **Beiyang Hotel** ((472) 417-5656 FAX 417-1440, 23 Nanmenwai Street, Donghe. It's by no means the lap of luxury, but it has simple, well-maintained rooms and a good restaurant.

HOHHOT

Hohhot (in Chinese, Huhehaote), the capital of Inner Mongolia, is a far more attractive city than Baotou. It only became the capital in 1952, and prior to this time it was a center for Mongolian Buddhism.

What to See and Do

Xilitu Temple is set into the old city walls. Built in the Ming dynasty, Xilitu has an architecture that is mainly Han Chinese with a main shrine hall and sutra hall in the Tibetan style; it features an eight-sided pavilion inscribed with

details in Chinese, Manchu, Mongolian and Tibetan of the Qing emperor Kangxi's victorious military expeditions against unruly tribes in the northwest.

The great sutra hall, or Dajingtang, has walls inlaid with peacock-blue tiles with silver decorations. The roof of the building is strictly Tibetan, mounted with an ornate gilded vase, prayer-wheel, flying dragon and a deer, all cast in copper.

Near the People's Park you'll find the **Jingang-zuo Sheli Pagoda**, popularly called Wu Ta (Five Pagodas) a series of five square brick and stone towers faced with glazed tiles and richly carved with Buddhas, Bodhisattvas and bodhi trees, images of lions, elephants and birds, mandalas, and a total of 1,119 small Buddha niches. These towers, mounted on a stone base, are all that survives of a much grander Cideng Monastery which was built there in the eighteenth century.

The **Wanbu Huayanjing Ta** (Pagoda of the 10,000 Volumes of Avatamasaka Sutra) is in the eastern section of Hohhot; you can call it the **Bai Ta**

LEFT: A yurt interior on the shores of Sky Lake. RIGHT: Sweeping double-eaved roof of Qing dynasty tomb. ABOVE: Unleavened bread at a market stall in Urumqi.

(White Pagoda), which most of the citizenry call it. It's a lofty 43-m-tall (141-ft) eight-sided tower of wood and brick, probably built between 983 and 1031 when Buddhism flourished again in the wake of the late-Tang dynasty crackdown, and it stands on the site of what was once a monastery called Daxuanjiao. It features an interesting display of ancient graffiti — inscriptions carved by visitors as far back as the twelfth century and written not only in Chinese but also Mongolian, Nuzhen (an old Chinese tribal language), Kitan, ancient Syrian and Persian.

For one of the city's most prized Buddhist relics you have to visit the **Dazhao Monastery** in Hohhot's southern district. The Chinese call

it Yinfo Si (Silver Buddha Monastery) in honor of its most treasured possession, an image of the Sakyamuni Buddha cast entirely in silver. Again, the monastery's design is half Chinese and half Tibetan, built in 1580 and extended during the reign of the Qing warrior emperor Kangxi.

Nine kilometers (six miles) south of Hohhot on the south bank of the Dahei (Great Black) River there's a tall loess mound, 33 m (108 ft) high, which isn't much of a sightseeing attraction — just a huge bump in the terrain — but is worth a picnic while you sit and ponder over the legend and superstition that goes with it. It's the **Tomb of Wang Zhaojun**, who is said to have been a concubine of

A decorated wooden door ABOVE and colorful interior hangings OPPOSITE BOTTOM grace a Kazakh herdsman's yurt near Urumqi. TOP: Mother and child of the Mongolian grasslands.

the Han dynasty ruler Emperor Yuan. When a prince named Huhanye of the dreaded Xiongnu came to the court and asked to marry Wang Zhaojun, the emperor naturally saw the union as a God-given opportunity for some peace and quiet on the northern border.

Despite the harsh conditions that she had to endure beyond the Great Wall and the fringe of the Han civilization, Wang Zhaojun is said to have been a dutiful consort and ambassadress, her stoicism and dignity keeping the barbarians under reasonable control. Since her death, her tomb has been endowed with the power to cure barrenness in women, and childless visitors take a pinch of soil from the mound and pray there in the hope that they will overcome infertility.

The **Museum of Inner Mongolia** features an interesting display of costumes, weapons, cavalry trappings and a traditional yurt — along with another huge skeleton of a mammoth that was excavated from a coal mine. The present-day yurts and their inhabitants are found in Mongolian communes north of the city, and group excursions, known as **Grassland Tours** and lasting two days or more, are organized by CITS and other agencies in town. Very few travelers who join these tours enjoy them. The reason is mostly the way visitors are shepherded around sights that would obviously not exist if tourists didn't either.

Where to Stay

Hohhot's top hotel is the **Zhaojun Hotel** ((471) 696-2211 FAX (471) 686-8825, 53 Xinhua Dajie, right in the center of town, opposite the Bank of China and just down the road from the Museum of Inner Mongolia. It's not the best hotel you'll ever stay in, but the joint Hong Kong management keeps things shipshape.

The two most popular hotels with foreigners are the **Xincheng Hotel** ((471) 696-3322, 40 Hulun Nanlu, and the **Inner Mongolia Hotel** ((471) 696-4233, Wulanchabu Lu, which is where CITS is housed. Both hotels are a couple of kilometers (a mile and a quarter) from the railway station, making it best to take a taxi. The Xincheng is the better overall choice, having a selection of mid-range and budget rooms, but the doubles and singles at the nearby Inner Mongolia are slightly more luxurious.

How to Get There

Access from Hohhot is by bus to Datong or Baotou, or by train to Baotou and Lanzhou or Datong and Beijing. There are also direct flights to Beijing, Guangzhou, Shanghai and Xi'an, among other places.

The Northeast

BEIJING IS THE GATEWAY TO CHINA'S NORTHEAST, an area that is neglected by many China travelers. The reasons are obvious enough. The areas north and east of Beijing, once known as Manchuria, are rich in mineral deposits and have become a base for nearly a third of China's heavy industry. Add to this a climate of extremes — furnace-like in the summer and Siberia-cold in the winter — and you have a destination that on the surface is less than inviting. Nevertheless, with China's state-owned enterprises facing hard times and massive layoffs creating wide-scale unemployment, the northeast is starting to take tourism seriously as a revenue earner, making it a friendly and increasingly open place to visit. Harbin is home to some fascinating old architecture and sports an increasingly popular annual ice festival. Dalian has beaches (only an attraction in summer, of course), Jilin is emerging as a skiing destination, and in the far north of the region are forested national parks.

BEIJING

China is many things, and here in the capital, at the heart of it all, you'll find something of all of them. Beijing is the Chinese world in miniature. You'll see grand palaces, pagoda-studded gardens, crowded markets, acrobatic troops, five-star hotels, late-night discos, old-time *hutongs* (alleys); in short everything that China is famous for, and quite a lot more that it isn't. Give yourself plenty of time. This vast, busy and exciting city will, like any great city, soak up as much time as you have to give it.

BACKGROUND

The capital of China is a city of broad ceremonial thoroughfares and monumental architecture that is more awe-inspiring than livable. It is a place of eminence and imperial might. Stand on the

squares of the new capital that Kublai Khan built were designed so that the Mongol cavalrymen could get a good unhindered run along them on their horses; where the illustrious rulers of the Ming dynasty bathed and caroused in the treacherous care of their eunuch courts, unable to see or hear the rage swelling beyond the walls; where the long and harsh Qing reign of the Manchus committed virtual suicide, encircled by its own angry masses and the armed might of the Europeans; where, amid billowing revolutionary flags, the biggest mass rallies the world has ever seen chanted and waved little red books in homage to their new and perhaps last Emperor, Chairman Mao Zedong. It is where, in April 1976, the same masses turned in rage on the same revolution — prevented by the Gang of Four from paying homage to the newly dead Premier Zhou Enlai — and the course of Chinese history swerved dramatically once again.

Beijing began its life as an insignificant border outpost, pitted with the sweeping dust-storms that blow regularly from the Gobi Desert. The barbarians beyond the wall were the first to take its location seriously. The Khitan Tartars of the Liao dynasty made it their southern capital, calling it Yanjing or Swallow City, and in AD 1125 their triumphant rivals, the Jin, established it as Zhongdu, their capital. In both cases the city appealed to them because it was close to their tribal domains on the Mongolian Plateau to the north.

Genghis Khan ravished, depopulated and looted the place and burned it to the ground, and his grandson Kublai, the Great Khan, rebuilt it completely and established it as the Yuan capital Dadu, the most splendid of all the cities of the Mongol Empire. Marco Polo stood amidst its vast halls, palaces, temples, walls and squares as awed and open-mouthed as any visitor who contemplates the grandeur of the city today.

Much of Beijing's present historic character and architecture is the legacy of the Ming rulers, who, after crushing the Yuan and razing their magnificent Dadu to the ground, rebuilt it as their capital, Beiping, or "Northern Peace." It was the Ming emperors who gave it its real strategic value — for them it was a powerful garrison, listening post and command center from which they could maintain a vigil on the dangerous tribal lands beyond the Great Wall. When the Manchus grabbed the imperial throne in 1644, Beiping was a convenient center of power for them because of that same close proximity to their own homelands.

Most of Beijing's historical heritage dates from the Manchu Qing dynasty. Much has been lost. When the Communists took over Beijing in January 1949 they found a city that was backward,

edge of the vast Tiananmen Square, in the sweeping courtyards of the Forbidden City, or before the majestic blue-tiled Ming roofs of the once-sacred Temple of Heaven and sense, even in this irreligious age of clamoring traffic, bicycles and tourist crowds, the power and unquestioned authority of the 24 emperors who ruled from here; imagine the fear that struck at the heart from the traditional exhortation that ended each of their imperial edicts: "Tremble and obey!"

In another sense it is China's Washington DC, another grand architecture of the ego, a repository of pomp, sentiment and grandiose pride, the tomb of all the mortal fantasies and follies that history endows with immortal greatness and nobility. It is where the triumphant Jurchens of the Jin dynasty quaked and cowered and awaited horrific mass murder and destruction as Genghis Khan's cavalries smashed their way through the Great Wall to the north; where the boulevards and

The Gang Wan (Harbor Bay) Food City provides an exotic taste of nautical luxury in landlocked Beijing.

dirty and chaotic. To their minds, there was only one way to modernize: They began to clear away the old *hutong*s, widen the boulevards, and to create a modern — Soviet-style — city of wide-open spaces with Tiananmen Square at the center. It has been pointed out that in this the Communists were simply following historical precedent and inaugurating a new period of dynastic rule with the construction of a new capital. This process is still ongoing. To be sure, "old Peking" lingers in some historical monuments, in the occasional *hutong*, but what you are most likely to remember of Beijing is its thrusting confidence, its intimidating overpasses, busy roads and perhaps more than anything else its pollution. Today, by the Chinese government's own admission, Beijing is the most polluted city in the world. Most locals are phlegmatic about such problems, seeing them as the price to be paid for modernization. "Modernization," after all, is the key word in the new China, and nowhere more so than in the capital.

ORIENTATION

Beijing's main boulevards and backstreets follow a neat and very convenient "chessboard" grid that was established in the Yuan reign and maintained through the Ming and Qing periods. Not that grid-like necessarily means easy to use. The vastness of Beijing's boulevards, some of them seemingly stretching forever, changing names confusingly every couple of kilometers or so, can be daunting to the new arrival. Even after you've been in the city for some time, that feeling of looking out of a taxi window and not having a clue where you are will be familiar to most Beijing visitors and even residents.

The main thoroughfare is Chang'an Jie — in its east (*dong*) and west (*xi*) sections — which runs between the two focus points of the city: the Forbidden City and Tiananmen Square. The latter, along with Beijing's modern revolutionary monuments — the Great Hall of the People, Monument to the People's Heroes and the Chairman Mao Memorial Hall — lie to the south of Chang'an Jie. To its east and west, radiating from the square, lie the main tourist centers — the central Beijing Hotel, Beijing railway station, the Friendship Store, International Club, Long Distance Telegraph Office and the major restaurants, department stores and bookshops.

The city center is surrounded by the Second Ring Road and the Circle Line of the Beijing Subway, whose 18 stations make most of the main cultural attractions readily accessible. The Third Ring Road (Sanhuan Lu) essentially encompasses the city proper—base yourself outside it and you'll probably have a longish commute in store before you can begin sightseeing.

New arrivals generally find the street names appallingly difficult. Some of them are mind-bogglingly long and full of q's and x's and zh's. The first step, if you haven't already done so, is to familiarize yourself with the official *pinyin* spelling system. The second step is to learn the following words: *dong* — east; *nan* — south; *xi* — west; *bei* — north; *nei* — inside; *wai* — outside; *men* — gate; *lu* — road; *jie* — street; *dajie* — boulevard. Thus Chongwenmenwai Dajie, is "Outside Chongwen Gate Boulevard." It's simple… with a little practice.

Incidentally, the *nei* and *wai* (inside and outside) distinction refers to the now-torn-down city walls. The gates were usually gates in the walls.

GENERAL INFORMATION

Before you do anything else, get yourself a good fold-out map of the city, preferably one labeled with both English *and* Chinese — the latter is essential for letting taxi drivers (and anyone else) know where you want to go. You should be able to get one at your hotel.

Some of the major airlines represented in Beijing are:

Air France ((10) 6505-1818; **Alitalia** ((10) 6591-8468; **British Airways** ((10) 6512-4070; **Canadian Airlines** ((10) 6463-7901; **China Eastern** ((10) 6513-3671; **China Northwest** ((10) 6601-7589; **Dragonair** ((10) 6505-4343; **Garuda** ((10) 6505-2910; **Japan Airlines** ((10) 6513-0888; **KLM Royal Dutch Airlines** ((10) 6505-3505; **Korean Air** ((10) 6505-4639; **Lufthansa** ((10) 6465-4488; **Malaysia Airlines** ((10) 6505-2681; **Northwest Airlines** ((10) 6505-3505; **Qantas Airways** ((10) 6467-4794; **SAS** ((10) 6518-6788; **Singapore Airlines** ((10) 6505-2233; **Swissair** ((10) 6512-3555; **Thai Airways International** ((10) 6460-8899; **United Airlines** ((10) 6463-1111.

American Express ((10) 6505-2228 has an office at Room L115D, in the Shopping Arcade of the China World Tower, 1 Jianguomenwai Dajie. The **Commercial Bank**, CITIC Building, 19 Jianguo-

menwai Dajie, is a good place to change money and get advances on credit cards. The head office of the **Bank of China** is at 410 Fuchengmennei Dajie, and the Beijing branch at 8 Yabao Lu is another good place to do bank business.

Some foreign embassies in Beijing include: **Australia** ((10) 6532-2331, 15 Dongzhimenwai Dajie; **Austria** ((10) 6532-2061, 5 Xiushui Nanjie, Jianguomenwai; **Belgium** ((10) 6532-1736, 6 Sanlitun Lu; **Canada** ((10) 6532-3536, 19 Dongzhimenwai Dajie; **Denmark** ((10) 6532-2431, 1 Dongwujie, Sanlitun; **France** ((10) 6532-1331, 3 Dongsan Jie, Sanlitun; **Germany** ((10) 6532-2161, 5 Dongzhimenwai Dajie; **India** ((10) 6532-3127, 1 Ritan Donglu; **Ireland** ((10) 6532-2691, 3 Ritan Donglu; **Israel** ((10) 6505-2970, West Wing Office, China World Trade Tower; **Italy** ((10) 6532-2131, 2 Donger Jie, Sanlitun; **Japan** ((10) 6532-2361, 7 Ritan Lu, Jianguomenwai; **Mongolia** ((10) 6532-1203, 2 Xiushui Beijie, Jianguomenwai; **Netherlands** ((10) 6532-1131, 4 Lianghema Nanlu; **New Zealand** ((10) 6532-2731, 1 Donger Jie, Sanlitun; **Russia** ((10) 6532-2051, 4 Dongzhimen Beizhongjie; **Spain** ((10) 6532-1986, 9 Sanlitun Lu; **Sweden** ((10) 6532-3331, 3 Dongzhimenwai Dajie; **Switzerland** ((10) 6532-2736, 3 Dongwu Jie, Sanlitun; **United Kingdom** ((10) 6532-1961, 11 Guanghua Lu; **United States** ((10) 6532-3831, 3 Xiushuibeijie, Jianguomenwai.

For the latest on **cultural events** in Beijing, pick up a copy of the free listings magazine, *Beijing Scene*.

GETTING AROUND

Outside the central core around the Forbidden City, Beijing is so spread out that it'll wear you down and send your shoe repair bills soaring if you try to walk it. One option is to rent a bicycle, though Beijing is nowhere near as pleasant a place to cycle around as it once was — the traffic is very chaotic nowadays. Nevertheless, it is still possible to rent bikes at hotels around town, and providing you ride with care getting around the city this way can be a lot of fun. Bicycle rental is widely available, though prices vary remarkably from place to place — at the better hotels, you might easily spend upwards of Y100 per day on a rented bike, while elsewhere Y10 to Y50 per day is the norm. Shop around.

Beijing has taxis, huge fleets of them in fact, operating from all the main hotels, and they are surprisingly cheap and for the most part honest (it still pays to be alert to rip-offs). Most of them have meters, and most drivers use them.

The subway runs right around the core of the city and west along Chang'an Lu and Fuxing Lu, from 5 AM to 11 PM. Rides cost next to nothing. It does, however, get very crowded, especially at peak commuting times when the vast bureaucracy of Beijing pours in or out of its offices — but not as crowded as the buses get, some of which are the stuff of which Guinness records are made.

WHAT TO SEE AND DO

Beijing is so huge, its attractions so various that a plan of action is essential. The place to start is the center of the city, and indeed the center of China — Tiananmen Square, with its Tiananmen (Gate of Heavenly Peace) and Palace Museum (Forbidden City). These three sights alone will probably fill an entire day.

The square itself, expanded to its present vast dimensions after the communist revolution, is a

Beside the monument, the memory of the Great Helmsman remains revered in the Mao Zedong Mausoleum, open to the public as a museum, where the leader who is now accredited with having been 70% right and 30% wrong during his tumultuous reign lies in state in a crystal coffin. Two other sacred institutions flank Tiananmen Square. To the east stands the huge museum building which houses the Museum of Chinese History and the Museum of the Chinese Revolution, to the west the equally huge Great Hall of the People, which is where the Chinese parliament, the National People's Congress, meets and where you can take a look at the 5,000-seat Great Banqueting Hall.

central place of congregation for the people of Beijing and a particularly popular spot for spring and summer kite flying — the colored paper and silk butterflies and various other designs darting and swooping against a backdrop of huge red revolutionary flags billowing across the front of the Monument to the People's Heroes. The 36-m tall (118-ft) granite obelisk and graphic stone sculpture, almost an epithet of the Maoist era — soldiers, peasants, workers and women in a dramatic revolutionary tableau — breasting the tide of the future, commemorates the revolution. Inevitably this focal point of revolutionary idealism has become the focus of new "revolutions." In 1976 thousands gathered to publicly mourn Zhou Enlai, and were roughly dispersed. In 1989 hundreds of thousands gathered to protest official corruption and rampant inflation. The result: several thousands dead.

The Forbidden City

Everything in Tiananmen Square focuses on one point — the Gate of Heavenly Peace and the Mecca of all pilgrims to China, the renowned portrait of Chairman Mao. Rallies of a million or more people took place before this gate, from where the communist leader and his party lieutenants acknowledged the thunderous slogan-chanting adoration and acclaim — standing where the dynastic leaders before them, going back to the great Ming reconstruction of the fifteenth century, had occasionally emerged from their divine seclusion to exhort and review the mood of their common subjects. Now, tourist parties are invited to stand where Mao and his lieutenants presided over the masses.

The Gate of Heavenly Peace opens the way into the huge Forbidden City, the largest complex of antique wooden buildings of such scale left in the world, and, all in all, a fascinating but daunting tourist challenge of 800 palaces, halls, shrines and pavilions and no fewer than 9,000 rooms. This vast museum, formerly the seat of power and isolated inner sanctum of the rulers of the Ming and Qing dynasties, is far too big to cover in fine detail unless you have a week or so in which to do it. All that you can achieve in a half-day or so is to identify its main halls and relics and contemplate the ghosts of autocracy, pride, wrath, intrigue, folly, debauchery and murder moving restlessly about you.

Take a Walkman with you when you go to the Forbidden Palace and you can be personally guided around by the dulcet tones of Roger Moore.

imperial birthdays, court banquets and the awarding of degrees to lucky would-be mandarins in the imperial examinations.

North of these halls you step through the Heavenly Purity Gate into the inner palaces or living quarters of the Forbidden City and reach **Qianqing Guan (Palace of Heavenly Purity)**, which is surrounded by more than 40 mansions, libraries, medical consulting rooms and quarters for servants, concubines and palace eunuchs. Qianqing is where the emperors chose their successors. Each ruler would write the name of his intended successor on two slips of paper, one to be kept in his personal possession and the other hidden behind a plaque inscribed with the words

Cassette players are also available at the front gate for a refundable Y100.

Beyond the Gate of Heavenly Peace lies a sweeping courtyard leading to the massive **Meridian Gate (Wumen)**, the exclusive gateway of the emperors and where, at the stroke of noon on certain days, they issued edicts, had miscreant mandarins publicly flogged and had common criminals executed.

Beyond the Meridian Gate, five marble bridges lead across the bow-shaped **Jin (Golden) Stream** to the **Supreme Harmony Gate**, which in turn opens on to the ceremonial quarter of the palace complex, a huge courtyard that could hold 100,000 people at imperial audiences and the three **great halls** of **Supreme Harmony**, **Complete Harmony** and **Preserving Harmony**, each of which played a particular role in the most important imperial rituals: coronations, New Year's observances,

"Upright and Bright." Upon his death his advisers would compare the papers, and if the names tallied, the new ruler would be announced.

One tragic aspect of the Forbidden City is that while it's big on imperial architecture it's surprisingly light on imperial relics and treasures. For that the world can blame Chiang Kaishek and his nationalists, who ransacked the palace of its most precious ceremonial artwork and shipped them to Taiwan, where are now on display in the National Palace Museum in Taipei.

This, in any case, is the official story. In fact the treasures were removed in the 1930s and transported on the backs of coolies to Chongqing to

OPPOSITE: The Ancient Palaces, better known as Beijing's Forbidden City, are the largest surviving cluster of wooden buildings on such a scale in the world. ABOVE: The grand landscaping and architecture of the Forbidden City's palace gardens.

protect them from the advancing Japanese. (It is claimed that on that march of nearly 3,220 km or 2,000 miles not a single object was broken.) In the late 1940s they were transported by American military aircraft to Taipei when it was clear that "Shanghai Jack" had lost the mainland to Mao. Bearing in mind what was destroyed during the Cultural Revolution by the Great Helmsman's marauding Red Guards, Chinese posterity owes the Nationalists an unfashionable debt of gratitude for ensuring the survival of the greatest collection of Chinese art in existence.

What's left in the Forbidden City isn't much, and some of it has been brought there from other parts of the country, but it includes the fabulous

You emerge, slightly dazed and footsore, by way of the Palace Museum's north gate, **Shenwumen (Gate of Divine Military Genius)** to face a climb up **Coal Hill Park**, directly opposite, where the last Ming ruler, Chongzhen, hanged himself after murdering his family as the Manchus hammered at the city gates. From there, the path leads to **Beihai Park**, which was the site of Kublai Khan's grand palace and now features the distinctive **Bai Ta (White Pagoda)** and the **Yongan Si (Temple of Everlasting Peace)**, both built on an islet in Beihai Lake in 1651 in honor of the visiting Dalai Lama.

On the southern side of the lake, the **Chengguang Dian (Light Receiving Hall)** has a beautiful jade Buddha presented by the Burmese to the

Suit of Jade and a collection of terracotta warriors on display in the **Hall of Preserving Harmony**; Qing dynasty sedan chairs in the **Hall of Complete Harmony**; an old water clock and several mechanical clocks presented by Western rulers in the **Hall of Union**; a magnificent collection of traditional paintings in the **Palace of Peaceful Old Age**; a **Treasure Room** filled with costumes, jeweled ceremonial swords, gold Buddhas and stupas encrusted with precious gems, a five-ton block of carved jade, bronzes, flowers fashioned from semi-precious stones and crafts of both dynasties in the aptly named **Palace of Mental Cultivation**; murals from the celebrated Qing dynasty novel *A Dream of the Red Mansions* in the **Palace of Eternal Spring**; and other palace halls displaying silks, furniture, jewelry, gold and jade artifacts and the personal possessions of some of the supreme rulers and the many concubines and high officials of their courts.

Empress Dowager Ci Xi, but shorn of one of its arms when British and "allied" troops stormed and occupied much of Beijing in 1900 to put down the anti-European Boxer Rebellion.

Temple of Heaven (Tiantan)

While the Ming and Qing emperors sat enthroned in the Forbidden Palace at the very center of Chinese civilization, and that meant the entire universe to them, the firmament itself was represented by four temples beyond the palace walls, one at each of four points of the compass. To the north stood **Ditan (Temple of the Earth)**, to the west **Yuetan (Temple of the Moon)**, to the east **Ritan (Temple of the Sun)** and to the south, close to the canal on the edge of the inner city, the most architecturally inspiring and spiritually significant of all these sacred places, Tiantan (The Temple of Heaven).

It was here, close to each winter solstice and in the spring, that the emperor was borne in a spectacular procession accompanied by his imperial guards, advisers, priests and musicians to pray for good harvests and to offer sacrifices to heaven — performing his most crucial role as the nation's spiritual messenger to the gods and translator to the nation of the favor or wrath of the deities.

The emperor was taken first to the **Imperial Vault of Heaven**, the smaller of the two ornate halls, to pray amidst the tablets of the gods of the firmament and elements — sun, moon, stars, rain, wind, thunder and lightning. Around this hall, built in 1530, stands the remarkable **Whispering** or **Echo Wall**, a circular wall with the acoustic

"magic" that you find in the oracle caves of the Mediterranean — where if you speak to the smooth stonework you can telegraph your voice to someone some distance around it.

From this complex the emperor was taken south along the marble terrace, **Red Steps Bridge**, with its tall carved arches, to the **Circular Altar (Huanqiu Tan)**, a three-tiered white marble terrace decorated with blue tiles that are arranged concentrically in odd numbers, considered to be extremely propitious in ancient times. Here, on the central dais, the forces of heaven and earth came together in the most crucial of the ceremonies as the emperor, surrounded by the sacred tablets, prayed from what was regarded as the very center of mortal existence and then presided over the sacrifice of a bull calf.

The magnificent **Hall of Prayer for Good Harvests**, with its renowned triple-tiered blue-

tiled roof, is where the ruler spent the night resting and meditating between the two great rituals. Built on a three-decked marble terrace, it ranks with the Great Wall and Tiananmen Square as a visual symbol of Chinese history and culture, and features a sensational carved, gilded and decorated domed ceiling as complex as a mandala, with a dragon set in the center of it. In fact, the temple is relatively "new." Built originally in 1420 it burned down in 1889 and was rebuilt the following year in the Ming design and using the construction techniques of that age — supported by 28 cedar pillars with not one crossbeam, nail or dab of cement anywhere in the structure.

The Lama Temple (Yonghe Gong)

This beautiful Tibetan Buddhist lamasery, the third most remarkable cultural attraction in Beijing, can be found to the northeast of the Forbidden City at the intersection of Andingmen Dongdajie and Yonghegong Dajie, and the best way to get to it is to bicycle north from the Beijing Hotel. A former palace of the Qing emperor Yongzheng, it was established as a Tibetan monastery in 1744, largely as a symbol of Chinese suzerainty over Tibet, and assumed a spiritual significance as important as that of the Jokhang Temple in Lhasa. It has several halls featuring some of the most splendid Tibetan Buddhist artwork and relics found anywhere in the Chinese "lowlands," including a 26-m-tall (85-ft) Maitreya Buddha carved from a single block of sandalwood, a large bronze statue of the founder of the Gelugpa, Yellow Hat Sect, Tsongkapa, a host of other Buddha images representing the various stages of Buddhahood and a bronze mandala portraying the Buddhist "Western Paradise."

Buddhas and Pagodas

There are many other temples around the city, some of them in reasonably good shape and others derelict or destroyed all but for their pagodas. The most attractive are the **Binyin Si (Temple of Azure Clouds)** in Xiangshan Park in the Western Hills, a Yuan dynasty temple extended under the Qing reign and noted for its striking white marble pagodas in the early Indian architectural style; the **Wofo Si (Sleeping Buddha Monastery)**, also close to Xiangshan Park, with a giant bronze statue of Sakyamuni Buddha in the reclining position, which is said to be the pose he took when discussing with his disciples his impending departure from all earthly matters; the **Dazhong Si (Big Bell Temple)**, two kilometers (one and a quarter miles) northwest of the city center near the Friendship Hotel, with an immense 46-ton Ming dynasty bell

OPPOSITE: Tiantan (Temple of Heaven) and detail of the temple's decorative gilding and tilework. ABOVE: A woman and her grandchild pose at the Spring Festival in Beijing.

with Buddhist sutras inscribed on it; the **Guangji Si (Temple of Universal Rescue)**, just west of Beihai Park, with many good Buddha statues; and the **Mahakala Miao** at the southern end of the Forbidden City, which is one of the centers of Mongolian lamaism in Beijing.

Other Sights

As you go east on Chang'an Avenue, heading toward the huge Friendship Store, you'll find on the right the ancient **Guanxiang Tai (Observatory)**, built in the Ming dynasty and now notable for its collection of Chinese maritime maps and instruments and astronomical gadgets built by Jesuit priests. These scholars, headed by Father

Matteo Ricci, were employed in the Ming court to work on a Chinese calendar, and in return were given the freedom to seek Chinese converts — not many of whom ever turned up.

CITS operate daily tours of **Underground Beijing**, a network of subterranean defenses and shelters throughout the capital, some of which have factories, shops, restaurants and even, it's said, some 100 "hotels." They're a legacy of the Cold War and Yellow Peril period when the Chinese feared nuclear attack by the United States or the former Soviet Union, or both.

The **Junshi Bowuguan (Military Museum)** on Fuxing Lu, the western extension of Chang'an Avenue, has exhibitions recounting the history of the People's Liberation Army, its role in the Korean War (and American jets that it shot down) and captured weapons and documents of its most recent military foray, the 1979 military

"lesson" that it attempted to teach Vietnam. In the Military Museum you will see staged photos of the Tiananmen incident attempting to show how the students massacred innocent soldiers.

The **China Art Gallery**, just east of Beihai and Jingshan (on Coal Hill) parks, has changing exhibits, mostly modern. Check the *Beijing Scene* listings to see what's on.

The **Former Residence of Soong Ching Ling** on the northern bank of Shisha Lake, just north of Beihai Park, is worth a visit for the symbol that it now represents of the chaotic republican era after the collapse of the Qing dynasty. Soong Ching Ling was one of three daughters of "Charlie" Soong, a wayward Hainanese Chinese who became a Methodist preacher in the United States and was sent back to China to convert the "heathen" nation with American-style holy rolling evangelism. Charlie decided to get rich instead, backing Sun Yatsen and his republican cause and becoming, in the process, the wealthiest magnate in China.

Of his three daughters, Ching Ling, the "thinking" one, married Sun Yatsen and this placed her in the annals of the revolutionary heroes, while Meiling, the "clever" one, became Madame Chiang Kaishek, thence to use her particular talents for power, guile and false piety to hoodwink the Americans into one of their biggest-ever diplomatic blunders, their dogged, shortsighted support of Chiang's corrupt military regime. If you go to the Soong Ching Ling museum, take along a copy of the book that exposes it all — Sterling Seagrave's epic *The Soong Dynasty*. It makes illuminating reading.

The area north of Beihai Park is the only part of Beijing still standing that remains a tangled skein of old *hutong*s. The best way to explore them and get a glimpse of old Beijing is to join a **CITS Hutong Tour** ((10) 6615-9097, which leave twice daily from the northwestern entrance to Beihai Park. Immensely popular, the tours are conducted in bicycle rickshaws.

Yihe Yuan (Summer Palace)

This Qing dynasty summer retreat, about 12 km (seven miles) northwest of the city center, was built in the early years of the Manchu reign but has since become more popularly associated with its most famous, or infamous, resident, the Empress Dowager. She put a great deal of money into the place — most of it, as already mentioned, grabbed from funds established to modernize the antique Qing navy — and had a great deal of trouble keeping it in one piece.

It was torn apart by an Anglo-French force in 1860, damaged again by foreign troops in the Boxer Rebellion in 1900, and, each time, the Dragon Lady put it all back together again. Nowadays it's a

The Temple of Virtue RIGHT in the Qing dynasty Summer Palace. ABOVE: A detail of its opulent architecture.

public recreational spot, perhaps the most popular around Beijing, reclining along the shore of Lake Kunming and featuring splendid gardens, pavilions, mansions, temples and bridges — and the remarkable **Long Corridor**, a 7,000-m (7,655-yard) long, covered gallery full of frescoes with mythical themes. And in the lake itself there's the ultimate in imperial kitsch, the Empress's white marble paddlewheel steamboat. In wintertime the lake is the place to go for one of Beijing's favorite seasonal recreations, ice skating.

The Great Wall

The greatest man-made barrier in the world, said to be — it's a myth — the only concrete sign of human existence visible from outer space, the world's longest cemetery, the abiding symbol of China, the scene of incredible bloodshed, the wall that ultimately faced the wrong way... All this, and more, you can reflect upon atop the sweeping, crowded Great Wall at **Badaling**, 75 km (46 miles) northwest of Beijing, the main section of the 6,000-km (3,720-miles) wall that is open for tourism. It's the ultimate and, in many respects, the final destination of the China pilgrimage.

It is everything that you can imagine it to be — monolithic, magnificent, sweeping and snaking up and over steep hills as though a blind man's blundering had directed its path. In fact, when the great Qinshi Huangdi built the ancient first sections of it, the surveying technique followed by his engineers was to send ponies dragging saddles behind them over the hills and peg out the path they chose.

Along its full length, much of the wall has fallen into disrepair, its watchtowers left standing like tombstones in the desert wastes and on the loess hills of the west. You can see decrepit sections of it north of Lanzhou and follow a reasonably intact winding section on the railway ride between Beijing and Datong. The section at Badaling was repaired with a view to attracting tourists in 1957, and since then other renovations have been going on in the province. **Mutianyu**, 90 km (56 miles) northeast of Beijing is less overrun with tourists and their hangers-on, and makes a good alternative to Badaling. To get there take a morning minibus from the area just south of the Great Hall of the People.

Another good Great Wall viewing area is **Simatai**, which is 110 km (68 miles) from Beijing. This is the least developed section of the Great Wall, with just a scattering of souvenir stands and hawkers. Get bus tickets at the Jinghua Hotel (see below) in Beijing. Farther away again is the wall's dramatic eastern terminus called Old Dragon Head at **Shanhaiguan** on the Bo Hai (Sea). There's a beach here, a small village and a couple of hotels too. Close by is Beidaihe, a seaside resort popular with China's elite.

It seems that every hotel in Beijing offers a Badaling tour, which probably accounts for all the tourists out there. Most of these tours will drag you to a dozen "attractions" before you set sight on the wall itself, and charge you ludicrously inflated prices to do so. You're better off catching a bus out there yourself from outside the Qianmen subway station — the green numbered Nos. 1, 3 and 5 buses all go to Badaling. The buses start at around 6 AM and run about every 20 minutes through the day. Doing it by train is much more troublesome.

Unless you have oodles of time or have a keen archeological interest, it's best to avoid tours that include the **Ming Tombs**. They may be the resting places of 13 of the 16 Ming emperors, but nowadays they are virtually empty of relics and artwork and are little more than decorated concrete blockhouses surrounded by souvenir stalls, tea gardens and tourist restaurants.

WHERE TO STAY

Luxury

The **Beijing Hotel ((10) 6513-7766 FAX (10) 6513-7307, 33 Dong Chang'an Jie, was Beijing's first true luxury hotel, and in many eyes it is still Beijing's best. Built in 1900, right in the center of Beijing, the hotel comprises three wings, each fitted out in a different architectural style. The west wing is the place for views looking out over the Forbidden City. Essentially, this hotel has everything—shopping arcade (from "traditional silks to Pierre Cardin fashions," the blurb goes), dancing, sauna, billiard room, gym, business center, conference facilities, and the list goes on. Restaurants in the hotel include the Sichuan-style Yiyuan Garden and the Japanese Gojin Hiakusho. Bear in mind that the Beijing is not universally lauded; it has its share of critics, who mostly find fault with the service.

For more central luxury accommodation, but at lower rates, two good choices are the **Palace Hotel (** (10) 6512-8899 FAX (10) 6512-9050, 8 Jinyu Hutong (Goldfish Lane), Wangfujing, and the **Holiday Inn Crowne Plaza (** (10) 6513-3388 FAX (10) 6513-2513, 48 Wangfujing Dajie. The Palace, run by the Peninsula Group, is obviously in close competition with the nearby Holiday Inn. Both offer very high standards of accommodation, and services such as 24-hour medical attention (only if you need it), gyms with training staff, swimming pools, and the full complement of international restaurants. They are equally superb international-standard hotels and recommending one above the other is a near impossibility.

The **Grand Hotel (** (10) 6513-7788 FAX (10) 6513-0048, 35 Dong Chang'an Jie, next door to the Beijing Hotel, offers far more intimacy than its famous

The ultimate destination of every China pilgrimage: the Great Wall.

The Northeast

neighbor, and plays on the imperial Beijing theme — stylish fake antiquities in the rooms and so on. Some of the rooms do have excellent views over the Forbidden City, as does the rooftop terrace, but some may find the efforts this hotel has taken to achieve a grand style slightly pompous.

Another well located five-star hotel is the **New Otani** ((10) 6512-5555 FAX (10) 6513-9810, 26 Jianguomenwai Dajie, a link in the well known Japanese chain. It's a contender for Beijing's top luxury hotel, though some may find its style a trifle stuffy.

The **Shangri-La Hotel** ((10) 6841-2211 FAX (10) 6841-8006, 29 Zizhuyuan Lu, Haidianqu, is somewhat remote (around a 30-minute drive from

For a little more comfort, the **International Hotel** ((10) 6512-6688 FAX (10) 6512-9972, 9 Jianguomenwai Dajie, is recommended. The building itself isn't too promising, but the rooms are top-notch for the price and the location is good, making it a good alternative to the luxury hotels at about half the price.

Inexpensive

For years now the most popular budget hotel in Beijing has been the **Jinghua Hotel** ((10) 6722-2211, Nansanhuan Xilu. It may not be in an ideal location, on the southern section of the Third Ring Road, south of the Yongdingmen bus and railway station, but with inexpensive dorm beds and

downtown) but the landscaped gardens compensate for this. With 657 well-appointed guestrooms, seven different restaurants and a 24-hour business center (among other services), the Shangri-La is rated very highly by those who stay there.

Mid-range

One of the best centrally located mid-range hotels is the **Chongwenmen Hotel** ((10) 6512-2211 FAX (10) 6512-2122, 2 Chongwenmen Xidajie. Rooms start at between US$50 and US$60, which for a hotel with such good access to Beijing's prime attractions is a bargain. Amenities are scarce — this is a hotel with few pretensions. Similarly priced is the **Taiwan Hotel** ((10) 6513-6688 FAX (10) 6513-6896, 5 Jinyu Hutong (Goldfish Lane), which is even better located just off Wangfujing. Again, this is simply a basic mid-range hotel, with nothing in the way of extras.

doubles with private bathroom cheaper than any others in Beijing, this place can't be beaten.

The popular **Sea Star Hotel** ((10) 6721-8855, 166 Yongdingmen Dajie, is another good budget hotel, and under the same management as the Jinghua. The attraction is less the somewhat grotty dorms than the spacious doubles, which come in at less than US$30.

WHERE TO EAT

Despite rival claims by Guangzhou and Chengdu, Beijing is the best place in all China to eat out. Simply put, the capital has the best of everything, and diners are spoiled for choice, whether it comes to local fare, a regional specialty, or even an ethnic surprise from beyond the Himalayas.

The local cuisine, classified as "Peking" style, comprises dishes served in the imperial court of the emperor. You can find restaurants serving imperial cuisine, particularly in the banquet departments of the five-star hotels, but it won't be cheap. The local street cuisine, on the other hand, is hearty and inexpensive. Unlike the south, where rice is the staple, in Beijing it's noodles, dumplings, and breads (baked, steamed or fried) that fill up the empty spaces between the tasty bits. A great treat in Beijing is to watch an experienced noodle chef turning a lump of dough into a skein of perfect noodles, or *lamian* (literally "pull noodles") as they're known.

But Beijing's most famous dish is, of course, Peking duck (or Beijing duck if you insist). Strictly speaking, this is a dish for a party of at least six people, but as a visiting foreigner you can eat alone or with just one friend providing you can pay the bill, which is rarely that expensive anyway. The crispy skin is the most prized portion — wrap pieces in thin pancakes with a little spring onion and a dollop of plum sauce. Nothing is wasted. What's left is fried up with bean sprouts; the bones are used to make soup.

Beijing's most famous dish has given birth to a chain that has itself become a Beijing institution. **Qianmen Quanjude Roast Duck** ((10) 6511-2418, 32 Qianmen Dajie, and **Quanjude Roast Duck** ((10) 6301-8833, 14 Qianmen Xi Dajie, are the two main branches, with the latter earning the moniker, Super Duck, for its expansive pack-'em-in dining hall. Expect to pay around US$20 per head for your duck at either of these touristy but fun places. Look also for **Wangfujing Quanjude Roast Duck** ((10) 6525-3310, 13 Shuaifuyuan, Wangfujing. For a budget roast duck meal, the place to head to is **Pianyifang Roast Duck** ((10) 6465-3388, 2A Chongwenmenwai Dajie. It's a good idea to get to this restaurant earlier in the evening than later, as it is popular and the ducks have been known to sell out. At about half the price of the Quanjude chain and equally tasty, it's a bargain.

Beijing has always been a good place to sample spicy cuisine of Sichuan, and although some of the more famous Sichuan restaurants have been cleared out of the old *hutong*s in the city's race to modernize, there are still some excellent Sichuan restaurants around town. Currently one of the most popular is the **Jinshancheng Chongqing Restaurant** ((10) 6464-0945, opposite the Kempinski Hotel on Liangmaqiao Lu. Its one drawback is that it is a little way out of town, past the third ring road, but it is worth the taxi fare out there. Standards such as *gongbao jiding* (diced chicken and chili) and *ganbian sijidou* (green beans and shredded pork) are revelatory. Reservations are recommended.

Back in town, slightly more expensive and in a more contemporary setting is **Berena's Bistro** ((10) 6592-2628, 6 Gongti Donglu, a foreigner-friendly Sichuan restaurant that packs in the

Sanlitun embassy crowd, and for good reason — the food is superb.

Another regional specialty is Moslem, or Hui. This is a cuisine which has taken Beijing by storm in recent years, and there are now a huge number of Hui restaurants around town, some of them offering dance and musical performances and geared mostly to tourists. To sample this cuisine at its best and in a reasonably non-touristic setting, try the **Sunny West Xinjiang Restaurant** ((10) 6417-5918, 21 Dongzhong Jie, Dongzhimenwai. The specialty of the house is its "lamb feast."

For Chinese vegetarian cuisine, which is actually Buddhist temple food, **Gongdelin** ((10) 6511-2542, 158 Qianmen Nan Dajie, not only serves

up superb and fabulously inventive vegetarian dishes (many of them duplicating meaty dishes that Chinese Buddhists must forego), but does so at rock-bottom prices.

You don't have to go to Hong Kong or Guangzhou for excellent *dim sum* — the Cantonese-style snacks on a trolley are hugely popular in Beijing. One of the most popular places in town is **Hoi Yat Heen** ((10) 6436-2288, extension 2614, Harbor Plaza, 8 Jiangtai Xilu. The all-you-can-eat lunchtime deal is a bargain.

For a glimpse of the great leaps forward Beijing's restaurant scene is making, take a look at the wonderfully retro **Red Capital Club** ((10) 8401-8886, 66 Dongsi Jiutiao, where 1950s Politburo decor meets contemporary Chinese regional

OPPOSITE and ABOVE: A bicyclist and some bystanders at a Ming dynasty guardian statue on the triumphal route to Ming tombs.

THE NORTHEAST

N

0 50 100 150 200 km	
0 25 50 75 100 125 miles	

Khabarovsk

Sunwu

HEILONGJIANG

Keshan

Tongjiang

Qiqihar

Jiamusi

Qing'an

Anda

Jixi

Harbin

Weihe

Baicheng

Mudanjiang

NEI MENGGU

Jilin

Changchun

Vladivostok

Tongliao

Yitong

JILIN

Siping

Jingyu

Chifieng

Fuxin

Shenyang

Fushun

SEA

Chaoyang

LIAONING

Anshan

OF

Yingkou

Dandong

NORTH

JAPAN

Chengde

KOREA

Zhangjiakou

Badaling

Qinhuangdao

Korea

Bay

Shanhaiguan

Datong

BEIJING

Tangshan

Dalian

Hunyuan

Hangu

Tianjin

Bo Hai

Baoding

HEBEI

Cangzhou

Yantai

Taiyuan

Shijiazhuang

SOUTH

KOREA

Nangong

Zibo

Weifang

YELLOW

Jinan

SEA

Handan

SHANDONG

Qingdao

Tai'an

Qufu

Jining

fusion cuisine. English menus with detailed descriptions of every dish make ordering easy. Reservations are essential.

Less ostentatious, but the perfect Beijing dining experience all the same, is **Chairman Mao's Family Restaurant** ((10) 6421-9340, 30 Yonghegong Lu, close to the Lama Temple, where the theme is Mao and all the iconography he inspired. The dishes offered are according to the Chairman's personal tastes — Hunnanese country fare with a spicy bite.

In Beihai Park (the east entrance), the **Beijing Fangshan Restaurant** ((10) 6401-1889 gives diners an opportunity to sample the culinary traditions of imperial China. Strong on imperial ambiance, the food does not disappoint, with a number of set courses, varying depending on how

much money you want to spend. The cheapest banquets are remarkably good value at little more than US$10.

There was a time when Western food was the preserve of the cavernous **Moscow Restaurant** — which served jam and bread with its main courses. Amazingly the Moscow still survives (on the west side of the Beijing Exhibition Hall), and will serve up an unremarkable but authentic enough borscht for you if that's what you require. Nowadays Beijing is teeming with Western restaurants: everything from **T.G.I. Friday**, on Dongsanhuan Lu, which is an upmarket American-style diner (part of a chain), to **McDonald's** and company (**KFC**, **Pizza Hut**, **Baskin Robbins**, and others), and from the much appreciated coffee and croissant chain **Vie de France** (there's one next door to the Friendship Store) to up-market establishments like **Maxim's de Paris (** (10) 6512-1992, 2 Chongwenmen Xidajie.

Beijing's current bistro craze got its start with **Mexican Wave (** (10) 6506-3961, on Dongdaqiao Lu, which has been popular with the city's expa-triate community for some years now, not least for its excellent set lunch deal.

Don't forget to explore Beijing's street markets for delicious snacks and even meals. One excel-lent place to sample not only local dishes but also regional specialties is the **Donganmen Night Market**, at the northern end of Wangfujing. The action takes place every night from 6 PM to 9 PM. Another place you can try is the **Dongdantoutiao Night Market**, on Chang'an street, and the **Chongwenmen Night Market**. The latter is very much a local affair, but there's nothing stopping you sitting down and slurping back a bowl of noodles.

NIGHTLIFE

The China Daily lists current exhibitions and events, but a better listings source is *Beijing Scene*, which should be available at most major hotels around town.

Beijing has seen an explosion of Western-style bars over the last few years. Just four or five years ago the city was a home to little more than a hand-ful of drinking and dancing venues; today it seems as if a new one opens every day. For a mind-boggling choice of watering holes, the place to go is Sanlitun Lu, which has seen such a prolifera-tion of bars over recent years that it now goes by the nickname Jiuba Jie, or "Bar Street."

One of the pioneers, Poachers Inn, is now so venerable that it goes by the name **Old Poachers Inn (** (10) 6532-3063, Sanlitun Lu (second floor of the Friendship Store). An English-style pub, it's back in form again, pulling in the crowds after a spell in the doldrums.

For a look at what's hip in Beijing, check out **Jazz Ya (** (10) 6415-1227, 18 Sanlitun Lu. A little hard to find, it's in an alley next to the Bella Café. A Japanese-style bar, the menu offers both Jap-anese and Western food, and there's an extensive drinks menu. Also very cool, and just around the corner from Jazz Ya, is the **Comma Bar**, a chic designer space, like many other bars in Sanlitun it has alfresco seating that in the summer months make it a great place to relax.

A new arrival that looks to become one of the area's most popular places to hang out is the **Serve the People Bar (** (10) 6515-3242, an unpretentious bar that serves delicious Southeast Asian fare along with drinks.

For Beijing Opera, again check *The China Daily* or *Beijing Scene* for the latest performances. Bear in mind that a real opera performance will last up to four hours, and unless you have a reasonable grasp of the proceedings or are happy to sit and wonder at the spectacle of it all, sitting through the genuine article is no mean feat. With this in mind, the somewhat touristy (but still very enter-taining) performances at the **Liyuan Theater (** (10) 6301-6688, extension 8860, Qianmen Hotel, 175 Yongan Lu, are the perfect teaser. Perfor-mances begin nightly at 7:30 PM. Book ahead at the hotel.

Beijing's only surviving real opera house is the **Zhengyici Theater (** (10) 6318-9454, 220 Xiheyan Dajie, where you can eat roast duck in a fascinat-ing old Peking atmosphere and watch authentic performances of opera nightly — a not-to be-missed experience. Again, advance bookings are essential.

China's 2,000-year history of acrobatics make its current practitioners among the best in the world. The best place to see a performance is at the **Chaoyang Theater (** (10) 6507-2421, 36 Dongsanhuan Beilu. Shows take place nightly at 7:15 PM. Tickets are available through CITS.

Beijing is no slow coach when it comes to late-night action, despite its reputation as a haven for fusty bureaucrats, staid diplomats and number-crunching correspondents. The biggie for some years has been **JJ's (** (10) 6618-9305, 74–76 Xinjiekou Bei Dajie, which is a warehouse-sized cavern of sci-fi effects and techno beat. While still popular, it is no longer cutting-edge, however. For a sample of the trendier directions Beijing's club scene is moving in, take a look at **Club Banana (** (10) 6599-3351, Twelfth Floor, Sea Sky Shopping Center, 12 Chaoyangmennei Dajie, an atmospheric space complete with comfy lounge sofas and imported British DJs.

HOW TO GET THERE

Beijing Capital Airport is well organized and trans-portation into town is convenient. The Route A bus, outside the arrivals terminal, leaves at regu-lar intervals for as long as flights are still arriving and stops at the Hilton Hotel and close to Beijing main railway station. Taxis are readily available and should cost around US$12 to the city center. Train travelers arrive at either Beijing main station or Beijing Xi (west). Both have taxi stands, and it's best to avoid touts and proceed to the stands.

Beijing has access by air and rail to all parts of China and to the Mongolian Plateau to the north and the former Manchurian territory of the north-east. For rail travelers, **Beijing Station**, with its cavernous halls, crowded concourse and unusu-ally decorative clock towers, is one of the most convenient in the country. No booking struggles here — you simply make your way to its Interna-tional Traveler's section, through the central hall and down along the left of the escalators, to find a CITS-style reservations room, just for foreign guests, with two big boards listing destinations all over China, train numbers, departure times and ticket prices.

Outside the reservations section this VIP inner sanctum has a large waiting room, with comfortable furnishings and a Friendship desk, where you can await your train far from the madding crowds and even be escorted to it by an attendant when it's time to go. By average rail travel standards in China it's so comfortable and efficient that it's almost decadent.

THE NORTHERN TRAIL

There are two main northern routes, the "over the top" Beijing–Lanzhou run to Datong and across Inner Mongolia, and the northeast Beijing–Harbin route with major intermediate tourist destinations at Chengde, Shenyang, Changchun and Harbin.

The region itself is one of the most physically dramatic in all of China, bounded to the north, east and southeast by four great rivers, the Heilong, Wusuli, Tumen and Yalu (where, in its eastern reaches, Chinese forces stormed into the Korean War), and featuring four principal mountain ranges. The most beautiful of these, the Changbai Range, includes Mount Baitou, the tallest peak in the northeast, capped with snow all the year round. On its upper slopes lies the pristine but moody Sky Lake (Tianchi), a huge volcanic crater lake surrounded by 16 lofty peaks, that can be beautifully placid and serene one day and a maelstrom of crashing wind-whipped waves the next.

The Changbai Range also produces the Songhua River, the major tributary of the Heilong River, which flows through the region's two most interesting and attractive "river cities," Harbin, completely iced in and a popular resort in the winter months, and Jilin (in Jilin province, the capital of which is Changchun), famous for its frozen "tree hangings," a riverside filigree of ice formed by warmer moisture on banks of willow trees.

Culturally, Shenyang and Chengde have magnificent buildings and relics reflecting the region's former status as the cradle of the Manchu expansion that overran China in the seventeenth century and established the last of the nation's imperial dynasties. The founding emperor of the Qing reign established Shenyang, now the capital of Liaoning province, as the imperial capital before moving triumphantly to the Forbidden City in Beijing. That brief moment of glory has endowed the city with the Imperial Palace, the mausoleums of two Qing emperors and some 70 courts and administrative complexes that rank in architecture with Beijing's "Great Within."

Chengde features the Imperial Summer Villa, built by the early Qing court at Shenyang, north-

east of which lie several interesting monasteries and the world's largest wooden Buddha statue. At the region's farthest edge, the town of Mohe on the bank of the Heilong Jiang, the northernmost inhabited point in China, is called the Arctic City for its bitterly cold winter climate as low as 50°C below freezing point (minus 58°F) and the City of the White Night for its spectacular summer displays of the aurora borealis.

DATONG

At first sight, Datong is an unspectacular industrial and coal mining center, situated in the north of Shanxi province close to the Great Wall and the Inner Mongolia border and eight hours by train from Beijing. But it has a surprisingly interesting monastery and another major cultural attraction that makes it an important place of pilgrimage — it lies close to the Yungang Grottoes, one of the four greatest examples of Buddhist cave art in China, started by the Toba rulers of the Northern Wei when they made Datong their capital in AD 398.

What to See and Do

In Datong itself, the main cultural center is the huge, brooding twelfth-century **Huayan Monastery**, set on two levels right in the center of the city. Currently under renovation, the monastery looks a bit derelict and drab, but inside, the main hall is crammed with fantastic Buddhist artwork. Not only does it feature five huge Ming dynasty Buddha images, gilded and flamboyantly decorated and seated on lotus thrones, but these in turn are flanked by honor guards of 31 Liao dynasty statues of soldiers, officials and Bodhisattvas. Around them, the walls are decorated with murals and paintings of Sakyamuni Buddha, *arhats*, thousand-eye Bodhisattvas and other deities added by the artist Dong An in the late Qing reign.

To the south of Huayan, the **Shanhua Monastery** dating back to the Tang dynasty features another five splendid Buddha images and many murals. There's also a far more modern, yet still antique, attraction in Datong which should not be missed — the **Steam Locomotive Factory** where, on visits arranged by CITS on weekdays, you can watch the last of China's beautiful early industrial thoroughbreds being assembled.

YUNGANG GROTTOES

These dramatic Buddhist caves, carved into the northern slope of **Mount Wuzhou** more than 1,500 years ago, lie 16 km (10 miles) north of Datong in the heart of the region's coal mining communities. To get there you can either organize a minibus or taxi through CITS or take the public bus, or rather two buses — No. 2 from a terminal west of

French tourists dwarfed by a huge Sakyamuni Buddha image at Yungang Grottoes, near Datong.

the city's main square, connecting with bus No. 3 on the western outskirts of the city for the direct journey to Yungang.

There are 53 caves covering about a kilometer (over a half mile) of the cliff face and containing about 50,000 Buddhist statues and bas-relief carvings. Along the western face, the complex is dominated by a marvelous sitting Sakyamuni Buddha, 13.7 m (44 ft) tall, with a slightly amused expression that is typical of the Northern Wei style.

To the east, three ornately decorated wooden pavilions with double eaves and several galleries, built right into the cliff, form the entrance to caverns containing immense Sakyamuni and Maitreya statues and wall carvings and niches reaching right up to the ceilings. These depict the life of Buddha and also include flower motifs, altars, musicians and instruments; some were added as recently as the Qing dynasty. Although three different periods of Buddhist art are represented at Yungang, each grotto contains a Buddha image at least 13 m (43 ft) high that is said to have been modeled on a Northern Wei ruler.

Where to Stay

For foreigners there are basically just two places to stay: The **Datong Guesthouse** ℂ (352) 203-2476, to the south of the city center and the **Yungang Hotel** ℂ (352) 502-1601. Neither of them rate as luxurious, but the Yungang Hotel has some perfectly adequate single and double rooms with air-conditioning, satellite television and international direct-dial phones, as well as clean dormitory rooms for budget travelers. The hotel also has a slew of useful services in its lobby. The nearby Datong is a less appealing place for an overnight stay, but is by no means to be avoided; it's slightly cheaper than the Yungang. Take bus No. 15 or a taxi to get there.

Where to Eat

There isn't much in the way of eating in Datong, but the two hotels have good dining rooms and there are a couple of restaurants just opposite the Yungang Hotel, notably the **Hongqi Restaurant**.

How to Get There

There's only one way to get to Datong: by train. Despite the fact the city does actually have an airport and constant rumors that commercial flights will start up soon, no flights have materialized so far. The long-distance bus station is reluctant to sell tickets to foreigners for some inexplicable reason.

By train, there are two ways of doing it — stopping off on the west-to-east Lanzhou–Beijing route, or taking the overnight express west from Beijing. Leaving Datong you can take a daytime train to Beijing, riding hard-seat, and enjoy remarkable views of the Great Wall snaking around

and over the hills to the east, and old walled towns along the way.

SHANHAIGUAN

This dramatic coastal location, six and a half hours by train out of Beijing, is where the Great Wall terminates in the **Old Dragon Head**, the place where the wall ends (begins really) its journey by tumbling down from the hills to the remains of a walled garrison on the shore of the Bo Hai (Sea). It's an opportunity to view the wall without the tourist hassle of the conventional visit to Badaling, and even though the structure at Shanhaiguan is in relatively poor shape, it still has a great deal of physical and romantic appeal. Still, bear in mind that Shanhaiguan has become a popular destination for Chinese tourists. It's not quite the rustic, neglected by tourists attraction it was five years ago. Avoid weekends if possible.

Apart from the so-called Old Dragon Head, the main attraction is the **First Pass Under Heaven**, a massive gate that for many centuries was the northern route in and out of China. Climb up on the wall, and you will discover a small military museum.

Shanhaiguan also offers a temple commemorating one of the many romantic legends associated with the Great Wall, or rather its reputation as the "world's longest cemetery." The **Temple of Mengjiangnü**, six kilometers (four miles) from the town, deifies a lady of the same name who went in search of her husband who had been pressed into service along with thousands of other conscripts during its initial construction in the reign of the ruthless Qinshi Huangdi. "Suddenly there was a great rumble," so the story goes, "and a gaping hole appeared in the wall. The bones of not one but thousands of dead workers were exposed to the icy winds." Those of Meng's

husband were among them. Life, tragically, was cheap in the struggle it took to build the defensive barrier. It's also said that a sorcerer told the Iron Emperor that the wall would not be completed until 10,000 men had been buried in it. Qinshi Huangdi immediately tracked down a worker whose name included the character meaning "ten thousand" and had him slain and buried in the foundations instead.

Where to Stay

Shanhaiguan's most popular accommodation is the **Jingshan Hotel** ((335) 505-1130, on Dong Dajie near the First Pass Under Heaven (Tianxia Diyi Guan). It's a wonderfully atmospheric hotel that gives you the illusion of resting up in a Qing

Yungang Grottoes near Datong date back to the Northern Wei dynasty and feature about 50,000 Buddhist statues and bas-relief carvings covering three great dynasties.

guesthouse. Rates are very reasonable for doubles with attached bathroom and television. The **North Street Hotel** ((335) 505-1680, 2 Mujia Hutong, is another surprisingly atmospheric accommodation; rates are slightly cheaper here than at the Jingshan, making it very popular with backpacking travelers.

CHENGDE

The Hebei provincial city, 250 km (155 miles) northeast of Beijing, Chengde was an insignificant backwater called Jehol until 1703 when the Qing emperor Kangxi took a good look at its surrounding natural beauty and hot springs and transformed it into his **Imperial Summer Villa**. He called his palace Bishu Shanzhuang (Fleeing the Heat Mountain Villa), and his successors expanded it until it reached such magnificent proportions that it covered an area the size of the Forbidden City and Summer Palace combined. It is still the biggest garden palace complex in China.

Emperor Qianlong later endowed the palace with three Tibetan-style temples, one of them, the Putuo Zongcheng, a smaller version of the Potala Palace, to bind his authority to the Tibetan Buddhist rule after bringing the mountain stronghold under imperial control. Today the palace's gardens and temples, surrounded by a 10-km-long (six-mile) red wall, are in varying states of neglect and disrepair, awaiting renovations that will obviously have to be carried out if it is to become a major tourist draw.

Getting Around
Chengde is a sprawling place, and seeing the attractions on your own is almost impossible unless you have infinite patience and almost as much time. The best bet is to take a tour. These can be arranged cheaply once you arrive in Chengde.

What to See and Do
Bishu Shanzhuang's main **Central Palace**, now a museum, is in reasonable shape; so too are its **Misty Rain Mansion**, **Pine and Crane Studio** and **East Palace**. Of the temples, only five of the original eleven remain standing, but they still present a striking reminder of the power and artistry of the dynastic age. The **Puning Temple**, featuring a beautiful five-story Tibetan-style pavilion, houses an impressive 22-m (72-ft) wooden Bodhisattva image — a Thousand-Hands-Thousand-Eyes Guanyin — fashioned from five different timbers and one of the largest images of its type in the world.

The **Pule Temple** has a main building which is almost a carbon copy of the Hall of Prayer for Good Harvests in Beijing, and inside you'll find a three-dimensional mandala, at the center of which is set a bronze sculpture of the Maitreya Buddha.

The Potala-style **Puto Zongcheng** features a huge statue of the Buddhist Heavenly Mother, mounted on a horse, while the **Xumi Fushou Temple**, built in 1780 to accommodate the sixth Panchen Lama on a visit from Tibet, is a near-replica of the Tashilhunpo Monastery in Shigatse.

Where to Stay
Chengde is quite a distance from Beijing, so you may have to stay the night. An unusual and fairly luxurious option (though with mid-range rates) is the **Mongolian Yurts Holiday Inn** ((314) 202-2710, in which you get to do the yurt thing with all modern conveniences inside the grounds of the Imperial Summer Villa. Closer to town, near

Bifeng Gate, the Qing dynasty style **Qiwanglou** ((314) 202-3528 is slightly more expensive but good value considering its tasteful decor and quality service.

In town, the **Chengde Hotel** (*binguan*) ((314) 203-3157, 33 Nanyingzi Dajie has basic doubles that hover somewhere between budget and mid-range. It's perfectly adequate for an overnight stay in Chengde.

How to Get There
There are daily early morning trains from Beijing to Chengde. The journey takes around four hours.

SHENYANG

This industrial hub of Liaoning province was a trading center for the nomads beyond the Great Wall 1,000 years ago. In the seventeenth century it became the capital of the Manchus, and after they fought and connived their way to the imperial throne in Beijing, it remained as the secondary seat of power, known by its Manchu name, Mukden.

The city has changed hands several times since then. The Russians controlled it as a center of their Manchurian enterprise until the Japanese booted them out with savage warfare in 1904 and 1905. The Russians took it back after the World War II defeat of Japan, and then Mao Zedong's communists marched in and established it as a key northern base from which they launched their nationwide campaign that led to the triumph of 1949.

What to See and Do

Of Shenyang's **Manchu tombs**, the **North Tomb** is easily the best. It is the burial place of Abahai, the son of Nurhaci, who founded the Qing dynasty in the early seventeenth century. The tomb is set in an expansive park and the approach is lined with statuary reminiscent of the Ming tombs near Beijing. Bus No. 220 goes to the park from the railway station. The **East Tomb** is the burial place of Nurhaci himself and, though less impressive than the North Tomb, is worth visiting if you have time; get there by bus No. 18.

The main reason for visiting Shenyang is of course the magnificent **Imperial Palace** in the

Nowadays, Shenyang is a huge industrial and manufacturing city supported by the region's coal and steel, and would be a venue for the joint-venture businessman rather than the tourist, were it not for its magnificent footprint of the Manchu march to power, the Imperial Palace.

General Information

CAAC has its office in the center of town at 117 Zhonghua Lu, while **China Northern Airlines** is at 3 Xiaoheyuan Lu. It's easiest, however, to make air bookings at **CITS** ((24) 8680-9383, 113 Huanghe Nandajie, next to Beiling Park.

The **Bank of China** is at 6 Shiwei Lu.

Shenyang has a **United States Consulate** ((24) 8322-1198, at 52 Shisiwei Lu. The North Korean and Japanese consulates are on the same road. The Pheonix Hotel, on Huanghe Nandajie, next to Beiling Park, has a **Russian Consulate** ((24) 8611-4963.

eastern section of the city, which was the Manchu court and seat of power until the takeover of China was completed and the first Qing emperor, the warrior Shunzhi, moved the court to Beijing in 1644.

In scale and architecture this palace rivals the Forbidden City, where the Qing emperors continued their long and dramatic reign. It was built in three sections, beginning in 1625, and expanded by successive rulers until it comprised some 70 pavilions and halls dominated by the octagonal **Dazheng Hall**, where Emperor Shunzhi was crowned before being borne triumphantly south. It has a militaristic design — rows of five pavilions on each side, extending north to south, that give the effect of two lines of tents guarding the commander-in-chief.

Two views of the magnificent early Qing Imperial Palace in Shenyang — seat of the Manchu warlords.

The nearby **Pavilions** off to the south are a series of administrative centers where the Manchu ruler's 10 most important lieutenants — two princes and eight ministers — got together and met each day to plot the combination of political intrigue and military strategy that was to win them the empire. These days it is a museum of Manchu armor, military costume, carriages, campaign banners and weapons — and a sword that was worn by the eighteenth century ruler, Emperor Qianlong, which today, more than two centuries after his reign, is still untarnished.

Back in town, close to the south railway station, look for Zhongshan Square, with its massive — for some the ultimate — **Mao statue**. He stands mightily over the busy traffic, his arm gesturing with a flourish, the sculpted proletariat brandishing little red books at his feet. It is a reminder of a China that is fast disappearing.

Where to Stay and Eat

Shenyang's premier hotel is **Traders** ((24) 2341-2288 FAX (24) 2341-1988, 65 Zhonghua Lu, a Shangri-La managed hotel with a superb location in the center of town. It has everything from a fitness center to Jacuzzi, and the rooms have electronic safes, in-house movies and coffee-making facilities.

The Gloria group have arrived in Shenyang in recent years and erected two luxury hotels, though like most upmarket hotels in this part of China their market is more business travelers than tourists. The best of the two is the **Gloria Plaza Hotel** ((24) 2252-8855 FAX (24) 2252-8533, 32 Yingbin Jie, close to the north railway station. The **Gloria Inn** ((24) 2482-5225 FAX (24) 2482-5875, 8 Wenhua Donglu, is around 15 minutes from the center and offers similar standards of comfort, though again catering more for the business traveler than the tourist.

Slightly cheaper and highly recommended is the **Phoenix Hotel** ((24) 8680-5858 FAX (24) 8680-7207, 109 Huanghe Nandajie, a friendly three-star hotel with gym, sauna and well appointed rooms. It has a pleasant location next to Beiling Park, and CITS is close by.

The **Liaoning Hotel** ((24) 2386-9166, FAX (24) 2389-9103, 97 Zhongshan Lu, is a good mid-range choice. Complete with views of the waving Mao statue, it was built by the Japanese and, with its art nouveau windows, is one of the most attractive buildings in town.

If you're looking to keep expenses down (not easy in Shenyang), the **Heping Hotel** ((24) 383-8188, 86 Taiyuan Beijie, has a wide-range of rooms, from dorms through to very attractive mid-range rooms. It's near the south station, and has a distinctive red-brick pyramid roof — you can't miss it.

Dining out is a chore in Shenyang. The hotels all have their restaurants, but with the exception of the two Gloria hotels and a couple of other luxury places, the meals are not great. An exception is the **Shang Palace** restaurant at Traders Hotel in the center of town. The *dim sum* here, prepared by chefs brought in from Hong Kong is excellent and well worth splurging on.

On the streets, Shenyang's food options are often disappointing. The **Laobian Eating House**, 6 Zhongjie, is a noted outlet for that northern specialty, *jiaozi* (dumplings), but while the *jiaozi* are indeed delicious the dining environment is grotty to say the least. Many visiting foreigners end up resorting to **KFC**, of which there are many branches in town. **McDonald's** has a branch on Zhongjie.

How to Get There

Shenyang has direct air connections with most major Chinese cities. Korean Airlines has direct flights to Seoul. Shenyang is also the junction of six major railway lines in the northeast, and lies on the route of the Beijing–Harbin express trains. Note that Shenyang-bound trains stop at either the north *or* the south stations.

Overnight sleeper buses to Beijing leave from the north railway station area.

HARBIN

The capital of Heilongjiang province, 385 km (238 miles) northeast of Beijing, Harbin was a sleepy fishing village — its Manchurian name meaning "where the fishing nets are dried"—until the Russians obtained parts of Manchuria as a concession in 1898 to give themselves access to the east, and built the railway line through to Vladivostok. They then lost the entire region to the Japanese as a result of their humiliating naval defeat of 1905 but continued to make a cultural impression on the area after the 1917 Bolshevik revolution, when Harbin became a refuge for White Russian escapees. This is largely what Harbin is famous for today: its surviving Russian character, particularly the architecture of its old Orthodox churches. That, and the city's harsh winter climate, when the temperature plummets as low as minus 30°C (minus 25°F) and when the city becomes a winter recreation resort and the venue for a spectacular winter festival.

General Information

CAAC ((451) 265-1188 is at 87 Zhongshan Lu, while **Shanghai Airlines** ((451) 263-7953 is down the road at 224 Zhongshan Lu.

There's a **Bank of China** at 37 Zhaolin Jie and another (the head provincial branch) at 19 Hongjun Jie. **CITS** ((451) 232-4114 is on the ground floor of the Swan Hotel, 73 Zhongshan Lu.

What to See and Do

Harbin is more of a recreational spot than a cultural center. While it's a big summer resort, with boating, swimming, hunting, trekking and cruises on the Songhua River, its most exciting season is midwinter. The Songhua freezes over and becomes an ice skating rink and a winter playground for ice yachting, ice hockey, sledding and sleigh rides. A long runway of ice for sledding sweeps 150 m (159 yards) down the riverbank and on to the ice at Stalin Park. Elsewhere you can take rides around the town on donkey and horse sleighs, clad to the eyeballs in fur fashions bought at the **Fur Product Shop** and **Harbin Fur Factory** at 88 Zhongyang Dajie, catching a glimpse here and there of a surviving cupola or onion-shaped dome and quietly humming the theme from Doctor Zhivago in your partner's frozen ear.

But the big attraction is the **Ice Lantern Festival** from January 1, to the end of February, when Zhuolin Park and other areas are decorated with fantastic ice sculptures of animals, plants, temples and pavilions, tableaux from Chinese legends and anything that strike's the ice artist's fancy — all lit up from the inside at night. The festival has become a major international attraction, and hotel rooms are at a premium for its duration.

Of Harbin's Russian architecture, the orthodox **Nigula Jiaotang (Nicholas Church)** is the only surviving structure in any reasonable repair. It was built in 1899 and was regarded as the finest of some 17 Orthodox churches that were eventually established throughout the short-lived Czarist concession.

Where to Stay

Being a summer and winter resort for the top echelons of the Chinese administration as well as foreign visitors, Harbin has no shortage of mainstream hotels and private *dasha*-style villa hotels for overworked party officials. But note that during the January and February Ice Lantern Festival prices go up at least 20%, and it's essential that you book ahead for stays at this time.

The best luxury hotel is the **Holiday Inn City Center Harbin** ((451) 422-6666 FAX (451) 422-1661, 90 Jingwei Street. As the name suggests, it has a convenient location and is about the only place offering true international standards. Given the standards at the Holiday Inn, the rates, which start at around US$100 are extremely reasonable.

The **Songhuajiang Gloria Inn** ((451) 463-8855 FAX (451) 463-8533, 257 Zhongyang Dajie, is a close runner up in the luxury stakes. This Hong Kong-managed hotel can also be booked in Hong Kong ((852) 2833-0298.

Harbin's most interesting hotel is the **Modern Hotel** ((451) 461-5845 FAX (451) 461-4997, 89 Zhongyang Dajie. Contrary to the name, this hotel was built in 1906 and despite a complete interior

overhaul it still oozes character. Almost European in character, and with a good Russian restaurant, the luxury singles and doubles at the Modern are excellent value.

Despite the fact many budget travelers stay there, the **Beiyuan Hotel** ((451) 364-2545, in front of the railway station, is not recommended. It is unfriendly and poorly maintained. A better, cheaper, place is the **Youlian Hotel** ((451) 468-6105, 225 Youyi Lu, next to Stalin Park and overlooking the Songhua River. Simple but clean singles and doubles are available here at bargain prices, and the staff are unusually friendly.

Where to Eat

Outside its many hotel restaurants and dining rooms, Harbin is noted for its Beijing duck, shish kebab, Mongolian hotpot, Korean dog soups and other less orthodox dishes, Russian bread the size of pillows and its *glacé* ice cream, all of which can be found in its eating houses and its streets.

One of Harbin's more famous places to dine is the **Huamei Restaurant**, 142 Zhongyang Dajie, a Russian restaurant that pulls in tourists and a smattering of locals, but which is surprisingly good.

Beijing-style roast duck is the specialty at **Futailou** ((451) 461-5278, 19 Xi Shishan Dao. Prices are very reasonable and it's popular with local diners. Unfortunately there's no English menu, but the staff are accustomed to dealing with the occasional hungry foreigner and will help out.

Currently one of the most popular places to eat with local Harbiners is the **Ri Yue Tang** (Sun Moon Hall), 502 Xinyang Lu, a cavernous place that offers generic modern Chinese cuisine that takes advantage of local ingredients such as the region's famous (in China at least) mushrooms.

How to Get There

There are direct air services to Harbin from Beijing, Guangzhou, Shanghai, Changchun and Shenyang, and daily express trains from Beijing. If you are flying out of Harbin, give yourself at least an hour to get to the airport, as it is more than 50 km (31 miles) from town.

THE ROAD SOUTH

The trail between Beijing and Shanghai is not littered with grand cultural attractions, but there are some worthy stopovers all the same. The city of Tianjin has a fascinating foreign concession district that rivals that of Shanghai (minus the river views), while in Shandong province, Qingdao, another treaty port, is home of China's most famous brew and some charming German villas. Elsewhere in the province, Qufu was the birthplace of Confucius, China's grand old man of letters, and nearby Taishan is one of the country's most famous Taoist peaks.

TIANJIN

Tianjin is worthy of note for two reasons. The first is its compact enclave of colonial buildings, a legacy of the Treaty of Tianjin, signed in 1856 and granting the right to the European powers to establish concessions. The second is its sheer size: With a population of close to 10 million, Tianjin is China's third largest city.

Although an important port since Ming times, nowadays the port has shifted 50 km (30 miles) east to Tanggu. Some travelers arrive in and leave China from Tanggu, which has shipping connections with South Korea and Japan.

General Information

Dragonair ((22) 2330-1234 has an office in the Hyatt Tianjin Hotel. **Korean Air** ((22) 2319-0088 is at Room 2415, Tianjin International Building, 75 Nanjing Lu. **CAAC** ((22) 2730-5888 is at 242 Heping Lu.

The **Bank of China** is at 80 Jiefang Beilu. **CITS** ((22) 2835-8499 is at 22 Youyi Lu.

Getting Around

Tianjin is a vast urban conglomeration, and getting around it is not much fun unless you're prepared to travel by taxi. The city has one subway line, which runs from the West Railway Station to Nanjing Lu.

What to See and Do

One of Tianjin's most worthwhile attractions is **Dabei Yuan Temple**, in the north of Tianjin, on an alley off Zhongshan Lu. It was built in the early seventeenth century, and to this day it remains very active. Note the nearby shops selling Buddhist accessories.

Other attractions include a **Confucius Temple** on Dongmennei Dajie and just east of here the main drawcard for both local and foreign visitors: **Ancient Culture Street (Guwenhua Jie)**. Essentially the idea is to time warp travelers into the China of centuries past and fleece them of their tourist dollars in the process. Still, it makes for an interesting couple of hours of browsing (virtually every imaginable Chinese souvenir is on sale here), and there's a small **Tianhou Temple** to take a look at as well.

In the city center, the European streetscapes are to be found south of the Hai River. A good place to start is the Zhongxin Park roundabout, which marks the heart of the old **French concession**, a delightful area to explore on foot. This central area is perfect for combining some architectural sightseeing with a little shopping. Go to Binjiang Dao, the length of which is virtually one long market, for clothes shopping, and go to Shenyang Dao for antique shopping. The **antique**

market here is probably the biggest in China. South of Nanjing Lu, is an impressive **Catholic Church** — you can't miss it. Five-minutes' walk farther east along Nanjing Lu, opposite the Friendship Hotel is the **Earthquake Memorial**, which commemorates the quarter of a million who perished in the Great Tangshan Earthquake of 1976; Tangshan is just 70 km (43 miles) to the north, and the earthquake destroyed much of Tianjin too.

Where to Stay

Tianjin has a couple of luxury accommodations, some very decent mid-range hotels, but virtually no budget hotels. Backpackers, indeed anyone who is counting their yuan, are better off visiting Tianjin as a day trip from Beijing, which is just two hours away by train.

Tianjin's two international class luxury hotels are the **Hyatt Tianjin Hotel** ((22) 2331-8888 FAX (22) 2331-1234, 219 Jiefang Beilu, in Central Tianjin, and the **Sheraton Tianjin Hotel** ((22) 2334-3388 FAX (22) 2335-8740, on Zijinshan Lu, in the south of town overlooking Yanyuan Park. Both are excellent luxury hotels, with little to discriminate between them except that the Hyatt has the better location by far.

At the top end of the mid-range scale is the **Friendship Hotel** ((22) 2331-0372, FAX (22) 2331-0616, 94 Nanjing Lu, an uninspiring but reliable option with a reasonably good location close to the Concessions part of town. The **Tianjin Number One Hotel** ((22) 2331-0707 FAX (22) 2331-3341, 58 Jiefang Beilu, makes up for what the Friendship lacks in charm, and does so at cheaper rates. Located in a turn-of-the-century colonial structure, it's highly recommended as a place to stay for mid-range travelers looking for some atmosphere.

Where to Eat

The first stop on any culinary tour of Tianjin (and the offerings are surprisingly good) is **Food Street (Shipin Jie)** just east of Nanmenwai Dajie. With two stories of restaurants, 50 or so per floor, it's easy to spend an hour or so just deciding where to eat. Regional cuisines are well represented here. The first-floor Sichuan restaurant, **Emei**, is highly recommended, though there's no English menu.

Tianjin's most famous restaurant is **Goubuli**, 77 Shandong Lu, which some claim serves the best dumplings — *jiaozi* — in all China. The name, ironically, means something like "a dog wouldn't touch them." Such claims are difficult to dispute. And if you didn't get your fill of duck in Beijing, Tianjin has a branch of the chain **Quanjude** ((22) 2735-0046, at 53 Rongji Dajie.

Shuishang (On the Water) Park is a pleasant retreat from urban Tianjin.

How to Get There

Direct flights from Hong Kong are available with Dragonair or with CAAC. Korean Air has flights from Seoul.

From Beijing, the easiest way to get to Tianjin is by bus. It saves queuing for train tickets, and the journey takes less than three hours. Buses leave frequently from the west section of the parking lot in front of Beijing railway station.

QINGDAO

For those with the time to make a slight detour off the Beijing to Shanghai trail, Qingdao (population 1.2 million) is a fascinating corner of Shandong. Being a former German treaty port, people often refer to Qingdao as a tiny slice of Europe, a town miraculously transplanted from Bavaria. For many decades, before China opened up to the west, when a Chinese director needed a European street scene for a production, chances are it would have been filmed here.

German troops took Qingdao in 1897, after two German missionaries were killed there. A year later China ceded the town to the Germans for 99 years. Before the locals could start muttering, "What have the Germans ever done for us?" a railway line was built to connect the town with the provincial capital Jinan, electric lighting was installed and — importantly — a brewery was established. The brewery is still going strong, and makes China's only internationally known beer: Tsingtao. The Germans lost their foothold in China (and their brewery), when the Japanese marched on the city in 1914.

General Information

Dragonair ((532) 589-6809 has its office in the Hotel Equatorial, 28 Xianggang Zhonglu. **Korean Air** ((532) 387-0088 has its office in the Haitian Hotel, 39 Zhanshan Dalu. **CAAC** ((532) 287-0057 has its office at 29 Zhongshan Lu.

The **Bank of China** is at 64 Zhongshan Lu, not far from the main railway station.

CITS ((532) 286-1513/4 is at 9 Nanhai Lu, behind the Huiquan Hotel.

Getting Around

There is no bicycle rental in Qingdao. Fortunately, with the exception of Zhongshan Park, central Qingdao is small enough to explore on foot. Taxis are abundant and are metered.

What to See and Do

Qingdao's main attraction is its **German concession**, and the best area in which to see what's left of it is in the vicinity of the railway station. Take a stroll up Zhongshan Lu away from the station and look for a fine **Catholic church** on your right. The church itself is only open for services on

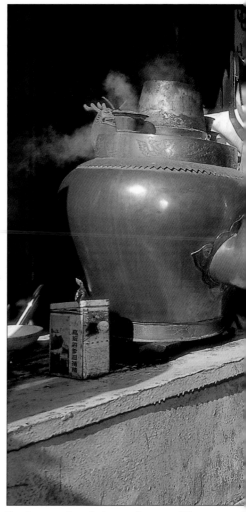

Sunday mornings, but a wander around the area to the rear of the church will reward architectural buffs the rest of the week.

The **Tsingtao Brewery** is, of course, a popular destination. Unfortunately the only way to get inside is to go on a tour with CITS (see GENERAL INFORMATION, above).

For Chinese visitors — and in the summer months the city is swarming with them — Qingdao is a beach resort. To Western eyes, the beaches will probably seem unappealing, and if you settle on one of them for a spot of sunbathing it's very likely that representatives of the China-wide fraternity of English students will descend on you in no time. Still, it's worth taking a stroll along the very pleasant esplanade that overlooks **No. 1**, **No. 2**, **No. 3** and **No. 6 beaches**. No. 6 is usually the busiest.

Northwest of No. 1 Beach is **Xinhao Park**, which has a beautiful old German mansion on its

grounds, now transformed into a hotel. Underneath the park is a bizarre underground shopping complex called the **Longshan Underground Market**. It's well worth visiting. **Zhongshan Park** is a huge garden made for strolling, and is famous for its cherry trees, which bloom between mid-April and early May.

Where to Stay

Qingdao's top hotel is the **Qingdao Shangri-La** ((352) 388-3838 FAX (352) 388-6868, 9 Xianggan Zhonglu, whose features include a 24-hour business center and a slew of recreational and dining options. Its only drawback is that it is a 25-minute taxi ride out of town, though its location near some of Qingdao's best beaches may be a drawcard for some travelers.

The **Badaguan Hotel** ((532) 387-2168 FAX (532) 387-1383, 19 Shanhaiguan Lu, is not the top hotel in town, but it has a good location close to No. 2

Beach, has some character and can also organize accommodation in villas around town.

The **Qingdao Huiquan Dynasty Hotel** ((532) 287-3366 FAX (532) 287-1122, 9 Nanhai Lu, is also well located, and is more a standard luxury hotel, if a little bland. The Gloria Group's **Huanhai Gloria Inn** ((532) 387-8855 FAX (532) 386-4640, 21 Donghai Lu, is another luxury hotel worth considering.

For mid-range accommodation, the central **Qingdao Hotel** ((532) 289-1888 FAX (532) 286-2464, 53 Zhongshan Lu, may look expensive from the outside, but room rates are very reasonable — discounts are often available if you ask politely. For sheer convenience, the **Railway Hotel** ((532) 286-6693, next door to the railway station, is hard to beat. Dormitory rooms make it popular with budget travelers, but the hotel also has some serviceable budget singles and doubles.

Souvenirs and tea served in bowls are highlights of a visit to Tianjin's Ancient Culture Street.

How to Get There

Qingdao has international air connections with Hong Kong and Seoul, and is well connected with domestic destinations. Jinan, the provincial capital is the nearest transport hub. The easiest way to get there is by bus, which take four to five hours and leave frequently from the bus stand next to the railway station. From Jinan, the provincial capital, there are buses to Taian (for Taishan and Qufu) and trains north to Tianjin and Beijing, and south to Shanghai.

TAIAN

Taian is a small dusty town and there would be no reason to stop here were it not for its Dai Temple, and the nearby cultural attractions of Taishan and Qufu.

The **Dai Temple** came into being as a pit stop for pilgrims visiting nearby Taishan — some say as early as the Qin dynasty (221–206 BC). It has gone through countless reconstructions since then, most recently in the mid-1950s. Today it's remarkably well preserved, and even if there is a museum-like atmosphere to the place, a visit is still an essential prelude to climbing Taishan; if you're feeling particularly energetic, you can walk up to the mountain, starting at the temple.

Notable sights in this large temple include a magnificent Song dynasty mural housed in the Main Hall, which depicts the god of Taishan in the guise of Emperor Zhen Zong, who commissioned the painting. In the temple grounds is a large collection of steles, some of them very ancient.

Where to Stay

Taian's top hotel is the **Overseas Chinese Hotel** ((538) 822-8112 FAX (538) 822-8171, Dongyue Dajie, which given its location does a very good job. It even has a swimming pool and a bowling alley, though after slogging up Taishan and back, bowling is unlikely to be foremost on your mind.

The popular place to stay, for backpackers and mid-range travelers alike, is **Taishan Binguan** ((538) 822-4678 FAX (538) 822-1432, on Hongmen Lu, just north of the Dai Temple and en route to Taishan. The doubles with air-conditioning and bathroom are very reasonably priced, while budget travelers pile into the three-bed dorm rooms.

How to Get There

If you're coming from Qingdao, change to a minibus in front of the Jinan main railway station. Taian is also connected by train to Jinan and to Beijing and Shanghai. The onward train journey to Shanghai takes around nine to 10 hours.

TAISHAN

Taishan is China's most sacred Daoist mountain. Its crags and peaks are littered with pagodas and temples and calligraphy, the legacy of inspiration-seeking artists, poets, and leaders. Imperial sacrifices were once held on its summit, emperors have toiled up its slopes, as did Confucius (who was born nearby) and more recently even Mao.

Taishan is the domain of the female Daoist deity Bixia, whose name is usually rendered in English as the Princess of the Azure (or pink, perhaps) Clouds. She has traditionally had a loyal following in Shandong, and among other things she is said to bestow long life on those who climb to the summit of her mountain — 100 years, specifically. But the most captivating thing about Taishan, after the views, is the tide of people. Don't be surprised if you see some gnarled old Daoist priest skip past you as you pant your way up the more than 6,000 stairs that climb ever upwards; move aside as the porters trip nimbly past carrying huge loads; watch for the honeymoon couples taking it easy on a two-man palanquin, a time-honored mode of conveyance on China's sacred mountains.

There are a number of different approaches to the summit. The combination of minibus and cable-car is the easiest one, and given that the proper pilgrimage trail from Taian to the summit involves four to five hours of uphill trudging it's tempting. One possibility is to "half cheat" and take a minibus to **Zhongtianmen**, which is where the cable-car starts, and walk from there, which takes around two hours — don't worry, your legs will know that they've been busy when you get to the top. Once you're on the summit, you can decide whether you want to walk back down or take the cable-car (it takes just eight minutes).

There is accommodation on the mountain at the **Zhongtianmen Guesthouse** ((538) 822-6740, and at the **Shenqi Guesthouse** ((538) 822-3866, which is at the summit. Neither hotel is particularly good value, though prices have come down

in recent years. Expect to pay in the vicinity of US$50 for a room in either.

QUFU

An interesting day-trip from Taian is the small hamlet of Qufu. Confucius, the Great Teacher, was born here in 551 BC and spent much of his life teaching with little in the way of recognition. His attempts to achieve influence foundered; his efforts, as he traveled around China, to reach the ears of the powerful were roundly ignored, and it was only after his students gathered together his ideas in a book known as *The Analects* that he achieved posthumous success.

Today it's easy to spend a day wandering around Qufu's **Confucius Temple** and the **Confucius Mansions**. Both of them are massive, testifying not only to the eminence that Confucius achieved after his death, but also to the extent to which his impecunious pursuit of his ideals enriched his ancestors. The Kong family (Confucius is spelled Kong Fuzi in Chinese) became the First Family Under Heaven, and they lived in their Qufu mansion for some 2,500 years, building on to it, enhancing its magnificence, until when the last family head of the Kongs, Kong Decheng, decamped (sensibly given his lifestyle) to Taiwan in 1948, the family residence, with its 466 rooms, resembled Beijing's Forbidden City.

Another worthwhile attraction is the **Confucian Forest**, which is the resting place of Confucius himself surrounded by the graves of his many descendents. It's a sprawling place — a real forest — and bicycles can be rented at the main gate. Rent one: the forest is far too big to explore on foot.

Where to Stay

If you decide you need more time in Qufu, there are places to stay. The **Queli Hotel** ((537) 441-1956 FAX (537) 441-2022 is an upper mid-range hotel that is right next door to the mansions and temple complex. Despite facilities like a bowling alley and conference halls, remarkably the hotel blends in with the surrounding historical architecture, and is a very comfortable and atmospheric place to spend a night or two.

The **Confucius Mansions Hotel** ((537) 441-2686 FAX (537) 441-3786, 9 Datong Lu, is the top budget hotel in town. Along with dormitory accommodation, it also has comfortable mid-range rooms. It's in the south of town, next to the bus stop.

Buses run from Taian to Qufu throughout the day, and there are also buses to the provincial capital, Jinan.

In modern China the sacred peaks that pilgrims once toiled up on foot are accessible by less exhausting means; here a cable car whisks visitors to the summit of Shandong's Taishan.

The Eastern Plains

THIS DRAMATIC EAST–WEST STRETCH of the long China trail offers an exciting and quite refined gateway to the heart of the nation for travelers starting from Shanghai — and for those taking the clockwise grand tour, it offers relative comfort, good cuisine and sophistication for the end of a China adventure.

The Yangzi River is the central axis on which all travel in China swings. On the rail route north from Guangzhou it provides access to Shanghai, Suzhou and Hangzhou in the east and Chongqing, Chengdu, Lhasa and Xi'an in the west. It offers the same east–west access coming, of course, south from Beijing. And from whichever direction you approach it, the two pivotal junctions are Zhengzhou and Wuhan.

ZHENGZHOU

A busy, prosperous industrial city, once a Shang dynasty imperial seat and now the capital of Henan province, Zhengzhou is one of the two most strategic railway junctions of central eastern China — the other being Hengyang on the east–west rail corridor to Yunnan and the west. It's also one of the most difficult cities in China for foreigners to tackle — very few locals speak English, and, unless you're staying in the Holiday Inn or the Novotel International, tourist facilities remain primitive. The main cultural attraction is Shaolin Monastery, 80 km (50 miles) to the southwest, considered to be the birthplace of Chan (Zen) Buddhism and the martial art kung fu.

GENERAL INFORMATION

CAAC has outlets in most hotels. The **Bank of China** is at 40 Huayuan Lu. **CITS (** (371) 595-2072 is at 15 Jinshui Lu.

WHAT TO SEE AND DO

Zhengzhou has only one overwhelming attraction, and that's Shaolin Monastery. Built in the time of the Northern Wei dynasty, it was established in tribute to Bodhidharma, the Indian monk (also featured on a mural in the Guangxiao Temple in Guangzhou) who brought the message of Chan (Zen) to China and is said to have been the first champion of the martial arts — teaching his disciples boxing and unarmed combat for self-protection in those unstable and dangerous times. Legend has it that he was so transcendental that he was able to cross a river on a flimsy reed.

In the monastery's most glorious age, during the Sui and Tang dynasties, it sported 5,000 shrines, halls, pagodas and pavilions. Only four major buildings remain — the Bodhidharma Pavilion, Thousand Buddha Hall, White Robe Hall and Bodhisattva Ksitigarbha Hall — but they do offer surviving artwork and relics that echo the monastery's martial role. In the White Robe Hall, for example, there are stunning murals depicting scenes and techniques of kung fu, including the epic "Thirteen Monks Rescuing the King of Tang" — a celebrated punch-up that took place when the monks of Shaolin acted as imperial retainers in the Tang dynasty. In the Thousand Buddha Hall you can study rounded hollows in the tiled floor — worn there over the centuries by daily kung fu training.

To get to the monastery, either take a CITS tour or a daily bus that leaves from outside the Zhongyuan Mansions opposite the railway station. Buy your ticket the a small white booth

on the edge of the station concourse. Note that if you take the daily bus, you should try to bring along a ticket request written in Chinese.

Aside from the monastery Zhengzhou provides easy access by train or bus to the cultural jewel of central China, Luoyang (see below).

WHERE TO STAY

Zhengzhou's finest is the **Holiday Inn Crowne Plaza (** (371) 595-0055 FAX (371) 599-0770, a hotel with an interesting history. It has been converted from a "foreign expert's" guesthouse built in the 1950s, but from the moment you step into the massive, glitzy lobby area there can be no doubt that the conversion has been a thorough one.

OPPOSITE: Daoist monk — in China, Daoism flourishes alongside Buddhism. ABOVE: Classic architecture in a gateway to a residential backstreet.

Close on the Holiday Inn's heels is the **Novotel International** ((371) 595-6600 FAX (371) 595-0161, 114 Jinshui Donglu, a sleek and imposing building at a location virtually next door to its main rival.

Although there are a few would-be contenders Zhengzhou's other hotels are either blandly mid-range or horrifyingly bottom range, and if you doubt the last take a look at the Dickensian Zhongyuan Mansions opposite the railway station.

The **Asia Hotel** ((371) 696-8866 FAX (371) 696-8877, 165 Jiefang Lu, is the best mid-range choice in town. It has a good location next to the Erqi Pagoda traffic circle, not far from the railway station, and discounts for the smart luxury doubles and singles are available on request.

Budget travelers are recommended to check in to the **Golden Sunshine Hotel** ((371) 696-9999 FAX (371) 696-9534, which is close to the railways station at 6 Erma Lu. The budget rooms come with shared bathing and toilet facilities, and some of them tend to be cramped and gloomy so look before you commit. The hotel also offers some surprisingly luxurious suites.

HOW TO GET THERE

Zhengzhou is connected by air with most major Chinese cities. For access by train, it's on the main north-south Guangzhou–Beijing express route, the cross-country Beijing–Xi'an–Lanzhou service and the east-west route between Shanghai and Xi'an. There are comfortable express rail services to Xi'an, which take around seven and half hours.

LUOYANG

Luoyang, west of Zhengzhou, is another city whose modern industrial façade obscures its long, illustrious history. Not only was it the founding center of Buddhism in China — the site of the Han dynasty White Horse Temple, built to celebrate the arrival of the first sutras from India — but it was the imperial capital of nine dynasties until it was destroyed by the armies of the northern Jin reign in the twelfth century.

Its most magnificent legacy is, of course, the Longmen Buddhist Grottoes, first excavated and decorated in the time of the Toba Northern Wei dynasty when Luoyang was the imperial court, and also the site of more than 1,300 Buddhist temples.

WHAT TO SEE AND DO

Around 16 km (10 miles) south of Luoyang on the banks of the Yi River, the **Longmen (Dragon Gate) Grottoes** were dug and carved around the year

AD 493 in the time of the Northern Wei and added to in the Tang dynasty. More than 2,000 of them are found along the cliff face overlooking the Yi River, packed with some 100,000 sculptured images, 40 stone towers and 3,600 stone carvings and inscribed steles and plaques. The Buddha images are magnificent, with their full, benign Han Chinese features that reflect the cultural assimilation that occurred as the Toba dynasty extended its control south.

The two most impressive galleries are the **Binyang Caves** at the entrance to the complex, featuring 11 large Buddha images of the Toba period, and the **Fengxian Temple**, now without its protective roof and actually an open-air

grotto, which was built in the Tang era and is dominated by 11 huge statues, the biggest of them a 51-m-tall (59-ft) Vairocana Buddha. One of the statues supports a pagoda in the palm of its hand and is in the act of crushing a demon underfoot. Aside from the Buddhas and attendant statues, there are sculptures throughout the grottoes of emperors, princes and nobles of the 400-year period over which the immense tableau was completed.

WHERE TO STAY

Luoyang won't go out of its way to pamper you. The top hotel in town is the very Chinese **Luoyang Peony Hotel** ((379) 485-6699 FAX (379) 485-6999, 15 Zhongzhou Xilu. It does a good job considering it's in faraway Luoyang, and the lobby restaurant is highly recommended.

The best mid-range hotel in town is the **Luoyang New Friendship Hotel** ((379) 491-1445 FAX (379) 491-2328, 6 Xiyuan Lu, whose lobby sees constant streams of overseas Chinese tour groups. It's inconveniently located in the southwest of town.

Budget travelers mostly stay around the railway station, which has a few inexpensive hotels and has the added advantage of being close to the minibus departure points for the White Horse Temple and the Longmen Grottoes. Choose between the **Luoyang Hotel** ((379) 393-5181, which is dinghy but very cheap, and the **Tianxiang Hotel** ((371) 394-0600, which is slightly more expensive and little better.

clustered at the confluence of the Yangzi and Han rivers. Hankou, on the Yangzi's west bank, is the main attraction. A former fishing village that became a major treaty port in the days of British and European military and trading pressure, its architectural character is similar to that of Shanghai.

Hanyang, south of Hankou, over the Han River, is a largely industrial center. Although it doesn't have the narrow teeming streets and old Victorian commercial buildings of Hankou, it features the city's most historically interesting attraction, the Qing dynasty Guiyuan Temple.

Wuchang, on the Yangzi's eastern bank, is the oldest, dating back to AD 221, but is ironically now more representative of modern China — wide

How to Get There

Luoyang is not very well connected to the rest of China by air. Consider flying to Zhengzhou and continuing from there to Luoyang by train or bus. The daily Zhengzhou–Xi'an express stops in Luoyang. Buses from Zhengzhou to Luoyang take around three hours. Minibuses to Longmen and to the White Horse Temple leave from in front of Luoyang station. Some of these buses are in fact Chinese tour buses, and their itineraries will include both sights. Tours are also available at the Friendship and the Peony hotels in Luoyang.

WUHAN

Hubei's provincial capital, one of the largest cities in the interior of China, Wuhan (population 3.34 million) is actually made up of three cities

boulevards and highrise administrative buildings — and includes the huge Wuhan University, the Hubei Provincial Museum and the popular recreational resort, East Lake (Dong Hu). Wuchang is linked to Hankou by the spectacular Yangzi River Bridge, built in 1957 and the first to span the great river, its eastern expressway sweeping under the beautiful multi-winged roofs of the city's most remarkable historic landmark, the renovated Ming dynasty Yellow Crane Mansion (Huanghe Lou).

Wuhan's place in contemporary history centers on an accidental bomb explosion on October 10, 1911 that triggered an anti-Manchu army rebellion and in turn became the long-awaited flashpoint of the republican campaign to sweep the Qing dynasty from power.

The sensuously rounded gateway OPPOSITE to the restored pavilion at Guiyuan Monastery ABOVE.

GENERAL INFORMATION

The Hankou branch of **CAAC** ((27) 8361-1756 is at 217 Liji Beilu. **Dragonair** ((27) 8580-6868, extension 80422-3 is in Shangri-La Hotel. The **Bank of China** is at 1021 Zhongshan Dadao. **CITS** ((27) 8578-4100, Seventh Floor, 26 Taibei Lu, is one of China's unusually helpful branches, where staff will go out of their way to provide information to individual travelers.

GETTING AROUND

Taxis are widely available, as are auto rickshaws. There are ferries and speedboats that run back and forth between Hankou, Hanyang and Wuchang, but they are often very crowded. Finding any place that will rent a bicycle is a near impossibility.

WHAT TO SEE AND DO

If Wuhan has a saving grace as a destination for travelers it's the street life in **Hankou**. There are no sights as such here, but take a stroll in the area between **Yanjiang Dadao** (beside the river) and **Jiefang Dadao**, and between the push and shove of the crowds and the delightful cultural clash between old Chinese and treaty port Victorian architecture, there's never a dull moment. Take a look at the Victorian-style Bank of China building on the corner of Jiangshan Lu and Zhongshan Dadao.

For those on a strict sightseeing agenda, **Guiyuan Temple** should top the itinerary. It's close to the waterfront in **Hanyang** — a Qing dynasty monastery, on the grounds of a Ming dynasty park, now springing back to life after the repression of the Cultural Revolution. Billowing with joss-stick smoke, it features a gloomy but fascinating main hall full of Buddha images, sculptures of *arhats* and a looming, moon-faced guardian deity, all staring from dark and dusty glassed alcoves. Its most treasured relic is a Burmese jade Buddha presented to it in 1935.

As for the **Yangzi Bridge** (the old one, not the new one in the east of town), you can climb up its stone towers and right onto its top traffic deck and cross the 1,156-m (3,800-ft) span enjoying a bird's-eye view of the river traffic and the packed city ferries disgorging hundreds of commuters and their bicycles along the **Wuchang** waterfront — the crowds streaming like hordes of ants up the ferry ramps, the chrome of their bikes flashing in the sun. Ahead of you, on the Wuchang side, you can also marvel at the towering, golden, multi-eaved **Huanghe Lou (Yellow Crane Mansion)**. It's really a rebuilt pagoda — the original is said to have been built in the Three Kingdoms days (AD 220–265) and rebuilt time after time. The last

but one, a Ming dynasty structure, burned down in 1884 — and although this one is completely new it's a popular recreation spot for Chinese and foreign visitors alike. The view from its upper balconies is a dramatic panorama of the bridge, its huge expressway, the Wuchang riverfront and the Hanyang foreshores.

East Lake (Dong Hu)

Out on the eastern fringe of Wuchang, East Lake (Dong Hu) is one of the largest freshwater lakes in China and a long-established recreational resort that has interesting pavilions, a botanical garden, good bicycling paths, boating and three lakeside restaurants, the **Renmin**, **Liyuan** and **Tingtao**.

It's also the site of the small **Hubei Provincial Museum** with a remarkable exhibition of bronze tripods, lacquered furniture and trunks, carvings, sculpture, jewelry and gold bowls and ornaments unearthed in 1978 from the tomb of the Marquis Yi of Zeng, one of the nobles of the Warring States period of 475–221 BC, just before the rise to power of the Iron Emperor Qinshi Huangdi.

The most splendid relic from the tomb is a huge ancient musical instrument, a bronze bell chime — 65 ornately decorated bells set on a heavy three-level frame which, as the museum's brochure explains, "were played by five musicians... Ancient and modern music, both Chinese and foreign, has been played on it, and the sound is melodious and beautiful."

OPPOSITE: The historic Ming-dynasty Yellow Crane Mansion, Wuchang. ABOVE: A suburban woman heads off to market.

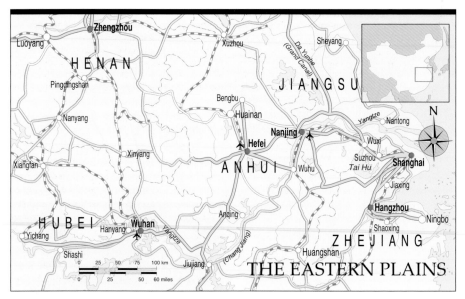

There's another notice that strikes a chilling tone in this important tomb excavation. It calls attention to the "immolated remains" of concubines and attendants found in 21 plain wooden coffins around the duke's sarcophagus. "Skeletons found in the coffins are those of young females, the oldest being about 25 and the youngest 13 years old. Obviously they were immolated for the master of the tomb. This is an indictment against the feudal exploiting class for their cruel oppression of the laboring people."

WHERE TO STAY

Most of Wuhan's accommodation is in the Hankou part of town.

Luxury

For international-standard accommodation in the heart of bustling Hankou, the **Holiday Inn Tian An Wuhan** ((27) 8586-7888 FAX (27) 8584-5353, 868 Jiefang Dadao, is easily Wuhan's best choice. With a superb selection of restaurants, a state-of-the-art fitness center and rooms starting at around US$100, it is popular with business travelers and tourists alike.

For those less in need of modern international standards, and for more in local ambiance, the **Jianghan Hotel** ((27) 8281-1600 FAX (27) 8281-4342, 245 Shengli Jie, is an excellent choice. It was built by the French in 1914, and although it has subsequently been completely refurbished, it still retains much of its charm. It is worth considering splurging on the period suites, which are cheaper than the Holiday Inn's rooms and ooze character.

The **Wuhan Asia Hotel** ((27) 8380-7777 FAX (27) 8380-8080, 616 Jiefang Dadao, was Wuhan's top

hotel until the arrival of the Holiday Inn. Slightly cheaper than the Holiday Inn, it offers an impressive range of amenities, including an outdoor swimming pool and a grand total of 10 restaurants and bars.

Mid-range and Inexpensive

Mid-range hotels are not thick on the ground in Hankou. Recommended is the **Victory Hotel** ((27) 8270-7241 FAX (27) 8270-7624, 11 Siwei Lu, an adequate and moderately priced hotel, though the location, north of the central Hankou district, could be better, and the hotel lacks character.

Finding a genuine budget hotel in Wuhan is difficult. Travelers used to rock-bottom dormitory accommodation in other parts of China will have to go a little upmarket in order to stay here. Best of the budget mid-range hotels is the **Guanshang Yuan Hotel** ((27) 8277-9069 FAX (27) 8277-8151, 117 Jianghan Lu, a characterless, but functional Chinese-style hotel that has some inexpensive singles and doubles with attached bathroom.

WHERE TO EAT

There's some good hotel food in Wuhan, notably at the Holiday Inn and the **Ramada Hotel** ((27) 8578-7968, 9 Taibei 1 Lu, which until the Holiday Inn came along held up the fort alone on the Western food front with its lobby coffee shop. The **Shang Palace** restaurant at the Shangri-La Hotel ((27) 8580-6868, 700 Jianshe Dadao, is an excellent Cantonese *dim sum* restaurant that is well worth a splurge.

Elsewhere around town, you might like to drop into one of Wuhan's longest-running and most famous restaurants, **Lao Huibin**, on the corner of

Minquan and Qianjin Lu. It's a good place to try Hubei dishes such as brown-sauce fish. The basic but wildly popular **Laotongchang**, 1 Dazhi Lu, is a cheap and friendly eating establishment offering very tasty and nourishing chicken soup in clay pots and a famous stuffed bean-curd snack known as *doupi*.

HOW TO GET THERE

Wuhan is China's central rail and Yangzi River access. It lies on the main Guangzhou–Beijing express route and the east-west routes from Shanghai to Kunming and Xi'an. The Yangzi River ferries ply east to Nanjing and Shanghai and west to

Chongqing. Both the main railway station and river ferry terminal are in Hankou. There are also direct air links with almost every airport in China.

Yangzi River Ferries

Tickets for the Yangzi River ferries are readily booked in Wuhan at any of the tourist hotels, or if you feel up to it at the Yangzi Ferry Terminal in Hankou. Departures leave daily for Chongqing (5 days) and Nanjing (two days) upstream and for Shanghai (three days) downstream.

If you want to enjoy the trip (and why else would you do it?) take a second-class passage. Second class is two-a-cabin, and is fairly comfortable: the third- and fourth-class berths are not only packed with people but dozens more crowd aboard at each stop along the river and bed down along the decks and corridors until there's hardly room to move. Because of the vessel's constant

hot water supply, the passengers all was clothes the moment they step aboard, a decks become festooned with flapping d~~ ~~ s, shirts, underwear and long-johns. But it's a restful run, with an occasional stop to pick up cargo and passengers along the way and, now and then, the sight of a passing moth-winged sailing junk thrown in for excitement.

NANJING

Nanjing (Nanking), the old southern capital of the dynastic age, now the capital of Jiangsu province, is a prosperous, attractive city with a fascinating history, dating back to 473 BC, in the Warring States period; it was later to become the Song dynasty capital. It was also the temporary capital during the early Ming period, and has always been regarded as an alternative to Beijing as a seat of power. Indeed Nanjing means "southern capital"; Beijing means "northern capital."

In 1842, British troops and gunboats laid siege to Nanjing in the first Opium War, forcing the Qing dynasty to sign the historic Treaty of Nanking which opened up the five treaty ports to free trade. In the Taiping Rebellion of 1853 the city was again besieged, conquered and established as the rebel headquarters. In 1911 it became the republican capital for a brief period and was where Dr. Sun Yatsen was declared president of the provisional government. In 1937 it was the headquarters of Chiang Kaishek's government until the Japanese advance drove it up the Yangzi to Wuhan and then to Chongqing. In April 1949, Mao Zedong's communist forces poured across the Yangzi and raised the red flag over its rooftops.

The city is now a leading center of culture and higher education, and a powerhouse for joint-venture business projects in Jiangsu. It is, in fact, a business city, but its strategic position on the Yangzi River ferry route and its cultural attractions make it well worth a stopover.

GENERAL INFORMATION

Dragonair ((25) 471-0181 is at Room 751-753, World Trade Center, 2 Hanzhong Lu. **CAAC** ((25) 440-8583 is at 52 Ruijin Lu. **China Eastern Airlines** ((25) 440-0102 is on the corner of Zhongshan Donglu and Changbai Jie.

The **Bank of China** is at 3 Zhongshan Donglu. **CITS** ((25) 342-1145 is at 202 Zhongshan Beilu, and does very little except sell airline tickets.

WHAT TO SEE AND DO

The commercial heart of Nanjing is the **Xinjiekou** traffic circle, where you'll find the upmarket Jinling

"Liberal era" young people sport the latest fashions.

Hotel, and where Zhongshan Lu intersects with Zhongshan Nanlu. North of here, at the intersection of Zhongyang Lu and Beijing Lu, you'll find the **Drum Tower** (Gulou) traffic circle, another center and useful landmark. The other area you need to know about is **Fuzi Miao**, a Confucian temple in the south of town, surrounded by many shops and restaurants.

East of Xinjiekou, on Zhongshan Donglu, the **Nanjing Museum** is wide ranging and always interesting. West of Fuzimiao, the **Memorial to the Nanjing Massacre** is a chilling account in pictures and displays of the darkest moment in the Japanese attempt to annex China as part of its colonial ambitions of World War II.

are likely to be more of a draw. Carved over the entrance to the mausoleum are the Three Principles, as expounded by Sun Yatsen (in Chinese, Sun Zhongshan), and still upheld by the Nationalist government in Taiwan: Nationalism, Democracy and People's Livelihood.

The **Zheng He Memorial Hall** and park and the **Qixia Monastery** are 20 km (12 miles) northeast of the city. The former commemorates the Ming dynasty eunuch admiral who led the seven great oceanic voyages to the African coast between 1405 and 1433, almost a century before Columbus discovered the New World. The hall and surrounding pavilions are packed with relics and exhibits of life in the Ming reign, graphs, maps

Xuanwu Lake Park, in the northeast of town is a landscaped park that provides a chance to watch the Chinese at play, but otherwise isn't much to write home about.

Farther to the east is **Zijin Shan** (Purple Gold Mountain), which has a number of famous attractions. Of most interest are the buildings around **Linggu Temple**, a small but very active Buddhist place of worship. The large **Beamless Hall** dates back to 1381, and was so named because its large frame is supported by columns without the aid of a beam. From here you can take a shuttle bus up to the **Sun Yatsen Mausoleum**. Although for many Chinese visitors — particularly the overseas variety — a visit the tomb of the man who the Nationalists refer to as the *guofu*, literally the "national father," is something of a pilgrimage, for most Western visitors the views over Nanjing and the surrounding hills

and models depicting the Moslem seafarer's expeditions and the 1,456 sailing junks that were under his command, and a brass bell that was cast to announce his safe return from the last of these "Silk Road of the Sea" odysseys.

WHERE TO STAY

Luxury

The pick of Nanjing's luxury hotels is the **Sheraton Nanjing Kingsley (** (25) 666-8888 FAX (25) 666-9999, 169 Hanzhong Lu, an international-standard hotel that contrives to create a cozy ambiance, and which, among other features, has a jogging track, indoor pool, a putting course, and even an Irish pub that serves Kilkenny's.

The magnificent 37-story **Jinling Hotel (** (25) 471-1888 FAX (25) 471-1666, Xinjiekou Square, may be Nanjing's oldest luxury hotel, but it has kept up with the times and is still competition to new arrivals such as the Sheraton. It has a total of eleven restaurants, including a revolving restaurant on the thirty-sixth floor, and other features include bowling alleys, a swimming pool, a fitness center, and excellent on-line facilities for the business set.

If you want to be based in the lively Fuzi Miao district in the south of town (the best area for dining and nightlife), the **Nanjing Mandarin Garden Hotel** ((25) 220-5555 FAX (25) 220-1876, 9 Zhuangyuanjing, is an excellent choice. Its facilities are on a par with the Sheraton and the Jinling, though it also has Nanjing's only squash court if you are in need of some exercise.

Inexpensive

Nanjing's least expensive hotel is the **Hua Kang Fan Hotel** ((25) 480-4181, 180 Huju Lu. The singles and doubles with attached bathrooms here are simple but clean, and the hotel has a good Chinese restaurant and basic business center.

Nanjing is unusual in that its university guesthouses (long a budget refuge throughout China for travelers in the know and with the right contacts) are open to all and sundry. The **Nanjing University Foreign Students Dormitory** ((25) 359-3589, Shanghai Lu, is where budget travelers inevitably end up, usually in double rooms with shared bathroom.

Mid-range

Highly recommended is the **Zhongshan Hotel** ((27) 336-1888 FAX (25) 337-7228, 200 Zhongshan Lu, a three-star hotel with a good fitness center and Internet access in its rooms. The location, in the heart of the town, is hard to beat.

The **Nanjing Hotel** ((25) 341-1888 FAX (25) 342-2261, 259 Zhongshan Beilu, has a wide variety of rooms. The bargains are in the old wing, but it must be said that it is not a particularly pleasant place to stay. The more expensive new wing is an altogether different affair, with well appointed rooms from around US$60.

The **Future Inn** ((25) 470-0999 FAX (25) 470-0123, 34 Guanjia Qiao, in Xinjiekou, combines a great location with extremely good value rooms. Aimed mostly at business travelers, its an efficient and friendly place that can handle onward travel bookings.

WHERE TO EAT

Nanjing is the perfect place to try Jiangsu cuisine at its best, and the best in Nanjing is the **Dingshan Spring Garden Restaurant** ((25) 880-1868, Dingshan Hotel, 19 Chahaer Lu, Daqiao District, in the north of town. There are couple of other branches of this famous restaurant around town nowadays, but the original is still considered to serve the best. The restaurant has an English menu, and English-speaking staff can guide you through the seasonal offerings.

Nanjing has its own, though not famous, regional cuisine, and it has started to become popular in the form of restaurants that celebrate home-

Two views of the Yangtze riverfront. OPPOSITE: A bridge spans the mighty river at Nanjing, Jiangsu Province. ABOVE: An evening ferry disgorges rush-hour commuters in Wuhan.

The Eastern Plains   *253*

cooking. For a taste of this interesting cuisine, go to the **Baixingrenjia Jiachang Restaurant** ((25) 340-0010, 4 Daqiao Nanlu. To really appreciate its offerings, however, you will need a local guide as there is no English menu and no English spoken on the premises. The house specialty is *laoyaguo*, "old duck stew."

For something less pricey and a lot less local, the **Maxiangxing Restaurant** ((25) 390-5807, 5 Zhongshan Beilu, on the Drum Tower traffic circle, does tasty, inexpensive Moslem cuisine. Try the sliced cold beef. Like many such restaurants, head upstairs for a sit-down meal — downstairs specializes in budget eats.

For a taste of Peking duck, the most popular place in Nanjing is the aptly named **Beijing Kaoya Restaurant (Peking Duck Restaurant)** ((25) 322-7929, 6 Hunan Lu. The duck is excellent and about half the price you would pay for comparable quality in Beijing itself.

If you're hankering for something closer to home, expatriates and business folk flock to **Danny's** ((25) 666-8888, extension 7775, on the second floor of the Sheraton Hotel in Xinjiekou. Apart from being able to order a draft Guinness, it's the only place in town where it is possible to get a platter of fish and chips with vinegar. The hamburgers aren't too bad either.

The adventurous might take a stroll in the area south of Xinjiekou in the evening to seek out cheap eats in one of the many Chinese snack shops. The unadventurous, on the other hand, will find Nanjing to be extremely well provided by all the familiar fast-food chains.

HOW TO GET THERE

Nanjing is connected by air with Hong Kong and with most other major domestic destinations. It's also a major port of call on the Yangzi River route west from Chongqing and east from Shanghai. Coming from Wuhan, this is the place to disembark for the trains on the Shanghai–Beijing–Xi'an route to Wuxi and Suzhou. The city also has a direct bus service to Hangzhou, a destination which otherwise can be reached only by train from Shanghai.

WUXI

On the eastward run to Shanghai, Wuxi is the first of the much touted Grand Canal cities. But, though it may once have been a picturesque place, nowadays it looks like most other Chinese cities in the region.

The real attraction is **Lake Tai** (Taihu), which in the summer is aflutter with picturesque square-sailed fishing junks. The two viewing points for the lake are **Plum Garden** (Meiyuan) and **Turtle Head Island** (Guitouzhu). The time to be in Plum Garden is springtime, when, if you're lucky the plum trees will be in bloom. But even if the trees are bare of pink blossoms, the garden area provides good views of the lake. Turtle Head Island, which is strictly speaking a peninsula, is the traditional viewing area for the lake, and is also the place to get a ferry ride to the small Three Hills Island (Sanshan).

If possible try to organize your itinerary to avoid an overnight in Wuxi. The Holiday Inn-managed **Milido Hotel** ((510) 586-5665 FAX (510) 580-1668, 2 Liangxi Lu, is the best place to stay if you have to.

SUZHOU

Suzhou has long been the pearl of the Yangzi delta and the Grand Canal — vibrant, exciting, beautiful, historic — a place famed for its gardens and beautiful women. Marco Polo was entranced by the city, and so too were many wealthy retired mandarins of the Ming and Qing dynasties who spent their last years there and are largely responsible for its greatest cultural drawcard — its famous villas and gardens. Unfortunately today, though the city's rich history provides much to see, Suzhou has lost much of its charm to the modernization that has claimed so much of China's history elsewhere. It's still a worthwhile destination, but it is a far less pleasant place to explore on foot than it was even five years ago.

Suzhou rose to prominence when the southern stretches of the Grand Canal were completed in the Sui dynasty 1,300 years ago. The city became an important trading and shipping link in the water transport chain, particularly for its most valued produce, silk. With its network of canals and waterways feeding off and into the Grand Canal, it was later hailed as the Venice of the East, a place of heaven on earth, the home of the most beautiful and accommodating women in China, a place of pleasure and sophistication, an ideal place, in fact, to spend one's waning days in the idyllic, meditative pursuit of higher thoughts and base instincts.

Not that it didn't have its upheavals. In the 1880s most of the city was destroyed and 70% of its population killed — and its silk industry devastated just as Japan was emerging as the major challenger to Chinese silk — by horrific fighting in the Taiping Rebellion. But Suzhou somehow survived the carnage and has since weathered the Japanese military occupation, the civil war, the 1949 revolution and the excesses of the Cultural Revolution, not to mention its latter-day

industrialization, to maintain much of its Old World refinement and charm.

GENERAL INFORMATION

CAAC ((512) 522-2788 has an office at 120 Renmin Lu, though Suzhou itself doesn't have an airport, the nearest being in Shanghai, about an hour away by taxi. The **Bank of China** is at 490 Renmin Lu. **CITS** ((512) 521-1054 is in the compound of the Suzhou Hotel, 115 Shiquan Jie.

GETTING AROUND

There's no better way to enjoy Suzhou than by bicycle; rentals are available from opposite the

Nanjing — OPPOSITE: Zijinshan Observatory. ABOVE: The majestic approach to the Sun Yatsen Memorial, the key revolutionary landmark in the city.

Suzhou Hotel. Taxis can be found cruising the streets and swarming around the railway station and the better hotels.

WHAT TO SEE AND DO

Suzhou, like everywhere else in China, is modernizing with zeal, but it remains a pleasant city to cruise around in by bicycle. Buy an English-language tourist map and follow the city's spiderwork of canals through streets lined with beautiful old low-roofed whitewashed housing, under the high cooling dome of dappled foliage of the huge plane trees, amidst great streams of bicycles, cars and buses, and alongside the raucous bellow and blaring horns and loudspeakers of the cargo boats and long convoys of barges on the canals.

The people of Suzhou are particularly relaxed and genial, especially the canal dwellers, and the first stop on any tour should be one of the bridges that cross the city's **Outer Moat** where you can stand for hours watching the concrete-hulled boats and barges cruise through hordes of sampans and moored craft. The **Renmin Bridge** to the south is a good spot, and there are other bridges, **Wannian, Wumen, Hongqi** and **Guangji** on the city's west side that provide interesting vantage points.

The main tourist hub is the **Guanqian Bazaar** area on Guanqian Jie, running east off the main north–south thoroughfare Renmin Lu. Part of the district has been closed off to traffic and turned into a pedestrian mall, and it's surrounded by arts and crafts and antique stores, bookshops, cinemas, confectionery stores and a number of famous old restaurants, most notably the 200-year-old Songhelou (see WHERE TO STAY AND EAT, below).

The **Suzhou Antique Store**, on Renmin Lu just up from the Lexiang Hotel and close to the Friendship Store, is one of the best in all of China — crammed with ceramics, porcelain, scrolls, paintings, jewelry and other artwork. It has one floor of particularly refined porcelains and other art that's not for sale — it hasn't been given the government's wax seal of approval for export.

On the northern side of Guanqian Jie you'll find the Daoist **Xuanmiao (Temple of Mystery)**, a big wooden barn of a place with a main hall, **Sanqing**, supported by 60 pillars and a sweeping double roof with "winged" eaves. The temple was founded in the Jin dynasty, around AD 275, but the main hall was built in 1181 after the original structure burned down. What makes the place more than just another temple is the bazaar that spreads through its courtyards and grounds — with so much buying and selling going on that the "religious" section, the altars and images, are roped off to prevent them being overrun by base commerce.

North of Guanqian along Renmin Lu, you can't help but notice the city's second most famous religious institution, **Bei Sita (North Temple Pagoda)**, a soaring, beautifully decorated nine-story pagoda. It's Suzhou's oldest Buddhist temple, built 1,700 years ago. The 72-m-tall (236-ft) brick and wood pagoda of today dates from 1131 to 1136. Close by is another particularly well preserved temple, the **Avalokitesvara Hall**, built under the Ming reign, and to the southeast of the city center, just south of a small canal that runs alongside Ganjiang Lu, you'll find the elegant **Shuangtasi (Twin Pagodas)**, which was erected in the time of the Southern Song.

For a fascinating study of Suzhou's silk industry, CITS will arrange a visit to silk farms and spinning mills, while the **Suzhou Silk Museum**, close to the North Temple Pagoda, has displays on sericulture and on the looms used to weave Suzhou's famous silk. **Suzhou Museum**, set in

the former mansion of Prince Zhongwang, a leader of the violent and ill-fated Taiping Rebellion, has some very good exhibitions of sample silks, brocades and *kesi*, a combination silk and gold thread, of the Song, Ming and Qing ages. The raising of silkworms is one of the most remarkable processes known to man — a batch of 700,000 silkworms weighs only half a kilo (just over a pound) at birth, and no less than five tons when they are fattened up on mulberry leaves and ready to spin their cocoons.

The Suzhou Gardens

These landscaped works of art, designed for harmony, meditation and tranquillity in the golden years of retired court officials, merchants and property owners, are the pride and joy of Suzhou. Many of them were built in the Ming reign, and at one stage there were about 100 of them scattered all over the city. Now there are only six, and thank-

fully they have been preserved for posterity. The one that's considered to be the most splendid is **Zhuozheng (Humble Administrator's) Garden**, to the north of the city adjacent to the Suzhou Museum. The name itself contains a tale: The garden was built by a Ming dynasty official who fell from imperial grace and was bundled off to Suzhou as a punishment. Among its most beautiful aspects are an ancient tea house, a large ornamental pool with a bridge that becomes crowded with visitors photographing each other, and beyond it **Mandarin Duck Hall**, a lovely pavilion that was once a small theater and has latticed windows with blue-glazed glass overlooking a smaller pond.

The most fascinating garden is **Wangshi (Garden of the Master of the Nets)**, which lies to the west of the Suzhou Hotel off Shiquan Jie. It is a

Softly rounded bridges in Suzhou, "garden city" of the Grand Canal.

very small place, less than half a hectare (one and a quarter acres), but its gardens, rocks, halls, pavilions and ponds have been artfully arranged to give the illusion of a far larger space.

Of the other gardens, the **Xiyuan (West Garden)** is perhaps the most interesting because it combines landscaping with temple architecture and Buddhist artwork. Situated to the northwest of the city beyond the Guangji Bridge, it includes the **Jiezhuanglu Temple**, originally called Guiyuan Si and built around 1271 in the Yuan dynasty. Under the Ming reign it became the residence of a high court official named Xu Shitai and was given its present name. In 1860 it was destroyed in the Taiping Rebellion, but was restored in the latter years of the Qing dynasty.

The temple has several well-preserved halls, including the **Hall of Celestial Kings**, **Main Shrine Hall**, **Avalokitesvara Hall** and the **Hall of the Arhats**, containing a striking display of 500 gilded clay statues of these immortals, along with several Buddha images and a statue of a guardian deity whose face is friendly on one side and severe on the other.

WHERE TO STAY AND EAT

Suzhou's most luxurious hotel is the new **Sheraton Suzhou Hotel** ((512) 510-3388 FAX (512) 510-0888, 388 Xinshi Lu, a 328-room palace built in Ming-dynasty style. It's a tastefully executed, international-class hotel, with some excellent restaurants and all the amenities to be expected of the Sheraton chain.

The **Bamboo Grove** ((512) 520-5601 FAX (512) 520-8778, 168 Zhuhui Lu, in the old section of town, was for a long time Suzhou's best. It's still a good place to be based, with a particularly good location close to the fascinating street life of the old quarter. It's set in pleasantly leafy grounds, and while the rooms and service standards can't match those at the Sheraton rates are less expensive.

Not far away from the Bamboo Grove, also on Zhuhui Lu, the **Friendship Hotel** ((512) 520-5218 FAX (512) 520-6221 is an excellent mid-range choice. The comfortable doubles are reasonably priced and some of them look on to the hotels gardens. There's a good restaurant at the back of the hotel.

The **Lexiang Hotel** ((512) 522-2890 FAX (512) 524-4165, 18 Dajing Xiang, in the central tourist area on the edge of Guanqian Bazaar, has both budget and mid-range rooms, and is geared to the needs of Western travelers. There are some inexpensive Chinese restaurants in the vicinity with English menus.

The most famous restaurant in Suzhou is the **Songhelou Restaurant**, where the Emperor Qianlong is said to have eaten. It won't be the cheapest meal you'll have in China, but it does provide an opportunity to sample Suzhou's famous cuisine in atmospheric surroundings.

HOW TO GET THERE

Suzhou's nearest airport is in Shanghai, which is just an hour away by taxi or on the Nanjing–Shanghai express rail route. It also has Grand Canal ferry services to and from Hangzhou. Tickets for the latter can be booked with CITS.

HANGZHOU

Like Suzhou, Hangzhou (capital of Zhejiang province) rose to prominence and flourished as a

trading center, key food supplier and a hub of the rich silk industry of the region when the Grand Canal was built in the Sui reign. The canal began at Hangzhou, eventually to link this southern city with Beijing, and this imperial bonding was not by trade and commerce alone. The Song dynasty — pushed southward by the "barbarian" Liao and Jin dynasty challenges from beyond the Great Wall — settled and established its capital in Hangzhou, and it was here that the most renowned age of refinement in China was born. It lasted until the Mongol armies of Kublai Khan marched south in 1276 to put Hangzhou to the sword and to destroy it in the campaign to bring the whole of the country under their heel.

The industrious Ming emperors restored the city, and in the Manchu Qing reign it became a popular imperial summer retreat rivaling that of Shenyang in the northeast. Then the Taiping rebels marched in and destroyed most of the city again in 1880, and much of its historic and cultural architecture and character went with it. But somehow it remains today one of the most renowned and beloved cities of China, famous for its balmy climate, its teas and silks, regarded as a place of romance and a Mecca for honeymooning couples, still paid homage to in an old saying that has been applied to it, and its Grand Canal sister Suzhou, for many centuries: "Above there is heaven, below there is Suzhou and Hangzhou."

Today, as in the past, Hangzhou is famous for its nearby recreational resort, **West Lake**, formed in the eighth century when an emperor ordered the dredging and diking of a lagoon off the

The **Bank of China** is located at 140 Yan'an Beilu. **CITS** ((571) 515-2888 has an obscure location on the north shore of the lake at 231 Baoshu Lu.

WHAT TO SEE AND DO

Having been razed to the ground a couple of times, Hangzhou is pretty thin on historic monuments and relics. The big attraction is West Lake, which is always crowded with Chinese vacationers paddling boats, taking walks, clambering over rocks and snapping pictures of each other. However, the city does have a remarkable temple, suitably named the **Lingyin Si (Temple of Inspired Seclusion)**, west of the lake. Originally built in

Qiantang River and landscaped and decorated with palaces, halls, temples, pavilions and gardens during the later dynastic reigns. It is now packed each summer with Chinese tour groups from Shanghai and the Yangzi cities and thousands of foreign visitors. Among its most distinguished contemporary visitors was the late President Richard Nixon in 1972. His sudden move to end years of Sino-American hostility was considered so momentous that the new airport 24 km (15 miles) from Hangzhou was built especially for his historic touchdown in Air Force One.

GENERAL INFORMATION

Dragonair ((571) 799-8833, extension 6091 is appropriately in the Dragon Hotel, Shuguang Lu, as is **Singapore Airlines** ((571) 798-5541. **CAAC** ((571) 515-2574 is at 390 Tiyuchang Lu.

AD 326, this temple has had a far rougher time than the city itself over the centuries: destroyed and rebuilt about 16 times through civil war, fires and other calamities.

It has managed to survive in a Qing dynasty renovated form with an impressive array of Buddhist relics — several large Buddha images, dominated by a 1956 camphor-wood carving of a Guatama Buddha, 26 m (85 ft) high, and about 150 smaller statues. There's a good vegetarian restaurant on the hillside near the temple. Also, on a hill facing the temple there's a cliff face filled with more than 300 Buddhist carvings going back as far as the year 951 and a huge sculpture of the Maitreya in the form of the rotund Laughing Buddha. Up in the hills you will also find the **Dragon Well** (with a temple), the namesake of

Elegant Song dynasty Twin Pagodas OPPOSITE and canal-side houses ABOVE in Suzhou's southeast.

China's most famous green tea, *longjing lucha*. Dragon Well Tea is cultivated on the terraced hills. You can wander through the tea bushes and in a tea house nearby you can taste this delicious brew. From here head southwards to the **Liuhe Ta (Six Harmonies Pagoda)** above the Qiantang River. On a hill above the pagoda you will find more Buddhist carvings. As for the pagoda itself, its main claim to fame is its historic role as a religious force to try to tame the notorious Hangzhou Bore, a current which rushes up the Qiantang River each late summer and with such ferocity that local sailing junks and sampans were specially designed over many centuries to withstand the force of it and ride it out.

section of West Lake (rooms with a view over the lake cost extra), and is the perfect luxury base from which to explore Hangzhou and its surrounding attractions.

The **Dragon Hotel** ((571) 799-8833 FAX (571) 799-8090, Shuguang Lu, is another luxury option, though it soaks up a lot of the overseas Chinese tour groups, making it somewhat of a busy place to stay. Its location in a dull part of town is not in its favor either.

In the wooded, very rural area southwest of the lake are a couple of mid-range hotels that are relaxing, if somewhat remote places to unwind for a day or so. The **Zhejiang Hotel** ((571) 797-7988 FAX (571) 797-1904, 53 Longjing Lu, is

As for the rest of the West Lake, you can walk around it and above it, paddle a boat on it, sit and contemplate it, and visit the islands, bridges, dikes, pavilions and mansions that were a part of the Summer Palace in Qing dynasty times. Unfortunately, it's unrealistic to expect much peace and quiet as you do so. Perhaps more than anywhere else in China, Hangzhou has become the focus of a local tourist boom, and the roads surrounding the lake are usually chock-a-block with buses and tour groups dutifully plodding along behind a uniformed guide brandishing a bullhorn.

WHERE TO STAY AND EAT

Hangzhou's top hotel is the **Shangri-La Hangzhou** ((571) 707-7951 FAX (571) 707-3545, 78 Beishan Lu. It has a superb setting, overlooking the northern

particularly pleasant, set amid the tea plantations, a perfect area for late afternoon and early morning walks. Room rates range from around US$50. Another good mid-range hotel is the **Qingbo Hotel** ((571) 707-9988, Nanshan Lu, on the southeast corner of the lake. Although this area gets a lot of through traffic (mainly tour buses), it has a village-like atmosphere and once the tourists have scooted off to dinner it is quite relaxing. Rates are comparable to the Zhejiang, and are good value if you can wrangle a lake-view room.

Hangzhou has long had a chronic under-supply of budget accommodation, and the situation has gotten no better in recent years. The best bet is the **Hangzhou Art Institute Foreign Students' Guesthouse** ((571) 702-3415, 218 Nanshan Lu, which will accept nonstudents in its basic rooms when it has vacancies.

The **Louwailou Restaurant** on Gushan Hill is Hangzhou's most famous dining establishment, but despite this is not particularly expensive. The sautéed eel slices and fresh shrimps with Dragon Well Tea are recommended.

For a mouth-watering breakfast or lunch buffet, head over the Shangri-La's lobby **Coffee Garden**. The Shangri-La's **Peppino** has the best Italian cuisine in town.

The Lingyin Temple has two excellent places to eat. On the ground floor is the **Gongdelin** vegetarian restaurant, where as usual meat dishes are duplicated inventively using *doufu* and vegetables. Upstairs is **Tianwaitan**, an immensely popular and inexpensive restaurant

HUANGSHAN

Though neither Buddhist nor Daoist, Huangshan is the most revered of all China's sacred mountains. To climb to its summit is to enter that peculiarly Chinese aesthetic of crags and peaks surrounded by swirling seas of clouds. For the Chinese this is the definitive mountain: climb it, the saying goes, and you will be done with climbing mountains. It's a sentiment that's hard to dispute, particularly when you're halfway up the seven-and-a-half-kilometer (four-and-a-half-mile) eastern ascent, and ahead lies a dwindling ribbon of cut-stone steps disappearing into the clouds.

that specializes in fish caught in the nearby West Lake.

For Chinese style cheap eats (you can dine at KFC beside the Shangri-La if your tastes run in that direction), Yan'an Lu, one street back from the northeast corner of the lake, is a good hunting ground.

HOW TO GET THERE

Hangzhou has international connections with Hong Kong and Singapore, and regular services to most major domestic destinations. Buses fan out across Zhejiang province, and there are long-distance buses to Shanghai from the long distance bus station on Hushu Nanlu. If you approach eastward down the Yangzi River, from Suzhou, say, traveling by train will force you to go to Shanghai first. Trains from Shanghai take around three hours.

There are three approaches to the summit. The most difficult is the 15-km (nine-mile) **western approach**. Unless you're in very good shape, consider *descending* via the western approach. It has some fabulous views — notably the precipitous stairway snaking up to the summit of the **Heavenly Capital Peak**, an optional detour of about an hour that is not recommended for those with a fear of heights, and the **Flying Rock**, which is at the summit, at the start of the descent. The western descent finishes at a **hot spring resort**, which has several hotels. The pick of them is the **Peach Blossom Hotel** ((559) 556-2666, where your room will have hot spring water piped into your bathtub — something your aching muscles will sorely appreciate.

Hangzhou Hotel ABOVE lies in an idyllic setting on the banks of West Lake. ABOVE: Hangzhou Railway Station.

The **eastern approach** to Huangshan is a vertiginous climb that can take three to four hours, depending on your level of fitness. No matter how fit you are, it is unlikely you'll have much bounce left in your stride by the time you've reached the top. But if you simply can't face the downward trek, there's the **cable-car**, which shadows the eastern approach, doing the journey in a brisk eight minutes.

Accommodation is available at the summit of Huangshan at the **Xihai Hotel** ((559) 556-2132, a beautiful place, but not cheap. Several hotels can also be found on the western approach. The best of them is the **Jade Screen Tower Hotel** ((559) 556-2540, which sits at over 1,600 m (5,250 ft) and has a stunning view of the Heavenly Capital Peak.

HOW TO GET THERE

The easiest way to get to Huangshan is to fly there from Shanghai, though flights are also available from as far away as Beijing, Guangzhou and Hong Kong, underlining what an important attraction the mountain is. Buses run direct from Shanghai to Huangshan, taking around 10 hours.

SHANGHAI

Shanghai is the fastest moving city in the world, a teeming place that is almost definitive of the expression "boom town." Curiously, it is also a journey back in time and a strange evocative combination of Manhattan, the Hong Kong waterfront and the Liverpool docks, circa 1930.

BACKGROUND

In Shanghai the British, the Americans, and their rivals the French, Germans and Italians, gained not so much a toehold as a colonial throat-hold, backed by military force, on the Chinese economy and society — turning a small and insignificant fishing town on the Huangpu River close to the Yangzi's wide estuary, into one of the richest, most frenetic, most desperate, exciting, freewheeling and wicked cities on earth.

In its heyday as the treaty port and International Settlement of China it had a foreign population of 60,000. Huge trading and financial houses built out of the nefarious "foreign mud" of opium rose up on the Bund, over the wharves, derricks and smokestacks of the Huangpu waterfront, alongside branches of some of the most respected and distinguished financial institutions of the West. Based on cotton textiles, an immense low-paid Chinese manufacturing workforce, and its position as a natural Yangzi River conduit of trade goods from the interior of China, Shanghai reveled in its wealth with flamboyant materialism, snobbery, vice and a kind of swaggering

modernity when compared to the rest of the country, while an epic power struggle took place around it between the nationalists, the communists and the Japanese.

In the late 1930s, when the Japanese blitz-krieged their way down into the south of China, the entire Shanghai dream collapsed into a nightmare of military repression, starvation and atrocity that cannot be imagined unless one was there at the time, or takes the time to read accounts like J.G. Ballard's disturbing *Empire of the Sun*, brilliantly brought to life in the 1987 movie by Steven Spielberg. When it was all over — World War II, the Japanese master-plan, the struggle for supremacy between Mao Zedong

and Chiang Kaishek — it was as though only a city as wicked as Shanghai could have been punished with such suffering.

It is perhaps because of that legacy of suffering that one of the most crucial power struggles of the revolutionary years was played out chiefly in Shanghai — the city was the hotbed of radical socialism, the power base of the Gang of Four, the place where the barricades of the People's Commune went up in the violent and ill-fated campaign to head off the "rightist tendencies" in Chinese society (who wanted to nudge the nation onto the capitalist path).

Shanghai has always been a place of ferment, and for many years the central government sim-

OPPOSITE: The Pagoda of Six Harmonies lies en route to Dragon Well Temple in Hangzhou.
ABOVE: Hangzhou's historically most important product, silk, is still a key export.

The Eastern Plains

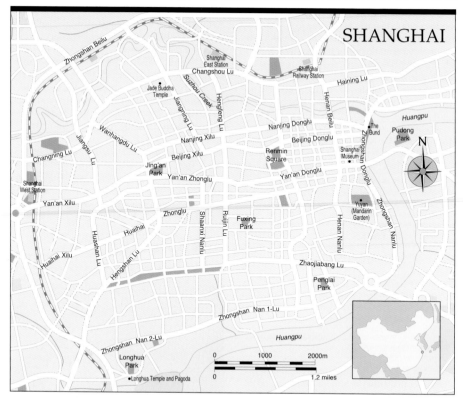

ply shut the place down. To visit Shanghai in the 1980s was to visit a city that was a pale shadow of its former self. All that changed in 1990, when Shanghai was given the go-ahead to exercise some open-door policies of its own. The results have been astounding. With over 13 million people toiling away, China's biggest city has turned itself into a powerhouse. It's impossible to visit Shanghai and not be impressed with how much has been achieved so quickly. This is a confident city with its eyes firmly set on a prosperous future, and for the foreign visitor it is the perfect place to start, or finish, the grand China tour (see A DAY ON THE BUND, page 15 in TOP SPOTS).

GENERAL INFORMATION

Airline carriers represented in Shanghai include: **Air China** ((21) 6327-2762, 600 Huashan Lu; **Air France** ((21) 6360-6688, Room 1301, Novel Plaza, 128 Nanjing Xilu; **Canadian Airlines** ((21) 6415-3091, New Jinjiang Tower, 161 Changle Lu; **China Eastern Airlines** ((21) 6268-6268, 2550 Hongqiao Lu; **Dragonair** ((21) 6375-6375, Room 2013, Shanghai Square Office Tower, 138 Huaihai Zhonglu; **Lufthansa** ((21) 6248-1100, Shanghai Hilton Hotel, 250 Huashan Lu; **Northwest Airlines** ((21) 6279-8100, Suite 207, East Tower Shanghai Center, 1376 Nanjing Xilu;

Qantas ((21) 6279-8660, West Tower, Shanghai Center, 1376 Nanjing Xilu; **Shanghai Airlines** ((21) 6268-8558, 2550 Hongqiao Lu; **Swissair** ((21) 6279-7381, West Tower, Shanghai Center, 1376 Nanjing Xilu; **United Airlines** ((21) 6279-8009, Suite 204, West Tower, Shanghai Center, 1376 Nanjing Xilu.

American Express ((21) 6279-8082 has an office in Room 206, Retail Plaza, Shanghai Center, 1376 Nanjing Xilu.

The head office of the **Bank of China** is at 23 Zhongshan Dong 1 Lu.

CITS ((21) 6321-7200 is on the third floor of the Guangming Building, 2 Jinling Road, on the Bund. Essentially, it is a booking office for flights, trains and boats. For general travel information, the **CITS office** ((21) 6323-3384 at 66 Nanjing Donglu, not far from the Peace Hotel, is the best place to go.

The following consulates are found in Shanghai:

Australia ((21) 6433-4604, 17 Fuxing Xilu; **Austria** ((21) 6279-7197, West Tower, Shanghai Center, 1376 Nanjing Xilu; **Canada** ((21) 6279-8400; West Tower, Shanghai Center; **France** ((21) 6437-1414, 21A Qihua Mansion, 1375 Huaihai Zhonglu; **Germany** ((21) 6433-6953, 151 Yongfu Lu; **Great Britain** ((21) 6433-0508, 244 Yongfu Lu; **United States** ((21) 6433-6880, 1469 Huaihai Zhonglu.

GETTING AROUND

Shanghai may be big, but it's one of the easier Chinese cities to get around. For starters it's fascinating to explore on foot. And when you tire of walking there's always a taxi (inexpensive and metered) or a subway stop nearby.

The public buses are best avoided unless you are an old China hand and used to the conditions in which ordinary Chinese travel. Just getting on the bus can be a battle, not to mention disembarking when your stop comes around.

Try to avoid having to be anywhere during the peak rush-hour periods, from 8 AM to 9:30 AM and from 4:30 PM to 7 PM. It can be hard to flag down a taxi at these times, and if you do get one you're likely to spend a lot of time sitting in the traffic.

WHAT TO SEE AND DO

With very little notable history beyond its treaty port days, Shanghai doesn't have much in the way of cultural attractions, but it is still a wonderful city to be in and to stroll around. It's the combination of the race-to-the-future development and the colonial era time warp that makes it interesting.

There are those who have a fetish about identifying every aspect of the **Shanghai International Settlement**, where the famous hotels, nightclubs, brothels, restaurants and great homes were. But such things are long gone. Besides, the Shanghai of today has 13 million walking, living, breathing realities that are far more relevant and interesting than all the ghosts of its past.

Every day, they crowd along the **Bund** and into the tiny **Huangpu Park**, overshadowed by the immense bulk of the Shanghai Mansions Hotel, strolling, chatting, picnicking, taking pictures of each other amid gardens that were once forbidden to all "dogs and Chinese." They pack the sidewalks down the long east–west shopping thoroughfare, Nanjing Lu, where you can find the **Shanghai No. 1 Department Store**, countless fashion boutiques, bookstores, arts and crafts centers and, finally, everything you'd expect to find on the main shopping strip of a big cosmopolitan city.

Along Nanjing Xilu you'll find **Shanghai Center (** (21) 6279-8663, where acrobatic performances are now held, from 7:15 PM. Buy tickets at the ticket booth the day of the performance.

Huaihai Zhonglu is the "Paris end" of Shanghai, with some of the city's best department stores and boutiques (virtually all the name brands are represented here). And this is appropriate; it was once the French concession, after all. In those days Huaihai Zhonglu was called Avenue Joffre.

South of this area, in what was once the French-town of the treaty port days, the **Site of**

the First National Congress of the Communist Party of China commemorates the city's role in the revolutionary ground swell during the chaotic republican years. Shanghai was where the communist party was founded in July 1921. To the south of the commemorative hall, you'll find more of the former **residences of Sun Yatsen and Zhou Enlai**, and, on Fenyang Lu, a mansion housing the **Arts and Crafts Research Institute** and another where the **Conservatory of Music** is based.

On Renmin (People's) Square, the **Shanghai Museum** is housed in an impressive urn-shaped building. Probably the best museum in China, it shouldn't be missed. Whereas most Chinese

museums are gloomy and poorly labeled, the Shanghai Museum is the wave of the future. It has a collection of over 120,000 cultural relics. The galleries for bronzes, ceramics and paintings, and calligraphy are the most highly rated.

Also on the square, and architecturally even more impressive than the Shanghai Museum, is the **Shanghai Grand Theater**. Daily English-language tours (** (21) 6327-6562 are available and are well worth attending.

Another Renmin Square attraction is **Great World**, an old and infamous entertainment center that has been resuscitated in a less raunchy version of its former self. Karaoke, acrobats, opera and music all share the same roof. There's even a haunted house ride and a Guinness Book of Records display.

Shanghai 's commercial center, where architecture reflects the city's past as a Treaty Port.

On the religious side, Shanghai offers the **Jade Buddha Temple (Yufo Si)**, in the city's northwestern Putuo District, not very old — it was originally founded in 1882 — but featuring a good collection of gilded Buddha figures, scriptures and paintings representing the major dynasties going back to the time of the Northern Wei. The **Longhua Temple and Pagoda**, on the city's southern riverbank, goes back a little further, to AD 247 and has an *arhats* hall, bell and drum towers and several other interesting buildings — along with its vegetarian early luncheon restaurant.

For a tacky but fun Chinatown experience, go along to the **Yuyuan (Mandarin Garden)**, south of the Bund. The garden itself is a compact affair,

covering only two hectares (five acres) and was built in the Ming reign. The shops and restaurants, all housed in mock Qing dynasty style, are the real attraction. The **Temple of the Town Gods** is a real temple; it failed to safeguard the gardens when Shanghai was attacked in the Opium War of 1842, and was again virtually destroyed by the French when it was used as a command base for the Taiping Rebellion. Yuyuan is a good place for lunch or dinner (see WHERE TO EAT, page 269).

Another pleasant outing is the three-and-a-half-hour, 60-km (37.2-mile) **Huangpu River Cruise**. Boats leave from an area north of the Shiliupu Wharf, next to the huge Diamond Res-

ABOVE: Shanghai makes no bones about its international ambitions, and parades them on the Pudong shoreline, which now bristles with skyscrapers like the Jin Mao Tower. RIGHT: Nanjing Road, China's most famous shopping street.

taurant, and tickets can be bought before boarding. Weather permitting, there are two departures daily at 9 AM and at 2 PM. The cruise not only provides a wonderful vantage point from which to view that famous shoreline, the Bund, but it also gives you a glimpse of the massive **Pudong New Area** development on the other side of the river, where history is in the making.

Pudong, which means "east of the Huangpu River" was, little more than a decade ago, an expanse of rice paddies. Today it is emerging as one of Asia's major business centers. Dominated by the **Jin Mao Building**—the world's fourth tallest — and the 457-m (1,499-ft) **Oriental Pearl Tower** (which has a lookout), Pudong is also set to be home to the world's tallest building if the troubled Shanghai Financial Center goes ahead. The area is easily reached in less than five minutes by subway from Renmin Square.

For a free aerial view of the waterfront and the busy **Suzhou Creek** back on the other side of the river, the best place is from the eighteenth floor of Shanghai Mansions.

Lastly, for a quick overview of Shanghai, take a red **Jin Jiang Tour Bus**. The buses leave every half hour or so from the side entrance of the Garden Hotel on Maoming Nanlu. Tickets can be purchased when you board the bus.

WHERE TO STAY

Luxury

Shanghai has a huge number of hotels that slip easily into the luxury category, and making recommendations is no easy matter. Nevertheless, some stand out from the pack.

Heading the list, despite the fact that it doesn't have a prestigious old-Shanghai address, is the new **Grand Hyatt Shanghai** ((21) 5049-1111 FAX (21) 5049-1234, which is perched in the clouds on the upper floors of the soaring Jin Mao Building in Pudong. This is arguably the wrong side of the river to be on, but nowadays it is a speedy 5 to 10 minutes by subway to downtown Shanghai, and the views from the Hyatt must rate as among the world's most breathtaking. With 555 rooms, unparalleled amenities, a spectacular 29-story atrium, 12 bars and restaurants, the Hyatt is virtually a luxury world unto itself.

Equally impressive is the **Portman Ritz-Carlton Hotel** ((21) 6279-8888 FAX (21) 6279-8800, 1376 Nanjing Xilu. The Portman is part of the Shanghai Center, where you'll also find most of Shanghai's foreign airlines, consulates and business representatives. In short, it's a perfect executive hotel. Amenities include four top-class restaurants, pool, business center, and extras include tennis and squash courts, and a theater. The tastefully decorated interior, complete with objets d'art, sets a high tone that is sustained throughout.

The **Shanghai Hilton International** ((21) 6248-0000 FAX (21) 6248-3848, 250 Huashan Lu, has a good location not far from the Shanghai Center, and inside is a veritable city of delights, with 775 guestrooms, eight cafés, restaurants and bars, a highly rated health club, tennis and squash courts, and a business center. The atrium has a splendid garden-setting café that is a wonderful place to sit with a coffee and a newspaper. Its rates are considerably less expensive than either the Hyatt or the Portman.

The **Peace Hotel** ((21) 6321-6888 FAX (21) 6329-0300, 20 Nanjing Xilu, doesn't strictly speaking deserve a place in the luxury stakes, unless you stay in one of the suites. Even then, be warned: You are not at the Peace for its exemplary service standards or its outstanding amenities; you're there because it is a slice of history. Formerly known as **The Cathay**, it was one the four big names of the East: the Peninsula in Hong Kong, Stanley Raffles in Singapore and the Taj in Bombay. Everybody who was anybody stayed at The Cathay, and Noel Coward wrote *Private Lives* in one of the hotel's suites. Today, despite renovations, there's still a 1930s ambiance about the place — note the revolving doors, the paneling, the deco windows, and pop into see the Jazz Bar in the evenings; the band members look to be as venerable as the hotel.

Mid-range

Shanghai has a large number of mid-range lodgings. For a combination of old Shanghai atmosphere and rates that won't break the budget the **Ruijin Guesthouse** ((21) 6472-5222 FAX (21) 6473-2277, 1111 Yan'an Lu, is recommended. The grounds themselves, an alluring retreat with ponds and pavilions, are winning feature alone, but the hotel's five different villas decorated period style clinch its status as a superior mid-range accommodation. The hotel has a number of highly-rated

Chinese restaurants (Cantonese, Sichuan and Beijing) and a Thai restaurant that is the toast of the town.

The **Donghu Hotel** ((21) 6415-8158 FAX (21) 6415-7759, 70 Donghu Lu, has a good downtown location, and is a no-nonsense operation that wins repeat visitors for its excellent value, spacious rooms. Sporting restaurants, along with a business center, tennis, billiards, even a swimming pool, its rates, which start at around US$50, are very reasonable.

Also recommended is the **YMCA Hotel** ((21) 6326-1040 FAX (21) 6320-1957, 123 Xizang Nanlu, which combines a superb location with top-rate facilities and bargain room rates. With a 24-hour lobby restaurant, a ninth-floor Cantonese restaurant, an efficient business center, gymnasium and shopping, the YMCA is one of the best deals in all Shanghai. Book ahead.

Inexpensive

And now for the bad news. Shanghai is not a backpacker heaven. The old standby for close on two decades has been the **Pujiang Hotel** ((21) 6324-6388, 15 Huangpu Lu, which has dorm beds in clean, high-ceilinged rooms, some of which sport views of the Bund. The Pujiang is still going strong, and now also has very reasonable doubles at around US$40. Given the location, it's one of the best deals in town.

The **Music Conservatory** ((21) 6437-2577, 20 Fenyang Lu, is a wonderful base if you can get a room. The refurbished doubles (formerly dorm rooms) are not bad at all, and at just US$30 are very good value, particularly given that you are just a short walk from fashionable Huaihai Lu and the Shaanxi subway stop. The only catch is finding the rooms for rent in the conservatory — don't give up; they're in there.

The **Changyang Hotel** ((21) 6543-4890, 1800 Changyang Lu, should be considered as a last option. It's too far out of town to make being in Shanghai fun (remember the traffic). Bus No. 22 takes about half an hour to get to it from the Bund. Rooms cost around US$40.

WHERE TO EAT

Shanghai is swarming with restaurants — and rates — up there with Beijing, Guangzhou and Chengdu as one of the great culinary capitals of China. The local cuisine tends to get a lot of flak for being too heavy on the oil and sugar, but this probably reflects regional frictions as much as anything else — Shanghai will always be the new kid on the block in the Chinese world.

For the best in Shanghai cuisine, the **Xiangqiangfang Folk Restaurant** ((21) 6372-9893, 57 Nanchang Lu, has been such a success it has spawned a host of branches around town. The most

notable of these, and the one that pulls in the most tourists, is the **Hongqiao branch** ((21) 6295-1717, 1468 Hongqiao Lu, which is housed in an old villa. Don't think for a moment, however, that the folk restaurants are tourist traps — the food is uniformly superb and the restaurants are as popular with locals as they are with out-of-towners.

Another highly recommended Shanghai cuisine experience is **30s** ((21) 6256-2265, 134 Nanyang Lu, where Shanghainese dishes are served in an intimate period-style setting. An English menu makes even the more adventurous dishes easy to order. Another extremely popular Shanghainese restaurant is **Lu Lu's** ((21) 6258-5645, 69 Shimen Yilu. Cozy, thoroughly authentic and inexpensive, again there is an English menu for easy ordering.

For a look at where locals go for a big feed, take a trip out to any of the almost innumerable branches of the **Shanghai Family Restaurant** ((21) 6531-3060, 41 Yunnan Zhonglu. These restaurants are low on ambiance but big on hearty portions. The often rowdy atmosphere can make for a fun night out if there are a few of you.

If you're the adventurous type, head out for the **Yunnan Road Night Market**, found on the street of the same name, just off Nanjing Lu. Mingle here with the crowds, pick up some cheap eats (point at something that someone else is dining on, if you have to), and you are as close to the heart of Shanghai as you are likely to get.

Curiously, given that Xinjiang is so far away, Shanghai has some very good Chinese Moslem restaurants. The pick of the pack is **Aini Bayi** ((21) 6278-7877, 2311 Yan'an Xilu. Given that so many Chinese Moslem restaurants are grungy places, Aini Bayi is a pleasant surprise. Not only is the ethnic decor tastefully executed, but the English menu comes with an extensive and enlightened drinks list.

For Peking duck, Beijing's famous **Quanjude** ((21) 6433-7286, 786 Huaihai Zhonglu, now has a branch in Shanghai. Standards are on par with those in Beijing, making this the perfect place for a meal if Beijing is not on the itinerary.

The cuisine of Xishuangbanna's Dai minority is the specialty at the **Dai Village** ((21) 6227-1465, 159 Aomen Lu. Something like a cross between Thai and Chinese, it's a fascinating and little known cuisine that is well worth sampling. Evening meals are enlivened by performances of Dai dance and song — be prepared to be dragged on stage.

For Sichuan cuisine, the best choices are mostly hotel restaurants, such as the **Bamboo Garden** ((21) 6415-1188, in the Jinjiang Tower, and the **Fu Rong Zhen** ((21) 6280-8888, in the Holiday Inn. One exception is a Sichuan hotpot restaurant, aptly

Shanghai's Great World Building is a cherished landmark that has been entertaining the masses for the better part of a century.

named **Sichuan Hotpot**. It's next to Shanghai Mansions. Locals claim that this is the hottest hotpot in Shanghai.

Moving away from Chinese fare, **Frankie's Place Restaurant and Café** ((21) 6247-0886, 118 Changde Lu, is a friendly Singaporean restaurant that has become popular with the foreign community, not least for its inexpensive beer.

Worthwhile as much for the atmosphere as the superb food, **Hazara** ((21) 6466-4328, in the Ruijin Guesthouse, is one of Shanghai's most popular Indian restaurants. The desert tent decor conspires to make diners feel like princes on a desert safari.

Just around the corner from the Shanghai Center is **Malone's** ((21) 6247-2400, 257 Tongren Lu, a Canadian-run sports bar that passes itself off as American. It pulls in the crowds, and the hamburgers continue to hailed as the best in town. Close by, **Henry's Home** ((21) 6247-1248, 267 Tongren Lu, also specializes in hearty American fare such as ribs and steaks, and is the perfect antidote to the stir-fry blues.

Lastly, for something different, **Sandoz** ((21) 6466-0479, 207 Maoming Nanlu, has won a loyal following for its Macau-style Portuguese cuisine. A charmingly intimate place for a meal for two, the house specialty is the succulent African chicken.

NIGHTLIFE

As in Beijing, there has been an explosive growth of bars in Shanghai's nightlife scene over recent years. Some of the old fixtures, like the **Peace Hotel Bar** and the **Long Bar** ((21) 6279-8268, Shanghai Center, have now become largely the haunt of tourists. For a glimpse of where Shanghai's local after-hours set goes to mingle, you will have to get out of the hotels and onto the streets.

The highest concentration of nightlife is in the Maoming Nanlu area, near the Shaanxi Nanlu subway stop. One of the coolest bars in this area is **1931** ((21) 6472-5264, 112 Maoming Nanlu, which goes all the way to achieve the retro concession-era ambiance that makes it perfect for a quiet drink. **Judy's Too** ((21) 6473-1417, 176 Maoming Nanlu, the longest-running of the area's bars, is still going strong. While it can turn somewhat debauched late at night, it's an atmospheric spot for a pint any time before around 11 PM.

Currently the hottest late-night venue on the Maoming strip is **Babylon** ((21) 6445-2330, 180 Maoming Nanlu. The clientele is young, but all are welcome, and it's a fascinating insight into the Shanghai scene.

Malone's (WHERE TO EAT, above) is a good sports bar around the corner from the Shanghai Center. **Shanghai Sally's** ((21) 6327-1859, 4 Xiangshan Lu, is an English-style pub with darts and pool.

It's Shanghai's pioneering British pub, and is remarkably as popular as ever.

O'Malley's Irish Pub ((21) 6474-4533, 42 Taojiang Lu, is near the United States consulate. For many foreigners living in Shanghai it is a home away from home. With Guinness on tap and countless corners in which to hide away with a book or friend, it is celebrated in Shanghai above all for its beer garden, a leafy retreat from the bustle of downtown Shanghai.

One of Shanghai's best kept secrets is the **Old China Hand Reading Room** ((21) 6473-2526, 27 Shaoxing Lu. Part library, part antique attic, there are few more atmospheric places to lounge in comfort in Shanghai.

If you find yourself out late and want to take a look at how Shanghai's high-flyers spend the wee hours, **Maya** ((21) 6415-2218, 1329 Huaihai Zhonglu, is currently the hippest late-night haunt in town. Expensive by Chinese standards, it still won't break the budget.

For something a little more alternative, **Real Love** ((21) 6474-6830, 10 Hengshan Lu, packs in less of the beautiful people and more of the rebels, who can be found dancing there en-masse nightly.

HOW TO GET THERE

Getting to Shanghai is like getting to China. There are countless ways to do it. Most major airlines have international flights to Shanghai, and as for domestic flights Shanghai is connected with almost every town that has an airport in China.

Unless you are arriving in Shanghai on an international flight, you will touch down at the old Hongqiao airport around 15 km (nine miles) west of the Shanghai city center, and taxis into town cost around US$8. International travelers arrive at the far less convenient new Pudong International Airport, which is around 45 km (28 miles) east of town. Taxis from Pudong cost upwards of US$12, depending on where in Shanghai you are going, but an inexpensive bus service also runs from the airport to the China Eastern Airlines office on Yan'an Lu.

CITS will sell you boat tickets to a number of destinations, including Yokohama and Osaka in Japan, and Hong Kong. There are also boats to Qingdao, and you can start the Yangzi River cruise here, if you don't mind spending many days on a boat.

It's best to buy train tickets either at CITS or the Longmen Hotel ((21) 6317-0000, extension 576, which is next door to the main Shanghai railway station, at 777 Hengfeng Lu. Shanghai is on the new Kowloon–Beijing train line, but tickets on this service are generally booked up for weeks ahead.

Shanghai's celebrated acrobatic troupe does the impossible on a daily basis.

Travelers' Tips

GETTING THERE

China's two main gateways are Beijing and Hong Kong, though there are an almost bewildering host of alternatives to these, involving everything from flights to regional Chinese capitals to rugged border crossings from China's neighbors.

BY AIR

For flights to China, you can choose from of a large variety of airlines, and a selection of standard and special fares. It's generally cheaper to fly to Hong Kong. For more remote destinations it may well be cheaper to fly to Hong Kong, travel overland to Shenzhen or Guangzhou and fly from there. Book your ticket though through a travel agent as airline companies tend not to give discounts. For very affordable flights, look in your local newspaper. But a word of warning: with any discounted fare there are bound to be restrictions so check the conditions thoroughly before committing yourself.

HONG KONG TO CHINA

By Train

The main route from Hong Kong to China is by rail from the Kowloon–Canton Railway's (KCR) Hung Hom terminus next to the Cross Harbour Tunnel's Kowloon exit. Trains depart for Lowu at the Hong Kong–China border from around 6 AM until 10 PM, every 6 to 12 minutes. From Lowu you walk across the border to Shenzhen and take a connecting train to Guangzhou. Direct to Guangzhou, the Hong Kong–Canton Express leaves five times a day between approximately 8:30 AM and 5 PM. It is now also possible to travel directly to Beijing, Shanghai and other destinations such as Hangzhou from Kowloon. While these services are frequent enough, they are usually booked up weeks in advance. (For train travel in China see GETTING AROUND, page 278)

By Air

China Air (CAAC) ((852) 2840-1199 (reservations) flies directly to most cities in China, and covers virtually the entire country from Guangzhou. You'll find them at two locations in Hong Kong: Ticketing, Ground Floor, Gloucester Tower, The Landmark, 17 Queen's Road, Central; or Thirty-fourth Floor, United Centre, Queensway, Central.

Dragonair ((852) 3193-3888 (reservations) FAX (852) 2810-0370 (reservations and confirmation) ((852) 2868-6777 (ticketing) has direct services to Beijing, Changsha, Chengdu, Chongqing, Dalian, Fuzhou, Guilin, Haikou, Hangzhou, Kunming, Nanjing, Qingdao, Sanya, Shanghai, Wuhan, Xiamen and Xi'an. They are located in Room 4609-4611, Forty-sixth Floor, COSCO Tower, 183 Queen's Road, Central.

By Bus

Air-conditioned bus excursions leave daily to Shenzhen, Dongguan and Guangzhou (separate services) from the Admiralty bus terminus on Queensway on Hong Kong Island and from the basement of China Hong Kong City, 33 Canton Road, Kowloon. For more information contact Citybus ((852) 2873-0818. The CTS Express Bus ((852) 2764-9803 only runs to Guangzhou, but does so 15 times a day from various Hong Kong locations.

By Boat

From the China Ferry Terminal, China Hong Kong City, 33 Canton Road, Kowloon, hoverferries make frequent daily passages to Shekou, a China–Hong Kong trading and manufacturing enclave west of Shenzhen, and four times a day to Shenzhen International Airport.

There are regular sea services, many of them daily, to a variety destinations in Southern China such as Guangzhou, Nanhai, Haikou, Xiamen and Wuzhou.

Also from the China Ferry Terminal, another interesting route to consider is going by hydrofoil to Macau across the mouth of the Pearl River, one hour away. Boats leave every half hour and can be booked through travel agents, CTS, CITS or at the Macau Ferry Terminal in the Shun Tak Centre, 200 Connaught Road Central — next to the Victoria Hotel, along Hong Kong Island's waterfront. (Hydrofoils also leave from the China Ferry Terminal.)

From Macau you can take a bus across the border to Gongbei in the Zhuhai Special Economic Zone and from there buses or minibuses to Guangzhou or elsewhere in Guangdong province.

Ducks OPPOSITE and picturesque square-sailed junk ABOVE on Lake Tai (Taihu) near Wuxi.

OVERLAND ROUTES

There are some interesting, though usually arduous, alternatives to flying into China. The most famous is the so-called **Trans-Siberian Express**, which is in fact two separate routes: The **Trans-Mongolian**, which travels from Moscow through Mongolia to Beijing after leaving Siberia; and the **Trans-Manchurian** which runs from Moscow almost the length of Siberia before cutting south through Manchuria to Beijing. Neither journey offers much in the way of creature comforts, and both involve navigating a minefield of bureaucratic paperwork — in the form of visas — before

and in the case of the Karakorum slightly dangerous. To travel onwards from Nepal to Tibet, you will have had to have obtained your visa somewhere other than Nepal — do not indicate your intention to travel this route when applying for the visa.

An increasingly popular overland route into China with budget travelers is from **Vietnam**, which also has overland connections with Laos, now allowing overlanders to travel all the way from Indonesia into China. Crossings from Vietnam to China are a straightforward affair these days, and can be undertaken either at Dong Dang for China's Guangxi province or at Lao Cai, for Yunnan.

the journey can be embarked upon either from Beijing or from Europe. The Manchurian train is slightly slower, taking around six days to complete the journey; the Mongolian takes around five.

Even more difficult, though undoubtedly tempting to latter-day world explorers, is the route so recently opened up through **Central Asia** to China's western Xinjiang province. Nevertheless, if you can get to the capitals of either Kazakhstan (Almaty) or Kyrgystan (Bishkek) — both of which are accessible from Moscow by rail and air — and you have a valid Chinese visa in hand, it is possible to continue on to China. The easier route is from Almaty, which is connected to Ürümqi, in Xinjiang province, by a twice-weekly rail service.

From the **Indian Subcontinent**, it is possible to travel to China either via Pakistan and the **Karakorum Highway** or via Nepal to Tibet on the **Friendship Highway**. Both are grueling routes,

ARRIVING (AND LEAVING)

VISAS

Tourist visas for one month are readily available at your nearest Chinese embassy or consulate, or through your travel agent. Anyone applying for visa anywhere other than Hong Kong will not have much control over the type of visa they get. If you a need longer visa, arrange your visa in Hong Kong, for which most nationalities do not need a visa. Permits are no longer really an issue in China, and no other travel documents are required, or at least useful.

From Hong Kong China visas can be obtained from the Visa Section, Fifth floor; Chinese Ministry of Foreign Affairs, 26 Harbour Road, or from almost any travel agency in town. It's a simple and efficient process, and the fee varies according to how long you want to stay in China and how quickly you want the visa processed. If you're willing to pay enough, a visa can be pushed through in a matter of hours.

Although Chinese authorities seem extremely tolerant of who visits China, it still pays to fill in your visa application conservatively. Avoid job descriptions such as "journalist" or "photographer" and refrain from mentioning that Tibet is on your itinerary.

CUSTOMS

Chinese customs are surprisingly relaxed about checking the contents of incoming bags. The rules are as follows: 400 cigarettes, two liters of liquor and 20 fluid ounces of perfume. In theory, foreign cash in excess of US$5,000 should be declared, but it's highly unlikely that this will be checked. It is forbidden to bring yuan in excess of Y6,000 into China.

DEPARTURE TAXES

China cottoned on to departure taxes early, and they are now levied at every airport in the country for both domestic and international flights. Typically, domestic departure tax is around half or less than international departure tax. Actual rates vary considerably from one airport to the next.

EMBASSIES AND CONSULATES

Important Chinese embassies overseas include:
Australia ((02) 6273-4780, 15 Coronation Drive, Yarralumla, ACT 2600; ((02) 9698-7929, 539 Elizabeth Street, Surry Hills, Sydney; ((03) 9804-3683, 77 Irving Road, Toorak, Melbourne.
Canada ((613) 789-3434 or (613) 791-0511, 515 Saint Patrick Street, Ottawa, Ontario.
Germany ((030) 4883-9722, 9 Heinrich-Mann-Strasse, 13156 Berlin.
France ((01) 4723-3677, 11 Avenue George V, 75008 Paris.
Ireland ((01) 269-1707, 40 Ailesbury Road, Dublin 4.
Italy ((06) 8413458, Via Bruxelles 56, 00198 Rome.
Netherlands ((70) 3065061, Adriaan Geokooplaan 7, The Hague.
New Zealand ((04) 4721382, 2-6 Glenmore Street, Wellington.
Spain ((01) 5194242, 113 Arturo Soria, 28045 Madrid.
United Kingdom ((020) 7631-1450, 31 Portland Place, London W1.
United States ((202) 328-2517, 2300 Connecticut Avenue NW, Washington, DC; ((212) 613-5500, 520 Twelfth Avenue, New York, New York; ((415) 674-2925, 1450 Laguna Street, San Francisco,

California; ((213) 807-8088, 443 Shatto Place, Los Angeles, California.

TOURIST INFORMATION

China is not a country with an efficient network of tourist information offices. Essentially Chinese authorities still expect that visiting foreigners are members of tour groups and as such all their needs are provided for. This despite the fact that increasing numbers of tourists visit the country under their own steam. The situation is unlikely to change any time soon, and outside of popular backpacker destinations, where enterprising locals often set up information services along with budget tours,

information is often not forthcoming from the authorities.

Originally CITS was established with the aim of helping foreigners in China, but these days it is unusual to come across a branch (every city has one) that is not specializing in money making tours to the exclusion of any other services. Hong Kong and Macau are both exceptions to this rule, and have excellent tourist offices (see the Hong Kong and Macau chapters for more details).

CHINESE TOURIST OFFICES OVERSEAS

China's overseas tourist offices operate very much like the tourist offices in China: aside from recommending tours and perhaps some giveaway brochures, they are not very useful places for planning an individual vacation in China. Offices can be found in the following countries:
Australia ((02) 9299-4057 FAX (02) 9290-1958, Nineteenth Floor, 44 Market Street, Sydney, NSW 2000.
France ((01) 4421-8282 FAX (01) 4421-8100, 116 Avenue des Champs Élysées, 75008, Paris.

OPPOSITE: Early industrial beauty and power are still in action on China's extensive rail network. ABOVE: Yangtze river ferries at Wuhan.

Germany ((069) 520135 FAX (69) 528490, Ilken-
hanstrasse 6, D60433 Frankfurt am Main.
Japan ((3) 3433-1461, Sixth Floor, Hammatsucho
Building, 1-27-13, Hammamatsu-cho, Minato-ku,
Tokyo.
Singapore (221-8681 FAX 221-9267, 1 Shenton Way,
No. 17-05, Ribina House, Singapore 0106.
Spain ((01) 548-0011 FAX (01) 548-0597, Gran
Via 88, Grupo 2, Planta 16, 28013, Madrid.
United Kingdom ((020) 7935-9787 FAX (020) 7487-
5842, 4 Glentworth Street, London NW1.
United States ((212) 760-1710 FAX (212) 760-8809,
Suite 6413, 350 Fifth Avenue, Empire State Build-
ing, New York, New York; ((818) 545-7505, Suite 201,
333 West Broadway, Glendale, California 91024.

GETTING AROUND

Travel inside China is surprisingly easy and efficient, largely because of the extensive air and rail
networks.

DOMESTIC AIRLINES

While China Air operates the international flights
into the country, domestic services are divided
among some 15 large and small airlines, headed
by **Air China** based in Beijing, **China Eastern**
(Shanghai), **China Southern** (Guangzhou), **China
Northern** (Shenyang), **China Southwest**
(Chengdu) and **China Northwest** (Xi'an). There
are also numerous smaller airlines. How safe they
are is anyone's guess.

Most hotels with three-star ratings and upwards will have an airlines booking desk, thus
making bookings very simple. Despite this, a large
number of the old CAAC offices linger on in China.

Most domestic routes are far better served
nowadays than they were half a decade ago, and
it's rare that you have to wait to get on a flight.
It always pays to book a few days in advance,
but it's usually possible to book the day before
providing you're not much concerned about what
time you fly.

BY TRAIN

If you have the time, the best way to get around
China is by train. It's the way to meet people. Even
in the relatively pampered soft-sleeper class, you
will find yourself in a compartment with three
other strangers. But, as you'll soon discover, the
Chinese are not content to allow people around
them to remain strangers for long. You'll probably be offered fruit and tea and generally drawn
into the give-and-take of the Chinese world.

There are three classes of travel on the trains
— soft-sleeper, hard-sleeper and hard-seat. Soft-
sleeper is the top of the range, offering separate
four-berth compartments, well serviced by the
attendants, equipped with a table and lamp between the bunks, white nylon curtains and carpet
slippers. It's the most comfortable form of travel
and if you can afford it (usually it works out to be
as expensive as flying) the perfect way to get
around China.

Hard-seat is the other extreme — open carriages packed with simple vinyl-covered wooden
seating, crammed with peasants, soldiers and
workers and their luggage, and anything from
crated television sets to factory spare parts. Such
travel is only for the hardened, as conditions can
be nothing short of horrifying on some runs.

Hard-sleeper is the compromise many travelers end up taking. These are carriages lined with
open three-tiered sets of bunks, rather like steer-
age class on a migrant steamer. But they are comfortable, nonetheless. Be careful not to select a
bottom bunk when you buy the ticket, as Chinese
travelers will sit on the bottom bunks late into the
night — eating peanuts, playing cards, slurping
on jam jars full of tea — whether someone is
asleep in the bed or not.

Essentials

Whatever class of train travel you choose, you need
to carry snack food with you, especially on the
long hauls. The dining cars get terribly overcrowded and the food they offer is generally basic.
The standard of cleanliness and hygiene in the
dining cars can also be a rude shock. On most routes
the trains stop long enough at main stations and
junctions for you to stretch your legs on the plat-
forms and buy hard-boiled eggs, buns, fruit and
cigarettes.

The toilets, marked "Cesuo," at each end of
the carriages are basic hole-in-the-floor conveniences over which you squat and hold tightly
to a rail, especially in the vicinity of the main
stations where the drivers tend to brake the trains
so abruptly that they sometimes actually skid to
a halt.

There is one infernal problem on all the trains
that Westerners find quaint and interesting at first,

and then increasingly aggravating — a constant blare of travel information, public announcements, Chinese pop music and Beijing or Cantonese opera from public address speakers installed up and down every carriage. The racket begins at 7 AM (sometimes earlier) and does not stop until 10 PM, and while you can switch the speakers off in the soft-sleeper compartments there's nothing you can do about them in hard-sleeper or hard-seat areas. Some have very flimsy wiring, if you care to inspect them closely, but otherwise you just have to accept that nothing moves in China without a lot of commotion and noise to help it along.

Reservations

It used to be that CITS handled train bookings for foreigners. This is very rare nowadays. Most train bookings can be done at the front desk of your hotel. If you're staying in a tourist class hotel this will be a simple affair; if you're staying in a budget hotel you may need the help of a phrasebook or a friendly interpreter. Only go to the railway station and book your ticket yourself as a last resort. Once you see the queues you will realize why buying a railway ticket is not a chore that anyone in China relishes.

As for the struggle to get to the trains, you'll find that at most of the major stations right down the east of China there are special segregated waiting rooms with soft chairs and sometimes even a coffee bar and souvenir counter for anyone traveling soft-sleeper. In some stations the alternative is very unpleasant. More often than not you are pitched in with everyone else, and even with the station police and attendants controlling the crowds, you can expect a rough free-for-all getting through the ticket barriers.

BY BUS

With a rapidly improving road infrastructure, long-distance buses are gaining in popularity. Increasingly popular is the overnight sleeper bus. These are mixed blessing. All berths are allocated by number (so there's no overcrowding), but unless you are traveling as a couple you will probably end up reclining in a space the size of a single bed with a complete stranger.

If it's possible to avoid traveling by bus, do so. They're generally slow, crowded, dirty and sometimes dangerous. In certain parts of China you will have no choice. A travel companion makes long bus journeys far more bearable.

BY TAXI

All major Chinese cities are well supplied with taxis nowadays, and you rarely have to wait more than a couple of minutes before one happens past. Communication is often a problem, even for foreigners who have studied some Chinese (accents vary greatly from region to region, and most foreigners have problems with tones that make uncontextualized place names difficult for Chinese to understand). Rates are reasonable by Western standards: In most cities you can cover a lot of ground for around US$3. As a general rule, avoid taxi drivers who loiter around railway and bus stations — they are usually waiting for a big payoff from an out-of-towner.

BY BICYCLE

Bicycles are slowly but surely being supplanted by motorscooters as the standard means of conveyance for urban Chinese. This is a pity, as it was not that long ago that most Chinese cities were fun places to explore on a bike. Nowadays, more often than not, it is difficult to find a bike for rent and the traffic conditions make riding when you do find one less than pleasant.

Previously the bikes were the standard proletarian Chinese models, all of them based on the design of the old British workhorse, the Raleigh, equipped with just two accessories, a security lock and a bell. Today, you'll see all kinds of bikes on the streets, with a basic road version of the mountain bike being the most popular. Out in rural China, of course, the old Flying Pigeon still rules supreme.

You can rent a bicycle by the hour or full day, paying an average Y20 to Y50 for eight hours, with orders to be back by nightfall. You pay in advance and will usually be required to provide Y400 as a refundable deposit. You also need to check the bicycle over first for loose components or tire leaks and make sure that the saddle is at a comfortable height. You then wheel out into the streets and find that biking in China is initially like venturing in a rented car into the Los Angeles freeway system. It takes some nerve and eyes in the back of your head to learn to flow along smoothly in the creaking, jingling floods of chrome, steel and rubber. A good English-language street-map showing the main tourist attractions is essential—these are usually available at hotel lobbies.

ACCOMMODATION

China's accommodation standards have improved immensely over the last decade. In all but the remotest destinations privately-run luxury hotels have moved in where once there were only mismanaged state-run guesthouses. And this in turn has forced the state-run guesthouses — or *binguan* — to lift their performances.

Trolley buses and bicycles are the main forms of transport on a frigid Beijing morning.

Nevertheless, with the exceptions of Hong Kong and Macau, hotels for travelers are a relatively recent phenomenon, and they are rarely more than functional places to spend the night — particularly in the budget and mid-range categories.

Luxury hotels in China are known as *da jiudian* or *da fandian*, or less frequently *da jiulou*. Not that the name is a guarantee of luxury. Standards vary enormously depending on location. In the big cities and destinations that see high tourist traffic international chains like the Hyatt, Holiday Inn and Peninsula group are usually represented, ensuring competition for the luxury market. In less well traveled destinations the best hotels in town are

likely to be comfortable but no-frills joint ventures. Rates for the luxury category of accommodation in this book vary accordingly, from anywhere as low as around US$50 in destinations like Dunhuang and Dali to US$300 or more in destinations like Hong Kong and Beijing.

Mid-range hotels are usually known as *binguan* or *fandian*. The former tend to be renovated older hotels that were originally built for traveling cadres and visiting overseas dignitaries. The latter are usually newer hotels. It is a very remote destination indeed where there will not be at least one or two serviceable mid-range accommodation choices, though as with luxury accommodation standards vary. In major destinations such as Hong Kong, Shanghai and Beijing, the mid-range hotels listed in this book range from around US$60 to US$120. In remoter destinations, expect rates to range from around US$40 to US$80.

Budget travelers are faced with ever-dwindling choices of places to stay along China's booming eastern coastline, but farther west the situation improves considerably. Away from the east coast, mid-range hotels often provide budget rooms or dormitories in older or still to be renovated wings. In very remote destinations it is sometimes possible to stay in budget hotels that are usually designated for Chinese travelers — these are known as *zhaodaisuo* (guesthouse) or *lüguan* (inn). Rooms in such hotels will usually be very cheap but lacking in any but the most basic amenities. Prices for the budget hotel listings in this book vary from as low as US$5 in destinations such as Dali and Yangshuo to US$30 in places like Shanghai, Hong Kong and Beijing.

EATING OUT

China's dining standards have improved enormously over the last decade. Nowadays, along with the international-standard restaurants in the luxury hotels, most destinations have a wide-range of restaurants to choose from.

If your budget does not stretch to the luxury hotel restaurants, it's a good idea to check any of the mid-range hotels listed in this book for restaurants. Chinese mid-range hotels invariably have one or more Chinese restaurants, and there will usually be someone on staff who speaks English, and in many cases there may even be an English menu. Such restaurants are usually good and can be surprisingly inexpensive.

Out on the streets communication problems can sometimes get between a hungry foreign traveler and a good meal, but with a little persistence this need not be the case. Don't be put off by the sometimes dingy appearances of Chinese budget restaurants. Very famous restaurants in China can sometimes look like they have not seen a coat of paint in decades, but that does not stop the crowds from coming and it should not stop you either. Nobody will take offence if you make your order by pointing at what other diners have ordered, and sometimes someone will even take you through to the kitchen to make your order from the ingredients on display.

Bear in mind that many Chinese restaurants are two- to three-story affairs. The first floor is always the cheapest, where people gather for a quick meal. The upper floors usually feature better decor and service, along with higher prices.

Most of the restaurants listed in this book will be accustomed to receiving the occasional foreigner and will have an English menu, and unless otherwise noted prices for a meal for one will range from around US$4 to US$10. Bear in mind that outside big cities like Beijing, Shanghai and Guangzhou a US$10 meal (including drinks) is a major extravagance.

Some cheaper restaurants expect diners to pay up front, but at better restaurants the custom is as in the West to pay after finishing the meal. Tips are not expected.

BASICS

BUSINESS AND BANKING HOURS

China basically follows a 9 AM to 6 PM working day, usually with a half day on Saturdays and a day off on Sundays. The only thing to watch out for is China's extended lunch breaks, known as *xiuxi shijian*—something like a siesta. In big cities such as Beijing and Shanghai, this custom is

dying out, but in rural China it is not unusual to find government offices and banks closed from noon until 2 PM.

TIME

Despite the size of the country, there are no time zones. When it's noon in Beijing it's noon everywhere else in China. China is eight hours ahead of Greenwich Mean Time.

NATIONAL HOLIDAYS

The biggest of Chinese national holidays, and one in which it is not a good idea to be in China is **Chinese New Year**, or Spring Festival, which usually falls some time in January or February. Officially, businesses close for three days over Chinese New Year, but it can end up being longer than

that if a weekend is loaded on either side. Transportation and accommodation becomes a nightmare at this time of the year, as it is traditionally a time for Chinese to return to their families.

Other national holidays are:
January 1   New Year's Day
March 8   Women's Day
May 1   Labor Day
June 1   Children's Day
July 1   Chinese Communist Party Day
August 1   Army Day
October 1   National Day

ELECTRICITY

Electrical current is 220 volts all over China, and the sockets are mostly two-pin. It's best to take battery-operated shavers, hairdryers and other gadgets.

CURRENCY

The standard Chinese currency is the *renminbi* (people's currency) or RMB, known officially as *yuan* but popularly called *kuai*. The highest denomination is the 100-yuan note (Y100).

Exchange rates for major currencies at press time are:
US$1 = Y8.27
J¥100 = Y7.68
UK1 = Y11.87
DM1 = Y3.62
HK$1 = Y1.06

The yuan is divided into 10 *jiao*, more popularly known as *mao*, and there are 10 *fen* to the *jiao*. The only time you are likely to see paper *fen* these days is when you change money, and they are needed to provide the exact amount. You may as well throw them away for all their worth—either that or keep them as mementos.

At first, the currency can be confusing, but it follows two simple, if illogical, rules: Wherever *renminbi* is written, it's called *yuan* and *jiao*; when you're actually buying something with it, it's *kuai* and *mao*.

The following credit cards are accepted: Visa, MasterCard, Federal Card, Million, American Express, JCB and Diners Club — but only in the major cities, and beware that among budget-category hotels, only by a handful accept them.

TIPPING

Tipping is appreciated in China—and nowadays it is expected in luxury restaurants and hotels — but it is not part of traditional Chinese culture.

OPPOSITE: Winter ice glistens on Kunming Lake, the landscaped centerpiece of the Summer Palace in Beijing. ABOVE: A rock hangs precariously, forming an arch in the Stone Forest.

In ordinary restaurants, the bill you get is the bill. There's no need to pay more.

COMMUNICATION AND MEDIA

POST

Every reasonable hotel in China has its own mailing desk for postcards and letters. Mailing costs vary from place to place, but are always reasonable. Most hotels provide stationery too, but the envelopes have no adhesive on them and must be stuck down with glue at the mail desk. All cities and larger towns have a centrally located post office as well, where you can mail letters, postcards and parcels.

TELEPHONES

Most hotels, even budget ones nowadays, have telephones in the rooms with international direct-dial lines. Local calls are not free but should cost next to nothing, and if your hotel doesn't have IDD for international calls, you can go telephone via an operator or fill out a booking form at the desk. Bear in mind, however, that it will be around 30% cheaper to dial from the central telecommunications office (usually in the same building as the general post office) than from the hotel.

TELEGRAMS, FAXES AND E-MAIL

The telecommunications office at the post office is the place for telegrams and theoretically for faxes too. In practice, important faxes should be done at a hotel business center where you can watch them go through and receive a slip confirming they reached their destination.

On the e-mail front, China is playing catchup extremely quickly, and an increasing number of hotels are "wired" nowadays. Cybercafés and services are also increasingly easy to find through the country. Internet access points do come and go, but getting on line is generally no problem — at least in urban China. Prices vary, although it's usually cheap. Check whether your server has a "roaming account" with China access numbers. Otherwise, you can access your account by proxy through almost any of the free e-mail services that abound on the Internet.

MEDIA

It's far more likely nowadays than it used to be that big hotels will stock the latest — or reasonably recent — copies of major weekly and daily publications. The *International Herald Tribune*, *Newsweek* and *Time* are the most readily available. In more remote places in China, it's often only possible to find the government's official mouth-piece, the *China Daily*, though it must be said this daily English-language newspaper has improved over the years and nowadays has some interesting reading.

Satellite television is widely available, even in the cheapest of lodgings, meaning that it is rarely necessary to resort to Chinese television programming, which language obstacles aside is almost uniformly dull.

ETIQUETTE

China is unlike anywhere else in Asia, or the world for that matter. Although foreign visitors will frequently find themselves the subject of unexpected

favors and solicitous inquiries about everything from their age to their marital status, China can also be a frighteningly push-and-shove place. Unless you're on a luxury tour, it is to be expected that you'll experience moments of culture shock.

Nevertheless, there are few mysteries to Chinese etiquette — the word "inscrutable" applies far more appropriately to Japan than it does to China.

Actually much of what is difficult for foreigners to initially understand about China stems from the "publicness" of Chinese life and a general lack of individual privacy. Meals and sightseeing trips are usually carried out in large, noisy groups. In cheaper hotels it is not unusual for cleaning staff to burst unannounced into occupied rooms with the tools of their trade. On long-distance sleeper buses, travelers find themselves nearly literally in bed with complete strangers. And in rural China, public squat toilets come with partitions so low you can read your neighbor's newspaper.

Despite this general lack of privacy, many rules of etiquette govern the day to day dealings of people doing business and socializing together, though as a foreigner you will not be expected to follow them closely. Basically, these rules boil down to people showing each other mutual respect, a concept that is often translated as "face."

Face, or *mianzi*, is not a complex concept. You can give it to somebody by listening respectfully to their opinions (interesting or otherwise), honoring them your presence at a dinner gathering (which they will pay for), or by presenting them with a small gift from you country. Alternatively

Although it is not so unusual to see public arguments in China, it is still considered very unseemly to lose your temper. When events reach an impasse in China, no matter how frustrating, it is always best to remain cool and maintain a smile. Shouting at someone will cause them to lose face and at best will probably result in a stony silence.

HEALTH

You don't need to show a vaccination certificate on arrival in China unless you've traveled from or through an area where there's been a recent outbreak of smallpox, cholera or yellow fever.

you can make someone "lose face" by too vehemently disagreeing with them, by turning down their offer of a favor, a gift or an invitation.

Showing people respect also translates into small daily rituals such as the exchange of name cards (it's a good idea to come prepared with some), for which it's polite to both offer and receive with both hands. When you receive a name card from somebody, make at least a pretence of carefully reading its contents (even if it is in Chinese) before putting it in your wallet or purse.

Drinking in social gatherings follows similar rules. Never pour a drink for yourself without first pouring for others, and before taking a drink, it is polite to raise your glass (always first to the host) in toast to somebody at the table. If somebody toasts you, it is impolite to refuse — if you don't drink or have already had too much, you can switch to tea or make a polite pretense of sipping at your drink.

China's most common health risk is the flu, and resulting chest and sinus congestion and a persistent cough. The flu always seems to be doing the rounds somewhere in China, and the combination of dampness and industrial pollution in the bigger cities often leads to lingering after effects. Plenty of fluids and rest are recommended in the early stages of the flu, but if you end up with a persistent cough, see a doctor — antibiotics can be very effective in clearing up such problems, though it is of course important to finish the course.

Some travelers in China are affected by intestinal troubles, though usually this is part of becoming accustomed to an unfamiliar cuisine rather than due the uncleanliness of the food. In the majority of cases, plenty of fluids and rest

Framed by dry foothills and rocky banks, the Lhasa River in remote Tibet receives the day's first welcome rays of sunlight.

is enough for such problems to pass in a day or so. Antidiarrheal medicine such as Lomotil does not cure diarrhea, it just treats the symptoms and should only be used in case of necessity — such as before a long trip in which finding a toilet might be a problem. If you are affected by an onset of acute diarrhea accompanied by vomiting and stomach cramps, it is essential you visit a doctor. Although intestinal diseases like dysentery and giadia (characterized by sulfur-flavored burps) are rare in China, they are sometimes known to strike travelers in remote regions like Qingdao, Xinjiang and Tibet.

Malaria is almost unknown in China, but it's a minor problem in tropical areas such as southern

straight to a hospital. This advice is best taken for any serious illness.

CHINESE MEDICINE

In the 1970s the World Health Organization and the United Nations recognized the benefits of acupuncture and Traditional Chinese Medicine (TCM), and in the following years both have won increasingly large numbers of adherents in the West. In China, most hospitals and clinics use a combination of both Western medicine and TCM, and if you visit one of these with a minor ailment the chances are you will be treated with Chinese medicine.

Yunnan province and Hainan Island. The best prevention is to avoid being bitten by mosquitoes — cover yourself up, use a repellent and at night sleep under a mosquito net. If you are planning to spend any length of time in a high-risk area, consult your doctor before leaving for China.

Hepatitis a is the main illness to worry about, because of the general lack of hygiene at eating houses, noodle and soup stalls and even some of the hotel kitchens. It's advisable to have a gamma-globulin shot before you go to China. Once there, always be careful of where and what you eat on the streets, use disposable chopsticks (or your own) wherever you can, always drink only the boiled water supplied in the hotels and on the trains for tea, and if you're unlucky enough to come down with extreme lethargy, nausea, fever, loss of appetite and a yellowing of the whites of the eyes, get right out of China, fast. Go to Hong Kong, and

TCM has a very long history — probably as long as Chinese civilization itself. Essentially it uses acupuncture and herbal remedies to restore the body's energy balance. Illness, in the TCM scheme of things, is a lack of harmony — a concept that is related to Daoism — and acupuncture and herbal remedies seek to restore that balance, thereby ending the illness and preventing its return.

Acupuncture addresses the body's life force, or its qi. The body's qi might be seen as its energy, which girds the body in a complex network of "meridians." Illness is prevented by the smooth flow of qi along these meridians, and acupuncture is used to stimulate or retard the flux of qi as the case may be. In total there are 401 acupuncture points on the body, and a skilled practitioner will have spent many years studying the significance of each of these points.

SECURITY

China is a wonderfully safe country to travel in, and its risks are associated more with traveling on its roads than with violent crime. Nevertheless, crime has been on the rise for years now, and it is wise to keep your wits about you on the streets if you are out and about late at night. Don't flaunt wads of cash about, and keep your money in a money belt of some kind.

Generally China's hotels are extremely safe, but it's obviously not a wise idea to leave valuables unattended in your hotel room — all Chinese hotels have a safe, where your passport,

Though summer is by far the best time to go, for reduced hotel rates and an assured berth on the train, travel in the off-season, from November to March, is not a bad idea. It means traveling through the northern areas of China in the grip of winter, when Arctic winds blowing from the Gobi Desert can chill you to the bone. You need to be heavily dressed, with several layers of clothing over long woolen underwear, to feel comfortable. Monsoonal cold fronts sweep right down through China at this time and in the southern provinces it can be quite chilly, but between the fronts, when the weather is from the south, it can be comparatively warm, even balmy.

travelers' checks and other valuables can be left for safe keeping.

China is a safe country for women to travel in, but it's still not a good idea to travel alone to remote parts of the country.

WHEN TO GO

The peak season for organized tour groups is April to October, and during this period there is a veritable conveyor belt of tour groups coming and going — and the inevitable mêlée at major attractions and shopping spots. With the rapid growth of hotel accommodation, individual travelers can now make their way through all this high-season clamor with a reasonable guarantee of a hotel room — an improvement on the mid-1980s when many found themselves virtually camping in guesthouse and hotel lobbies and corridors waiting for a bed.

WHAT TO TAKE

In summer, wear the lightest clothing possible, obviously. Drip-dry garments that can be rinsed through and dried overnight are preferable, though most hotels offer inexpensive same-day laundry services. In winter, long thermal underwear, thick socks, a Chinese-style hat with earflaps and good gloves are a must if you're going north. In all seasons, dress for comfort rather than fashion — soft-soled walking shoes, jogging shoes or hiking boots rather than high-heels, for example. If you plan to tour Tibet in the summer, take warm clothing and a lightweight sleeping bag — there have been many instances of trekkers caught

OPPOSITE: Steamed bread and noodles, the staples of northern cuisine, at a food stall in Beijing. ABOVE: Young Kazekhs from northwestern China ride horseback in traditional costume.

without adequate protection on mountains where the temperature plunges to freezing point at night.

Individual travelers should travel as lightly as possible if they want to keep their trip from becoming an endurance test. One large but comfortable backpack, and preferably not the type with a bulky aluminum frame — they're cumbersome in crowded situations, and they get snagged in train and bus doorways. Add one other soft hold-all and a camera case — but no more than that; you'd be surprised how grueling it is to negotiate the length of an average Chinese railway platform after a long journey, if you're loaded down with heavy luggage. Other basic necessities that should be taken along are as follows:

Chapstick. In winter, particularly, the climate in the north and in Tibet is harshly dry.

Coffee. This is readily available in sachets at department stores, but outside the big cities is rarely served in any place other than luxury hotels.

Vitamin pills. Definitely of supplementary value in Tibet and in the northern provinces in winter.

Swiss Army knife. You never know.

Batteries. These can be bought in major cities, but in rural China often only weak, local brands are available.

Flashlight. Optional, but comes in handy in the dead of night on the way to toilets in Tibet.

Chopsticks. Optional, but certainly cuts down on health hazards when eating communally.

PHOTOGRAPHY

Generally the Chinese are very relaxed about photography. Few people are likely to refuse having their photograph taken, and in most circumstances there are no official restrictions on photography. Exceptions to the latter are in force at certain museums and in particularly famous tourist attractions such as the Entombed Warriors in Xi'an. Generally, however, you can snap away to your heart's delight.

The other area in which there are official restrictions on photography is in the event you find yourself close to a sensitive military base. Sometimes the same restrictions are enforced on bridges in remote parts of the country, particularly those near border areas.

LANGUAGE BASICS

Mandarin, or Putonghua, is the official language of China. Mutually unintelligible dialects are legion: Cantonese, for example, is the dialect in Guangdong and Hong Kong, though Chaozhou is spoken in the north of Guangdong, and north of there again the locals speak Minnan (Hokkien). To complicate things even further, there are the Turkic tongues of the Moslem northwest and Tibetan in Tibet.

Although Mandarin is grammatically a very simple language, its written form is probably the most difficult in the world to learn, and as a spoken language it is made difficult for foreigners by its tonal aspect. There are four tones, and depending on which tone you use, a sound can mean any of four things. Thus, famously, the sound *ma* can mean variously "mother," "hemp," "horse" or "scold." The possibilities for miscommunication should be immediately apparent.

The best advice is to get yourself a Mandarin phrasebook that includes the written Chinese for everything you need to say. At least you can then point your meaning out and be understood. You will find the Chinese on the whole very patient with non-Mandarin speakers. Be sure too that your reference is in Pinyin, the new Romanized form of Chinese, as distinct from the old Wade-Giles system. It is Pinyin that has changed Peking to Beijing, Mao Tse-tung to Mao Zedong, Soochow to Suzhou and Chungking to Chongqing. From the tourist's point of view, the Pinyin is rendered indecipherable by five letters, which will draw a blank if they're not pronounced properly:

"x" pronounced "s" (but slightly more slurred than in English).

"q" pronounced "ch" (but harder than in English).

"c" pronounced "ts," as in "it's."

"zh" pronounced "j," as in "Joe."

"j" pronounced "ds," as in "fads."

There are two phrases that you will find useful just about wherever you go, "Ni hao" (pronounced "nee how"), which means "Hello. How are you?" and "xiexie" (pronounced "seeyuh, seeyuh), which means "thank you."

The polite way to get things done in China is to preface your request with the expression "mafan ni," or literally "bother you." Once you've said that you can say "wo yao…", meaning "I want…" But this is hardly the place for a crash course in Mandarin. With a phrasebook and some perseverance, you should have a repertoire of basic phrases together within a short time.

The following are some terms frequently used in this book:

lu, dao, jie   road, street

da   big, major, great

dajie, dadao   main street or avenue

dong   east

xi   west

bei   north

nan   south

Beijing *Nanlu*   Southern Beijing Road

hu   lake

si, miao, yuan   temple or monastery

shan   mountain

ta   pagoda

gongyuan   park

yuan   garden

cun village
qu district

WEB SITES

China-related web sites seem to come and go with even more rapidity than web sites elsewhere. The following were the best at the time of publication.

www.chinanow.com/
One of the most comprehensive China web sites available, you can find information on travel, hotels, restaurants, daily news, and make discounted reservations online.

www.chinaonline.com
A comprehensive China news channel with everything from breaking news to features about Chinese pop culture. A superb background source.

www.beijingscene.com
An online (and print) magazine aimed mostly at China expats with the low-down on dining, hotels, embassies and having fun in Beijing, Shanghai, Nanjing, Chengdu and Guangzhou.

www.chinatour.com
Somewhat random but nevertheless extensive overview of tours, travel hot spots and news, together with a map of China.

www.tibetinfo.net
The place to go for the latest information on events in Tibet, also including travel reports.

Recommended Reading

BAUM, RICHARD. *Burying Mao: Chinese Politics in the Age of Deng Xiaoping.* Princeton University Press, 1994. The best portrait of the enigmatic inheritor of Mao's empire.
BECKER, JASPER. *Hungry Ghosts: China's Secret Famine.* Henry Holt, 1998. A fascinating account of the "secret famine" caused by Mao's Great Leap Forward.
BLUNDEN, CAROLINE AND MARK ELVIN. *Cultural Atlas of China.* Phaidon Publications, 1983.
BONAVIA, DAVID. *The Chinese: A Portrait.* Penguin, 1987. An out of date but highly readable roundup of the Chinese people, their history and society.
FAIRBANK, JOHN KING. *China: A New History.* Harvard University Press, 1994. A lively history by a highly-respected China scholar.
FLEMING, PETER. *One's Company: A Journey to China.* Penguin, 1934. Probably the classic China travel book, both funny and illuminating, written in the warlord years leading up to World War II.
GERNET, JACQUES. *A History of Chinese Civilization.* Cambridge: Cambridge University Press, 1986. A classic round up of China's cultural achievements.

HOPKIRK, PETER. *Foreign Devils on the Silk Road.* Oxford Paperbacks, 1984. A highly readable history of Europe's discovery and pillage of Chinese Turkestan's ancient Buddhist art treasures.
HOPKIRK, PETER. *The Great Game.* Kodansha International, 1994. A fascinating history of the machinations of the European powers for influence in Xinjiang and Tibet at the turn of the last century.
JENNER, W.J.F. *The Tyranny of History: the Roots of China's Crisis.* Penguin, 1994. A tendentious but intriguing other history of China that examines the country as a place tyrannized by its history of tyranny.
KRISTOF, NICHOLAS D. AND SHERYL WUDUNN. *China Wakes: The Struggle for the Soul of a Rising Power.* Vintage Books, 1995. A popular look inside China of the mid-1990s; already dated but interesting reading all the same.
REID, DANIEL P. *Chinese Herbal Medicine.* Hong Kong: CFW Publications Ltd., 1987. A guide for those looking for a deeper understanding of China's long medical tradition.
ROBERT, K.G. *China: Land of Discovery and Invention.* Weldingborough (UK): Patrick Stephens, 1986.
SALISBURY, HARRISON E. *China: 100 years of Revolution.* André Deutsch, 1983. A workmanlike history of China's twentieth-century travails and upheavals.
SALISBURY, HARRISON E. *The Long March.* Pan, 1986. A longtime China watcher follows the trail of the Chinese Communist Party's Long March.
SEAGRAVE, STERLING. *The Soong Dynasty.* Sidgwick & Jackson, 1985. A fascinating, if at times somewhat fanciful, history of one of early twentieth-century China's most powerful families.
SPENCE, JONATHAN. *The Gate of Heavenly Peace.* Penguin, 1982. A highly recommended alternative history of twentieth-century China that relives the experience through some of its main actors.
SPENCE, JONATHAN. *The Search for Modern China.* Second edition, Norton, 1999. Arguably the most comprehensive history of modern China available, though nowhere near as lively or as compelling as *The Gate of Heavenly Peace.*
SNOW, EDGAR. *Red Star Over China.* Grove Press, 1968. Snow achieved worldwide fame by sneaking in to join Mao and his revolutionary "bandits" and then writing this definitive account of the early CCP.
THEROUX, PAUL. *Riding the Iron Rooster: By Train Through China.* Penguin, 1989. A quirky journey through China of the 1980s by a travel writer you either love or hate.
THUBRON, COLIN. *Behind the Wall: A Journey Through China.* Penguin, 1987. The most thoughtful and best written travel book about China of the last 30 years.
ZHU JIAJIN. *Treasures of the Forbidden City.* Viking Press, 1986. A guide to the Forbidden City.

Quick Reference A–Z Guide
to Places and Topics of Interest with
Listed Accommodation, Restaurants and
Useful Telephone Numbers

The symbols Ⓕ FAX, Ⓣ TOLL-FREE, Ⓔ E-MAIL, Ⓦ WEB-SITE refer to additional contact information found in the chapter listings.